FRANCIS WILSON'S LIFE OF HIMSELF

HIMSELF

FRANCIS WILSON'S LIFE
OF
HIMSELF

WITH ILLUSTRATIONS

"I laugh for hope hath happy place with me"

BOSTON AND NEW YORK
HOUGHTON MIFFLIN COMPANY
The Riverside Press Cambridge
1924

The Riverside Press
CAMBRIDGE · MASSACHUSETTS
PRINTED IN THE U.S.A.

TO MY WIFE
EDNA
MY SON
CRAYCROFT
AND MY DAUGHTER
MARGALO

CONTENTS

I.	LOVE OF THE THEATER	1
II.	"EMILY"	10
III.	THE POOR RELATION	27
IV.	A WANDERING PLAYER	36
V.	"CARRYING ON"	55
VI.	"ERMINIE" OF YESTERDAY	75
VII.	"STAR-GAZING"	98
VIII.	TOUCHING HANDS WITH EDWIN BOOTH	118
IX.	THE THEATRICAL SYNDICATE	148
X.	EUGENE FIELD AGAIN	168
XI.	JOSEPH JEFFERSON — "RIP" AND "THE RIVALS"	197
XII.	WALT WHITMAN AND "LEAVES OF GRASS"	228
XIII.	THE ACTORS' STRIKE	243
XIV.	STORY OF AN AMBITION, A PLAY, AND A DRAMATIST	279
XV.	TOLD AT THE CHIMNEY CORNER	292
XVI.	"ERMINIE" OF TO-DAY	336
XVII.	A WORD TO BEGINNERS	362
XVIII	ADVENTURES IN LOVE	396
XIX.	THOUGHTS OF THE THEATER	423
	INDEX	447

ILLUSTRATIONS

HIMSELF	*Frontispiece*
PÈRE HYACINTHE	4
EMILY	10
CHARLES EDWIN WILSON	20
MACKIN AND WILSON	42
COLONEL MONSTEREY	46
WILLIAM EMERSON	50
WILLIAM H. CRANE	50
ANNIE PIXLEY	56
CHARLOTTE CRABTREE (LOTTA)	60
WILLIAM T. CARLETON	64
JOHN A. McCAULL	64
E. JACOBOWSKI	72
FRANCIS WILSON AS CADEAUX IN "ERMINIE"	76
HENRY IRVING AS ROBERT MACAIRE	80
From a Caricature in *The Sketch*	
WILLIAM DABOLL AND FRANCIS WILSON IN "ERMINIE"	84
CHARLES ALBERT FECHTER AS ROBERT MACAIRE	88
From a photograph	
FRÉDÉRIC LE MAÎTRE AS ROBERT MACAIRE	88
From a lithograph	
PAULINE HALL	92
ISABELLE URQUHART	92
RUDOLPH ARONSON	96

MARIE JANSEN 100

FRANCIS WILSON IN "THE OOLAH" 104
From a drawing by A. J. Goodman

LULU GLASER 108

EDWIN BOOTH 118

LIBRARY AT 24 GRAMERCY PARK 122

READING-ROOM AT THE PLAYERS 138

EDWIN BOOTH AS HAMLET 142
From an etching with autograph quotation, by courtesy of Mrs.
Grossman

FACSIMILE OF EUGENE FIELD'S "THE LITTLE PEACH" 168

HUBBARD T. SMITH 172

MARIE JANSEN AND FRANCIS WILSON SINGING "THE LIT-
TLE PEACH" 176

EUGENE FIELD 180

FACSIMILE OF EPITAPH BY EUGENE FIELD IN THE MANNER
OF SKELTON 186

FRANCIS WILSON AND EUGENE FIELD AS CHERUBS 192

JOSEPH JEFFERSON AS RIP VAN WINKLE 198

HORACE HOWARD FURNESS, JR., AND FRANCIS WILSON
PLACING A MEMORIAL TABLET TO JOSEPH JEFFERSON 204

FRANCIS WILSON AS BOB ACRES 222

WALT WHITMAN 230

AUTOGRAPHED POEM OF WHITMAN 238

VIOLET HEMING 260

PATRICIA COLLINGE 260

CLYDE FITCH 284

ILLUSTRATIONS

Austin Strong and Francis Wilson   288

Francis Wilson in "The Little Father of the Wil-
    derness"   290
    From a drawing

Caricature of John Drew   294

Mark Twain   298

Sarah Bernhardt   302

The Loving Cup   358

Ada Rehan   378

Edwin Forrest   390
    From a daguerreotype

Julia Dean   406
    From a painting by Eastman Johnson

Francis Wilson at Home   416

Mary Devlin Booth   420

Brander Matthews   442

Dr. Henry W. Bellows   442

FRANCIS WILSON'S LIFE OF HIMSELF

.•.

CHAPTER I

LOVE OF THE THEATER

I DO not know how I came by my love of the theater, my desire to play on the stage and become a professional actor. None of my people before me were so minded. Quite the contrary, in fact. I had a near relative who, when success was assured, supposed I would continue to prosper, but who could not, he regretted to say, wish me success because the "thing" I was doing (adding a little to the general sum of cheerfulness and, incidentally, relieving him of the burden of family support) was so wholly against his religious scruples.

That was a point of view, of prejudice, with which I could not sympathize. It made me laugh, even to his beard, as, with foreboding shake of the head, he predicted direful results.

With the deference due older persons, I listened with what gravity I could to one, as it seemed to me, whose mental train was being run on a decidedly narrow-gauged track. While he never understood nor quite forgave my continued success, he was consistent enough not to question Infinite Wisdom in permitting it.

On a day when I thought he had long ago given over the intention to mention the matter again, he put his hands on my shoulders and sadly remarked:

"It would not surprise me to see you suddenly struck with a bolt of retribution! Then the laugh will be with me!"

If I could have been assured of sufficient time to witness that laugh, my relative being a grim man, I should have been greatly inclined, however costly, to pay the price, sacrifices in the interest of laughter being dear to the heart of comedians. They are building relatives of wider vision, these days.

He has gone now, and is basking, I hope, in the sunshine of Supreme Beneficence. He has left me not wholly inconsolable at his departure, with little to solace me, however, but health, comfort, family, and friends, "that which should accompany old age."

Long since, of course, he has revised his pitiful little earthly conception of the Infinite, and, confident of this, I bear him no grudge — even now he may be interceding for me.

At one time there was in our family, I remember, talk of apprenticing me to the law and, later, while still holding forth on the stage, I went about picking up pearls of legal wisdom dropped by Blackstone, Coke, Littleton, *et al*. These gems of judicature written down on scraps of paper, were memorized during enforced delays on trams and trains — all this at the instance of an acquaintance, a gentleman of the long robe, who was interested, presumably, though he never said so in as many words, in rescuing me as "a brand from the burning."

I am convinced that failure to continue my legal studies, failure to embark on a legal career, worked no irreparable injury to the profession of which Chief Justice John Marshall was so signal a representative.

Looking back, I recall an appalling number of well-meaning people who were deeply concerned in redeeming me from a "career of shame." I was " such a bright boy," such "a studious young man," that it was a great pity I did not devote my "life and energy to something worthy."

I had another relative, by marriage, Père Hyacinthe, the famous French divine and orator, who exacted a promise that when I had "made my fortune" I would abandon the stage and assist him in his church work. At Neuilly, one day, with much enthusiasm and absolute seriousness, he told his wife of my promise. I had scarcely thought to be taken so literally. There was no intention or wish on my part to make such a promise, but I was willed to it by the masterful power of the man in front of me. I was in the position of Swift's publisher, Faulkener, whom the Dean had refused another helping of asparagus until he had finished what was on his plate.

"What, sir, eat my stalks?"

"Aye, sir!" Swift replied. "King William always eats the stalks!"

The publisher told this story to his friend Dr. Leland.

"And were you blockhead enough to obey?" Dr. Leland asked.

"Yes, Doctor, and if you had dined with Dean Swift, tête-à-tête, you, too, would have been obliged to eat your stalks!"

It was so with Père Hyacinthe. If this magnetic man made one of his eloquent appeals, he was not easy to resist. Lovable, charming, genius that he was, Père Hyacinthe had been unfrocked for daring to forswear his vows and do so natural a thing as to fall in love and marry.

For a long time he was hopeful of securing a following which, while adhering in every detail but one to the belief of the Mother Church, reserved to their religious leaders the right of marriage. He was a great man, a powerful orator, but not great or powerful enough to accomplish such a reform. I attended his sad little church in the rue Lafitte and heard him make several of his superbly eloquent efforts, moving his hearers to tears and cheers. He stood much in need of adherents. I was his guest, and seeing that my promise to aid would make him happy, I could not withhold it. It would have been cruel. I ate my stalks, with apparent gusto. It gave me pleasure to agree to abandon my profession, the only thing for which I was fitted, certainly the only thing I wanted to do and in which I thought to accomplish some good. I was mischievously inclined to make just such promises. It was a dull year when I did not make several of them.

How was I supposed to know, as well as other people, just what I ought to do with my life? There seemed no way that I could possibly be as much concerned with it

PÈRE HYACINTHE

The French priest who knew how to thrill with his eloquence. He fell in love and married, and so lost all chance of becoming a cardinal.

as they! To be sure, there was grave danger that it might be a failure as the result of their meddling, but what is a little life more or less, in a world teeming with such a common commodity?

I had another friend, Eugene Field, not much known at that time, and we canvassed the situation. He agreed perfectly with me that it was my bounden duty in the interest of general glee to go on making such promises. I am not quite sure that we did not adopt a scheme of his to hint to our ministerial friends, that, if "labored with," I might be willing to give over the "sock and buskin" for the cloth. He got to printing things about it in a paper, after which, much to my regret, the opportunities to promise grew fewer.

To be sure, I had my "doots" that the object of my ambition was as unlovely as depicted, buoyed thereto by what the poet Campbell had said of the drama in the "Ode of Farewell" to John Phillip Kemble:

> The youngest of the sister arts
> Where all their beauty dwells;

— by what Byron was saying to Edmund Kean:

> Thou art the sun's bright child!
> . . . . .
> I herald thee to immortality;

— again, knowing that Johnson had said, with permitted exaggeration due to intimacy and affection, that Garrick's death had

> eclipst the gayety of nations;

— and, coming a little further on in time, I recalled the

hymn of praise which Tennyson sang to Macready, that irascible snob, when he bowed himself away forever from the scene of his triumphs, a hymn which Laurence Hutton happily paraphrased when our own Charlotte Cushman made her really final farewell to the public:

> Go! take thine honors home, rank with the best;
> Kemble, statelier Siddons and the rest,
> Who made a nation purer through their art.
> Thine is it that our drama did not die.

I remembered, too, that an enraptured audience, on this farewell night of the Siddons, forced the play, "Macbeth," to end when the great tragedienne had finished Lady Macbeth's sleep-walking scene. After that night she passed into private life, to her constant regret.

"Oh, dear," she moaned to Samuel Rogers, "this is the time I used to be thinking of going to the theater. First came the pleasure of dressing for my part, and then the pleasure of acting it; but that is all over now!"

After many years of service to her art, during which she had touched the highest peak of admiration, respect, and affection, the only regret this wonderful woman could find to utter was one of sadness that it was "all over, now!" What a tribute, what a tribute to her profession! There must be something worth while in this art of acting, I reasoned, to fill the heart and soul of people so intensely that, even when they have devoted a long life to its practice, they grieve at separation from it. What can it be? I asked myself. Let us

look further, I said, into what worth-while people
think of it and its followers. Soon I found what the
gentle Elia, Charles Lamb, had written of a comedian
whose art and power he had loved:

Magnificent were thy capriccios on this globe of earth,
Robert William Elliston! for as yet we know not thy new name
in heaven.

How happy Elliston would have been to hear that,
from Lamb! How fine, how generous of Elia to write
so about a comedian, a mere maker of sunshine! But
if that homage pleased me, I was startled at the testi-
mony the great essayist bore to the power of another
comedian, Joseph Shepherd Munden, whose "whimsical image" stuck by him, in a manner to threaten sleep
when he had retired to his pillow:

I have seen this gifted actor in Sir Christopher Curry, in Old
Dornton, diffuse a glow of sentiment which had made the pulse
of a crowded theater beat like that of one man, when he had
come in aid of the pulpit, doing good to the moral heart of the
people.

Then, too, I knew of a modern critic of real power
declaring that Joseph Jefferson's art was a blessing to
mankind and his career a public benefaction. I grew
more and more puzzled. But presently I realized that
all these people were poets, dramatists, actors, and
critics, and, with strong sympathy for the stage, might
have been prejudiced. Where, I asked myself, shall I
find a layman with an unprejudiced mind to guide me?
Not Jeremy Collier, I thought, for many of his stric-
tures were just and led to needed reforms. I then came

upon a little book, long out of print, "The Relation of
Public Amusements to Public Morality," by the
Reverend Henry W. Bellows, D.D., and among many
able and eloquent arguments, met the following phrases
which took away my breath:

> The drama stands in its own right, and in the right of its
> great priests, the wonderful interpreters of humanity, and the
> great re-creators of the race; and all the apostates and criminals
> who have desecrated its pure and beautiful shrine cannot make
> its nature otherwise than lawful and honorable, and entitled to
> the protection of universal reason and justice. . . .
> The theater is the most brilliant, complete, and untiring of
> public amusements.

Now, when I thought of these tributes to the drama
and its people, I could not reconcile them with the
declaration from my well-wishers that I was headed
precipitately for "the outer pit of darkness." It
dawned upon me that, though the intentions of my
would-be advisers might be good, even noble, it was
within the limit of possibility — I mention it reverently,
if timidly — for them to be mistaken.

I knew about the hairs of a man's head being numbered. On some heads I could even count the number.
I had read, too, of the strict account that was kept of
the fall of a sparrow, but I was unable, poor weak thing,
to convince myself that in a decision of such unimpor-
tance I should be running counter to any real will,
divine or otherwise.

A finer feeling of pride in what I was attempting took
possession of me. I struggled all the harder for recognition, acknowledgment that I was contributing, how-

ever mildly, to the public stock of harmless pleasure. If only recognition could be attained, the incident attending Garrick's life — to wit, his death, which had eclipsed the gayety of nations — might, so far as I was personally concerned, be indefinitely postponed.

CHAPTER II

"EMILY"

MOST fellows who come forward to tell the story of their lives to the Indulgent Reader have been blessed with a mother whom they celebrate as the one person to whom they are indebted for whatever success has come to them. With what felicitous words they can command they pay her a tribute of affectionate acknowledgment. I am absolutely conventional in this respect.

The splendid mothers I have known and of whom I have read have had many appealing qualities, of course; that is why they were splendid mothers. But few of them, I find, under trial and tribulation have more successfully maintained their sense of humor than my mother, and this it was, no doubt, which kept her sane.

I suppose there was a time when I must have called her "Mother" or "Mom," as the other children did, but I do not remember it. To me she was always "Emily." It may be that the habit of so calling her began in jest, but, for whatever reason or in what manner it began; she was something more than mother; she was a friend, a companion, an all-round good fellow; in a word, she was "Emily."

She never objected to my calling her by her first name; quite the contrary, I think she liked it. It was something different, individual. Once, when I tried to

"EMILY"

She never objected to my calling her by her first name. I think she liked it. She was eighty and refused to put her signature to the picture. She admitted she was no longer beautiful, but nothing could convince her that she "looked like that!"

address her otherwise, she smiled and shook her head as if to say, "Better let it rest as it is!" So it rested at "Emily." Fate so willed it that she and I became the responsible heads of the family, with an understanding and appreciation of each other all our own. I was her led captain.

"Emily" was not what you would call a "superior" woman, if by that you meant a woman of flashing intellect. She was swayed rather by sentiment and feeling than by deep logical conviction. Neither was she a religious woman, in a straitlaced sense of the word. She had scant time for the observance of outward forms of declared faith, but she was no Laodicean. She saw to it, however, that her children said their prayers and went to Sunday School. She did not presume to be acquainted with the special designs of Providence, and she had a swift, impatient judgment of actions right and wrong. While those about her had narrow views as to the pleasures upon which Deity frowned, "Emily" saw no harm in dancing, card-playing, or theater-going.

After her marriage she had little leisure or means to indulge in these, but she always encouraged young people in healthful, innocent games and sports. I never saw her play cards. She never danced except the once or twice when I caught her sportively by the arms and urged her on. On one occasion, after watching me dance for her — she had been much depressed that day — she went through a few rhythmic motions to show me how it was done in her time. I loved it because she danced with expression of face and hands as well as feet. It was quaint and graceful. She was pleased when I applauded. In trying to cheer her, I must often have been *gauche* and ridiculous. She would not notice it, but instead would smile into my eyes and pat me on the shoulder. She had a comforting feeling that God would not hold it against her if, in the exacting, even distressful, care of her family, she were less worshipful, save in her heart, than others. Shocking to say of one's mother, she had grave doubts as to the dogma of "eternal damnation." She could not bring herself to believe that the Book of Genesis "was a standard scientific treatise." This gave great concern to that serious-minded relative who had grieved over my choice of a profession. He could see no chance of "Emily's" being "saved," but, insisting upon being wiser than both in fathoming Divine Will, I gave her many assurances which she was inclined to accept and much comfort for which she was grateful.

She had an old-fashioned way of withholding any display of feeling before others. Her greeting was always tender, but reservedly so. It would greatly amuse her when, as a grown man, insisting upon being "held," I would lumber across her lap as she sat in her rocking-chair. I observed, though, at such times, in the old-fashioned mother manner, she never failed to enfold as much of me as possible in her arms, and was soon rocking to and fro and crooning to me in a pleasant, tuneless, humming way as in the days of childhood. It was but a tiny step back in her memory, in fact no step at all, and she made the transition readily, adorably.

She had, too, all the old-time conventional modesty. The things of nature, of health, that children now of necessity and right discuss and decide upon with their parents, were eschewed by "Emily" as indelicate or shameful. The modern manner of wearing the hair draped over the ears, as we see it in pictures of "George Eliot," would have put her "in style" again in that respect, and she would have remarked, with meaning, that she was glad to find the old days had something worth imitating, but the modern cut of frocks, with the accompanying display of legs, occasionally bowed, would have horrified her. She would have said pointed things about it and shaken her head ominously. She would have wondered what the world was coming to and that women had so little modesty. In her day, women burdened themselves with three or four petticoats, to disguise the suggestion of form.

I see myself in her constantly, in quickness of movement, in speech, in the swift, direct, deadly-earnest way she had of doing things, often mistaken for excitement or anger. She was an extremely sensitive woman and, with the least suggestion of criticism or reflection, would flash back with heated look of eye, and heated tone of voice, though not loud. She did not recover too readily from anger, but was amenable and did not long harbor resentment.

She had married the most promising young man of her acquaintance, the only son of a Quaker family of birth and refinement. It was a love-match. She had left a home of comfort and taste and the marriage had not prospered pecuniarily. His mercurial temperament and finally his acquired habits, led her far down and away from the things to which she had been accustomed, and, though her relations at times came to her assistance she never lost faith in her husband. She too readily accepted his predictions of to-morrow's mountain against to-day's molehill. With his Micawber-like temperament a wonderful something was always trembling on the edge of delivery. She constantly began life anew with him after recurring appeals. Her pride was concerned. She ever hoped, as many another woman has hoped, that he would justify the faith she had reposed in him, when she had accepted him from among her other suitors.

I said to her, "I can easily imagine you gave yourself some liberty, in your day, and led your admirers a pretty dance, for all your criticism."

"You mean you can imagine that I was young, and acted like it."

"Yes."

"One can be young but once, but I hope I was never like girls of the present day."

"How?"

"Huh!" — this with a disdainful sniff; "the girls of the present day make no bones of *telling* the young men that they admire them."

"Have you actual knowledge of this?"

"Don't question me like a lawyer! Of course I have. They boast of it. Make conversation of it."

The enthusiasm and patriotism of her husband took

him into the Civil War, through the entire length of which he fought, first in the Fourth Pennsylvania Reserves and next in the Fifth Pennsylvania Cavalry. From him I probably got what combativeness I have, also love of the written word. He would read on silently and then suddenly burst out, as if nothing else mattered with a repetition of what he thought a humorous or well-turned phrase. I find myself doing that, despite my struggle to resist.

"Emily" had three great loves, a love of children, a love of animals, a love of humor. For a good part of her early married life, she had always a child in her arms — and another "concealed about her person." All told, she had nine children, five of whom persisted. She talked to every child she met on the street, and if in a hurry when she met one, she gladly permitted herself three collisions to the block for every backward look.

For many years she was in herself a society for the prevention of cruelty to children and to animals. She considerably antedated these two humane institutions. They advanced to her stage of benevolence, not she to theirs. She halted, shamed, and berated innumerable culprits, and was the means of prosecuting others. She surrounded herself with cats and a dog, who would gladly perform extraordinary "stunts" at her always gracious bidding.

When a very old lady, and somewhat deaf, she imagined the breaking-up sounds in her ears were the cries of animals in distress, and was with great difficulty persuaded to the contrary. The illusion frequently took her out of doors with the hope of rescuing the victim and apprehending the culprit. When she was in her early nineties, suddenly one night, a freezing winter wind swept through the house. The front door was found open and "Emily" was gone, to put an end, as she later explained, to the ill-treatment of a dog she imagined she heard whining down the street. The alarmed family ran swiftly in search of her and were met by the neighborhood policeman kindly conducting her home. He had hold of "Emily's" arm with one hand, and with the other he returned a part of her attire, which she, in the eagerness of her humane pursuit had been unconscious of losing. Her excitement over, she was covered with shame, though ever after she laughed till she cried if the matter were even hinted at. Previously she had been friendly with the policeman, but she never after noticed him. He understood and smiled.

She had all a Southerner's prejudice against the negro. When first she heard the phrase, "Nigger in a fit," it greatly amused her. Shortly afterwards when an elaborately over-dressed darkey got into the same street car with her, the phrase recurred to her and insisted upon associating itself with that particular darkey. This so amused her that she could not refrain from laughing outright and continued to do so despite her best efforts at control.

"Nigger in a fit! Nigger in a fit!" she kept whispering to herself and, looking toward the darkey, would laugh increasingly. Embarrassment obliged her to quit the car long before her destination had been reached.

"Why did you do that?" she was asked.

"It was dreadful, wasn't it?" she replied. "I couldn't help it. All I could think of was that ridiculously attired darkey, losing his pomposity in a fit."

Once, when visiting her, she refused sternly to extend even the usual greeting until I promised her "a raise of salary and a burial lot in Oddfellows' Cemetery." Like most women of Southern origin, she was proud and sensitive and would resent instantly any seeming show of inattention or disrespect.

"When you have time, I'll mention the matter again. I'm afraid you didn't hear what I said!" she would say.

Once, when we were walking together, she tugged at my sleeve and said: "Don't look! Don't look! Keep on talking!"

When I thought the time prudent, having followed directions, I asked what was the matter.

"That was Dr. N—— we just passed," she replied. "I didn't want him to think I saw him. He has become rich and important. He was one of my suitors when I was young." This not too proudly.

"Did he propose?" I asked.

She was silent for a moment and then said softly: "Yes."

"Why did you refuse him?" I pursued mischievously.

"I didn't love him," she retorted quickly as if that were a good and sufficient reason.

"Don't people marry sometimes without loving each other?" I ventured.

"No doubt about that!" was her reply. She pursed her lips and looked at me with a smile and added: "However, my not accepting him was an extremely fortunate thing for you."

"In what way?"

"You would never have been here!"

"Does that matter much?"

She squeezed my arm and replied tenderly:

"Oh, very much!"

When I thought the subject had gone quite out of mind and even after we had talked of other things, she said with feminine pride of conquest:

"He never married."

Past ninety, she rebelled against being "watched like a child" and resented being assisted upstairs. Seeing her opportunity, she would venture when sure of not being followed. On one such occasion she grew dizzy and fell the entire length of the stairway. She was thought to have been killed. Opening her eyes, she said, calmly: "As I am not dead, it might be advisable to help me to the sofa."

In a letter, written in convalescence, she said, "You'd better come and see me pretty soon, before all the bruises on my face and head have disappeared!"

"Why did you wish me to see the bruises?" I asked when we met.

"I wanted you to see how much an old lady could stand without complete annihilation," she said.

Probably such fondness as I have of a book comes from my father who, when at leisure, read constantly. If I have any humor, or love of a quip, it comes, with some vivacity, from "Emily." But she had little time to cultivate literary graces. She was maternal perforce, unselfish, helpful, willing, tender and sympathetic. In her youth, there were no Wellesley and Smith Colleges, and "higher education" for the female was a jest. However, she had the education of the better class of women of her day; that is, she possessed an excellent knowledge of "the three R's." She quilted, embroidered, did fancy needlework, and pointed a fascinating toe at cotillions. I know especially about the cotillion matter. Did she not exemplify? She wrote an excellent letter and was proud of her penmanship, which was neat and feminine. Letter-writing, though, was never a joy to her. To the later years of her life she retained some excusable vanity. She refused to put her signature on a photograph for me, because it did not do her "justice," and she would powder her face, even using flour, if nothing else were at hand, "just to take off the shine." As to the photograph she said, "I know I'm no longer young, and what good looks I had" — this significantly — "have long since vanished, but I cannot believe I look like *that*." I have heard my father say she was one of the most beautiful girls of her day. I would have thought him prejudiced, but her friends and her daguerreotype corroborated his statement. I never heard but one of her enemies speak of her, and it was not in terms of admiration.

"Old cat!" was the characterization, but then "Emily" had been the means through the proper authority of preventing the cruel treatment of the enemy's stepdaughter.

It is said that sorrows purify and ennoble the spirit of men. Likely that is how "Emily" came to be so sympathetic, so broad in her views, so tender, so unmindful of what any one had been or said or done if he stood in need of help. She had been sorely tried.

She did not talk about it much, but the great sorrow of her life was the loss of her first little girl, aged five, who had grown into her affection as I think none of the rest of her children ever did, and who was never quite absent from her thoughts. She was freer from superstition than most women of her time and station, yet nothing could shake her absolute belief that the little girl, whom she had worshipped, had reappeared to her from the other world. It was vain to suggest to her that the closeness of the tie, the care, the suffering, the longing and loss might easily have created so deep an impress upon her mind that, at the time, she could have called it up at will. She waved that all aside with an indescribable ejaculation of dissent that left no possible doubt of the nature of her unalterable conviction.

"Why," she said, "she never stood more real before me in life than she did on that day, but, as I rose from bed and stretched out my arms to her, she vanished."

"What do you think it meant?" I asked.

"Nothing," she replied sadly, with a look of one who held a cherished image in her eye.

CHARLES EDWIN WILSON

An impractical man, never succeeding though always confident of success.
Notwithstanding his Quaker origin, he fought through the entire length of
the Civil War.

"Nothing! She just wanted to see me and she knew how much I wanted to see her. I'm so glad she came!"

Of course I could not hope to rival a love like that, but "Emily" gave me many assurances of tender affection. She gloried in such measure of public favor as came to me. Her side of the house, she said, was a generation late in making its presence felt, but to her prejudiced view there was no doubt that with me it had now come finely forward. For years she occupied a box at the Broadstreet Theater opening performances in Philadelphia. It came to be known that she was there, and when the people of the upper tiers chorused: "Good-evening, Mrs. Wilson!" she was delightfully abashed, but far from displeased.

Not infrequently at first performances, scared almost rigid with a sense of responsibility, I have peeked out at her from behind the curtain and recalled the old saying: "God could not be everywhere, therefore he made mothers." Just that glance at her made everything right.

Inheriting the roving spirit of her side of the family where romance had had place, I greatly tried her soul when I was a boy by disappearing from home, following a detachment of men sent from Philadelphia to Havre de Grace, Maryland, during the Civil War, to reinforce a body of soldiers there to protect a threatened advance on Washington. In efficiency and courage that "detachment of men" more nearly approached Falstaff's army than any I have since seen on or off the stage. The chief *service* rendered, to my keen boyish observation, was chicken dinners three times a day supplied by adjacent hen-houses and a stampede during the night on a cry of "The enemy!" that would have done credit to the swiftest Marathon contenders.

Once again I wandered forth as a boy prodigy in singing and dancing to Alexandria, Virginia, where I played in a theater packed nightly with soldiers and to the sound of cannon in the distance. In the steamboat trips from Washington to Alexandria, I passed the prison fort and saw the mounted guard over the prisoners concerned in the conspiracy and assassination of Abraham Lincoln. I was absent for two weeks and thought to be dead.

When I came back with my "wardrobe" done up in a red cotton handkerchief and slung over my shoulder on the blade of a "combat" sword, peered in at the family seated at dinner, and asked, "Are you going to whip me?" the joy of my return as from the dead outweighed all else.

There is no doubt that I was a restless, mischievous, uncomfortable little person and gave "Emily" many days and nights of anxiety. It was not until I was an old man of twelve or fourteen and had quite settled into my stride as the family's steady bread-winner that I brought her any real comfort. There was little occasion to think about choice of profession for any of the children. The simple problem before us was existence and, with "Emily," as has been said, existence without separation. We were probably not an ideal family, but, thanks to "Emily's" great love and splendid determination, we were united, and so remained. Somehow her teaching, her example, and the remembrance of what she had endured got between me and everything I knew she would not like to have me do, and with occasional slips, I let it rest at that, for life.

It was about this time that she forgave me every foolish thing I did, confident that I had done it for the best, even to the dreadful auctioning-off of all her old mahogany furniture that had come to her with her marriage and "setting up housekeeping." I do not understand how she permitted it, except that it had become too painful a reminder of unhappy associations. I seemed to have been glad for her sake to get rid of all that lovely old-fashioned "stuff" and to replace it by new-fashioned worthlessness.

I was eight or ten years of age before I had a pair of trousers made of anything but Uncle Ben's old "pants." Being a man of wealth, he wore good clothes, and "Emily" wielded the needle of a wizard. I did not think much about it then, but I realize now that the wonderful similarity in color and texture of "Emily's" short sacques and my long breeches was due to her skill in economical revamping of the same tall trousers. It seemed all right to me then, but there was ever a spirit of rebellion in "Emily's" breast that would not down; and so, almost with my first earnings, nothing would do but that I must have a store suit, a tailor-made suit, and it came to pass. As I strutted along when nearing home in my new clothes, I was as proud as a peacock, and it was generally agreed in the narrow little neighborhood in which we lived that one "gentleman" at least, was due the district. "Emily" said nothing. It was unnecessary. Just the beautiful look in her soft face was sufficient. Then, almost immediately, there came a tragic happening. "Emily" ruined the suit.

I was fond of teasing her, and, boy-like, was not always, if ever, discreet about it. She forgave me many times, of course, when, as I always knew too late, I had exceeded endurance. On the day of the tragedy we sat at table together and, as she would try to raise her cup to her lips, I would catch her arm, and, chattering like a magpie, halt her action. She warned me repeatedly. Amusing at first, my prank became annoying, and of course intolerable, and I was finally told that a repetition would be met with a deluge of coffee. Instantly measuring what I regarded as a safe means of retreat in the steep stairway which I was accustomed hourly to ascend and descend, three or four steps at a time, and confident that no mere woman could reach me before I had touched the top, I dared to repeat the offense.

I was gone in a flash, made every leap accurately, and stood at the top, soaked with coffee, sugar, and milk. I was amazed, stunned. I could understand how she might be indignant with me — I had deserved that — and even while offending her I was planning to apologize, but my beautiful first-born tailor-made suit of which she had been so proud, how *could* she have ruined that! I sank to the floor overwhelmed with grief. She came to me presently and mingled her tears with mine, but I was never courageous enough to confess to her that I exacted the fullest measure of demonstrative consolation.

It is provoking to admit a weakness in one's heroine, but "Emily" had it. Ice-cream! She reveled in it. Often I have heard her say apologetically that, after a Saturday's heavy marketing, she felt herself entitled to "at least one plate." Then she would pause for the assurance she craved that she had not been unduly extravagant. When the modern ice-cream freezer came into the home, an eventful occurrence, it found a place in some strange way at a point which "Emily" passed frequently during her household duties, so that, like Sairey Gamp, she could put a spoonful of its contents to her lips when she felt so "dispoged."

"Emily" had a sweet voice and sang in perfect tune, though with no great range or power. All the songs popular in her day, "The Last Rose of Summer," "Sweet Ellen Bayne," "Round the Corner Waiting," "Suwanee River," and others were hers by heart; and she delighted to sing them as she plied her needle on the "odds and ends of sewing" gathered for the purpose ever since she had been eighty-five. In the summer of 1916 we spent a very happy evening together. She sang "The Last Rose of Summer" for me, every word, but, alas, with what a tiny voice, full of cracks and quavers! The power to sustain the pitch was nearly gone. How pathetic it was! If the voice was impaired, the humor still remained. During the last verse some one being called from the room, yet leaving quietly, "Emily" stopped instantly and said: "Good Lord, is it as bad as that?" She then finished her song, but put nothing more of pathos in it. When I could have seen her again, she had gone on before.

If there are such things as celestial garments, I am sure she is plying the celestial needle, humming the while in her old soft, true voice, and probably suggesting kindly but impressively that in the sphere of clouds a band of flannel about the stomach for infants as well as adults is a sensible precaution against cramps and colds and, if she is permitted further to have her motherly way, there will be much fluttering about her for the privilege of dipping into her bottle of camphor and old-fashioned Balsam-apple steeped in spirits, that is, if "prohibition" is not omnipresent.

God cannot help liking her. She is His kind.

CHAPTER III

THE POOR RELATION

MANY things occurred in 1854. I myself was one of them. It was decided the day should be the 7th of February, and then what I have long known as me came into existence.

When as a kiddie poor relation I visited my Quaker kinsmen, who, in a small way, were mostly bankers and farmers in New Jersey, my childish mind was much attracted by the "second person singular" and I fell naturally into its use. I could "thee" and "thy" with the best of them. I do not remember that we ever "thoued" at all, and I believe we did not, and, so far as I know, no harm has come of the omission.

The "plain attire" of the Quaker, the

> . . . ample brim,
> A hat that bowed to no salaam,

never seemed as comic to me as to many Philadelphia boys in that it appeared always to have been, as my hand or my toe, but when I grew old enough to know that this "plain attire" was meant as a protest against the frivolity of dress, against its lace and frills and ruffles, a frivolity that no longer exists, I could not, cannot yet, repress a smile when it comes into view because it itself has now the very thing that Quakers condemn, conspicuousness.

Among these good people I heard something of the

Mayflower, of George Fox, not the comedian-benefactor whose pantomimic "Humpty-Dumpty" brought joy to millions of children, something of Elizabeth Fry and of William Penn. However, such things made no very awesome impression upon the mind of a homesick child of tender years, and I finally persuaded my older brother that the only way to satisfy our intense longing for home and mother was to cut our protracted visit short by taking French leave. This we did in high spirits, borrowing enough *en route* from former employees of "Uncle John" to take us, after a nine-mile walk, by train to Philadelphia.

Oh, the joy of reaching home safely after such an adventure! Oh, the welcome of "Emily" to her boys! Yes, of course we had done wrong in running away without warning, but that was the zest of it, but no matter, we were still her boys! We had been out in the world alone with only one object in our flight, her arms! A little later, so eager was she to excuse us, she was not at all certain but that we had been driven to flight by unkind treatment, and she recalled that somebody had told somebody else that "Uncle John" could be very harsh if he had a mind. We did not dispute the point. Uncle John Curtis not only had a mind but a heart, and would have found difficulty in being "harsh" to a hoptoad. I had reasons to feel that the sojourn of "Cousin Charles" and "Cousin Francis," especially "Cousin Francis," was looked upon by our relatives, the Friends, not so much in the light of a visit as a visitation.

Mine was a restless, roving spirit. I was ever
agitating change, something different, and, while I do
not wish to do my early self an injustice, I believe, in
behalf of strict truth, that it must be stated that I was
probably an uncomfortable little creature. I doubt if I
was wholly uninteresting, but it is likely that I was
interesting in the way that pin-pricks interest. They
do not stop us from the pursuit of an object, but they
annoy most infernally. The angelic disposition which
is now mine is an acquisition. It has come only as the
result of intense philosophic thought and spiritual
humility.

Looking back at myself as a child has always furnished
me with much food for merriment. Not the least
reason for this amusement being the careless ease with
which I used to determine to accomplish the most
difficult things in life and the absolute confidence I had
that I could. That there might be obstacles to overcome bothered me not at all. As I saw it, it was merely a
question of deciding what to do and then doing it. At
one period, like most boys, there was some hesitancy
on my part as to whether I should become President of
the United States, or emulate the example of "Jack
Sheppard," the highwayman, with strong leaning in the
direction of Sheppard. There was a great deal being
said from time to time about the Presidency, and it had
its attractive side, in that it was the head, the chief of
things, as of the Nation, and nothing short of being
chief of things would be acceptable. However, interest
in the office sagged when I discovered there was a

formality to be gone through with in connection with the matter, that people actually got together and decided by vote who should be their chief. The independent, Jack Sheppard method seemed by comparison to be so much easier, so much more direct. Jack just said: "Let there be a Chief, and I am it!"

As a time-saving device this had my hearty endorsement. In addition to this — no small consideration — Jack wore stunning clothes, rode beautiful horses that could jump tollgates which, if they toppled over in the first leap, could be yanked upright by the obliging stage-hands for the second successful effort, to be followed by applause.

If a highwayman needed money to pay his inn bills, some one with a well-filled purse which resembled a sausage tied in the middle was always coming forward and obligingly turning it over with no other formality than a little polite conversation and the pointing of a pistol. If overwhelmed momentarily by people who objected to this procedure, one had only to call upon his burly companion, the faithful and ever-ready "Joe Blueskin," who would promptly pop up from nowhere with a pair of tremendous horse pistols and further arguments ceased.

I was emotionally impressed with the fact that this taking of other people's money was for no ignoble purpose, for did not the highwayman always declare with moving voice: "What I take from the rich, I give to the poor!"

With my own eyes had I not seen him give the poor

woman and her child — I know the woman was poor
because she wore a shawl over her head, an unfailing
stage indication of poverty — the whole purse which
he had been at such pains to filch from the rich citizen?
Not even enough had been extracted from the purse to
pay the score at the inn, haste in departing, coupled
with pursuit, preventing, doubtless. It did not matter,
for innkeepers and landlords, running true to form,
seemed to have a sympathetic feeling for highwaymen.

Now this generosity, this tender regard for the poor
and unfortunate on Sheppard's part (or was it "Dick
Turpin," another noble gentleman of the road?) ap-
peased whatever doubts I had of the right to make
people " stand and deliver," and I determined, once
launched upon the career of a Highwayman, that I
would never be less generous to women with shawls
over their heads than "Jack Sheppard" or the redoubtable "Dick Turpin."

Just to show how the best-laid plans of mice or men
may come to naught through stupidity or the upturn-
ing of the unexpected, or both, I may say at once that
this whole projected career of mine was knocked into a
cocked hat by so trivial a thing as a poke in the eye. A
strapping boy to whom I had unfolded my plans, and
who had consented enthusiastically to be my "Blueskin," undertook to act without me, too impatient to
wait until we had saved enough to purchase a horse
pistol. He had selected a dark evening and, the moment being propitious, had called upon another boy
to "stand and deliver!" The poke in the eye he had

received as the result of that command completely shattered our confidence in the successful working of the scheme.

The boy who had been commanded to stand and deliver did exactly as he was told, only what he delivered was wholly unexpected, and not at all as laid down in the rules of the game. When we met, my man-handled companion was in some absurd way inclined to hold me, as projector of the scheme, responsible for what had happened, and I had some difficulty in halting his threatening attitude, in convincing him that his presuming to "go on his own" had had a natural result.

After discussing the matter thoroughly, we easily persuaded ourselves that there might be, as we had seen, unpleasant consequences in such a career, that putting the project into practice had turned out so different from the stage version, it might be well to revise our ideas on the subject.

We instantly resolved ourselves into a "Committee of the Whole" to determine one of two questions, whether it was better to persist in the plan to adopt the career of Knights of the Road, or, Go Swimming. We went swimming.

The plan of becoming a Knight of the Road, thus summarily and unromantically checked, there remained, of course, the stage. When all else fails, when one has shown exceptional weakness in every other endeavor of life, one always adopts the stage, where, not infrequently, even the gifted of the gods fall flat! When one sees so many social mistakes fairly flash their

way into the drama and then, of course, speedily fade
out again into obscurity, why not make the effort?
There is nothing to do on the stage, except to think up
things to say, and be natural. What could be easier?
The schemes of becoming President and emulating the
example of Jack Sheppard having presented embarrassing features, the stage now seemed a welcome refuge for
which, as I speedily discovered, I had always possessed
a predilection, no week passing but saw me as childish
amateur in the midst of heroic or zeroic antics. I was in
no way incommoded by social prestige, or ambition-
defeating wealth. The more I thought about the
matter, the louder became the knocking for egress of
the spirit of dramatic expression.

Of the requirements of natural gifts and technical
skill for the stage, I was much too young to know but
little. With no "home-run" record, and no diamond-
studded pugilistic belt, and too young to be a blazing
divorcé, which have been open sesames to opportunity,
it might be thought that I should have rough going. I
was not to be halted, however, and with the courage of
youth I plunged ahead determined, if possible, to win
on my merits.

It may seem a little odd that a boy of Quaker forbears should have gravitated so early toward the stage.
I was not older than eight or nine when I made my first
appearance. I can explain it only on the theory that it
was an overdue protest against the solemn repression
suffered by generations of ancestors. To me it has always seemed that those antecedents of mine must have

had a sad time with all the wonder, all the joy of the
theater debarred them. It probably was not so, but it
is beyond me to imagine it otherwise. I feel that their
telepsychic demands upon me have always been of the
sternest character, that the pendulum be swung as far
as possible in the direction of cheer. Had they been
less exacting, I might have compassed the career of a
mere tragedian, but their insistence upon a full and
complete compensation, if not revenge, obligated me to
a sphere of the broadest comedy.

In his charming "Appreciation of Charles Frohman,"
Sir James Barrie says:

> This passion for the theater began when he was a poor boy
> staring wistfully at portals out of which he was kept by the
> want of a few pence. I think when he first saw a theater he
> clapped his hand to his heart, and certainly he was true to his
> first love. Up to the end it was still the same treat to him to go
> in; he thrilled when the band struck up as if that boy had hold
> of his hand.

One of the real joys of my life is the retention as actor
and auditor of all the old enthusiasm, all the old
passion for the theater. I am not ashamed of the tears I
am able to shed with "the heroine in seduced circumstances," nor the glee I still share with the comedian,
provided he is comic. It is not until a second or third
visit to a play that I at all observe the wheels go around.
I am in hearty sympathy with the woman who said:
"I had a lovely time at the matinée. I cried all through
the performance."

There are many unfortunate people who cannot, or

will not, surrender themselves to the spell of the dramatist, the illusion of the play, and I think they are to be pitied, such surrender being the chief object of one's visit to the playhouse, the only way to a full enjoyment of that visit.

To the present day I "thrill when the band strikes up," and I gratefully confess I have not been able to subdue that delightful sensation of hushed expectancy that comes over me when the lights go down and the curtain is about to rise. Then, as Barrie says, I know I "have that boy by the hand," that boy of long ago who shares with me my inmost thoughts, my every joy, which, unlike my hair, are still ungrayed.

I never button up my coat and tuck my programme into my pocket without thinking how utterly impossible it would be to invent another amusement comparable with the theater for the delight and recreation of mankind.

It has taken a long time to bring it to its present captivating condition. Like "Topsy," it "just growed," and like many sacred and profane things which people revere and set aside in a special class, the theater, the drama, has "just growed" with the growth of the people, as a giver of pleasure and a stimulator of thought, until it stands to-day preëminently the people's temple, "the most powerful of all the arts," because the most popular.

CHAPTER IV

A WANDERING PLAYER

MOLIÈRE's mother is said to have left him five thousand livres as a start in the world. If anybody had left me five thousand livres, I should not have known what to do with them except give them to "Emily." It was not money, but opportunity and experience that I wanted. "Emily" could give me but affection and encouragement, and that was about all I craved of her. My boyish conviction was that, with opportunity, success and the livres would speedily follow, and they did.

Notwithstanding a tenacious grip on "Emily's" precepts, the wonder to me has always been that, away from home influence, left completely to my own resources, guided only by an ambitious boyish instinct for a goal, I did not, like Oliver Twist, fall a prey to some alluring Fagin who taught the gentle art of securing everything for nothing.

"Emily's" first thought was always of keeping the family together, an undertaking in her situation involving risks that racked her heart and brain. She could only guess at the dangers and temptations that must beset a boy out in the big world.

As a mere youngster, I chanced to hear of a minstrel performer named Wright, "Billy" Wright, who had encouraged ambitious youths and directed them to stage engagements. I sought out Wright, and while he whistled I danced the "essence of Old Virginia," not nearly so interesting a "turn" as the "Jim Crow" that Joseph Jefferson danced with "Daddy" Rice.

Wright got me an engagement in a "concert hall" in the Kensington district of Philadelphia. It was a heavenly place to me then, because it gave me the coveted stage appearance, but as I look back upon it now it must have been of no repute whatever. What matter? It had a stage — that faced an audience! Wright, who rattled the "bones" as an "end-man" or, as occasion demanded, thumped a long-suffering tambourine, was also, when quite himself, a skillful "knife-thrower." It was his delight to make an outline in knives of any friend whose courage was sufficiently "stimulated" to stand against a board and permit the hazardous undertaking. Wright could even throw knives between the outstretched fingers of his "subject." One night, though, he sent a knife through the thick part of a friend's nose, and the friend was very nice about it. Wright was profusely apologetic and laid the mishap to the fact that he was not quite himself. This appeared to be consoling to the friend, who went home with his nose in a rag.

In the search for novelty, the "concert" management thought to have me sit up as "interlocutor." My readiness, off stage, to repeat the jokes of the comedians convinced the stage manager that I was capable of filling the position, and so I was, until the "Sambo" or was it the "Brudder Bones"? — took it upon himself to "ad lib" and launch into an old, unrehearsed joke the ending of which, though familiar to

every one else, was Greek to me. Too confused to take
the hint or promptings of every member of the minstrel
semicircle, there came a disastrous finish and the "boy
prodigy" was deposed and relegated to his "turn" of
song and dance.

Wright gave me a note to that Father of Minstrelsy,
Samuel S. Sanford. He was an excellent actor of negro
farces, such as "Bone Squash," "The Virginia Mum-
my," etc. He had been popular in his day, but at this
time was busy furnishing entertainments made up of
half-baked talent and seldom-employed players who enlisted their services with him "for what they could get
out of it," and the joy of recurring public appearance.
An abandoned church served, with some cheap refitting,
as theater. The Saturday night's attendance was depended upon to cover the expenses of the week. It
was that type of playhouse, and that kind of performance. It seemed wonderful, though, to me who, for
the first time, was a salaried member of a theater where
lines were spoken and plays were given. It appears
pitiful enough to me now as I look back on it. My first
week's salary, five dollars, was paid in pennies. Done,
I fear, to impress me. And it did. In that form it
seemed a lot of money, even though it was a dollar
short, with a long promise, never fulfilled, of early payment of the balance. The money was of little consequence, however, except to "Emily"; the thrill of
knowing that I was a regularly enrolled player of a
theater and actually had my foot on what I believed
was the ladder of fame, was enough for me.

I appeared in little sketches, adaptations from farces by Sanford, danced and sang, and, in short, did pretty much everything I was called on to do. The sight of a small boy impersonating a lover and uttering sentiments far beyond his power to comprehend must have been droll enough for any auditor of intelligence, if any such visited that theater. Yet, as I remember it, "Sam" Sanford, who had a genius for negro impersonations, played with as much earnestness and attention to detail as if an audience of astute critics sat in front. My opinion is, he was in love with what he did. He told me that he imagined that he was the character he was portraying, that he was actually going through the happenings of the play. — I was impressed by that, for somehow I had come by the belief that that was one of the real secrets of acting.

About this time the tragedian Edward L. Davenport was the lessee of the Chestnut Street Theater, Philadelphia. His "Sir Giles Overreach" in "A New Way to Pay Old Debts," and especially his "William" in "Black-Eyed Susan," had won my love and admiration. I wondered if, somehow, I could not secure an engagement in this theater. It would be a prodigious leap from Sanford to Davenport. I dared not breathe the secret desire to any one. The idea of a youngster like me seeking an engagement of Davenport would have been ridiculed. At last, however, I mustered up courage to speak to Sanford. He was astonished and said something about "the courage of youth." I pleaded and, to my joy, he gave me a note of introduction. He wished

me luck, but feared I was too young and too small to be
of service. He did not seem at all disturbed at the
prospect of my going. Now I had my hands on what I
regarded as the open sesame to a brilliant future.

How would my "Sir Giles" or my "William" receive me? Would he put on that piercing, suspicious
mien of "Overreach" that I had often seen from the
peanut gallery, or would he, as I fondly hoped, hear to
the end the story of my ambition, and in the hearty
tones of "William" grasp me by the hand and bid me
welcome at the threshold of a glorious career? It never
occurred to me that he might not see me at all. The
flattering letter of my first real patron assured me that
my reception could not be other than kindly.

Realizing that I was about to enter the august
presence of the great tragedian, I must needs study well
how to approach him. Hugging the precious bit of
script to my bosom, I went to Fairmount Park, walked
the paths and pondered. Halting on a bridge that
spans the Schuylkill, I drew the precious paper from my
pocket and scanned it for the fiftieth time. A whiff of
wind, a sudden grab in the air, a cry of despair, and my
beautiful letter was sailing down the stream. The old
agonizing fable of the "Pot au Lait" was being re-
enacted. It was heart-breaking. I never mustered
courage to ask Sanford for another letter, and I never
met my "Sir Giles" or my sailor "William" who
"played the fiddle like an angel." I was disheartened,
and, unlike Peter Pan, I longed to grow up, that I
might do the thing I loved. Back I went to my
burnt cork and my jig steps at the "concert" halls.

About this time I met a boy by the name of James Mackin who was in partnership with a boy named Sullivan, both of them unusually skillful dancers. Mackin liked me, and out of this acquaintance came an indefinite sort of an agreement to unite our efforts. There was no longer need for running away from home to play upon the stage. The situation there was such that whatever income could be gained was now not only welcome, but necessary. There being no theaters open in the summer, I took to the "concerts" given after the performances of circuses in the large tent.

It made no difference to me where I played, so long as I played, so long as I faced an audience. I recognized that fact as of vital importance. In circus life there was every chance for learning acrobatics, to which I was not attracted. The travel was hard, and I was such a puny youngster, nobody seemed interested in me, except the Cannon-Ball King, George Cutler, who sometimes made me the subject of his jests. I remember how he opened his eyes in astonishment one day when I had the courage to tell him it was no credit to him to be unkind to a small boy. That shamed him. He grabbed me up as if I were a chip and, exhibiting me to the Clown James Maguire (easily the most intelligent man in the company), to the Bareback Rider James De Mott, the Lion-Tamer George Conkling, and others in the canvas dressing-room, apologized to me and said I was quite a little gentleman. Thereafter he was my friend.

Another season, I traveled briefly with an All-Star Circus Performers Company, engaging only in the "concert" part of it. The name of the "aggregation" escapes me, but it was headed by George Kelly, the wonderful "Leaper," Peter Conkling, the Clown, and his brother John Conkling, the Strong Man, and Ringmaster. There was no menagerie, and the company traveled on two canal-boats especially fitted out for the purpose. One boat was used for the circus trappings, horses, and hostlers, the other for the performers, dining-room, bunks and sleeping-apartments.

This boat, lightly laden, would shift about at the mercy of the winds. One night, when all were asleep, the wind blew the boat against the stone abutment of a lock. The shock of the collision and the noise of the water pouring over the lock gave the impression to the startled sleepers that the boat was going down.

"She's sinking!" some one cried, and then followed a scene of indescribable confusion and uproar, of fear and terror, as the people, mostly trained athletes, leaped and scrambled from their bunks or burst from their rooms, bent upon escape. In the center of the cabin there was a long dining-room table which went to the floor with a crash as the top "bunkies" landed upon it in force. It was the days before pajamas were much in vogue, and there was a generous and desperate swishing of old-fashioned nightgowns, together with a liberal display of shapely legs. Bass drums, cymbals, and tuba horns got hopelessly in the way and were badly smashed. Bruised bodies and limbs and abraded faces were unnoticed in the scramble for the narrow companionway. Serious consequences might have resulted had not a

MACKIN AND WILSON

Marking time in minstrelsy until old enough to graduate to the drama.
Meanwhile in nightly contact with audiences and, incidentally, earning
a competence. Edwin Booth, Joseph Jefferson, John Sleeper Clarke, and
many other prominent players served in minstrelsy.

boy's treble voice (mine) shouted, what had been told him the day previously, that there were not three feet of water in the canal!

I was not sorry to leave the circus. The boy, Mackin, was at Indianapolis, not so far away. He and Sullivan had dissolved partnership. Mackin and I therefore agreed to tour the country under the name of Mackin & Wilson. He had been simply a dancer. At my suggestion we decided to create something embracing song, speech, and humor, and to devote ourselves to minstrelsy. It was the only field open to us except the "Variety" stage.

The "Variety" theaters, so called, from which developed Vaudeville of the present day, were not much esteemed at that time. They catered to a male audience which was thought to relish freedom of jest and speech. Minstrelsy was much in vogue and numbered among its ranks many wits and men of talent, as Dan Bryant, Frank Brower, "Eph" Horn, Charles White, "Nelse" Seymour, Frank Moran, Charles Backus, "Billy" Birch, "Billy" Manning, Ben Cotton, John R. Kemble, "Billy" Arlington, Cool Burgess, Hughey Dougherty, J. W. "Watermelon Man" McAndrews, "Lew" Simmons, John L. Carncross, E. F. Dixey, E. N. Slocum, "Billy" Carter, George Thatcher, William Sweatnam, and "Billy" Emerson of the "Big Sunflower" fame, and many others. Some were coarse in their fun, but the humor of men like Manning was as delicate in texture as the threads of a fine cambric handkerchief.

When the "Variety" theater, deciding to cater to women, banished vulgarity and changed its name to "Vaudeville," it became one of the most popular forms of American amusements. There were no women on the stage in minstrelsy, and few or none in the audiences of "Variety," because of its coarseness.

Mackin and I originated a new type of song and dance, combining, we believed, the lightness of execution of those superb artists Delehanty and Hengler and the clever acrobatics of a singer and dancer named Charles Walters, who had come to Indianapolis with a company headed by Tony Pastor. We two boys practiced acrobatics all one summer in the sawdust of an abandoned ice-house on the outskirts of Indianapolis, laboring diligently to acquire the "flip-flaps" and neck-springs essential for our performance. We may not have been as skillful acrobats as Kean and Forrest were in their earlier days, but what we learned was enough. It served.

It was far from the thing I craved, but it was a means to an end, and I thought, if done at all, it should be done as well as possible. It won almost instant success for us. We had our first little triumph in Boston, at the Howard Athenæum, then under the management of that "Mrs. Partington" of the drama, John Stetson.

For many years Mackin and I were able to command a salary of one hundred, one hundred and fifty dollars a week, each, a princely sum for those times. He was, therefore, much astonished, some eight or nine years later, when I brought my folded costumes to him, dresses of the various "acts" we had "created," and told him that I meant to go no further in minstrelsy, that the time now being ripe, I had accepted a position as "utility man," at fifteen dollars a week, at the Chestnut Street Theater, Philadelphia. He was incredulous, and said that a few weeks would cure me of my folly, and that I would then be glad to resume the old relations.

I appreciated the experience I had had in minstrelsy which has served as the nursery of some of our best actors, but I was glad to take up the task which afforded greater opportunity. That period of my probation was over, at last. I was now twenty-three. I had delayed a year or two in making the change in order to provide maintenance for home and to bear me safely over to the period of greater earning. With the perky confidence of my age, I felt this would not be too long in arriving.

"Emily" rejoiced when the change was made. She was confident that it was for the best — "the only thing to do!" It was especially pleasant to sever relations with my boy partner. We had little in common. He had no further professional ambition. His taunts relative to mine were irksome. Had he halted there perhaps I had not minded, but once he resorted to fists to drive home the point of an argument. He was rather skilled in boxing. It was not a pleasant experience. I determined on a salutary lesson, to strike a balance for the rough usage I had suffered at his hands. I sought out Colonel Thomas H. Monsterey, a scientific teacher of self-defense, and soon

acquired sufficient knowledge of the art to compete
with my pugnacious partner, and this I did with the
result that I succeeded in gaining his real or assumed
respect. At that, I was not too sure of the outcome.
The element of surprise to Mackin was as enjoyable to
me as the conquest. Occurring years before the dissolution of our partnership, the "salutary lesson" had,
of course, nothing to do with our separation, but I
understand that he could never be brought to think so.

Colonel Monsterey, who taught Junius Brutus Booth,
Edwin Booth's older brother, Frank Mayo, and other
players, the use of arms, was a Dane, and probably the
most expert swordsman who ever made America his
home. After months of careful instruction, he persuaded me to enter the sword contest in the games of
the New York Athletic Club at Gilmore's Garden
(Madison Square Garden) in 1878, and through his
coaching I managed to come off victorious.

Monsterey had "a redeeming weakness," he was
boastful, but in all the years of his acquaintanceship I
never knew him to fail in making good a boast. He had
great facility in tongue wagging.

> He loved its gentle wobble,
> He loved its fluent flow,
> He loved to wind his tongue up,
> And loved to hear it go.

He is dead now, else I had not been so bold, perhaps, in
my characterization of him. After the amateur cham-
pionship contest, he aimed to prove that none of his
pupils, however skillful, could compete with the

COLONEL MONSTEREY

"master" and he proved it, but not until, catching him off guard, I had disarmed him. When I tried to follow up the advantage, he deftly disarmed me with his bare hand and turned the point of my sword against me.

As in Chicago, so in San Francisco, in minstrel days, I had gone instantly from the theater in which I was playing to the Baldwin Theater, where there was a finely capable "stock" company, doing the things I was most ambitious to do. Here I came to know such actors as James A. Herne, James O'Neill (who was an old and valued friend of Chicago days — Adelaide Neilson regarded him as "the best Romeo" with whom she had ever acted), Louis James, M. A. Kennedy, "Ned" Buckley, and William H. Crane, all members of the Baldwin Theater Company, and some of them destined later on to be leaders in the theater world.

From no member of the dramatic profession have I ever received more encouragement than from William H. Crane and his wife. They knew of my inclination toward the drama. Their friendly, candid advice, their presentation of a huge box of stage costumes capable of fitting a young man out for a round, a season of legitimate plays such as was then in force, was a tender thoughtfulness that went straight to the heart.

Here, too, I often saw, as "Richard III," the Irish tragedian Barry Sullivan, whom provincial England praised and sophisticated London derided. His fight on Bosworth Field, when "Richmond" brings the tyrant to book, was intensely realistic, lacking only in effect the curved fall at the death which Edwin Booth gave in the same character, before he had been injured in an accident. Sullivan's "Richard" had an impressive bit of "business" lasting for minutes, of "Richard," sword in hand, tracing the disposition of his forces of the morrow's battle. Suddenly he halts, puzzled. Something is evidently lacking, has been overlooked. He retraces his movements, but halts again on reaching the same point. After a meaningful pause, he leaves the field, puzzled and in heavy doubt. It was a presage of "Richard's" defeat on the morrow at Bosworth Field.

With Mackin, while in San Francisco, I was a member of the minstrel company headed by William (Billy) Emerson, at the Bush Street Theater, managed by that elderly Adonis of the Pacific Slope, "Tom" Maguire, so intimately associated with the dramatic history of California.

Probably no one will write the life of "Billy" Emerson, that black-faced player of varied talents who gave so much pleasure to myriads of people in the days of which I speak, and so, in saying farewell to minstrelsy, I am paying my tribute to this proficient public servant who was endowed with a charming stage personality. In his time the mass of our people knew much more of this Emerson of minstrelsy than of the Emerson of Concord, of whom, to my certain knowledge, the Emerson of minstrelsy knew nothing.

"Billy" Emerson then was an exceedingly gifted player who had a genius for comedy, his "Hungry Jake," in a negro sketch of that name, was a masterpiece, imbued with an earnestness and drollery not excelled by any player in the legitimate drama. It was of a piece with the superb character acting of Luke Schoolcraft in "Mrs. Dittymus' Party," or with the equally intense playing of Ben Cotton in similar negro sketches. It had all the mirth-provoking quality that Hughey Dougherty (that brainy fun-maker) produced in his humorous performance of the frightened guest in "The Haunted House," but was more subdued and artistic. Emerson never permitted himself a vulgarity in his playing, a quality for which he was recognized and appreciated. Dougherty made his audience a part of the play, took them ever into his confidence, while Emerson ignored the fourth wall of the room, where the public sat. Both methods succeeded.

In addition to this talent for comic interpretation, Emerson had a singing voice of unusual range and quality which he used with charming effect. He had been a balladist. He danced with skill and in perfect rhythm. Except in the matter of gesture, he was grace itself. He was knowing enough, however, to gesticulate infrequently.

Without having come under the spell of the man's charm, it was difficult to understand his extraordinary popularity, not so much in the East, perhaps, as in the Middle and Far West. In such melodious songs and dances as "The Big Sunflower" and "Nicodemus Johnson," he was captivating. The tunes were on everybody's lips and were played by barrel organs at every street corner and much sung in homes. Emerson made a great deal of money, lived high, and squandered his income. I saw him in his decline which came while he was comparatively young. He was still dapper in appearance and almost debonair. He had come to the condition of being willing to solicit small loans.

No two men in minstrelsy ever provoked more spontaneous laughter for wit and humor than "Billy" Birch and Charles Backus, of the San Francisco Minstrels, New York. In an association of a season or two when with Mackin, I had an opportunity to note their manner and methods which were, as to their sallies, of a peculiar, personal nature. Birch was bald and Backus had false teeth. Birch was mild with a light voice, and Backus was heavy and stentorian. His imitations of popular actors were famous. In the wordy contests which took place between them nightly as they sat on their respective "corners" in what was called "the first part," the good-natured and flashing repartee was filled with covert digs at each other's weaknesses. Oftentimes the "stories" they began to tell, between each song, were almost lost in the byways into which they strayed by force of alert and refreshing comment and reflection. Their acquaintance was large and their friends constant. Their audiences were not merely spectators, but participants, and relished, as audiences will, the association. A visit to the tiny hall of Birch, Wambold, and Backus Minstrels, southwest corner of Thirty-Ninth Street and Broadway, was usually an enjoyably intimate event. They were a metropolitan institution.

WILLIAM EMERSON

A famous "minstrel." He had a beautiful voice
and was a versatile character actor with an
engaging personality.

WILLIAM H. CRANE

Long associated with Stuart Robson. Crane was
one of the earliest of our native actors to
encourage American dramatists.

Except for the meager experience gained at the tawdry Sanford Opera House, Philadelphia, this season of 1878–79 in Philadelphia, at the Chestnut Street Theater, under the management of William D. Gemmill, was my first enrollment in a regular dramatic company. Gemmill was a stage-struck amateur with taste and refinement whose misfortune it was not to be able to realize on the stage the aims of his ambitious mind. Regretfully enough, no doubt, after essaying "Hamlet," he was told by the critics of the Quaker City that Gemmill the manager should forthwith discharge Gemmill the actor.

In my first season, the company consisted of William E. Sheridan, W. J. Ferguson, Charles Stanley, George Holland, Joseph J. Holland, Ernest Bartram, George Erroll, Harry Bave, Francis Wilson, Lillie Glover, Mrs. E. J. Phillips, Alice Mansfield, Nellie Barber, Annabelle Dudley, etc. Few of these are now living. In the second season, 1878–79–80, Sheridan gave way to James Hardie, Ferguson to Henry Lee, Mrs. Phillips to Mrs. Stoneall, while I was advanced from the position of "Utility" to "Second Low Comedy."

I was wise not to have waited longer before making the change from minstrelsy to the drama. The present system of traveling combinations was already rapidly supplanting the old resident "stock" companies in which I was hoping to obtain valuable schooling. The careful, intelligent rehearsal of that interesting old comedy of "London Assurance," our opening play, was a positive revelation to me. My part of "Cool" brought favorable mention from the press and gave encouragement. An opportunity to advance a little came much sooner than I expected and in a comic rôle for which at the time I was not ambitious. At rehearsal the Second Low Comedian, Harry Bave, had been tried and found wanting as the theatrical manager "Lamp," in "O'Keefe's Wild Oats." I was given the part, presumably because of my familiarity with the foil, which figured prominently in the scene. When shunted, I had been rehearsing "Farmer Banks," who had in one of his scenes a highly dramatic speech refusing to permit any one to cross his threshold save over his lifeless body, and I was flattering myself that I should deliver the passage with conviction. I grieved over the loss of the opportunity to deliver that speech. In the scene in which "Lamp" engages "Rover" as his leading man I was rewarded with a "recall," the joy of which nearly unbalanced me, though I tried to give no sign of it. I dare say the applause was sufficient for the "recall" or I would not have gotten it, but to me, a beginner, it was thrilling. No applause since received has been sweeter.

When I was assigned the part, I had taken it to the vicinity of Broad and Master Streets and reviewed it under the eaves of the Edwin Forrest residence with the hope in some way of absorbing inspiration. "Emily's" joy was as great as mine when, at her bedside on that wonderful night, I recounted the story of my success. Like Monte Cristo, we felt indeed the world was ours!

As the season went by, many of the leading comedy parts in plays such as Robertson's "Caste" and "Ours" fell to my lot. I was encouraged to feel that there would be a decided advance in salary for the following year; perhaps I would be offered seventy-five dollars or fifty dollars per week. But twenty dollars per week was as much as Manager Gemmill felt he could afford. I was disappointed, but, considering the opportunity, the schooling I was obtaining, a point which he did not fail to press home, I was not so foolish as to refuse.

It was a valuable experience, indeed, an education. Of my own choice I was the understudy of all the players in the company. I stepped instantly from "Salarino" to "Gratiano" during the performance of the "Merchant of Venice" when a bit of petulance on the part of "Gratiano" sent him from the stage in the middle of the play, in the hope of embarrassing the manager with whom he had had a tiff. In the thoughtful and picturesque production of "Hamlet," I was but "Osric" the "waterfly," but I arranged "the contest with foils" between Hamlet and Laertes, and gave it color and form. My understudy ambition did not carry me as far as the part of "Hamlet." My aspiration had some limitations which I recognized. However, I could have spoken the lines, and once, on a wager, I attempted to repeat the entire acting copy of the play with no more than a dozen mistakes. I lost, but came off with credit close to the finish. This was not so difficult a task, the tragedy having been many weeks in rehearsal. This merely to indicate the educational and professional advantages of the "stock" companies to the beginners of that time.

The previous experience in minstrelsy was proving of incalculable service through the familiarity it had given me over many years with audiences. As the swordsman comes to know the "feel" of his blade, so, by contact, I had come to know the "feel" of an assembly of people.

Besides the Shakespearean plays and the classical old comedies, the Chestnut Street Theater Company gave the plays of modern authors. I recall that Bartley Campbell, of "The White Slave" fame, and Archibald Gunther, who wrote "Mr. Barnes of New York," came to us with dramas about the merit of which they—and others — had doubts. The doubts proved to be justified. Campbell was a peculiar man whose egotism was boundless, brought about probably by the great popularity of his plays. Augustus Thomas is responsible for this story in connection with him:

Campbell's letter-head was adorned with two busts, one of Shakespeare and the other — of Campbell. Underneath Shakespeare's effigy was a pile of the poet's plays in book form, carefully titled. Underneath Campbell's bust there was a pile of Campbell's plays, also carefully titled. Beneath this all came the remarkable inscription: "A friendly contest for supremacy." If self-appreciation has ever gone further, it was probably in the case of the noted lyric artist, Catalani. She quietly met the severe criticism of a popular local musician by saying: "When God has given a mortal such marvelous talent as I possess, it should be applauded as a miracle."

CHAPTER V

"CARRYING ON"

Edwin Forrest declared that an actor should possess three accomplishments: singing, dancing, and swordsmanship — grace for the voice, legs, and hands. This saying made such an impression upon me as a youngster that I set about the acquirement of these graces. Dancing seems to have been a gift. The Danish *maître d'armes* Monsterey helped with the sword, but, though Nature did her best to make it impossible for me to become a coloratura vocalist, for which I had no ambition, I acquired some practical knowledge of the throat and its action in speech.

Turning now from things physical to things mental, I soon came upon a discovery that was of immediate professional advantage and a real stimulant to thought and creation — a trick to which I often felt myself impelled to resort for the sometime paucity of acceptable material provided for my utterance. There is less necessity for its use nowadays, because of the brilliant invention of our present-day playwrights, but I offer it as a safe harbor of refuge to those of my profession who find themselves beset.

The trick has unquestionably prolonged the life of many a play, and saved more than one play from actual failure. Its successful use will greatly depend upon its earnest and intelligent employment, and there is no excuse whatever for its use in plays of classic texture. Here is the discovery:

To make the unthinking roar (and the unthinking constitute a good half of any audience), it is not necessary that the author's lines be clever or humorous, and occasionally they are not. It is merely necessary that your comedian shall cock his voice into a peculiar intonation, as if the things said were the acme of wit and wisdom. The effect is instantaneous. I dare say it had often been done before my time and I know it has been done since, but so far as I myself am concerned it was an original conception. It is not too complimentary to the discriminative, but as it is only a bridge, a stop-gap until the arrival of what is needed, the discriminative only suffer temporarily. At times, even *they* are fooled.

It came about in self-defense, through disappointment that the author had failed to provide material at points in the play where instinct told me the audience would expect to laugh. The audience, which involuntarily writes many plays, does not blame the author for his shortcomings, indeed, it hardly ever considers him; it is the player whom they hold responsible, a large part of every audience regarding the players as the authors of the play.

I was forced then to accept the responsibility. If I were to be held responsible for this disappointment, I naturally felt an immediate desire to remedy it. Sometimes I was fortunate enough to supply immediately the author's lack and to answer the audience's expectation with the right words and inventions, and the fire

Yours Truly,

Annie Pixley.

A beautiful woman and an excellent actress who won success in "M'liss," a play made by Clay M. Greene from Bret Harte's story of the same name.

flamed, but not infrequently the muse was coy, and it was then that I had recourse to the enticement or deception spoken of. The more knowing would laugh at the audacity of the thing and, because laughter is infectious, everybody would laugh. If failure results, or the *coup* comes tardy off through lack of earnestness or dullness of wit, you must expect both manager and playwright upon your back at once. If success attend your efforts, you are to look for no word of appreciation. It will be told only in the increased demand for your services.

Through this artifice on the player's part, many authors have been persuaded their plays possessed wit and humor, for which there was no justification whatever. Some authors, wiser than their fellows, have even been known to say to the comedian: "These lines are not too remarkable, old chap, but given in your inimitable way they cannot fail to be received with shouts of laughter." They have not really believed this. They used what they thought was a subtle form of flattery to inspire the comedian to greater effort, thereby enhancing the prospect of success.

And now to come back to my story. If Gemmill could not afford to pay more than twenty dollars a week for my services after the promising first season at the Chestnut Street Theater, I had the satisfaction of finding those services in demand elsewhere at a higher figure. At the close of the regular season, I accepted an engagement with Annie Pixley to play the "Judge" in Clay Greene's drama of "M'liss," a dramatic version of the Bret Harte story. Miss Pixley was a successful "star" and a charming woman.

Sitting in the hotel office after the play, one evening, I overheard two men discuss the merit of her acting in racing terms:

"I think she has a better gait than Lotta," said one.

"Why?"

"Well, she gets down to her work cleaner."

There was no comparison between the two actresses. Both were capable artists who delighted their audiences. Annie Pixley was more convincing, perhaps, in a serious dramatic situation, which she was better fitted by nature and temperament to sustain. Lotta seldom, if ever, attempted this; but it is my belief that Lotta, with a winsomeness of personality, touched comic heights attained by few other comediennes. Others satisfied and delighted; Lotta did this also, but swept you into a whirl of enthusiasm. She was a rare spirit, and well deserved the extraordinary popularity that was hers through many years. A woman so highly attractive as Charlotte Crabtree, Lotta, must have heard many a *chanson d'amour*, but never one that was tender enough to persuade her to marry.

During the season with Annie Pixley, through the defection of a member of the company, I assumed, on short notice, a rôle in the play on which much of the success of Miss Pixley's part depended. I was flattered before the engagement ended at receiving an offer to co-star with her. I could not feel myself ready to assume so important a position, and declined.

On the opening of the season of 1879–80 at the Chestnut Street Theater, Philadelphia, I found myself again back in the ranks. I determined nothing should keep me out. Called to the stage-door one evening, I met my old minstrel associate Mackin. He had come to urge a renewal of our former partnership. He could not understand my refusal, and I could not well explain that I was so completely absorbed in what I was doing that it seemed years instead of months since we had met. He went away, discouraged. I never saw him again. A few years later, I read of his death at Sturgis, Dakota. We had labored industriously and had enjoyed many little successes. His passing gave me a real twinge. As said previously, I was appreciative of my apprenticeship in minstrelsy for many reasons, and for none more than the acquaintanceship it gave me with the public.

Years later, when a member of the "All Star Rivals Company," as we sat at table in the private dining-car, the subject of minstrelsy came up for discussion.

"I suppose," said Mrs. John Drew, "there are few, if any men in this company who have not at one time or another been connected with the minstrels."

Jefferson spoke up, saying: "For years I danced 'Jim Crow' in black-face, in imitation of Daddy Rice."

"I can vouch for that," continued Mrs. Malaprop Drew, "for I once sat in front and saw you do it."

"I was on the tambourine 'end' of Pell's Minstrels," added William H. Crane.

"Francis Wilson knows that I was in the minstrel

business, for he and I were in the same company —
Emerson's Minstrels, at Chicago, in the fall of '85,"
said Nat Goodwin.

"Did Edwin Booth ever black his face professionally?
I forget" — asked Mrs. Drew.

"He did," said Jefferson.

"Indeed, he did," corroborated Crane. "He told me
so himself, at Cohasset, when he was there on a visit to
Lawrence Barrett. He said that he had played the
banjo in a minstrel company in which John S. Clarke
was the 'Brudder Bones.' When Edwin Booth accompanied his illustrious father, the banjo was his constant companion in the dressing-room."

Not even my good fortune in comedy rôles, at twenty
dollars a week, my earnestness as a "utility man,"
backed by an efficient Shakespearean Stock Company
and a manager with the best will to succeed, were able
to halt the doom to which change of times and methods
were condemning the effort of managers like Gemmill.
The "ghost," as it is called in dramatic parlance, "did
not walk" promptly; that is, salaries became irregular,
and, as the season waned, I sought and obtained release in order to accept an engagement with Mitchell's
Pleasure Party in a musical comedy entitled "Our
Goblins," written by William Gill. The play was one
of the first and best of the Salsbury-Nelly McHenry
"Troubadour" sketches. My part of "the Baron,"
originally a serious one, was handed me with permis-
sion to "develop" it. I did the best I could.

We were given a chance, during the heated term

CHARLOTTE CRABTREE (LOTTA)

The best beloved and most popular comedienne of her time

(1880), to appear at the Fourteenth Street Theater, New York, then under the management of the redoubtable J. H. Haverly. The play made an immediate and unexpected success, and I suddenly found myself in favor with metropolitan audiences, a desideratum of all players. There now were many offers of engagement, but I elected to remain with a success, rather than risk a "prospect." My salary was advanced to one hundred dollars per week.

The future looked inviting. I saved money, I became confident. I married Miss Mira Barrie, of Chicago. I became venturesome, purchased a large interest in "Our Goblins," took it to San Francisco one summer, and failed. It seemed impossible that this little play, which had proved so successful in New York, should lack appreciation in San Francisco. It did, and it was something of a shock. I had hesitated over this investment and a European journey. However, I paid all the bills, brought the company home in a Pullman, and found myself in New York penniless. *Ainsi va le monde.* I have always wished there had been some other way than the one I adopted of paying that San Francisco indebtedness. A fortune, even though little, looks so much more extensive in gold, particularly a fortune that has been earned in driblets by hard work. It was no joyful experience, three thousand miles away from home, to sit at a table with yellow coin, and to pass the accumulation over to others, even though that tiny accumulation of a right belonged to those who were receiving it. But youth, health, and strength remained, so why be pessimistic? We did not long remain so. We resolved not to yield to disaster, but to press on more bravely. My young wife and her husband were at an age to smile away cares. We smiled.

However, I now had my first fling in a real musical play, one that had been the rage of the hour, and was destined, because of its humor and tunefulness, to have many recurring hours of popularity, "Pinafore."

With the failure of "Our Goblins," it was thought to help our finances with the Gilbert and Sullivan master-piece. Whether because the novelty of the thing was off for San Francisco, or because I was "off" as "Sir Joseph Porter, K.C.B.," or both, I cannot now determine. But the sad truth to me was that it did not attract the public.

Public taste as to plays runs in cycles. The entire country at this time was mad over comic opera. The "legitimate" companies, with their dramas, were having difficult days. A new order of things had arrived. Theaters were given over to comic opera, operettas, to all kinds of performance with music. It was a reflection of the European craze in the same field where Strauss, Millocker, Audran, Gilbert and Sullivan, Czbulka, Genée, and others were triumphant.

It has always been curious to me that my life should have been so closely associated with musical plays for which I had no training and which to me, comparatively, make no appeal. As a player or an auditor, I have always been a lover of the theater, but I have not often elected to attend those plays in which music prevailed. This is not in any way a reflection, but merely a statement of fact. I am, I always have been, more interested in the drama, in comedy, the skill of its construction, the lesson it teaches, and the charm and cleverness of its impersonation, than in other forms of public entertainment, yet, except in later years, a good part of my professional life has been spent outside it.

There was now nothing promising but musical plays to which to turn when I had come back from my disastrous first effort at management on the Pacific Slope. If, then, I could attain a position in the musical field, I would accept it as a stop-gap, just as I had accepted minstrelsy as a means to something I preferred.

Colonel John A. McCaull, a brusque ex-Confederate soldier, was coming to the front as a manager. We had several interviews as to terms, and finally, when he had complimented me on my doggedness in holding out for one hundred dollars per week, a contract was signed. He had, in association with Rudolph Aronson, manager of the Casino, opened that novel venture in theaters (at Thirty-Ninth Street and Broadway, which was believed by many to be miles too far uptown for success) with "The Queen's Lace Handkerchief," by Johann Strauss. The theater was unfinished and after a week or two the company, withdrawing until the building should be completed, went to the South Broad Street Theater, Philadelphia. Here I joined them. It was the beginning of several years of successful and enjoyable association with McCaull.

I replaced George Gaston as "Don Sancho." Considerable latitude was permitted me, it being understood by this time that I was a "creative" player, whatever that might mean. To me it meant a struggle "not to be obscure, not to be flat, and, above all, not to be tedious." The field was a new one, the salary high for a beginner, and much was expected of me. I had replaced a gentleman whose fine qualities made him popular with his associates, the coarser of whom resented my supplanting their friend. The responsibility of a "first night" in a new field of endeavor was heavy enough, but was made unhappy by an attempt to make a dressing-room butt of me. At first I would not notice this, and hoped my persecutors would now hold off; but when the thing reached the barefaced stage, I challenged the leader so forcibly that no further affront followed. By this time, however, I was in no condition to do myself justice. Later, in the evening, as I stood much depressed, leaning against the rail of a "star trap" underneath the stage, McCaull came by, and, speaking of the performance, his "Well, you were pretty damned bad, weren't you?" was not reassuring. However, I had marked out the squares of my stage picture, and, with his encouragement, I gradually filled them in to such satisfaction that before long he voluntarily increased my salary to one hundred and twenty-five dollars a week, and openly referred to me as his "find."

The opera, slight in plot, beautiful in production, charmingly attractive in music, ran many weeks in Philadelphia. I could well afford to leave the musical

WILLIAM T. CARLETON
A popular baritone of his time

JOHN A. McCAULL
The lawyer-soldier-manager who wanted all the chorus to "sing as high as the prima donna." When told that that was impossible, he compromised by commanding them to sing as high as they could!

side of the entertainment to such capable artists as the manly, vigorous William T. Carleton, the graceful, handsome Signor Perugini (John Chatterton), Joseph Greensfelder, Lillie Post, and a large and handsome chorus under the able direction of that dignified reproduction of the first Kaiser Wilhelm, Herr Ernst Catenhusen. He had come to us direct from "the Waltz King" composer, Johann Strauss, bringing with him an authoritative correctness of *tempii*, the mere living-up to which was an inspiration.

Catenhusen was a master. Such were his bearing and the confidence he gave that, when at the end of each act he had put down his divining-rod and ducked, as near as his dignity would permit, under the stage out of sight of the audience, the orchestra pit was empty, no matter how many musicians it still contained. Respect for his position, as he viewed it, did not permit him, except by a slight expression of face, to show his enjoyment of the stage fun, but in the dressing-room and with delightfully broken speech he would recount and expatiate on what made its appeal to him, and then laugh until tears ran down his face. Are you, which I doubt, still in the land of the living, *Vieux Maître*, or *Herr Kappelmeister*, as you would prefer to be called, back in that "*spurlos versunkt*" Germany, still cowardly in defeat? If so, I send you greetings in memory of the joyful hours we knew together.

Vocal excellence was not expected of me, and I never vouchsafed any happy disappointment in this direction. I gave every consideration to the comedy in our performances and little to anything else, except the "topical" songs, which I insisted should have point and wit. The "Dotlet on the I" in "Prince Methusalem," for instance, was a brilliant piece of writing by Sydney Rosenfield, and helped by its lilting melody, won extraordinary popularity.

Topical songs are an interruption to the drama of a performance, and so, for that matter is any song or solo. The dramatic part of grand opera has always appeared ridiculous to me, with the dying tenor and primadonna staying departure long enough to deliver themselves of difficult arias, and I have always appreciated that witty rejoinder made to the individual who was clamoring for "happy endings," even as applied to opera: "To me, any ending of a grand opera is happy!" We overlook these inconsistencies for the beauty of the music and the skill of its rendition. So, too, for the happy conceit, the timely comment and the humor, we not only pardon but welcome the topical songs. They pay for themselves, or did. As Brander Matthews says of good comedies which seem to have no moral, the moral lies in the fun of the thing and in its salutary effect upon the auditor. I have always disliked topical songs as such, but I have keenly relished an audience's enjoyment of them.

The "ensemble music" which woefully tried my patience to acquire received, I know, scant justice at my hands. I was infinitely better at it, though, than William Gilbert, who, later, became one of the comedians at Daly's Theater.

"I know all my music, perfectly, but I don't know just where it comes in," he said to the conductor.

"Never mind!" was the reply. "Watch me, and when I wave my baton at you, sing!" The opera was in three acts, but, as the conductor seemed always to be looking at him and pointing his baton in his direction, Gilbert sang every note allotted him in the first act.

McCaull knew less of music than any one else, but, as is the foible with some managers, he would commandingly offer ridiculous suggestions and then fail to realize the meaning of the silence that followed. Once he stopped orchestra, principals, and chorus to insist that the chorus should take the high note with the primadonna. It was explained to him that such a feat was beyond the vocal power of anybody but the primadonna herself. He saw the point, but, not to be outdone, he exclaimed: "Very well, then, all sing as high as you can!"

The artistic power behind the throne in the McCaull enterprise, the discreet and capable person who said little and guided everything, was the experienced Madame Mathilde Cottrelly. She was the singing comedienne who, like myself, had brilliant incapacity as a vocalist. Truth to tell, we both sang well enough, but, as Dr. Johnson said of a dinner, "It was nothing to invite a man to." Secretly, I think I sing very well — I have even met people who like my singing, Heaven bless them! — but it is not painful to poke fun at something in which you know you do not excel.

"The Queen's Lace Handkerchief" was taken back

from Philadelphia to New York for the reopening of
the now completed Casino. A successful run followed,
and then came the "Princess of Trebizonde" in which I
played "Tremolini," the clown, to whom his master,
who had won a castle by lottery, deferred in all social
customs. Later, Strauss's tuneful "Prince Methusalem" was given. My rôle was that of the minor
monarch "Sigismund" who waited till the issue of the
morning papers to know how he should act toward a
visiting monarch.

Returning to Philadelphia, "The Merry War" and
"Falka" were successfully given, I playing "Bal-
thazar," the tulip-grower, in the first, and the pompous
old military crust "Von Folbach," in the second opera.
At the close of the season I made my first trip to
Europe. I mention this, not because it was my first
trip to Europe, but because at Venice I met an embryo
Goldoni, who, though but seven or eight years old, was,
I felt, quite as young as myself. I had been told that
one might walk around the Queen City of the Adriatic
if one were patient and tireless. Exploration by means
of gondola was easy and delightful, but the declared
pedestrian possibility seemed attractive. By venturing
into a seeming *cul de sac* I had suddenly come out upon
a broad piazza in the center of which stood a bronze
statue of Carlo Goldoni, the little comedian who was to
Italy what Molière was to France. It was an unexpected, a delightful experience. A comedian in
bronze! I had seen them in "brass," even in "ivory,"
but never before in bronze. At that moment, I longed

for nothing so much as the presence of all those whom I had promised in the interest of religious ethics to give up the stage. I wanted them to witness my recantation.

On my way back to the hotel, I came upon an alert, eager-eyed boy, whistling. As I passed him, I imitated his melody. We halted, and, standing a few yards apart, whistled in imitation of each other. Exhausting that, I began in succession to gesticulate with head, hands, body, arms, and feet, all of which he reproduced perfectly, with an added grace of his own. Passers-by stopped, and a crowd gathered around us. We paid no attention. The people were more interested in the young Goldoni's clever mimicry than in the foreign *lunatico*, who was spurring him on. Being unable to "stump" him, I was about to raise my hat to the boy in acknowledgment of defeat, when I bethought me of a significant motion which my friend Perugini had told me was used in Italy as a picturesque indication that one was not to be taken for a fool and imposed upon, the swift right-and-left movement of the forefinger without moving the hand. I did it. The young Carlo tried it, and, to my joyful surprise, failed. He made a second determined effort, but, try as he would, when he wiggled that forefinger the hand wiggled with it. The crowd uttered a sympathetic "Ah!" The boy gave a shout of laughter and disappeared down a narrow street. I ran after him to press a coin upon him, but was unable to find him. I think he was looking at me covertly from the window of one of the near-by houses. I dared not enter. Among these superstitious people I might be mistaken for a foreign kidnaper, *un stregone*, whose mission it is to wish evil upon children.

The next season with McCaull at the Casino brought forward "Apajune, the Water Sprite," and gave me a chance for dramatic characterization as "Prutchesko," the rakish but wrongfully suspected husband. An opportunity occurred, legitimately, to play, or pretend to play, a cornet. Jules Levy, the really wonderful soloist, was then much in the public eye. I imitated his marked mannerisms. One evening, as I was preparing for this imitation, I caught sight of Levy looking down upon me from a box. The audience grasped the situation and rose to it. At the conclusion, Levy tactfully applauded and seemed greatly pleased. Some days later, when we met, he inquired solicitously if he actually went through such gyrations when he played the "'orn." I replied that I thought he did, except in a much less exaggerated form. I was careful to add that the fun of the thing, of course, lay in the exaggeration. "Well," he said, tucking his monocle into his eye and looking dubiously out of the other, "what an 'owling idjit I must be!"

During the early part of my association with McCaull a trip was made to San Francisco, with "The Queen's Lace Handkerchief" and "The Merry War." The long journey was broken by a night's stop at Omaha, where a performance of the first-named opera was given.

During the opera, the baritone William T. Carleton sang an interpolated song entitled "Woman, Fair

Woman," the cue to which was, "Oh, woman, lovely woman, what would we not do for thy sweet sake!" Having delivered himself of which he would make the conventional up-stage tour gazing most unnaturally at the muslin clouds and sky, returning to the front at the exact moment for the first note of the ballad. I bethought me to give him something worth looking at and that might add a touch of naturalness. As he brought his eyes earthward, I set before him, in the wings, but out of the audience's view, a rather awful caricature of a woman I had found among the rubbish of the property room. Carleton gave the picture one glance and, in trying to sing, snorted. He tried again and burst out laughing, and was forced to explain to the audience that because of something ridiculous which had just happened behind the scenes and, convulsed as he was, it was impossible to sing a serious song.

The effect on me was as surprising as to Carleton. Ever a stickler for stage discipline, had I dreamed that an artist of so extended an experience would not be able to control his feelings, I had not been guilty of the prank. I had difficulty in making my peace with our manager, Colonel McCaull, who was incensed at the unwelcome interruption of the performance. Though not pacified by my suggestion that the audience would also have laughed if they had been in on the joke, he finally forgave me. I have a distinct recollection that my salary that week was minus ten dollars and that I deemed it prudent not to call attention to the fact.

McCaull and Aronson had differences and separated, Aronson deciding to provide the Casino entertainments without the aid of McCaull. The latter wanted the Casino and the former was determined he should not have it. Being Aronson's creation and his life's chief effort, it was natural that he should have that feeling. But Aronson had a positive genius, I think, for quarreling with his best interests, which ultimately made for his managerial and financial undoing.

If it had been a question of money and personal preference, I had been better off with McCaull, but it was one of opportunity and permanent place in New York, and I elected to go to the Casino under the management of Aronson.

Colonel John A. McCaull was a soldier who fought all through "the late unpleasantness" on the Southern side. He was twice wounded, made prisoner and carried to Fort Warren, from which he was pardoned by Abraham Lincoln. Of Scotch-Irish extraction, he had all the impetuosity and pugnacity of his progenitors. He had been trained to the law, and, defending some theatrical suit brought to him by Emily Melville, I believe, became interested in that branch of the theatrical profession with which he afterwards became allied. A proud man, he was swift to take offense: he could be a firm friend and a bitter enemy. His impulsiveness often warped his judgment.

He was cordial, a gracious host, and the soul of generosity. He sustained serious injury in being thrown from a carriage. A stroke of paralysis followed. He

MR. JACOBOWSKI

The composer of "Erminie." He accommodatingly interchanged the
music of two operettas he had written. The result, musically, was the
popular "Erminie."

was patient and courageous through it all and had complete confidence in his ultimate recovery. As his resources dwindled, the theatrical profession came to his aid, and, by a single performance at the Metropolitan Opera House, raised for him the sum of twelve thousand dollars — enough money to make him comfortable for the rest of his life. He died at Baltimore, on November 11, 1894. This benefit performance concluded with an act from "Erminie" in which Lillian Russell, then in the height of her popularity, first appeared in the part of "Erminie." The writer played "Cadeaux."

I made my first appearance in the Casino's new company under the sole management of Aronson as "Marsillac" in "Nanon," by Genée, an opera, with a tuneful waltz that caught public favor and ran for one hundred and fifty performances. Sadie Martinot and William T. Carleton sustained the rôles of the lovers, Carleton doing the singing, Miss Martinot doing the loving. Later on came "Amorita," followed by "The Gypsy Baron" in which the tenor William Castle, of the "Emma Abbot Kiss" fame, played a leading rôle, all produced under the superintendence of Heinrich Conried, a very able stage director, who afterwards, as impressario, became associated with the Metropolitan Opera House when Maurice Grau retired. Conried had all the industry and thoroughness belonging to the German system of stage management. He had been an actor in German and had managed German-speaking theaters in America. He was short, pompous, not distinguished-looking, and ridiculously vain. He thought it a great pity that German was so slow in becoming the chief language of America.

"The Gypsy Baron" did not run as long as was hoped, and, its successor not being ready, a substitute was found in "Erminie," by Paulton and Jacobowski. The composer was of Polish extraction and long resident, perhaps born, in England. Years later, at the time of the first revival of "Erminie," I invited him to come to America for the initial performance. He wrote a new melody or two and conducted the revival première. I had him as my guest at The Players. We were joined at table by the poet Robert Underwood Johnson. I announced that the dessert was pie, and that all Americans ate it with knives.

"Very well," said the unsuspecting musician, "we'll eat it with knives"; and when the pie came, he and I accordingly attacked it boldly. This was too much for Johnson who felt called upon to explain that I was joking. I have not quite forgiven Johnson to this day.

CHAPTER VI

"ERMINIE" OF YESTERDAY

THE first time I played "Cadeaux" in "Erminie," I was hissed. It was a terrifying experience. That is, I thought I was hissed, which amounted to the same thing. It is not often that an actor faces such an ordeal in connection with a play with which he is to be long and intimately associated. Actors seldom face it at all. It is as vivid to me now as when the thing happened, thirty-odd years ago. There came over me a sense of helplessness and a sense of something else that may only be adequately described by the word *doom*. I felt as " Cadeaux's " wily companion " Ravennes " feels when, seeing the web of detection drawing closer and closer about him, he exclaims: "Only the sudden death of the rest of humanity can help me now!"

The thing was all the more panic-striking in that up to a good half of the performance the audience had given warm evidence of delight in play and players, and now here was I spreading a funeral pall over the whole proceedings.

Charles Lamb had the melancholy satisfaction of joining in the hissing at the failure of his own comedy. Sitting in front as an auditor, one can hiss a comedy, even if it is his own, but one cannot very well hiss one's-self; such a thing is a shade too agonizingly personal. Then, just as I thought the world must come to an end, it suddenly grew beautiful again. There was an electric burst of applause, and I knew instantly that the hisses were meant for the verse that had been sung, and the applause, a reassurance of personal favor. Now, indeed, "the rest of the world" might go on living and I knew that I should postpone that sudden visit to home and "Emily" which had been my immediate second thought when I felt the blow of disfavor had fallen.

The audience, having shown its disapproval of a sentiment that had been expressed (a playful allusion to a poem of doubtful delicacy then being much recited by a woman of social prominence), settled down anew to the enjoyment of what was said to be, as it really was, "the most successful operetta of modern times." It has been declared to rival in interest, and importance, Gay's celebrated song play "The Beggar's Opera." At the Casino alone, where "Erminie" had its première May 10, 1886, it had twelve hundred and fifty-six performances. At that time a run of "one hundred nights" for a play was an event.

"Erminie" was a happy marriage of tuneful melodies and interesting story which, under various titles, had become more or less of a classic throughout Europe and even in America. The addition of these taking melodies and the introduction of new material with a quaint twist by the composer and authors gave it high charm and attractiveness. It gained extraordinary popularity, being whistled, hummed, sung, and quoted everywhere, from drawing-rooms to legislative halls. The splendid feature about it — some-

FRANCIS WILSON AS CADEAUX (1921)

(The costume is the same as worn in the original production in 1886)

"Curiously enough, a secondary rôle became the stellar one, thanks to Mr. Wilson's racy interpretation . . . withal of a comic force undeniable . . . as full of the joy of life as Sam Weller, and of original sin as the Artful Dodger." — James Huneker.

thing of a novelty, too — was that it was clean, wholly free from dirty intrigue and nasty allusion. It was preëminently a play to which, as the saying went, one might take his mother, and these mothers went in great numbers. It grew to be a habit with them. Relatives joined them, and soon the fathers of the land, many of whom had gotten over "the theater habit," were drawn into the maelstrom. Everybody went.

"Erminie" lost a fortune for Rudolph Aronson before he, as manager, secured it for the Casino. However, when he did get it, it made one for him, so they were even. While it was playing at the Comedy Theater, in London, with fair success only, the American rights to the piece were offered to Aronson for five hundred dollars. Wholly wed to German music, German composers, German ideas, Aronson hesitated and, with the usual result, lost. He lost not only the play, but the fortune spoken of.

Nat Goodwin, in Europe at the time in search of material with which to succeed the extraordinary success made by Henry E. Dixey in "Adonis" at the Bijou Theater, in New York, bought several plays, among which was "Erminie." When he read his purchases to his managers, Miles and Barton, Barton pooh-poohed "Erminie," which he declared was a mere revamping of "Robert Macaire," and not a good revamping. Goodwin relinquished his rights in it to Frank W. Sanger, as agent for the owners Willie Edouin and Violette Melnotte. By this act Goodwin lost one of the many fortunes he might have made as an actor, larger, perhaps, than any of the many fortunes he did make, and never kept.

Goodwin's first play at the Bijou was "Little Jack Sheppard." When business began to decline, Barton called for "Erminie's" appearance. Goodwin was sorry, but, as suggested by Barton, he had parted with it. Goodwin took a carriage (no taxis in those days) to Sanger's office and explained that he wanted "Erminie."

"Why you had it," said Sanger.

"I know I did, confound it, and I want it again!" the auburn-headed comedian replied.

"Isn't that too bad!" said the sympathetic Sanger. "I have just disposed of the rights to Aronson for the Casino, and Francis Wilson will play 'Cadeaux.'"

That is how Goodwin lost a large fortune, and how Aronson came into possession of one. When Aronson had finished paying royalties on a play he might have had for five hundred dollars, he paid, according to his own statement, one hundred and twenty thousand dollars for its rental. And that is how Aronson first lost and then won a fortune.

When "Erminie" was at the height of its success, Goodwin sat in a box at the Casino, one night, to get what enjoyment he could out of his lost opportunity. It was the saddest effort at enjoyment I have ever witnessed. As peal after peal of laughter was evoked, and curtain call followed curtain call, he made a poor effort, indeed, to conceal his chagrin. Not knowing the history of the play at the time, I imagined that it was

my impersonation of the character of "Caddy" that
was distressing him, but he explained later that it was
only when he actually saw how the play took hold of
the audience that he realized what a fool he had been to
part with it.

No manager was ever more out of sympathy with the
production of a play than Aronson with "Erminie."
He regarded it as distinctly inferior to the previous
offerings he had made to the public — "The Queen's
Lace Handkerchief," "The Merry War," "The Beggar
Student," "Prince Methusalem," "Nanon," and "The
Gypsy Baron," charming operettas, musically, and
which had won considerable success. Dear, delightful
"Erminie," what a time you had making everybody's
fortune, except Nat Goodwin's, concerned with you
here in America! How patiently you bided your time
to prove that, instead of being the "stop-gap" play for
which you were purchased, you were destined for years
to outshine all other plays in the affectionate regard of
the public!

The great vogue of "Erminie" was not merely that it
had heart-warming, foot-tapping melodies. These it
had aplenty. It had besides, or first, I think, a strong
interest-keeping story well and humorously told, a
story which as a drama, "Robert Macaire," many of
the great actors of the world — Lemaître, Fechter,
Irving, in their prime, and even Booth in his youth, had
played with distinction and effect. Theirs was ever the
chief part of vital interest in the play. There appeared
never to have been any effort, by characterization, to

develop the possibilities of the companion rôle of "Cadeaux," or "Jacques Strop," as it was named in the drama.

The quality which I like to think I contributed to this impersonation was that of sympathy, wistfulness. I tried to emphazise not only the unwillingness with which the little rascal did the things which his burly, superior companion cowed him into doing, but the very tones in which the protest was made. I sought to make it evident that "Cadeaux" was a knave not so much by nature as by force of circumstances, and brutish association; that, with all his blundering and comic *gaucherie*, there was a human, tender side to the character. It was evident that, if this were not done, I should simply be following the course pursued by all previous interpreters of the part. Mere imitation has never attracted me. By a different treatment, which seemed plain enough, I hoped to bring the portrayal up to a level of interest and importance with the chief character of the play.

As "Erminie" rolled on and on at the Casino, past the first year of its run into the second and on again into the third, I wondered if it would ever end. It was interesting to contrast its tremendous success with the doubt and timidity which surrounded its rehearsals and production. Harry Paulton, the comedian-author of the piece, who came from London to rehearse it, predicted failure.

"What with the many interpellations," he said to Aronson, "and the antics of some of the people on the

HENRY IRVING AS ROBERT MACAIRE
Caricature in *The Sketch*

stage, Francis Wilson's in particular, 'Erminie' will be a fiasco."

"All I care about, all I ask of 'Erminie,' is that it will last for four or five weeks until I can get the new opera ready," Aronson declared. His belief was that everything in music, drama, taste, "kultur," originated in Germany or Austria; that the people of America needed these, and these only, for pleasure and development; that he was marking, wasting, time on anything so plebeian as a simple English classic which by education and inclination he had little power to recognize. He lived in America with his mind in Europe. "Erminie," then, was pitchforked on to the stage, in costumes made up mostly of altered dresses of previous productions. "The new opera," which was to come in for the usual lavish outlay, was named "The Marquis." When its time came for an American appearance, it failed lamentably.

At the outset of the play my own mind was far from being contented. I was not too eager to appear in "Erminie," and that excellent comedian Paulton almost got the coveted opportunity to create the part of "Cadeaux" in America, as he had done in England. I wanted to get on with the thing for which I had trained myself, toward which my ambition beckoned, the drama. I wanted to reach out and, if possible, find a play and character with which I might be forever associated, as Jefferson had reached out and found "Rip," Owens, "Solon Shingle," and Mayo, "Davy Crockett." I could not imagine that such a play and character could be in association with music! I had little or no vocal training and the thought of a career in musical plays sat heavily on my conscience and my chest, as I feared it might upon that of the public. I had gone into this mixture of song and story only from necessity or accident, and was counting hopefully upon escape; but fate decided against me. Thus I fought desperately but futilely away from the play with which I was most intimately to be known.

There was a good deal of mistrust, particularly on my part, of the dialogue of the two chief comedians. As written, it consisted largely of strained plays upon words. "That last and saddest evidence," as Mark Twain called it, "of intellectual poverty, the pun." It was my attitude toward these puns, my absolute refusal to use many of them, that brought me into disfavor with Paulton. Such things were in high repute in England, he said, and would be received with great favor here. I knew they would not. It was his rock-ribbed prejudice for that type of humor, and the possible omission of any part of it which had once been used, which gave him the keenest doubt, I think, for the success of the play. He lent himself with more or less grace to the changes and interpolations that were insisted upon, notably the "Downy Jail Birds'" duet for the two vagabonds. Never by any stretch of imagination, as I believe, did he conceive that "Cadeaux" had a human side; that while the audience might laugh at him, they might also be brought to sympathize with him.

We went on with "the stop-gap" play. The public spoke. Before long, it needed no *diseuse de bonne aventure* to point out that both reputation and fortune were being plumped into my lap. It became merely a matter of sitting down quietly and making as big a lap as possible. The public was charmed with a new type of amusement that combined delightful melody with wholesome fun which was neither an insult to their intelligence nor yet a shock to their taste.

The cast of "Erminie" at the Casino was well selected; each player seeming to fit the part to which he was assigned. Pauline Hall, in the title rôle, caught the public fancy at once. She was young and handsome and equal to the musical demands made upon her. The "Lullaby" was her artistic opportunity, and, backed by a stageful of capable, neatly costumed people, and especially by that "Pink Ballroom Scene," a freakish sort of thing that created no end of admiring comment, Miss Hall sang her way swiftly and firmly into the public heart.

For a long time I wondered about the propriety of "Erminie" singing a tearful lullaby in the center of a pink ballroom, but one day the composer, Jacobowski, explained it to me by saying that, originally, there was no "Lullaby" in "Erminie"; that, in fact, the music of "Erminie" belonged to another opera and "Erminie" belonged to other music. The managers to whom both operas had been submitted liked the music of one and the play of the other. The plays were switched, and "Erminie" was the happy result — only, the "Lullaby" had to be sung in the "pink ballroom" scene or not at all. It was too tuneful to be omitted, so into the "pink ballroom scene" it went with splendid inconsistency.

The character of "Ravennes" ("Robert Macaire") was one that made great demands upon its impersonator. He must be tragic, comic, debonair, convincing, and have ability to sing and dance. William S. Daboll was happily selected for the part. He had all the qualifications with a dash of romance, and his fine interpretation of the plausible rascal, whose confident bearing makes possible the acceptance of his awkward and timid fellow scoundrel "Cadeaux," was a real creation.

Daboll had attracted notice when he was playing with the Salsbury Troubadours. Gladly he accepted the chance to play in an important Broadway production that would greatly help his reputation, but, like all artists, he was mindful of the responsibility he was assuming, and when the "first night" came, he went to bed from sheer fright and had to be hunted up and encouraged into making his appearance. His success was most pronounced.

I never knew Daboll well. We seldom or never met outside the theater. I was a "commuter" in those days from New Rochelle to New York. But I was ever his admirer. He was a handsome fellow, a fine actor with an ingratiating stage presence. He was nervous, quick, and very sensitive. He was a college man. On gala nights at the theater his fraternities were loyal in their floral remembrances, as I found out to my embarrass-

WILLIAM DABOLL AND FRANCIS WILSON IN "ERMINIE" (1886)

ment. Once I smilingly gathered up a bouquet intended for him, and *shared* it with him. Only when I had reached the dressing-room did I discover the mistake. He forgave me readily. He had a touch of melancholia running through his make-up. In a fit of despondency one day, overcome by some trouble he thought too great to bear, he suddenly ended everything.

Marie Jansen was not in the original production of "Erminie." Agnes Folsom, a niece of Mrs. Grover Cleveland, played "Javotte." Miss Jansen came later, with an interpolated song, "Sunday, after Three." It was the charm and skill of that artist which made the "little German song" acceptable. Her successors, and there were many, always failed in it, or never attempted it.

There was another interpolated number, already mentioned, which greatly helped the success and brought the two vagabonds brightly forward, "Downy Jail Birds of a Feather." Aronson was responsible for this. He took the music from Plauquette's "Les Voltigeurs du 32$^{me.}$" and Paulton supplied the words. It fitted the situation admirably, and it is hard to believe it was not a part of the original play.

Following the winning and graceful Marion Manola, who was the original "Cérise," there came to the cast of "Erminie" the stately Isabelle Urquhart who, as I think, had much to do with the trend of modern dress in American women, now the best undressed women in the world. It was the custom to wear several petticoats in the mistaken effort to conceal as much as possible of the feminine form divine, so worshiped of men.

Isabelle Urquhart, so far as outward appearances gave indication, was moulded on perfection's lines of the Venus de Medici type and had some inkling of the fact, but she bore herself with as much modesty as would be possible for any lovely creature glorying in the possession of such an endowment. Having no desire, however, to hide her light under a bushel, or her beautiful outline under petticoats, she began to shed them, and, finally, divested herself of them entirely. All the world was then going to "Erminie." Over this innovation of the Urquhart, men raved, and women, taking the hint, became imitators. Petticoats disappeared from female attire. In place of the bulging hourglass type of dress, adored by the Dutch, American women became an anatomy, a slender, clinging thing of beauty.

Far be it from me, a mere man comedian, to set myself up as an authority on the evolution of women's dress, but this startling change in female attire followed so pat upon the appearance and action of Miss Urquhart that I have ventured to credit her with its origin.

To the praise accorded Pauline Hall as "Erminie," to Daboll as "Ravennes," to Marie Jansen as "Javotte," and to Marion Manola and Isabelle Urquhart as "Cérise," let me add a liberal quantity to the sterling characterization of the "Princesse de Grampaneur" by Jennie Weathersby. As the susceptible, simpering old dowager person in ballooned skirts and pyramidal headdress, she was inimitable. With what exuberant admiration and placid confidence she would say: "Where is the dear Baron? He *is* so clever! He changed my diamond bracelet into a pair of old gloves and a bunch of grapes, and declared that I shall find it on my dressing-table when I return to Paris." How we smiled over the reason she gave for not securing her door: "I am so afraid of ghosts!" — the easy inference being that, if the ghosts came, the unlocked door would afford a swift means of exit for "Her Grace."

"Erminie" was first played as a drama under the title of "L'Auberge des Adrets" at L'Ambigu-Comique, Paris, on July 2, 1823. No character in the play was of special importance except "Robert Macaire," which was impersonated by the gifted comedian Frédéric Lemaître, much admired and lauded by Victor Hugo. It served to crown Lemaître as a master player. As written, it was intended to be a lurid melodrama. The authors, Benjamin Antier, Saint-Amand, and "a certain Doctor Polyanthe," believed they had composed another "Cid."

Lemaître was convinced from the first that the play was impossible, and that the public would not accept it; that it was the climax of a type of blood-and-thunder drama (there is a murder in the original) rapidly growing into disfavor. He could see nothing but ridicule for it, and in this, naturally, he did not care to be concerned. While studying the lines, turning and returning the pages of the manuscript in despair, it suddenly occurred to him one day that the situations, especially those concerning the "two thieves," would lend themselves tremendously to serio-comic treatment. Greatly taken with the idea, he confided it to his fellow actor Firmin, who was to be the "Bertrand" ("Cadeaux"), and who, like himself, was uncomfortable in the thought of playing the part seriously. Firmin thought the idea "sublime" (*il la trouva sublime*), and the two determined, come what might, to put it into execution.[1] They rehearsed their conceptions of the characters in secret, and, on the first night of the play, launched them upon the unsuspecting authors and the public. The effect was overwhelming, according to Lemaître (*L'effet fut écrasant*). The drooping fortunes of L'Ambigu-Comique were revived, Lemaître was hailed as a genius, and everybody was delighted, except "a certain Doctor Polyanthe," one of the authors, who could not bring himself to forgive Lemaître, and ever after bore him an implacable hatred (*une rancune implacable*).[2]

Later on, Antier and Saint-Amand joined with Lemaître in writing "Robert Macaire," of which part of "L'Auberge des Adrets" formed hardly more than the prologue. "Robert Macaire" became the chief play in Lemaître's repertoire, and, with other French dramas, found its way into English.

Robert Louis Stevenson, in conjunction with William Ernest Henley, wrote "Macaire: A Melodramatic Farce in Three Acts," Edinburgh, 1885. It was for private circulation only. It is the old play of "Robert Macaire" with speeches rewritten by Stevenson and Henley,

[1] *Souvenirs de Frédéric Lemaître.*   [2] *Ibid.*

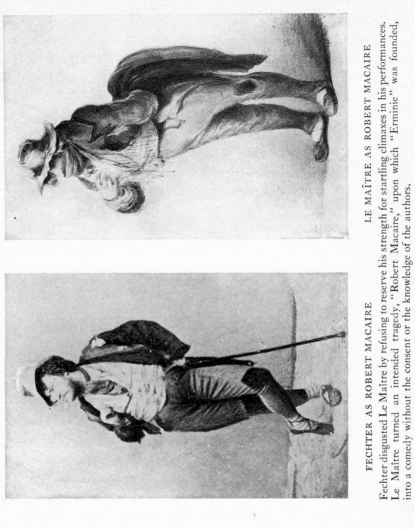

FECHTER AS ROBERT MACAIRE   LE MAÎTRE AS ROBERT MACAIRE

Fechter disgusted Le Maître by refusing to reserve his strength for startling climaxes in his performances. Le Maître turned an intended tragedy, "Robert Macaire," upon which "Erminie" was founded, into a comedy without the consent or the knowledge of the authors.

who knew nothing whatever of the technic of play-writing. "Stevenson's idea of dramatic writing," says Pinero, "was that fine speeches, and fine speeches alone, would carry everything before them."

It finally occurred to Harry Paulton, the English comedian, to write a version of "Robert Macaire" and give it a musical setting. He got Edward Bellamy to make the lyrics. Edward Jacobowski wrote the music. And that is the story of "Erminie," and of the circuitous route by which the play, which delighted myriads of people, came into existence. Dion Boucicault used to say wisely that plays are not so often written as they are rewritten.

The Casino at Thirty-Ninth Street and Broadway, where "Erminie" was first played in America, was Rudolph Aronson's art dream come true. It was a new and attractive example of Moorish architecture and, for a long time, was one of the sights which all visitors to New York must see. The Woolworth and Municipal Buildings, together with the Hippodrome, have somewhat dulled its edge in this respect. It was opened first to the public with Johann Strauss's "Queen's Lace Handkerchief," October 21, 1882, and it was the world's first roof-garden theater.

"Erminie," though not flawless, was the chief jewel in the Casino's crown of plays. It had a radiance all its own, in comparison with which the other play-jewels of that theater, though bright, were almost lusterless. As it was originally constructed, with the theater on the second floor reached by a winding staircase, the Casino was a veritable fire trap. Once it came near proving so.

During one of the numerous souvenir performances, the five hundredth, or the eight hundredth, I forget which, there came a muffled cry of "Fire!" and what might easily have been a lamentable occurrence was narrowly averted. The two vagabonds "Ravvy" and "Caddy" had just made their entrance upon the scene. With that dreaded cry instantly all was commotion and suppressed excitement, for not everybody had understood the cause of alarm. Many blanched faces could be seen, and women here and there in the audience leaned weakly against their escorts. It was a critical moment. Something had to be done, and done quickly, to prevent the threatened stampede which could only result in injury and loss of life. The right word spoken now might avert that. Often before, "Cadeaux" had heard the fire engines go clanging by, and he was confident now that the theater was in no danger. Unfortunately smoke from a passing engine had curled itself ominously through the sides of the partly open roof, and, in the excited state of mind of the audience, foreboded the worst.

"Ladies and Gentlemen!" shrieked the ragged "Cadeaux" in tones that he was glad to see commanded attention, "there is no danger! Please sit down! If you behave like men and women, and not like sheep, a great danger will be averted; but if you do not accept my word that there is no fire, no cause for fear, nothing in the world can prevent a great disaster. Please sit down!"

Not everybody obeyed, but many did, which made a diversion in the state of affairs, and set an example which could not but act beneficially, as it did, upon the overcharged imaginations of those present. Then "Cadeaux" explained further that if there were the least danger he would be the first to run like a March hare, that as long as the audience could see him standing there, they might rest assured that all was well; and he especially explained the cause of the smoke.

"Cadeaux" knew that he had spoken the right word at the right time, yet it would not have been half so effective but for the heroic behavior of a number of the most uncompromising-looking fashionables, "Johnnies," who had been occupying the front-row seats, and who, to a handsome, well-groomed man, seated themselves, and, leading the applause, called, "Sit down! Go on with the performance!"

I had heard of the English "toff" who to-day drawls his words in the most affected manner and on the morrow, as a soldier, gives up his life with the utmost coolness and heroism, and I was now thrilled with admiration for those American elegants in the front row who, though only half assured of safety, behaved so courageously.

Looking back at that lengthy period of continued performances, year in and year out, when the tired players, on one excuse or another, were dropping out of the race, an incident always comes to mind, that of Aronson's father meeting me from time to time at the stage-door and plaintively saying:

"You feel goot, vot?"

"Yes."

"Please, Mr. Vilson, don't *you* get sick!"

My professional position was now much improved. More than ever I realized the wisdom of having made monetary sacrifices for greater metropolitan opportunity. The one soon vastly enhanced the other. I was not only reconciled to whatever additional good fortune fate held in store for me, but quite prepared to welcome it with open arms.

The public was leaving me in no doubt as to its continued favor, but I did not realize how strongly I was entrenched in managerial estimation until, after several seasons, I was sent for and told flatteringly that people regarded me as much a part of the "Home of Comic Opera," as the Casino was called, as one of its Moorish arches, and, with the coming season, I was to be the recipient of a certain percentage of the profits of the theater, provided I would enter into a long-time agreement, in order that the management might be sure of my services.

I was weak with astonishment. As I viewed it, Aronson, as representative of the Casino, was trying to force upon me an additional thirty or forty thousand a year with no inclination in the world on my part to resist. To this very end I had been devoting every particle of mental, physical, and emotional power I possessed, hanging on at the theater through winter storm and summer heat, when nearly every other member of the cast was disporting himself or herself in European or

PAULINE HALL

Erminie in the first American production of the operetta by that name.

ISABELLE URQUHART

The regal beauty who played Cerise in "Erminie."

American seashore vacations, but I had not dared to hope that this good fortune would arrive so soon.

My dream was coming true, my ship, laden with all the treasures of my fancy, was coming in! At last the future of the family was to be secured. The reward for the struggle up through the poverty of childhood and youth was in sight. The life of the nomad was over. I could even fancy myself, like William Warren, of the Boston Museum, actually possessed of "a local habitation and a name." Now, now, the *real* search was to begin for coveted treasures, the things with which one surrounds himself in an atmosphere of refinement, the bookish prizes, this bit of pewter, silver, and mahogany, and that small but choice array of pictures over which I had been so long mooning! Could it be possible that I was to be so happily gratified? I was, indeed, startled at the proposal of Aronson, but I kept countenance and agreed to what was proposed in as measured a way as my palpitation permitted, and then, as one rudely shaken out of a dream, I woke up!

I had had a beautiful reverie, extending over many a week, a reverie that in some strange way was yet real enough to leave in my possession (I still have them, unsigned) a set of contracts, made out in the handwriting of the Casino's manager, setting forth terms and conditions, precisely as I had dreamed them. Lapsing into dreamland again, presumably, I found myself insisting upon the naming of a day and hour for the signing of the contract. For one evasive reason or another, but never the same, the act of signing had been postponed from week to week, and, this time, in actuality, I was finally told that it had been found that the manager's contract with the stockholders of the Casino would make such an agreement as mine illegal! Perhaps this was true. I did not think so. To me it seemed unquestionably nearer the truth that Aronson, after his first generous impulse had found himself in the position of Mark Twain's dog, which had a disagreeable habit of eating heavily and then going to his master's room to repent. Aronson was still willing to enter into an agreement, but only on a stated salary basis. As it was now past that period of the season when I could treat with other managers for engagement, I believed, whether rightly or wrongly, that I had been misused, and, refusing to enter into further arrangements, packed my trunks for a journey to Europe.

Before sailing, however, I was again approached by Aronson and asked to name a salary for my services. With no little bitterness of feeling I named a sum which I meant to be prohibitive. To my astonishment, the terms were accepted. The contracts were signed, for a sum greatly in excess, I am told, of that paid any other player of the period. There must have been something appeasing in all this, for I have a distinct remembrance that much of the enjoyment of that European vacation was abated by the desperate fear that I should never live to receive my first week's princely salary!

It seemed impossible that any one could value my services at such an extraordinary sum. But with a fine burst of philosophy, when the time came, I readily adjusted myself to the situation and, so amazingly elastic is the human ego, I even came to feel that I was worth more.

The voyage home from Europe had compensating features for the fear entertained that fate meant to cheat me out of the joy of receiving such a fabulous wage. I give an account of the "compensating feature," not so much from the enjoyment that came to me from the experience as for the lesson it contains for the superstitious.

Late in securing passage and coming on board at Southampton, I was assigned to Stateroom Thirteen which many another superstitious passenger had been unwilling to accept. On going into my cabin for the first time, I was conscious of a good deal of awed attention from a number of people standing by, and one man said, loud enough for me to hear, that he thought I had my "courage" with me. Notwithstanding what the passengers said was an inauspicious beginning on my part of an ocean voyage, I was lucky enough next day to win the "pool" made up in the "Smoke Room" the evening previous on the day's run of the ship, those wagers in which one permits himself to indulge in order to relieve the monotony of the voyage, and hopes fervently the "relief" will be a substantial one!

There were many congratulations and a disposition on the part of the passengers to be more friendly with one who has flown in the face of superstition, and, besides, the "relief" *was* a substantial one, and that always makes a difference. But when I also won the "pool" the following day, with an equally substantial "relief," there was much commotion on shipboard. It furnished a topic for excited conversation. No one ever heard of such luck coming to a creature for whom Thirteen had no terror. But even this climax was to be outclimaxed, for, Dame Fortune, being in her merriest mood, resolved to make it " three times and out," for, the following day, I again won the "pool" with equally substantial "relief." The "three times" was for me and the "out" for the passengers, who, with ill-concealed feelings of disgust, resolved to stay out of further ship pools, refused even to consider one.

For a day or two the boat went along betless, with great quandary on my part as to my gains. I was puzzled whether to turn the money over to charity or build a home on the Hudson. I am still puzzling. We were nearing land and expecting the advent of the pilot. The passengers got together and decided, it seems, to "frisk" me. They resolved once more to risk a generous pool on the number of the pilot boat and, to make sure that I should not win *that* pool, I was allotted, being absent, the number of a pilot boat that had been lost at sea a few months earlier. Of this I was ignorant. It was to be a great joke on me, and the passengers were to enjoy a hearty laugh at my expense. I was told afterwards that there was much winking in anticipation of the roar that would go up at my discomfiture, and much nudging with elbows as I went by on my "constitutional."

Dame Fortune, however, had not even yet aban-

RUDOLPH ARONSON
To whom America is indebted for the first roof-garden theater

doned me, and, in a strange and humorous way, provided a boomerang for my would-be scoffers. During the day a Hebrew passenger asked me to buy a half interest in his ticket. It was no good, he declared, unless, with my luck, I took an interest in it, then it would be sure to win. Why should I buy an interest in his ticket, I argued, when I had one of my own, a whole ticket, with which I was quite satisfied? He was so insistent that, to end the matter, I offered to purchase the ticket outright; this offer he positively refused. I finally consented to take a half interest.

At an early hour the following morning, the door of "Stateroom Thirteen" was stormed by a committee of hilarious passengers, headed by the Hebrew, who told me that our number had won! At the same time a lot of money was forced into my hands as the result of my copartnership. There was much talk of my "great run of luck," but, as a believer in the law of averages, it did not seem strange to me.

Let me add that in all my ocean voyages I had never before, nor have I since, won a pool on the run of the ship.

CHAPTER VII

"STAR–GAZING"

As the story goes, the Persians abused their privileges with respect to divorces. In a fit of nerves, wives would fly off the handle and, declaring themselves unwed, which was one of the ways to freedom, would find themselves automatically without husbands — and visible means of support.

To make people think twice before divorcing once, a law was made which forbade repentant divorced wives to remarry their former husbands unless they had been remarried *ad interim* to another man. This led to the creation of a substitute husband, a temporary hubby, so to speak, who, "for a consideration," would legally marry the woman, and then, at a statutory period, plump her intact into the arms of "her first and only."

It was an office of great discretion and delicacy, this Persian "Hulah," a popular and highly lucrative one, and men became renowned in it in proportion to their trustworthiness, for the privileges it carried might easily be abused with many resultant embarrassments. The story was in vogue in the early part of the nineteenth century, and as I remember reading, was one with which the Napoleonic exiles regaled themselves at St. Helena.

In the narrative, two beautiful people of rank have quarreled a day or two after marriage, but, having in the presence of witnesses uttered the fatal words that divorce them, and having as swiftly repented, seek the services of the accommodating "Hulah." Not the least amusing part of the story was the anxiety of the royal husband to take the "Hulah's" place, "for a consideration," as husband and protector, incited thereto by the fear that the "Hulah" in some way might be deceived or forgetful.

"Sir," replies the "Hulah," puffed to the highest by the consciousness of his integrity, "I have been married a hundred and fifteen times and have never been deceived once!"

When I spoke these lines, in a play which was made from this story and which we called "The Oolah," the audience seemed properly impressed and smiled, but when it occurred to me to add, "I have known men who were married but once, but who were deceived a hundred and fifteen times," the audience roared.

It was this play that I brought to the attention of the Casino management. Manager Aronson liked it, or said he did, and entered into an agreement to produce it. But when the time approached to put it into rehearsal, he ignored the matter. It was only after much delay and incivility that I managed to secure the return of play and forfeit. Aronson puzzled me. There was no reason or necessity for him to be unjust or discourteous to one whose services he regarded as practically invaluable. He labored under a common error that all such actions may be effaced by money. I thought this an excellent vehicle and the time opportune to begin preparations for "setting up in business" on my own account, and, greatly encouraged and helped thereto by Albert H. Canby, a long-time friend, newspaper man, manager, actor, and critic, I now lost no time in making toward that goal.

It was not easy to leave the Casino, where I had had much success, to take up the uncertainties of management in the attempt to launch myself as a "star," and my going would have been delayed for years had my position at the theater been happier. When all arrangements for departure were complete, the inducements to have me remain were somewhat staggering and tempting, but it was too late. I have been glad all my life that it was too late.

Rudolph Aronson had stumbled accidentally into something for which I felt he had little qualification, management. Intending one thing, he fortunately blundered into another, and that other nothing less than success, which died on his hands through incapacity. Endeavoring to establish himself as an impressario, a conductor, in the field of band concerts, orchestral music, and summer "gartens," after the manner of Johann Strauss, he had toppled over into successful theater management. Like many managers, he overrated his own powers and underrated the people with whom he worked. The power to employ has always made a great difference in the attitude of the employer toward the employee, and it probably always will but, as it seems to me, the czar-like attitude, now happily changed since the advent of The Actors' Equity

MARIE JANSEN

Association, has less reason for existence among managers than among people of other trades and professions, allowing it to have any reason to exist at all.

Having decided to use "The Oolah" as the opening play for my "first appearance on any stage" as a "star," I began to cast about for a supporting company. Charming Marie Jansen, the popular comédienne, agreed to trust her professional fortunes with me, but there remained lesser lights to be engaged. Making sure they were not under engagement of any kind with the Casino management, I entered into contract with a number of them for my new venture. Somehow this chagrined Aronson. It was proof that I intended to leave the Casino. He ordered the people dismissed, but would reinstate them, provided they gave up their future contracts with me. I thought this rather high-handed, and was much at loss to know how to act. However, Aronson's stage manager, one Max Freeman, solved the difficulty by taking it upon himself, in his employer's interest, to declare me irresponsible and likely to strand people whom I employed somewhere "on the road," minus salaries.

I met the burly stage manager that evening in the alleyway of the theater in which we were playing — Grand Opera House, Chicago, — and asked for an explanation. Oh, dear, he could not think of such a thing! He would not explain, much less retract or apologize, and he wanted to know what had lent the idea that he would. Of course I could have ended the incident by saying, with "Bob Acres," that I thought my traducer a "very ill-bred man," which would have been polite and anæmic, and, not unlikely, that is what I should do now that the blood does not run so hot. Be that as it may, of one thing I am certain, no man wearing a pot-hat ought to engage in a fistic contest. Every time Freeman met the earth his pot-hat met it, too, but at a different angle. I grew tired of seeing it replaced so carefully by his henchmen. Freeman also grew tired. On my pointing out to him that it would be advisable to reinstate at once the illegally dismissed players, I was delighted to find that his views had undergone a change. He coincided readily with the suggestion. He was even mild of tone. Later, under threat of a suit, Freeman demanded an apology. Refusing, I was put under bonds to keep the peace within the State limits, the magistrate being unable to conceal an amused smile, and laughing outright when I inquired the exact distance to the State line, a bit of parade on my part, as I had lost all resentment on the players being reinstated.

Aronson, of course, was greatly incensed. His managerial dictum had been thwarted. Few things in this world are worse than thwarting a managerial dictum. In a theatrical company, absolutely nothing. I suspected that revenge was being planned, and I wondered what form it would take. I had not long to wait. Crossing Park Square, on my way home one Saturday night from the Brooklyn engagement, I scanned the bulletin boards, as usual, in front of a newspaper office. There was the revenge plastered up as large as life — "Aronson drops Wilson." The act was a distinct violation of contract, and it was evident the Casino manager meant to make my dismissal as humiliating as possible. What he was really doing was giving me the time I had been craving to attend to the launching of my own ship of state, which was now in swift preparation.

I stood in front of the bulletin board and laughed, thanking my lucky star for the dismissal. I went about the preparations of my play with increased vigor for a week or two, and then something happened to Aronson. My name being in the Philadelphia contracts, the managers there refused to permit the performance of "Erminie" in the Quaker City unless I were a member of the cast. Aronson was obliged to eat crow, obliged to consent to everything, restoration of position and lost salary, etc. The only thing that induced me to return to the play was my love for it and the fact that I had no legal right to refuse — and I did have a mischievous desire to see the effect of the boomerang Aronson had prepared for himself. I rather incline to feel that this latter motive outweighed the legal consideration.

The welcome back was enthusiastic. People had taken sides, and acted in a way hard to understand in these days of many theaters and many public favorites. It was as if something of real importance were taking place. To me, the center of it, it was wonderful!

"The Oolah" opened at the Broadway Theater in May, 1888, and on that night, in his desire to do his utmost for the man who believed he had done as much as any one to make the Casino a success, and the Casino in those days was an "institution," Aronson, with a heart full of gracious appreciation, gave a dinner on the roof of the Casino to the dramatic critics, possibly with the idea of influencing them in my behalf by keeping them away from that first performance. However, newspapers, notwithstanding dinners on a roof, have a way of making assignments to cover events, and our play did not lack attention. What it did lack was skillful construction, and the newspapers said so frankly.

When the curtain fell that May night — the 13th, by the way — it was not the only thing that went down. My heart went down with it to a greater depth of discouragement than it had ever known before. But the heart of a young man is an elastic thing, and mine came back with a spring. I forgot all about the possible rejoicing of Aronson at my discomfiture and gave all my energy and determination to the oxygenizing of our near-corpse of a play. We pumped new ideas, new scenes, new songs into it, and soon it began to show additional signs of life. Of what use was it, where the sense in being "a creative comedian" in the performance of other people's plays if I could not follow it with similar service for my own? And I did, with the aid of the best help I could command. One night I dared to hold the curtain down for an unusual length of time after the first act while we rehearsed a newly written ending to the second act, an ending which, when given a few minutes later, made a vital difference, causing the near-corpse of a play to sit up and wag its head.

FRANCIS WILSON IN "THE OOLAH"

Hoolagoolah, the Oolah, was the Persian marriage-broker who obliged by becoming the husband *pro tem* of divorced wives. He declared he had been married one hundred and fifteen times and had never been deceived once. He knew men who had been married but once and had been deceived one hundred and fifteen times.

When all possible was done, I invited that wizard of playwriting and construction, the elder Dion Boucicault, in for inspection and criticism. "I have seen much worse plays," he said, "run a hundred nights." Through summer heat, our play ran well past that figure and to the joy of friends — and myself — closed a very successful season. If, like some unfortunate racers, we had gotten off to a poor start, we certainly made a "Garrison finish," if that is the correct term. For a brief period there, it looked as if we might be obliged again to trail at the Casino cart as a led captive. Determination, much energy, and some inventive power spared us that humiliation. Who can tell, though? Perhaps our return would have saved Aronson the loss of his Casino, than which no theater in New York was nearly so successful. If my going back had brought me less happiness than I have enjoyed, I cannot find it in me to be sorry that I came away.

There was no doubt, however, about the next play produced, "The Merry Monarch." I have never done such a thing before or since, but I was so confident of its immediate acceptance that I sat in the box-office of the Broadway Theater on the first night until the last ticket in the rack was disposed of, 8.10 P.M. I was wholly free from that nervousness which has attended many other plays I have given. The story was unusually strong and would have made a winning performance quite independent of any musical accompaniment. As it was, the dainty "When I was a Child of Three," "The Ostrich Song," and "Love Will Find the

Way," by J. Cheever Goodwin, with the appealing music by Woolson Morse, deeply emphasized an unusual and lasting success.

This is how I came by the play. Sitting in a Paris theater, I had chanced to observe the theater's successes painted in a circle of the ceiling. As I read I wondered what the story of "L'Étoile" could be.[1] I got it, read it, and was interested. Having adapted it, I turned it over to J. Cheever Goodwin, and "The Merry Monarch" was the result. Much of its success was due to J. Cheever Goodwin, a Harvard man, whose wit and humor and graceful lyrics were ever in evidence. He wrote the libretto for the musical play of "Evangeline" which so attracted an earlier generation of playgoers, and in which Henry E. Dixey and Richard Golden made their appearance as front and hind legs respectively of the "heifer," that heifer which won enthusiastic applause for her dance. One must always be careful in mentioning "Adonis" Dixey's connection with the "heifer." While he does not at all object to the statement of the fact of his having been a pair of the "heifer's" legs, he is punctilious about having it known that it was the *fore* legs. Innumerable were the tricks, when in that front position, he played upon his Golden partner in the rear. The great Lemaître made *his* first appearance on "all fours," as a lion in "Pyramus and Thisbe."

In a previous season I had come upon two colored

[1] The star (*l'étoile*) of fate which governed the lives and actions of monarchs, especially superstitious monarchs.

boys, John and Jess, in Washington. They were street
urchins who danced along the curb for pennies. I found
them in tatters, but ordered them properly attired and
forwarded to New York. When they arrived months
later on the stage of the Broadway Theater for rehearsals, they were so fancifully dressed as to be greeted
with shouts by the entire company. Colored boys, with
canes and ultra-fashionable straw hats on abnormally
oblong heads, shriekingly loud clothes, and patent-
leather shoes, were not met every day, at that time, on
Broadway. I fitted them into the play by dressing
them in "trunks" and Eastern headgear and making
them the barelegged, be-sandled African attendants
of the "Merry Monarch." When the King had delivered himself of the manner in which "Love Will Find
the Way" to open the door to all difficulties, and had
withdrawn, these darkey "attendants" gave themselves
over surreptitiously to the dance. They were surprised by
the monarch, who found the dance so infectious that he
completely lost all dignity and joined them. The music
was so contagiously lilting and the dancers so earnest,
and apparently unaware of observation, as wholly to
delight the audience. When it came time for the "scene
rehearsal," our English stage director Richard Barker
was horrified to discover that the merry monarch's
throne was of peacock design. He declared it to be "a
sure omen of failure!" However, I insisted. I remembered that Whistler had a famous room all of peacock design. I remembered "Stateroom Thirteen," and
I failed to understand how a little thing like a theatrical

peacock throne could influence the success of a play. Anyway, what was the use of being a "star" and a merry Monarch into the bargain, if one could not indulge a taste for peacock thrones? I had my way. A happy memory, that "Merry Monarch"!

During the run of "The Merry Monarch" at the Broadway Theater, our musical conductor Signor Antonio DeNovellis introduced a voice to me through the half-open door of my dressing-room. The owner of the voice had shown intelligence and spirit at a morning rehearsal and DeNovellis recommended her warmly as a likely candidate for understudies and as a decided addition to the chorus. I had no wish to make a special journey from the country to hear any one sing for a chorus position, so, as I dressed, I listened to the new candidate while she sang in the wings. It was a fresh, sweet voice, and the spirit of the song's rendition made me eager to meet the singer. When I came from my dressing-room, I was surprised to see a very young girl, wearing a chip hat and a short dress — only young girls wore short dresses and chip hats in those days.

"This is Miss Glaser," said the conductor. Lulu Glaser showed great aptitude, and, because of the early professional opportunities she met and to which she was equal, rose speedily in her chosen career. She was graceful in form and action and had wonderfully luminous eyes. She was an ambitious young lady, a more than average musician, even owned a bookplate, and had the health of the German Spa. She became an understudy and, when told that she had to take the place of Marie

LULU GLASER

Jansen who had fallen ill, she promptly fainted, which gave great hopes of her. It was strong evidence that she appreciated the responsibility of the undertaking. She was too frightened to do herself justice. Then, when the opportunity came again, she acquitted herself admirably. She succeeded Marie Jansen in "The Lion Tamer," and, later, had the leading female rôles in our plays "Half a King," "The Little Corporal," etc., and I shall always remember her best as "Pierrette" in "Half a King," where her youth and spirit fitted so admirably, and where her talent, daintiness, and intelligence had full play. She came from Pittsburgh, but lived to gain not only a great victory over the undulating "r" one hears in the speech of many western Pennsylvanians, but to head her own company. The operetta called "Dolly Vardon" was her chief success. Besides Miss Glaser, other young women who afterwards became professionally prominent, made humble beginnings in companies of mine. Miss Christie Macdonald was one. At a rehearsal of The Players Club production of "She Stoops to Conquer" (June, 1924), Elsie Ferguson reminded me that she also had so begun — in "The Strollers."

About this time there began an inundation of naïvely humorous letters from ambitious people, mostly women, eager to try their wings in a stage flight. Setting forth their qualifications in varied ways, they begged for an opportunity. Sometimes, though not too frequently, they were willing "to begin humbly and work to the top," but more often they wished to startle the world at once with their genius. They had had every assurance from friends and acquaintance, and from success attained in amateur effort, that only a chance was wanting. Would I give it to them? I not only would, but I did, according as they deserved, though it was not always easy to persuade some that, without technic and experience, "startling the world" had its difficulties and delays.

Some of the letters of appeal were especially welcome because of their unconscious humor. One ambitious mother wrote, " . . . my daughter is five feet six and full of music." No accurate gauge could be made, however, because no width was given. Another young lady said, "My dear Mr. Wilson, my voice is so powerful I wish you would appoint a large hall to examine me in." It is unnecessary, perhaps, to say that I did not avail myself of this opportunity, as attractive as it may have proved. This naïve correspondent closed her letter with this insidious dab at my age:

"My mother saw you in one of your plays, but that was a long, long time ago when she was a very, very little girl."

Not less amusing was the incident of the young woman who sought me out and applied for a position, declaring that she had two voices. I was interested, curious.

"Two voices?" I asked.

"Yes."

"Indeed! What are they?"

"A singing and a speaking voice."

But she capped the climax by adding that she would be glad to sing and so give me a taste of her quality, but, unfortunately, she had lost her singing voice. Then, hastily and reassuringly, she volunteered: "I am expecting it back, though, in about a week."

Somehow I had no distinct feeling of excitement at the prospect of being present on the Tuesday or Thursday of its possible arrival.

Few people have any idea of the power of rehearsals to exhaust nervous energy. The monotony of endless repetition, the necessity of care in order to produce the appearance of spontaneity, and the dull waiting, waiting while others, more stupid than ourselves, so we always think, are rounding out their characterizations with deadly, nerve-racking reiteration.

I was in just such a state as this at the end of one of "The Merry Monarch" rehearsals and had wended my way to the Grand Central Station to take the train home to New Rochelle. I had barely given a nod of recognition to an acquaintance or two I had met *en route*, I was so tired and off guard, as it were. Suddenly, after entering the "Waiting Room," there appeared before me, dressed in his Sunday clothes, a stubby, stocky little Irishman with a crescent of scarlet whiskers. "Galways," I have heard them called — the kind that runs like a rivulet under the chin from ear to ear. Each particular whisker seemed to have been the recipient of recent and meticulous attention, the whole shining with coral brightness. I knew that mischievous boys on meeting such whiskers were wont to imitate the sound of the wind, "zizz-z!" sifting through trees. In thinking of this I, unconsciously, gave utterance to the "zizz-z!" As I hope for grace hereafter, that is the truth of it. Instantly the Irishman, his ears quickened to what was evidently a familiar if unpleasant sound, was upon me. With both fists clenched and himself balancing on one leg, exactly after the manner of Edward Harrigan in a stormy part of "The Mulligan Guards," he shouted:

"G'out o' here! G'out o' here, for a dam loafer!"

"That guiltiest feeling," which cartoonist Claire Briggs depicts so faithfully, took complete and immediate possession of me. I could not deny that I had offered the taunt, but I realized how futile it would be to attempt an explanation to an exasperated man, fighting mad. He would not believe me. In his place, I also would not believe me. I did not know what was going to happen, but I did know that I was too fatigued to care. I swiftly determined to protect myself if struck at, but not to strike in return. That much I could and would do.

"G'out o' here!" he repeated threateningly. "G'out o' here!"

"But my dear friend, I don't wish to go out," I said calmly. "I have just come in — for the purpose of taking the train, and, if it is all the same to you, I'll proceed to do so." Pat was much taken aback at this, and, I thought, a little relieved. He evidently expected a greater show of spirit. His fists unclenched and he looked at me as if he thought I were demented, while my indifferent tone and action, as I hoped, deceived passers-by as to the real situation.

"Is it the thrain yure takin'?" he said sneeringly.

"It is," I answered peacefully, trying to move on.

"Wait a minyute, wait a minyute, me bould bucko!" he said quickly, stepping in front of me with reclenched fists. Wagging his head at me in an indescribable way, he delivered himself of the following accommodating threat: "It's meself that's goin' out for a minyute or two. Whin I come back, if yure still here, I'll kick you into the sthreet fur a durty loafer!"

And with these civilities, we parted. My wife, who had accompanied me, quite properly abandoned me on the first hint of hostilities. I could never convince her that I had not invited an attack. She was somewhat disappointed at my escape from punishment. Half my joy at that escape was her disappointment.

A most important member of that "Merry Monarch" cast was Marie Jansen, a born comédienne. She was gifted with an appealing stage presence. Modest and sensitive, she had a real love of the written word. She owned books, some of them scarce, read them and quoted aptly. Men raved about her, and Eugene Field wrote verses to her. She came first into actual prominence with the McCaull Opera Company by singing a winning song called "Ohe, Mama," with which she became extremely popular.

Before the play "Black Hussar" was produced in which it was sung, she had sprained her ankle which

caused her to limp badly. Nothing daunted, she
utilized the limp by making it an attractive part of the
rendition. Perhaps the best thing she ever did professionally was "Nadjy," in Chassaigne's opera of that
title. She had no thought of playing the part even a
few days before the opera was given. It was in the last
period of rehearsal at the Casino. Some one, Sadie
Martinot, I believe, in a fit of petulance, withdrew
abruptly from the cast at the eleventh hour. The
manager, Rudolph Aronson, was in despair, and
appealed to Jansen who was under contract to me. It
was between seasons, and points of legality and courtesy were involved. Jansen, eager to seize the opportunity, asked my advice and consent. I gave both.

It was assuredly a fine opportunity, but I could not
believe it possible, in the brief space of two or three
days, for the comédienne even to commit the lines to
memory, let alone give the character an adequate
rendition. I said so, and added that by accepting I
thought she would be in a fair way to do herself an injustice from which nobody would suffer as much as herself. She was a level-headed little lady and, I felt sure,
would see the force of my advice. This is how she
followed it:

When the ordeal of the "first night" came, she
was "perfect" in the lines, made an instant success,
and greatly enhanced her reputation. Degas never
painted a lovelier picture of a ballet girl than that
presented by Marie Jansen in "Nadjy." Why can we
not always stay young!

Here is the poem that Eugene Field wrote and dedicated to her:

To Marie Jansen

'Tis years, soubrette, since last we met;
　　And yet, ah yet, how swift and tender
My thoughts go back in time's dull track
　　To you, sweet pink of female gender!
I shall not say, though others may,
　　That time all human joy enhances;
But the same old thrill comes to me still
　　With memories of your songs and dances!

Soubrettish ways these later days
　　Invite my praise, but do not get it!
I still am true to yours and you:
　　My record's made, I'll not upset it!
The things they say, the pranks they play,
　　I'd blush to put the like on paper!
And I'll avow they don't know how
　　To dance, so awkwardly they caper.

I used to sit down in the pit
　　And see you flit, like elf or fairy,
Across the stage, and I'll engage
　　No moonbeam sprite were half so airy;
And everywhere about me there
　　Were rivals reeking with pomatum;
And if perchance, in song or dance,
　　They caught your glance, how I did hate 'em!

Oh, happy days, when youth's wild ways
　　Knew every phase of harmless folly!
Oh, blissful nights, whose keen delights
　　Defied gaunt-featured melancholy!
Gone are they all beyond recall;
　　And I, a shade, a mere reflection,
Am forced to feed my spirit's greed
　　Upon the husks of retrospection.

And low, to-night the phantom light,
That as a sprite flits on the fender,
Reveals a face whose girlish grace
Brings back the feeling warm and tender!
And all the while, the old-time smile
Plays on my visage, grim and wrinkled,
As though, soubrette, your footfalls yet
Upon my rusty heartstrings tinkled.

As I began my professional career as a "star," with "The Oolah," and also began this chapter with some account of it, let me finish with an incident in connection therewith which I think not wholly devoid of humor.

"The Oolah" was an adaptation from the French of "La Jolie Persane," the chief female rôle of which Jane Hading had played in Paris. When that incomparable comedian, Constant Coquelin, fresh from his secession from the Théâtre Français, came to this country to delight us with a series of classic performances, Jane Hading was his co-star. We appeared at the same time in Chicago, in opposite theaters, and learning that "The Oolah" was her old friend "La Jolie Persane," the Hading expressed a lively desire to see it. A box was set aside for her. She greatly delighted in the performance and apparently relished a few speeches which I remembered from the original French, though she may not have understood me.

Nothing would do at the end of the performance but that she must see and personally thank Monsieur Francees Weelson, "l'artist incomparable." The door from the boxes was thrown open and Madame was escorted to the center of the stage, where, in the flurry of her appreciation, she gave me the French salute on each side of the face. I flattered myself that I got along pretty well with my best back-of-the-dictionary French. She insisted upon an autographed photograph, and, not to be outdone, I asked for a lock of her hair, which came in due time tied with a bit of dainty blue ribbon, and arranged with all that delicacy of taste for which the French are famous. I really believed that I had made something of an impression upon Coquelin's *compatriote*.

When her season in America had finished and Madame Hading was giving her farewell interview to a reporter, just previous to sailing to *la belle France*, she said, among other things: "One of the most delightful evenings I have spent in America was in Chicago at a performance of 'The Oolah,' the chief character in which was played by a young man whose name, I think, was Watson."

CHAPTER VIII

TOUCHING HANDS WITH EDWIN BOOTH

ONE of my happiest remembrances of "Erminie" is in connection with Edwin Booth. We often sat opposite each other at the long reading-table, on the main floor of The Players, which, as he wrote a friend, was his "abiding-place in New York for all future time that may be mine."

On an afternoon when we sat there alone, reading, a pellet of paper dropped into my lap. I guessed readily who threw it, there being a suspicious earnestness in the way "Hamlet" bent forward over his magazine. On unfurling the tiny roll, I read:

"I've played in 'Erminie.'"

Booth had torn off the margin of a newspaper, written his message on it, shied it at me, and resumed reading. Following his unworthy example in the destruction of club property, I wrote and tossed over the top of his magazine:

"What part did you play?"

"The part opposite yours," he shied back in the same manner. "Then it was not called 'Erminie,' but 'Robert Macaire.'" [1] I wrote and flung back:

[1] After Lemaître became famous as "Robert Macaire," the play was translated into various languages and given everywhere. In the days of "stock companies" here in America, Friday nights were "benefit nights." The leading players of a company, for example, would be engaged for the season and given a "benefit," or, "a half clear bene-

In his Hamlet no cock crowed, as in Garrick's time, that the Ghost might start "like a guilty thing."

Irving introduced Booth to Ellen Terry. She says: "He looked up at me swiftly. I have never in any face, in any country, seen such wonderful eyes."

"Will you sometime play 'Robert Macaire' to my ('Cadeaux') 'Jacques Strop'?"

He smiled and nodded amusedly in the affirmative. Not a sound had passed between us, though we were but a few feet apart. Knowing how much sorrow he had had in life, it was a great pleasure to see him smile — and to contribute thereto.

Shortly after this, I had printed a large, oblong, old-fashioned programme, as shown on page 120.

In a large envelope conspicuously marked "Police Headquarters," I enclosed one of the two or three bills I had had struck off and sent it to Booth with a letter saying, in effect, that such bills were being distributed about the streets of Hudson City, and that, believing the intent to be fraudful, the writer, as Chief of Police, would stop any such performance if it were attempted. I then gave the matter no further thought.

At The Players, Booth's mail, it seems, was sorted by the Superintendent with the idea of saving time and annoyance. The envelope with the "Police Head-quarters" caught this worthy's eye and was pounced upon, opened, and scanned. I was suspected, and seriously haled to the "desk" and questioned. This situation was funny if my joke were not, and there was no one by but myself able to enjoy it. I was asked to explain. If there were any humor in my prank, which I was rapidly doubting, I thought it must be apparent.

fit." He would put forward his favorite play and, for contrast, to show his versatility, a character comedy, or farce, as an afterpiece. "Robert Macaire," condensed, would frequently be that afterpiece.

One Night Only

Hudson City, N. J.

FRANCIS WILSON

— And —

EDWIN BOOTH

in the well-known drama

ROBERT MACAIRE

JACQUES STROP — FRANCIS WILSON

ROBERT MACAIRE — EDWIN BOOTH

Remainder of cast to be composed of people of social distinction, and under the direction of Mr. ARTHUR BRISBANE.

Pieces of ice will be distributed during the performance.

SEATS SHOULD BE SECURED EARLY

I began to sympathize with my poor little effort and, realizing that its feebleness would never survive an explanation, I finally said that, if the delivery of the mail to Booth were not thwarted, I should be willing to risk expulsion. What with meddling, I scarcely knew what turn the matter would take. When we met shortly afterwards, Booth gave me a quizzical little smile and said:

"When do we rehearse?"

Living at New Rochelle, and acting in New York, brought me frequently to The Players for dinner, and here, at the Round Table, Booth was often at his de-delightful best, narrating in humorous vein events of the past. His mind would often run back to the "early days" in California and to his association with the comedian David Anderson — "Dave," he called him — for whom and his wife he had a loyal affection. This intimacy held till death. Quaintly he told of "Dave" and himself keeping "bachelor ranch," five miles from "Frisco," and of the "ranch" being infested with fleas and rats.

"I have visited San Francisco many times since," he said, "but have never been so troubled as in those early days. The rats and fleas have spared me, I suppose, because of the lively times they gave me in the days when I was more succulent. That ranch," he said tenderly, "must now be in the heart of the city!" Wherever it is, it was certainly deep in the heart of his remembrance.

He regretted that he had never visited Yosemite

Valley. He and Lawrence Barrett had intended to do so when they made their joint trip West, but Barrett, who managed the tour, having failed to arrange with the company for a vacation, had dissuaded Booth. Barrett, as Booth put it, was more careful as to the cost of the journey, being at that time both the responsible manager and the chief supporting actor.

In those days carrying such a company across the continent and back was an expensive undertaking. What would Booth and Barrett say to the cost at the present time? Now, however, the price of theater tickets have advanced, and profits are larger! With his artistic nature, the loveliness of Yosemite would have given Booth great joy. What would he have said to the overwhelming majesty of the Grand Canyon of the Colorado, or the marvels of the Yellowstone with its geysers and mountains of glass? He told us of having been to the Garden of the Gods, but its exact location had for the moment slipped his memory.

He wondered how I could live all winter in the country, yet play in town. He drew a humorous picture of his wife and himself trying to spend the winter at Cos Cob, Connecticut. His daughter Edwina, coming home for the Christmas holidays and finding them both as blue as indigo, had labored unsuccessfully to cheer them up. He had even gone in for planting trees at this same Cos Cob. The land was so stony the maples died, but elms did better. He had many huge holes dug during the fall to receive the trees in the spring, but the snow filled the holes and he had forgotten all about them. Shod in a

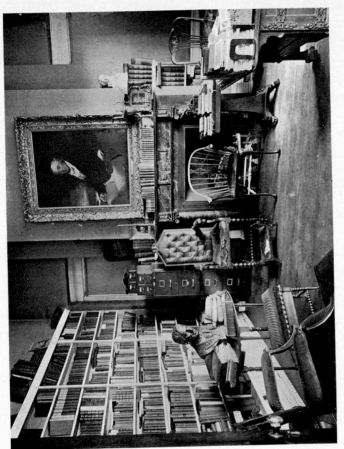

LIBRARY AT 24 GRAMERCY PARK

Showing Sir Thomas Lawrence's portrait of Francis, Fourth Earl of Guilford. The bronze bust of F. W. is by Edmond Quinn, who did the Booth statue of Hamlet which adorns Gramercy Park. The tall armchair by the mantel was given by Scott from his Abbotsford library to Landseer.

pair of boots made by the versatile stage-door keeper of Booth's Theater, boots so long that had he been split further up they would have reached his ears, he sauntered forth for a stroll over his estate. He had not gone far when slish! he went into a snow-covered hole. The boots, being more for ornament than use, had little room for knee action. Try as hard as he would, he could not get out of that hole, and there he lay, alternately laughing at his predicament and yelling for help, until his hired man yanked him forth.

Another time at the same Round Table, with the poet Aldrich, William Bispham, Laurence Hutton, and Charles Carryl, Booth amused us by telling of the Indian skeleton Joseph Jefferson had discovered on his farm at Buzzards Bay. Jefferson thought it a veritable Cyclops, with but one eye — in the center of the forehead, the place where all true Cyclops wore that organ — and Booth, curious to see the thing, went over to "Crow's Nest," Jefferson's home, for the purpose.

"From long practice, I knew how to hold a skull," said Booth, "and when Jefferson, with great pride, had placed the thing in my hands, I was able to show him conclusively that he had been regarding the gullet as the place where the eye of a Cyclops should be!"

Under the date of February 17, 1891, I have a note of dropping in at The Players and being thanked by Booth for an enjoyable evening at our performance of "The Lion Tamer." He had been feeling well all day, had done some walking, and was quite happy. He told a story I had never heard before of the elder Booth.

"Once, in playing Richard," he said, "father was about to deliver himself of a fit of stage rage when, looking down, he saw the tyrant's hump lying in front of him on the ground, that hump which it was my duty as his dresser to see securely fastened. Father gave it a kick that sent it scurrying into the wings. Strange to say, nobody in the audience laughed. It was quite different behind the scenes. Everybody, except myself, was laughing and enjoying the mishap. I knew what a blowing-up I should get as soon as father reached his dressing-room."

I asked him if, as a young man, he had played much in — comedy. I meant farce, but, looking as I was into Hamlet's eyes, I changed the word.

"Yes, and I always enjoyed it, too," he replied.

He seemed surprised when I said that I, also, had enjoyed it. In reply to his look of interrogation, I mentioned "Don Cæsar," "Benedick," and "Petruccio."

"Oh, that!" he answered; "I meant something broader — farce, 'Robert Macaire,' 'Little Toddlekins,' 'The Rough Diamond,' 'The Serious Family,' and so on — you know."

"It is not easy for me to imagine you doing anything extremely farcical," I said, "but I'll bet you did it well."

"Good for you, Wilson!" he replied. "I thought I was fine," he continued, "but I was probably wrong, for I took to tragedy, and now look at me!" I wanted him to say: "and now look at the damned thing!" —

but he did not. Then, shaking his head reflectively, he added: "Oh, I went through it all, I went through it all! Except at the beginning" — by which I took him to mean the advantage he had had in association with his father — "my experience has not been much different from other actors of my time." [1]

When his daughter Edwina (Mrs. Grossman) published her father's letters, I found this among them bearing on the matter:

"When I was learning to act tragedy, I had frequently to perform comic parts, in order to acquire a certain ease of manner that my serious parts might not be too stilted, so you must endeavor in your letters, in your conversation, and your general deportment to be easy and natural, graceful and dignified."

By the same token, a dose of tragic rôles would be a good thing for comedians.

"I doubt if you have ever posted your own playbills," said Booth laughingly.

I admitted that I had, as an amateur player.

"Well, I did it professionally."

"No! Actually pasted them up on walls and fences?"

"Yes."

"Where?"

"Honolulu."

[1] There are programmes at The Players with Booth's name on them as the "Ghost," in support of an amateur actor, C. C. Clapp, as "Hamlet." Other programmes there show that at Sacramento, California, in 1855, he also supported as "stars" Adelaide and Joey Gouggenheim in a romantic little trifle entitled "Love's Fetters," Booth playing the part of "Anton Latour, a Creole."

"I should like to have seen Edwin Booth posting his own playbills!"

"Somebody did see me — somebody who recognized me, a New Yorker."

"Good Lord! weren't you ashamed?" I asked.

"Somewhat," he replied, "but it had to be done, and I'd no money to pay for it."

I laughed over the story, and had no difficulty in picturing it, particularly as in recounting it Booth pantomimed it completely with an imaginary paste-brush, even to its final flop into the bucket preparatory to his taking up the bill for its adjustment to the fence or ash barrel, if ash barrels form a part of Hawaiian domestic necessity. Then came the dabs and the over-wipes for the banishment of the wrinkles in the paper, and the thing was done in the most approved professional manner.

Booth was alert to a humorous situation, even when playing, and would at times surprise the players with an aside or interpolated speech. In his "Fifty Years of Make-Believe," Frederick Warde tells us that once at Mobile the company had been much annoyed by mosquitoes. On this night the play was "King Lear." Booth, of course, was the "King." Warde was impersonating "Edgar." Sitting on a log, the demented monarch asks "Edgar":

"What is your occupation?"

To which "Edgar," humoring "Lear," replies:

"How to prevent the fiend, and to kill vermin."

On this occasion, Warde was astounded when

"Booth," as Warde tells it — "without change in the vacant eye or in a muscle of the pain-drawn, reverend face," asked: "Skeeters and sich?"

Charles Gotthold was once playing "Horatio" to Booth's "Hamlet." Bending over the body of the dead Prince, at the end of the tragedy, "Horatio" should say:

> . . . Good night, sweet prince;
> And flights of angels sing thee to thy rest.

But "flights" would not come to Gotthold and, for want of it, or something else, he spluttered out:

> *Flocks* of angels sing thee to thy rest;

which I think was not a poor substitution, in the emergency. However, as the curtain was slowly descending Booth, in a half whisper, called:

"*Flights*, Gotthold, flights! *Geese* flock!"

Booth was reserved in manner and speech, in fact diffident. So much so that people in and out of his profession sometimes misgauged the quality of his mind and his general ability. One of these doubters was Stuart Robson, a stanch admirer of Edwin Forrest and a warm friend of Lawrence Barrett. Robson was as quaint a comedian as America has produced. He had a personality so marked and a voice so fantastically keyed that laughter followed his every speech. There was much more to Stuart Robson than what was designated as his "squeak." He had a fine light in his eye and had an exceedingly intelligent facial play. He was a man of culture and delightful enthusiasm.

Talking one day with Robson, before the founding of The Players, the subject turned to Booth:

"I had always maintained," said Robson, "that Edwin Booth had too little intelligence to be at the head of our profession, that the mantle dropped by Edwin Forrest had not fallen squarely upon Booth's shoulders. I realized that I was prejudiced in Forrest's favor, but I tried to be fair. Let me tell you how my conversion was brought about. Edwin was visiting Barrett at Cohasset, where, as you know, we all live, and when Lawrence brought him over to call on me I did all I could to bring him out in conversation, I was so anxious to dispel the unfavorable opinion I had formed of him. Then, too, there were friends staying with me who were ardent admirers of Booth, and I did not wish them to be disappointed in their idol. I launched subject after subject, and then gave up in despair. Booth was not to be drawn out of his shell of reserve, or else he had nothing to offer, which I feared."

"Perhaps he knew you were trying to draw him out, which would be the surest way to keep him silent?" I ventured.

"Of course he did!" said Robson, "as I now know, knowing him better. Then for a while we talked on aimlessly and uncomfortably until by good fortune I happened to mention the name of 'Dave' Anderson, the comedian, with whom Booth had been professionally associated in the early days. Presto! the sky cleared,

Booth became eloquent and fairly scintillated. The subject changed many times, but he was not to be denied and talked brilliantly. What he said, and particularly the way he said it, delighted everybody and made me rejoice in him as a worthy leader."

"Do you think your friend Barrett will ever be able to contest leadership with Booth?" I asked.

"Mentally, yes," said the loyal Robson, "but professionally, I hae ma doots. But here's something that Barrett said about it, at his home, where a lot of us had foregathered. It was during this same visit of Booth's to Barrett. Lawrence was saying, with characteristic earnestness, that he would be willing to work for fifty years for nothing if at the end of that time he were thought to be at the head of his profession."

"Did Booth hear him say that?"

"Yes."

"Did he comment on it?" I inquired.

"Listen, laddie!" said Robson, with a chuckle. "Edwin put down the paper he was glancing over, took off his spectacles, and, turning toward Lawrence with mock seriousness, said:

"'Now what good would it do you, if you had this leadership?'

"'You ought to know,' Lawrence replied, 'you have it!'

"'Well, it is far from being a bed of roses!' Edwin said. 'It hems you in like a cat in a bag. You want to be free and you find you are restrained. You want to be jovial and jolly, to roam out with your comrades and drink a glass of beer without being stared at, and you can't. You must always subordinate your outdoor actions to the public eye. In a large measure you must always be acting without seeming to be acting, all of which makes you infernally self-conscious. Leadership is fine in many respects. It has its compensations, its glories, but it also has its discomforts, its thorns.'"

My own knowledge, acquaintance, and association with Booth began at an early date. I saw him play many times in all his stage creations. That joy came to me in this way. After Chicago's great fire, in 1871, one of the first theaters to be rebuilt there was McVicker's, on Madison Street. Myer's Opera House, on Monroe Street, backed up against McVicker's, with intervening and side alleys. As a seventeen-year-old boy, I was employed at the Opera House in the minstrel company headed by such shining lights as (William) Arlington (Ben) Cotton, and (John R.) Kemble, real masters of their art.

The part I took in the performance with the boy Mackin, already mentioned, often lasted but a few moments, and then, with a dash through the adjoining alleyway to McVicker's, I would soon be seated as auditor to all the notable players of the day — Booth, Barrett, James W. Wallack, Jr., Jefferson, Salvini, the elder Sothern, Charlotte Cushman, Adelaide Neilson, Mrs. D. P. Bowers, Maggie Mitchell, Lotta, etc., etc., etc. — what a treat, what an advantage for a young man pining to shine in the world of the drama! In those days the houses were not always crowded, but as my friend the doorkeeper used sometimes to remark as I passed in: "We're sure of one person, anyway!"

Comedy seemed to me to be so easy, so much a matter of course, that I permitted nothing to engage my serious attention except the highest flights of tragedy. Jefferson would do, yes! and so, too, would Sothern and Lotta, but to me the real, worth-while thing in acting was Booth as "Hamlet," or "Bertuccio" in "The Fool's Revenge." That I was low in stature was no discouragement, for I had measured my height with that of Booth's as he came from the stage-door to his carriage, and as I occasionally followed him along the street. To my supreme satisfaction I had *proved* that he was *not much taller* than myself, with the added pleasurable thought that I had still time to grow. I seem not to have considered the trifling matter of height of intellect — and personality.

Junius Brutus Booth, Booth's eldest brother, was to add further fuel to my ambition for tragic playing. I was one of the pupils of the Danish master of sword and self-defense, Colonel Thomas H. Monsterey. So, also, had been the eldest of the Booth boys, Junius. Visiting his old preceptor, and on my ambition being aired, Junius Booth told us — the bewaxed moustached Colonel and myself — that, if one had ability, height did not matter. Then I bethought me that none of the Booths were over medium height — nor, for that matter, had been either Garrick or Kean!

Convinced, then, that lack of stature was no disadvantage, was perhaps an earmark of genius, I made it a point to familiarize myself not only with many Shakespearean rôles, but also with the great names of history, preceding and succeeding Napoleon who, though long in genius, had been short in person. It was even possible to be secretly patronizing to people of height, and to take comfort in the slanderous Baconian dictum, that in all tall houses the attic is ever the worst furnished.

What puzzled, however, was that on the stage, in the tempest and very whirlwind of passion, in the climaxes of innumerable noble situations, Booth seemed suddenly to tower to gigantic proportions! I have seen him at times as the defiant "Richelieu," the noble "Brutus," the frenzied "Bertuccio," the revengeful "Shylock," and the procrastinating "Hamlet," who would "take the Ghost's word for a thousand pounds," when, as it seemed to me, the actor's dimensions were only limited by the height and width of the proscenium. But I assured myself that that was "a part of the game," a power that must come with the ultimate fitting into the picture.

Meanwhile, possessing my soul with patience, I must render homage to the merry muse Thalia, until such time as I were old enough to attempt a flirtation with her sister, the more serious Melpomene.

As a young man I had seen Booth not only on the stage and on the street, but even at funerals. At the dedication of the Actors' Fund Monument, at Evergreen Cemetery, Long Island, in 1887, I heard him make the opening address. His "Comrades!" thrilled all us hoi polloiers. A few moments later, the crashing platform on which he stood came perilously near forcing him to make a most undignified exit. I noted well his calm in danger. But never until a lovely day in July in the same year had I met him "front to front." The opportunity was a welcome one. He was the foremost American actor, and I was eager to see upon what meat this our Cæsar fed that he had grown so great. I wondered if he would laugh when tickled, just as I supposed he would bleed when pricked. From all that I had heard, this our "Hamlet" had a noble capacity for everydayness, and so it proved.

I was invited aboard the steam yacht Oneida to make Booth's acquaintance. I accepted gladly. The Oneida, on which took place the inception of "The Players" Club, was owned by Commodore E. C. Benedict, the banker and enthusiastic yachtsman. Booth and he were fast friends, having met as neighbors at Cos Cob. Over many years "the tragedian," as he playfully called himself, made many happy voyages on the Oneida. "Erminie" was then enjoying an unprecedented run, and everything in connection with it was popular. Booth's greeting was cordial, and when some of the guests had been dropped at their homes along the Sound and the talk became more intimate, he was kind enough to say that the Benedict family had spoken so often of me that he wanted to make my acquaintance. As he turned now and then to reply to questions put by others, I had opportunity to study him.

Booth was then in his fifty-third year. His face had begun to show not only the "wear and tear" of his profession, but also the sorrows through which he had passed. His hair was graying. The fine eyes, always the most beautiful feature of his countenance, were still lustrous. The mouth had taken on that wistful expression which has been happily caught in the Sargent portrait now hanging in The Players and their most prized possession.

The conversation became general, and many anecdotes were told. One story of a droll mishap in a theater especially pleased "the tragedian." While he did not, at that time, contribute to the story-telling, he was an appreciative auditor. He regretted that his brother-in-law Clarke were not present to enjoy and to add to the merriment.

Presently Booth and I were left alone. He talked of many things, but mostly of the theater which, as I had heard, he seldom did. We stood at the yacht's rail. Booth, hands on ratlin, occasionally swayed himself lightly from side to side. All his grace of form and action were apparent. After a while, he said, hesitatingly:

"You are now on a wave of success, and — and — if I knew you better, I'd ask you to promise never to be led into the mistake of building a theater."

The remark was prompted, of course, by his own disastrous experience. I remembered this advice, and years later, when John Stetson tried to induce me to become his partner in the ownership of the Casino on

Broadway, and agreed to furnish the capital, I declined. No doubt it would have been a good investment and, beyond question, an unhappy experience. I believe I made choice between riches and longevity.

It was flattering to find that Booth had been making inquiries about me, for he spoke of sword-play of which he had heard I was fond. I had then recently been fortunate in a public contest with foils. He declared that he had little skill in swordsmanship. This surprised me, having often seen his fencing bout in "Hamlet."

"My brother Junius," he said, "taught us boys" (himself, John Wilkes, and possibly his brother Joseph) "and we got most of our knowledge of it from him." Junius was an excellent teacher, it would seem, and his brother Edwin an apt pupil. The fact is that, along with their good looks and richly toned voices, the Booth boys inherited from their illustrious father aptness in the handling of the foil and broadsword. The youngest and the handsomest of them, the ill-starred John Wilkes Booth, unquestionably inherited also a streak of eccentricity.

"I have been much criticized," said Booth, "for my use of the foil in 'Hamlet,' particularly for throwing the foil back of me and thrusting and hitting while in that position." I replied that I thought it permissible in a friendly contest for points, or "touches," such as "Hamlet" and "Laertes" were having. That I had often seen it done, had done it myself. That in a friendly contest, when the fencers had come too close, throwing the sword behind the back was about the only way to score. In a duel, of course, a fatal blow could not be given in that way and, therefore, would not likely be attempted. Booth listened, seemingly with great interest, but I was startled when I realized that I had been posing as an authority.

"When I was last in London," said Booth, "one of the English players at rehearsal proposed an entirely new 'fight,' one probably with which he was familiar." Then, with a twinkle in his eye, our "Hamlet" said, "But I told him that, having done the contest for so many years in a particular way, I deemed it unwise to change."

The elder Booth was renowned for the intensity of his sword-play on the stage, fighting with such frenzy as to frighten his "Richmonds" and "Macduffs." I spoke about it and of having heard and read he once became so engrossed that he followed his scared "Richmond," or "Macduff," into the alleyway at the stage-door, fighting all the way. Booth's lips curled with an expression of amused dissent.

"There is no doubt that father fought his stage battles with deep earnestness. It wouldn't be much of a battle done tamely, would it? Father did everything earnestly. But, oh, I have been to a world of trouble all my life contradicting absurd stories about him," said Booth, which, after all, was not too strong a denial of the story.

On down through the years I followed him, losing no opportunity to see him play, noting regretfully the diminishing elasticity of full manhood and welcoming the mellowness of time that ripened and beautified his art. When The Players was founded in 1888, I was among the group that formed the actor members. Booth and I met frequently at the club. He was always considerate and kind. In all his life he had few intimates. At the beginning, the comedian David Anderson and the soldier Adam Badeau were such. In his last years his natural diffidence and weight of sorrows made him shrink more and more from people. The poet Aldrich, Commodore Benedict, William Bispham, and Lawrence Barrett, though loved by Booth, were never so deeply seated in his affection, I think, as either Anderson or Badeau.

If he ever had a regret at giving The Players to the people of his profession and to the members of the kindred arts, it must have been when he discovered they wanted to fill it with memorials of himself. Had this occurred to him, I think he might have delayed the gift until after his death. At New Rochelle, I lived near the artist Oliver Lay, who painted Booth as "Hamlet." I acquired a replica of the picture and wished to present it to The Players. I mentioned the matter to Booth, who said:

"Please don't! Even now I can't go anywhere about the house without bumping into a Booth!"

The *chef d'œuvre* of all the possessions of The Players is the portrait of Booth by Sargent.[1] It hangs over the mantel in the Reading Room on the main floor. It is

[1] Presented by E. C. Benedict.

so fine in color and composition, and so happy in expression, as to endear itself to all beholders. How precious it is to The Players may be imagined. There was difficulty in obtaining Booth's consent to sit for it. Nor was it easy for Sargent to get the result he aimed at.

"I had sat long that day," said Booth to Edward Simmons the artist. "Sargent had tired me greatly."

Suddenly he turned and said: "There, Mr. Booth! Look! If you like what I've done, we'll do no more. Please give me your opinion."

"But," said Booth, "my opinion is of no importance. The picture is not to belong to me. I'm not even to pay for it."

"Nevertheless," replied the artist, "I'd thank you for your opinion. Do you like it?"

"Frankly," said the tragedian, after a few moments' examination, "I don't think the expression is characteristic of me."

"Are you very tired?" asked Sargent. Booth would not admit that he was.

"Well," remarked the great painter, "if you'll give me a little time, I should like to try again." Booth acquiesced.

"With some sort of an instrument," continued Booth, as reported by Simmons, "Sargent scraped out the head and face entirely, and in three quarters of an hour had repainted them as they now stand!"

About this time I was in the toils of a fad, autograph-letter collecting, one of the many crazes that take

READING-ROOM AT THE PLAYERS

Showing Sargent's portrait of Booth, and Jefferson as Dr. Pangloss, also by Sargent. E. C. Benedict presented the Booth. He also gave the mantel ornaments on condition that the clock be placed in front of Booth's legs, which were thought to be overdrawn.

possession of normally developed people for their educative well-being. It seemed to me that I got nearer to the world's great people if I knew them in the intimacy of their correspondence; with Washington, for instance, if I owned a few of his letters, whether they commended Thomas Paine for his services to the American Revolution or merely ordered clothes from his London tailor. I surely knew Byron better for having his letter to Captain Roberts offering his boat, the Bolivar, to be used in search of Shelley's body.

Coming into possession of a fine large photograph of Booth, I was keen to have him autograph it, to hang up with others which Barrett, Jefferson, Florence, Mrs. Drew, and McCullough had given me. I wrote him to that effect. His reply follows:

PHILA., *Nov.* 17, '90.

MY DEAR MR. WILSON:

It pleases me very much to comply with your request since it affords me an opportunity to say what I meant to say many weeks ago, but didn't, anent your delightful performance of "The Merry Monarch." Mr. Barrett and I both convulsively enjoyed it, and I think seriously of borrowing your first entrance for that of "Richelieu," in Act 4th, where he threatens "the curse of Rome." May I?

Your freedom from effort is admirable.

Sincerely yours
EDWIN BOOTH

The entrance which Booth was "thinking seriously of borrowing" was that of "King Anso IV," who, arriving in a gorgeously bedraped palanquin, carried on the shoulders of sturdy blacks in tiger-skin garments, slips as he is descending the portable steps, and is ignominiously thrown to the ground.

Booth was slow to keep his promise and continuously apologetic for not having done so. I knew from experience just how he felt, and I tried to make light of his bothering about the matter. All the while I was fearful that he would take me at my word. He was growing frailer, and I longed for this particular souvenir of him.

When I would visit him in the apartment he had reserved for himself on giving over his house to The Players, I would see that "counterfeit presentment" askew on a corner table awaiting the autograph of its original. Later on I beheld the lop-eared thing, looking as if it had had some heavy fall, or some one had stepped on it, and I began to wonder humorously about its ultimate fate. Once, on becoming human, I was tempted to snatch it up in triumph and rush shrieking from the room. This would have amused Booth, perhaps relieved him. No, I could not bring myself to be as brave as that. I was nothing but the brutal type of autograph-seeker, guilty of the thing I so often deplored in others, demanding my pound of autographic flesh! I was ashamed, and wondered at my callousness. Noting my puzzled expression, one day, he said:

"There's that photograph."

"So I see," I replied.

"What do you wish me to do with it?" he asked, laughingly.

"You promised to sign it."

"So I shall, but you wanted a Shakespearean quotation. What quotation?"

"Do you mean that you'd like Francis Wilson to supply Edwin Booth with a Shakespearean quotation?" I asked.

"Yes."

"Now, my dear Mr. Booth," said I, "I can see that this request is bothering you, and I am sorry. Bid an affectionate farewell to that photograph. I am going to take it out of your sight forever"; this last not too emphatically.

"No, don't do that," he said, much to my relief. "The request doesn't bother me at all, it's the quotation. I'm just too lazy to look it up or think it up. If you'll provide it, I'll write it gladly, anything."

Several times when we met afterwards, he would ask if I had thought of that quotation, and it did seem as if everything were conspiring to prevent my doing so. One day, however, I was able to answer in the affirmative. On giving it, he listened and said:

"I've spoken that. What's it from?"

I was not surprised that he asked. Unless very familiar, a line of a poem or play, detached from its context, will nearly always puzzle as to its source. When I had about given up all hope of receiving either photograph, autograph, or quotation, to my joy, one day, they all three arrived. Fate avenged Booth for the annoyance I had given him, for, with many other treasures, I lost that photograph in a fire that consumed our country place, in 1918. I recall that the quotation was a selection neatly combined from two or three plays, and was exactly what I wanted Booth to say. But if the dead have cognizance of things in life, the great player is probably smiling sardonically at my unsuccessful efforts to remember what it was he wrote. At another time, while exchanging experiences as to autographs, photographs, etc., he said:

"What has given me much annoyance all through life is the repeated demand to know if I thought 'Hamlet' insane! This has always surprised me, for I have ever aimed to make it clear in my performance that 'Hamlet's' insanity is assumed." Corroborating this, Mrs. Grossman, Booth's daughter, allows me to reproduce an etching of her father as "Hamlet" and underneath which the tragedian has quoted:

I essentially am not in madness, but mad in craft;

which should set at rest for all time the view which Edwin Booth held of the so-called "Hamlet mystery."

There was a fine feeling of mutual admiration and affection between Booth and Dr. Horace Howard Furness. We catch a vivid glimpse of both in the following letter which my friend Dr. Horace Howard Furness, Jr., contributes (the letter is written to the two younger Furness boys, H. H. F., Jr., and W. H. F., at Harvard):

PHILADELPHIA
222 W. WASHINGTON SQUARE
19 *April*, '85

. . . The outside record of my week might be summed up in almost one word: Booth. His visit here terminated last eve'g and we have all greatly enjoyed him. He dined here every day,

"I essentially am not in madness,
But mad in craft."

EDWIN BOOTH AS HAMLET

Not by any means as picturesque a head as that of the Launt Thompson
bust at The Players.

except yesterday when he had a matinée, and each evening I spent with him in his dressing-room, smoking and laughing and criticizing. When he went on the stage, a chair was put for me in the wings and there I sat, believing myself to be one of the participants in the scene, very much tempted at times to emerge as a Deus ex machina and set things all straight, to tell "Hamlet" to peg away at his old uncle without the least compunction and to jog "Shylock's" elbow and suggest the word "blood" in his bond.

Booth seemed to enjoy having me at hand, and I think my friendly presence stimulated him, in fact he said that one of the actors asked him why it was that ear trumpets helped a performance, and Booth's asking for an explanation the actor said that they noticed that his performance was enlivened by the presence of an ear trumpet at the wings. One afternoon Polly [1] gave an exhibition of magic to Mr. Booth's intense mystification: he was a very satisfactory spectator, yielding credence to every artifice; he took a great fancy to Polly whom I took to his dressing-room when he was playing "Ruy Blas" which greatly gratified Mr. Booth and he explained to her all the mysteries of costume, etc., etc.

Booth adored his profession, and was ever doing his utmost to further its interest and that of its followers. The last important act of his life was to found The Players, a club in which, through the mingling of congenial spirits, of the arts of acting, painting, sculpture, literature, etc., he sought to bring out the social qualities of all concerned. Perhaps no club in America has such a distinctive atmosphere of intimacy, of refined taste, and worthy wit.

Shakespeare's birthday, April 23d, at The Players, is the well-known "Ladies' Day." Because of his modesty, Booth could seldom be persuaded to appear on

[1] Caroline Furness, afterwards Mrs. Horace Jayne.

this occasion. Once, however, I got him to make the journey from his apartment on the second floor, down the broad stairway, through the crowd, across the Lounge to the Stanford White dining-room. He became abashed at the rush of people to do him honor, and, clinging to my arm (he was not very strong), he said, in a low tone: "For God's sake, Wilson, don't leave me!"

So many people were eager to greet him that he was confused and disturbed, and asked to be taken back to his rooms. Once there, he seated himself with a great sigh of relief at what he called his "escape."

It is known, of course, that the life of Lincoln was taken by a Booth, but it is not nearly so well known that a Booth saved the life of a Lincoln. The tragedian told his friend William Bispham, The Players' first treasurer, of having saved the life of Lincoln's son Robert. The account, as told to me by Bispham, and published by him in "The Century Magazine," November, 1893, is as follows:

"He [Booth] had started for Philadelphia from New York, and while he was standing on the platform of a car, still in the Pennsylvania Railway Station, at Jersey City, and just as the train was about to move, a young lad, going from one car to another, stumbled, and would have fallen between them, had not Edwin Booth caught him by the collar of the coat and landed him in safety by his side. The boy, whom Edwin had never seen before, evidently recognized him, and, holding out his hand, said to him: 'That was a narrow escape, Mr. Booth!' and thanked him warmly. Two weeks later, Edwin received a letter from General Adam Badeau in which the latter mentioned that Robert Lincoln had told him that it was his life that had been thus saved."

"The Century" goes on to state: "Asked recently if he recollected the incident, Mr. Robert T. Lincoln replied:

" 'The account is essentially correct, but not accurate in its details. The incident occurred while a group of passengers late at night, were purchasing their sleeping-car places from the conductor who stood on the station platform at the entrance of the car. The platform was about the height of the car floor, and there was, of course, a narrow space between the platform and the car body. There was some crowding, and I happened to be pressed by it against the car body while waiting my turn. In this situation the train began to move, and, by the motion, I was twirled off my feet, and dropped, with feet downward, somewhat into the open space, and was personally helpless, when my coat collar was vigorously seized and I was quickly pulled up and out to a secure footing on the platform. Upon turning to thank my rescuer, I saw it was Edwin Booth whose face was, of course, well known to me, and I expressed my gratitude to him, and in doing so called him by name.' "

This having been disputed, I wrote to Robert Lincoln, stating what I remembered of the story, and asked if he would be kind enough to verify or deny it. His reply follows:

3414 N St.,
Washington, D.C.
April 1, 1921

My dear Mr. Wilson:

Your memory of the account of Edwin Booth's intervention for my safety at the Jersey City railway station is probably entirely correct.

His action was very prompt and vigorous, and I, recognizing him, thanked him by name.

Very sincerely yours
Robert Lincoln

Francis Wilson, Esq.,
Washington, D. C.

If ever man were pursued by a sinister fate it was Edwin Booth. I thought him the most pathetic figure in dramatic life, one of the world's sad men. His boyhood was spent as companion to a brilliant but erratic father. When the father had died and the son had begun to make headway in his profession, death suddenly robbed him of the young wife to whom he was ideally mated. When he had gained sufficient courage to go on, the theater in which he had invested heavily and which contained many of his own valuable possessions as well as priceless souvenirs of his father, was destroyed by fire. He pushed forward again, and had touched the high point in his career when the illustrious name he bore suddenly came to be reviled by the mad act of his brother in taking Lincoln's life, an act horrifying no one more than Booth.

Determined not to play again, he was finally persuaded to return and ultimately built a temple to the drama the like of which America had never known. Not long thereafter he found himself wrecked in health and a bankrupt. Bravely he continued, only to have every favorable advance accompanied by rebuffs of pain and sorrow. Thrown from a carriage, he was reported dead, but escaped with serious injuries. In a stage encounter he was stabbed by an awkward actor, and then a crazy creature named Gray, who imagined Booth barred his way to success, fired several shots at him during a public performance at McVicker's Theater in Chicago. He married again, and again became a widower. Finally, life grew a little less harsh, but the victim had been fooled to the top of his bent. All the success which followed, and it was not a little, seemed as but ashes to his taste.

There was now a great difference in the Booth who could act so swiftly and vigorously in rescuing the young Robert Lincoln, and the slow-moving gentleman with the wondrous eyes who went about The Players waiting, waiting for somebody or something which he seemed never to find.

It was now 1893. As the weeks went by, he grew frailer and frailer and kept more closely to his rooms. One evening, as he stood talking to friends at the club, he tottered and would have fallen but for some of us who supported him. He felt well, he said, but was weak. He had eaten nothing all day. I asked why.

"I never even thought about it," he replied.

Not long thereafter death came. He was indifferent to it. Perhaps he had found what he wanted.

CHAPTER IX

THE THEATRICAL SYNDICATE

Up to 1895, the theatrical profession was mainly in the hands of actors and actor-managers. In that year a number of men, mostly Hebrews, and formerly silent partners, advance agents, box-office attendants, etc., banded themselves together in a close corporation and, through affiliation and leases, got possession of the principal theaters throughout the country and closed the doors to all actor-managers who would not submit to their terms.

This managerial "closed shop" was known and is still known as the "Manager's Lockout" or "Theatrical Syndicate." It was composed of six men. Al Hayman, of San Francisco and New York; Klaw and Erlanger, of New York; Nixon and Zimmerman, a theatrical firm of Philadelphia, and Charles Frohman, of New York. Frohman was a reluctant member of the organization and often said that he got a lot out of it — but it was mostly trouble. This statement, however true when made, scarcely tallies with the fact that the Klaw and Erlanger part of the Syndicate "assisted" the Frohman part at times to the extent of nearly, if not quite, a half-million dollars.

Whatever the attitude of the Syndicate may have been toward the actors it employed, and it certainly has not been one which it could regard with pride, it has unquestionably shown a sustaining generosity toward itself.

The drastic action of the Syndicate in compelling actor-managers to submit to its terms or go elsewhere, there being nowhere else to go, did not apply to the rank and file of actors, but only to those who headed or controlled their own companies, the so-called "stars." These "stars," whose talent had won great favor with the public, were the most important attractions in the country, but were outnumbered by the "starless" companies which had been organized, or had come under control of the men forming the newly composed "Syndicate."

Managers of theaters in cities and towns outside of New York mostly resented this Syndicate as much as did the "stars," but were forced into affiliation with it by the threat of not being permitted to play the numerous Syndicate attractions, the formation of a powerful opposition, and the fear that the "stars" would ally themselves with the Syndicate. As it well knew, the Syndicate had the out-of-town manager on the hip; for, if forced to play only the Syndicate's comparatively inferior attractions, while it might keep his theater open for a longer period during the season, it would mean great loss of prestige with the public and still greater loss of profit. But, as was cunningly suggested by the Syndicate, if the out-of-town manager joined with it, there would be no theaters in which the "stars" could appear, and the out-of-town manager would soon have not only the Syndicate attractions, but also the "stars" as well. It was as plain as day. The out-of-town manager yielded. The actor-managers were unorganized, had no stomach for organization, and were, therefore, an easy and natural prey.

The contention of the Syndicate was that it must control the "bookings" of theatrical companies throughout the country in order to avoid the ruinous opposition that happened from two prominent companies appearing in the same city or town at the same time; also that it could not run its theaters and pay the percentages demanded by some unattractive "stars" whom it did not wish to "book" at a loss. There was reason in the first plea, none in the latter. Refusal to play unprofitable "stars" was the answer. It was only too evident that the Syndicate had "cornered" the theaters throughout America and was attempting to shut out all competitors and to bend everything in one direction, namely, the commercializing of the drama. When it was suggested that, given the power it was seeking, it might well lead to the boycotting of many worthy plays and players, that nothing would be easier than a yearly scaling-down of the player-managers' incomes until these player-managers were under the domination of the Syndicate, the Syndicate to a man was shocked that its intentions should be so misconstrued.

"What, take possession of that which had always belonged to the actor, which of a right should always belong to him! Dominate the drama? Never!" It was unkind and unjust to suggest such a thing! A simple

protection of minor financial interests they declared
was all that was sought. We shall see later how sincere
was this disclaimer.

The application of the "third degree" methods of
the Syndicate to the dramatic profession as a whole
was considerately postponed to a later period when the
Syndicate should have more firmly entrenched itself
and felt surer of its ground. Just at this moment, with
such players as Joseph Jefferson, Richard Mansfield,
Fanny Davenport, Nat Goodwin, James O'Neill, Mrs.
Fiske, and Francis Wilson arrayed against it, the Syndicate felt itself skating on thin ice and the outcome of
its startling action much in doubt. It was also opposed
by David Belasco.

Strongly organized, expert in matters of commerce
and "business," its struggle was with nervous, sensitive,
temperamental people to whom, as a rule, matters of
business were distasteful, and especially to whom the
thought of organizing to protect an art, their art, as
mechanics organize to make employers unhappy, was
repellently objectionable. "No," said most of these
players, Richard Mansfield in particular, "let us not
band ourselves into an association to oppose this Syndicate threat. It would be a mistake to lose the dignity
and strength of individual, independent action"; and,
so saying, helped to seal our doom. With such ideas the
players never had "a Chinaman's chance" of success,
as the saying goes.

Jefferson, nearing the end of his long and brilliant
career, and fearful, in the event of the Syndicate's

success, of what might happen to his sons, all in the acting profession, grew lukewarm and straddled the issue. Richard Mansfield opposed the managers, but played in their theaters and remained importantly "individual" and independent. Nat Goodwin, who was determined to build a chain of theaters from Maine to Oregon, and, seconded by A. M. Palmer, meant to drive the Syndicate into the sea, fell a victim to alluring offers of increased percentages and the promise, later fulfilled, to play in a theater on Broadway where he had never before appeared. Fanny Davenport, who was going to do anything rather than surrender, soon changed her mind. Belasco was scarcely considered, it being felt that sooner or later he would ally himself, as a theater manager, with other managers.

I never had much confidence in either the stability or business acumen of that "eccentric planet" Goodwin, and I viewed with special distrust his large idea of a transcontinental chain of theaters. I felt that we had a man's-sized job on our hands in trying to defeat the Syndicate. I still think, with proper coöperation and direction, that defeat would have been accomplished. The situation was a serious one. To my mind, the managers had determined to wipe out of existence the control of any company by an actor, because such control was inimical to their plans. It was evident to me from the beginning that, with the Syndicate in control, the receipts of all companies must satisfy the greed and caprice of that organization, or the companies would be abandoned. They would have no theaters in which to play. It was a foregone conclusion that the kind of play produced would be that which drew the most money, irrespective of its quality or character. There would be but one thought as to that. The receipts were the thing. It was an easy step to the conclusion that the financial returns from the smaller cities and towns throughout the country would ultimately fail to satisfy. Yet when I uttered such a thought, I was declared to be an alarmist. I did not foresee the complete abandonment of the smaller cities and towns, as to dramatic amusement, which has come to pass, except for moving pictures.

Sure enough, with the coming of the equally commercial Shuberts, there was soon no actor-manager in America, even at the head of his own company, and no matter how large his name might appear, who was not directed and controlled by Syndicate managers. Furthermore, if these jointly opposed, there is not now an actor-manager great or small in America who could follow his profession. How did these managers, this Syndicate, obtain a footing in the theatrical profession which was once, not long since, in possession of the actor and the actor-manager? How came they in a profession in which they are really unnecessary? If ever there were such a thing as a fifth wheel to an enterprise, they are it. There are just three essentials to this whole beautiful matter of the drama, no more; the author, the actor, and the audience. They are of equal importance and hold the same opinion of managers. All the rest can, and should, be hired. It is probably entirely due to the actor's lack of appreciation of his duty to himself and to his profession that managers as we now know them have come into existence. And there they are dominating the situation and quite convinced that they are the sun around which the entertainment, refreshment, and instruction of the world revolves, yet caring nothing for the ethical part of it.

Like Barnum, they are "showmen." Like him again, they are proud of it, but unlike him they never boast that "my show is one of the greatest moral influences of the age." They have too many Woolly Horses, Mermaids, and Joice Heths in them. Barnum's last question to his secretary was: "What were the receipts of yesterday?" And then followed the expression of regret that they were not so good as at the Olympia, in London. The Syndicate are very like Barnum in this. Indeed, of such is the kingdom of the Syndicate.

In the old days, the actor-manager maintained a "stock" company the year through, or nearly so, in various cities throughout the United States, as, in New York, the Mitchells, Burtons, and Wallacks, the Burtons and the Davenports in Philadelphia, the Conways in Brooklyn, the McVickers in Chicago, the Popes in St. Louis, the Fords and the Albaughs in Washington and Baltimore, etc.

To these theaters came as traveling "stars" the Edwin Forrests, the Booths, the Charlotte Cushmans, the Mrs. D. P. Bowers, the Lucille Westerns, the Maggie Mitchells, the Joseph Jeffersons, the W. J. Florences, the Barney Williamses, the Lottas, etc., who depended on the resident stock company for professional support in their tragedies and comedies. Causing many rehearsals and often resulting in uneven performances, particularly in the early stages of the engagements, the "stars" finally traveled with their own companies. This involved the employment of assistant managers and advance agents to aid the "stars" in matters of routine, and so allow them to conserve their energies for the more congenial task of acting. An assistant manager is seldom less than "a courtier-like servant" with a natural ambition to become associated financially through investment or what not with a winning enterprise. Sometimes these "investments," in form of loans, could not be repaid readily by the actor-manager and an interest was exacted or given in lieu of cash. The right, then, to suggest, even to dictate, grew.

From this condition of affairs to independent management was still not an easy step, but it was made possible by the detachment and comparative freedom of the agent or assistant manager to come and go in the actor-manager's interest, and by that agent's indefatigable energy in searching out new material for his "star," who, with proper activity, could and should have done it for himself. Routine knowledge once acquired, soon the more venturesome and speculative of these assistant managers, agents, etc., swift to realize how much the actor-manager would welcome freedom from all financial responsibility, assumed that responsibility, too often, alas, with little to support it but a glib tongue and irrepressible optimism! It is because the men composing the Syndicate thought faster, not better, moved quicker, than actors that the latter lost direction and control of their profession. An analogous case is that of the artists and the dealers in art. The dealers often not only control the prices of the pictures, but dictate the vogue of the artist.

Finally awake to the danger of the situation, it became important to know how this attempt at control on the part of the commercial manager was to be fought. Among the youngest but not the least successful of the actor-managers, at the time, I did not presume to advise. I was present when Goodwin, carefully coached by A. M. Palmer, and several others, met for consultation in Chicago. Goodwin had to leave quickly to fill an engagement in New Orleans. *En route*, he telegraphed me long messages of enthusiastic appeal to which I soon replied that I would surely join with my fellow players in what I felt was a just cause. A few days later I was astounded to read in the daily papers that the irresponsible Goodwin had gone over to the Syndicate, declaring he would have nothing to do "with Francis Wilson's mad scheme to oppose it"!

It was no "mad scheme" of mine. I had not originated the opposition. It arose spontaneously. But I approved it heartily, and was proud to be invited to participate in it. Once in, I stayed in until beaten down hopelessly by the defection of my fellow actor-managers. Of all who started out so bravely to oppose the usurpation of the Syndicate but two "stars" of any influence remained — Mrs. Fiske and myself. So situated, we had about as much chance of halting the Syndicate as a couple of old women armed with brooms would have in trying to keep Niagara from sweeping over the Falls. It is no disparagement of Mrs. Fiske to say that, though always an artist, she had not then the professional distinction she now enjoys. She had just returned to the stage after an absence of four years. While it is true that she had had success in Ibsen's "A Doll's House," two years were yet to pass before she would be seen in "Tess of the D'Urbervilles," and four years until her presentation of "Becky Sharp," which was to delight the world and bring her real renown. From a financial point of view — and that was the only view it cared to take — the Syndicate did not regard Mrs. Fiske as a star of the first magnitude whatever may now be said to the contrary. They were unwilling for this reason to *allow* her the same terms as other stars.

It may be admitted, then, that at this juncture of the struggle, I practically stood alone. Though I did what I thought was best, I probably did the wrong thing. The principle of the matter had not changed, of course. There were just two alternatives open to me — to commit hari-kari on the doorstep of the Syndicate, or leave the country. Being but a human being, I stayed to fight on when opportunity and stronger wills would insure success.

In those days, all dates to play at theaters were tentative. Later, they were either canceled or confirmed. No dates were sure until contracts were signed. Not knowing which of the two theaters in Washington would or would not go into the Syndicate, if it prevailed, I had dates held at both theaters. This was but ordinary protection. The Syndicate, always put to it to justify itself, on learning of this protective measure, cried "Treachery!" and declared I was to be "made an example of as a shining mark, for the benefit of lesser offenders." If the assumption and arrogance of all this had not been so comic, it might well have been maddening. Here was I, a member of a profession in which actors ought to have something to say as practitioners of the art, being publicly proclaimed as "an offender," because I opposed an assault upon my profession by a band of commercial exploiters.

Prohibited, except in New York, from playing in any theater of importance, I was obliged to rent the "Variety" theaters of the various cities throughout the country. The public did not understand and cared little about the theatrical squabble; and, not understanding, would not follow those of us who went into unaccustomed places to play. It is strange even now, it was shocking then, to know that so great an artist as Sarah Bernhardt, refusing to be "controlled" by a syndicate of managers, was obliged to play under a tent.

The little fortune that I had saved was greatly diminished in the unequal struggle, and I determined, rather than surrender, that I would abandon America and attempt to make my way to success in England. I hated England because, under the wretched teaching of our schools, I had been taught as a boy that she was to be despised as our greatest enemy and oppressor — that nothing could be more despicable than a monarchy, however liberal and however much desired by people living happily under it. Like many another narrow American, even long past adolescence, I was still fighting the War of Independence. However, my hatred of England was mild as milk by comparison with the feeling that was mine for those who were literally driving me out of my own country. The more I studied the situation, the less I liked it, and I began to feel that I deserved to be driven out if I could not find a way to circumvent my friends the enemy. Of what use was the thing with which I was doing my alleged thinking if it did not serve me in such an emergency.

The fight was over. The enemy had decimated our ranks by flattery, cajolement, and tempting offers of increased monetary certainties and comfortable book-ings, and so, had won the battle. Our people, meeting for the first time in their existence an emergency of this character, had fallen victims to what should have been easily detected as cheap cunning, and had especially fallen victims to their own selfishness and egotism. There was a lesson in all this, and I made up my mind that, if ever again the two parties met in conflict, the specious cunning of the one side and the disloyalty and egotistic selfishness of the other should be exposed, so far as I had the power, to a full measure of ridicule. The two sides did meet again in conflict, a bitter one, and the loyalty of the actors, brought about by a half-dozen years of industrious education, won the day. But that was The Actors' Strike, an account of which will be given in another chapter.

Meanwhile, how was I to extricate myself from the dreadful position in which I found myself, how avoid expatriation? Was I to sit down and calmly permit the money-changers in the Temple to walk all over me? The matter gave me many an anxious, many an indignant, thought. Then it occurred to me that there was such a thing as fighting the Devil with fire. It was only too evident that independence as to where and with whom one should play was lost to the American player, that henceforth he must appear only where he would be allowed! An extremely bitter, uncoated pill for any well man to swallow, yet there it was, to be taken or rejected as prescribed.

I was cribbed, cabined, and confined. As was said by a writer at the time, "I confessed myself, after a year and a half's fight, overwhelmingly defeated." Yet I could not bring myself to ask for what had previously been solicited of me, the privilege of appearing in a series of first-class theaters throughout the country. I knew instinctively, because of the determined opposition I had offered to the plans of the Syndicate, that I, as the "shining mark," the most outspoken opponent, was not going to come off too easily if I were "to crook the pregnant hinges of the knee" and, bowing to the managerial "thrift," did a little "fawning."

The plan I conceived to avoid the necessity of appealing to these men for an opportunity to appear in leading theaters was as follows: I was playing my company in a "Variety" theater in Philadelphia. With my trunks half packed to leave the country, if my scheme miscarried, I purposely bumped into Samuel F. Nixon-Nirdlinger, of the Philadelphia firm of Nixon and Zimmerman. Nixon was a vain little person with a tremendous appreciation of Nixon as an astute business man. In different ways he could squeeze more juice out of a business orange than any man I have ever met, and I have met many such squeezers. This quality in him was to be feared, but it was not to this side but to his vanity, I meant to address myself, and he succumbed like a meek and lowly Christian. I had always been greatly in favor with him. At the theaters he managed in conjunction with Zimmerman (quite another kind of person), I had played many long and successful engagements. Once he had refused to permit "Erminie" to be given without me at the Chestnut Street Theater, admittedly to his greater profit.

It was lamentable to be obliged to appeal to any one at all for the privilege of pursuing my profession, but there it was, and I must face it or begin life anew in another land. I did not want to begin life anew anywhere. The chances were much against those who so began. It was sure to be a long, hard, and doubtful pull. I had had that long, hard pull once, and had come through it victoriously, and I rebelled at being forced, like a newly released criminal, to make any such new and hazardous beginning. My feeling was not the less bitter in reflecting that these people, scarcely once removed from aliens, were forcing out of his country a man with several generations of American ancestors back of him.

As my indignation grew at the thought of expatriation, I realized that, though I could now do nothing against such odds, it was possible to live to fight another day, and that I could not fight if I did not stay. I stayed. Under humiliating circumstances, to be sure, but I stayed.

Out of the wreckage I was adroit enough to make a part of that Syndicate pay what amounted to fifty thousand dollars for the privilege of associating itself with me, when with a little more patience the Syndicate must have forced that association for nothing.

This was not a poor bargain for one who had broken his fortune in fighting for a principle which he consistently hugged to his heart while biding his time for another opportunity. It seemed a thousand years in coming. When it did arrive in the formation of The Actors' Equity Association, advantage of it was taken to the full, to the discomfort of the Syndicate, the triumph of justice and the placing of the actor in his present position of respect and power.

I had stood firm against the Syndicate until long past the time when there was a possible chance of success to the actors' side of the controversy, and until our power to resist had been shot to pieces.

After the greeting, which was polite, Nixon began, as I felt he would, by saying how foolish I was to fight on against the all-powerful Syndicate; the struggle being now in its second year. I declared myself satisfied with the situation, and that the Syndicate was not unlikely to meet with an unexpected opposition that would soon give matters theatrical an entirely different aspect. Busy with the thought he had in mind, this weak threat did not have any terrifying effect. "You'd better come on in," he said, "and resume playing to the old-time receipts at the Broad" (Street Theater). "We have always gotten on well together, and I'd like to be the one to take you over to our side."

"What," I replied, "go cap in hand to the Syndicate and say, 'Please may I play in your theaters?' Never!"

"*You* won't have to go to the Syndicate and ask for dates," he said quickly; "I'll be only too glad to get you all the dates you want!"

"No," said I; "I have no doubt you miss these old-time receipts, but with a business I have built up through my own efforts and energy I shall never consent to share it gratuitously with anybody. Ask for a 'date,' I never will, for I know that will lead to a demand that I surrender an interest in the thing, which, whatever else it may be, is, and always has been, my own. To that I never would consent."

There was a long pause, and then he said: "Why don't you sell an interest in your company, and make the purchaser your business partner? He could attend to securing a route from the Syndicate, which seems to stick in your crop."

I appeared to be taken with this idea, as if it might in some way lead to the solution of the difficulty. Taken

with it as if it had in no way been something upon
which I had spent nights of thought, and the very
thing I had been leading him on to suggest.

"That's not a bad idea," I replied, "for it would keep
me from personal contact with the Syndicate. But I
had thought never to part with any portion of my
enterprise. The man that gets it would have to pay a
good figure."

"What figure?" he asked.

"I am not prepared to say," I answered, "the thought
of it is so new, but any one who will meet me at his
office to-morrow morning at ten o'clock with a certified
check for so much money" — naming the amount —
"can have a half interest in my business for five years.
I thought never to consent to such a thing, but since
talking to you, I have changed my mind."

We parted with one of us — not Nixon — acting, as
never before, the part of utmost indifference. That
night at the theater I got a telegram from him saying
he would meet me at his office and with the check the
following morning. He kept his word. I got the check
which, with only moderately computed interest for the
time of our agreement, amounted to fifty thousand
dollars.

This was surely something saved from the struggle,
in addition to the formidable menace of banishment
which was the consideration at the moment that gave
me most concern. As I viewed it, it also was a million
per cent greater than the treatment that would have
been meted out to me had I gone to the Manhattan

contingency of the Syndicate. I had been outspoken in opposition to the conduct of the drama falling into the hands of a "trust"; into the hands of men who meant only too evidently to exploit that drama purely as a commerce. For months in speeches before the curtain and in the press I had pictured that Syndicate as a band of marauders who had the drama by the throat and were slowly but surely choking it to death. In the circumstances, now that they had won their point, I felt, if they could have willed it, my punishment, as Gilbert expresses it, would have been something lingering and accompanied with burning oil.

Had I determined to remain in America at whatever cost, Nixon, or any member of that Syndicate, must have acquired that business interest for nothing, as I have stated. I could not have helped it, for there was no other move for me to make in the theatrical field. A few days later, I explained this fully to Nixon. He gave me a swift look, and said something about what was to become of him in the next world, as "Well, I'll be d——d!" I hope he has escaped, for, with all his foibles, Nixon bore the financially inevitable with a chuckle.

I had fought the Devil with fire, and won — what? The privilege of remaining home, of being a citizen in my own country. I should have been humble and grateful, I suppose, but I was not. Instead, I was rebellious and resentful, and stayed so for years.

There was a little satisfaction in dealing the enemy a heavy blow in the financial "solar plexus," the region of his conscience, but I was not too proud of my "victory"; it had the taste of myrrh in the mouth. I was soldier enough to make my defeat as costly as possible. Circumstances were such that I had to bend or break. Broken, I could do nothing. I accepted the momentary taste of myrrh. I say momentary, because it became evident to me that such a sweeping victory as the Syndicate was having would lead to injustices from which the people of the dramatic profession would be sure to suffer. Present, I might be of service. I had been a witness to leadership on the actors' side of the question, and was not favorably impressed with it. Given the opportunity, I began to believe that I might do better. It was not possible to do worse. Years later, when The Actors' Equity Association was formed to check the intolerable injustices of this Syndicate and other managers, and I was asked to be its president, I accepted with more cordiality than I permitted to be seen.

The Syndicate went on unhindered for years, doing as it pleased, making things easier for itself and more difficult and intolerable for everybody else, actors, dramatists, and other managers outside its ranks. It decided when and where a play should appear, or whether it should appear at all, and even what monetary share it should have in the play. It decided what changes a play should undergo after acceptance, no matter to what well-meant but ignorant maltreatment it was subjected. It decided that a season's engagement should last but a few nights, and were brutally frank about it. It paid what it pleased, when it pleased, and where it pleased, and under conditions and agreements so one-sided, so far as the actor was concerned, as to be laughed out of court when, as occasionally happened, they reached there. Of course it produced and countenanced the type of play that "pulled the dough." With that, all thought, all ambition ended. It was a noble institution!

Then came the Shuberts.

They were no better and, in some respects, worse. It was a sad day, though, for the Syndicate when the Lord said, "Let there be Shuberts!" They were "the little willful thorns" in the rosebud side of the Syndicate. They have become its master. How they contrived to interest capital to construct theaters throughout the country and became the powerful competitors of the Syndicate is one of the mysteries of the theatrical profession. The history of it would make interesting reading, perhaps interesting disclosures.

Strong and extraordinary as the Shuberts have been in construction, competition, and opposition, strong as the Syndicate has been, they would have been weak by comparison with the coalition formed against them by the actors had the actors held against them in the 1890's as they did in 1917.

CHAPTER X

EUGENE FIELD AGAIN

Writing the names of those I love the best,
Lo, Francis Wilson's name leads all the rest,
As let this gift of mine to him attest.

THUS Field, in a Japan paper copy of his "Second Book of Verse." It was scarcely true, but none the less dear on that account, and the gift and the inscription are tender possessions. It is not easy to resign first place in the affection of a man like Field, but candor compels me to say that I believe he had a greater regard for Sol Smith Russell than for any of his many friends in the dramatic profession. I was a little more intimate in a bookish way, perhaps. Among his journalistic friends, no one surely was nearer and dearer to him than Slason Thompson. It was through him that Field published in the magazine "America," with which Thompson was associated, "Little Boy Blue," which, swifter than anything Field ever wrote, went to the hearts of the people and brought the author the fame he deserved. How familiar and endearing has become

The little toy dog is covered with dust,
But sturdy and stanch he stands,
The little toy soldier is red with rust
And his musket moulds in his hands.
Time was when the little toy dog was new
And the soldier was passing fair,
And that was the time when our little boy blue
Etc., etc.

The Little Peach

A little peach in the orchard grew —
A little peach of emerald hue;
Warmed by the sun and wet by the dew,
    It grew.

One day, walking the orchard through,
That little peach dawned on the view
Of Johnnie Jones and his sister Sue —
    Those two.

Up at the peach a club they threw —
Down from the stem on which it grew
Fell that little peach of emerald hue —
    Par bleu!

John took a bite and Sue took a chew,
And then the trouble began to brew —
Trouble the doctors couldn't subdue,
    Paregoric, too.

Under the turf where the daisies grew
They planted John and his Sister Sue,
And their little souls to the angels flew —
    Boo-hoo!

But what of the peach of emerald hue,
Warmed by the sun and wet by the dew?
Ah, well, its mission on earth is through —
    Adieu!

Eugene Field.

Field and I met before he had attained popularity or fame, before he had published anything in book form of which he was really proud. Harry Hamlin, son of the theater manager John Hamlin, of Chicago, brought Field one night behind the scenes of the Grand Opera House (Chicago) and introduced him. I was playing there in an operetta called "Nadjy," in which I sang a quaint poem written by Field and called "A Little Peach in an Orchard Grew." At the time I did not know, strangely enough, that Field had written it. A very dear friend, Hubbard T. Smith, connected with diplomatic life in Washington, had composed a bewitching melody for it, also not knowing of Field's authorship. Smith had found the verses, unsigned, in the corner of a country newspaper. My own acquaintance with the composition had come about through hearing it sung at a Lambs' Gambol, by Sidney Drew.

On a trip to Europe, I came across "The Little Peach" again in sheet-music form with both words and music credited to some one else! Bringing a copy home, I had John Braham, nephew of David Braham, of Harrigan and Hart fame, compose a dance for it. Arranging it as a duet, Marie Jansen and I interpolated it with marked favor into "Nadjy," and, later, carried it over into "The Oolah," the play in which I first disported myself as a "star." It was a long time before I confessed to Field that I often gave "The Little Peach" (Johnny Jones and his Sister Sue) before I knew he had written it.

Field gave the poem as a recitation in public and in

private. Sol Smith Russell, Henry E. Dixey, John A. Mackay, and many other comedians also recited it, though I never happened to hear them. It became popular. At first Field rather discounted its worth, once characterizing it as "rotten," but, agreeing with Slason Thompson, I think he wrote few things more irresistibly touching the chords of mirth. Later, Field revised his adverse pronouncement on the poem. It is, of course, but an amplification of a trifle he had written for his first tiny book, "The Denver Tribune Primer," where the story was told in a few lines:

The Peach is hard and green. He is Waiting for a Child to come along and Eat him. When he gets into the Child's little Stomach he will make things Hot for the Child. The Child Who eats the Peach will Be an Angel before he Gets a Chance to Eat another. If there were no Green Peaches there would not be so many Children-sizes of Gold Harps in Heaven.

I had copies of everything Field wrote, except this "Denver Tribune Primer." He plagued me about it; sent me catalogues in which the item was advertised. However, before sending, he would carefully cut out the price and the bookseller's name.

This "Primer" was in paper covers. Field's first book in boards, "Culture's Garland," was published in 1887, by Ticknor and Company of Boston. It was composed of material selected from his newspaper writings. Julian Hawthorne wrote the Introduction and called the book "delightful badinage." It did not win popularity, though Slason Thompson, Field's biographer, thinks it the most entertaining of all Field's books.

Originally, Field angled to have that Chesterfield of American men of letters, Edmund Clarence Stedman, the poet, write the Introduction, but the wary Stedman thought the material too light to be given such distinction. Likening Field to Shakespeare's Yorick, "whose motley coverd the sweetest nature and the tenderest heart," a "complex American with the obstreperous bizarrerie of the frontier and the artistic delicacy of our oldest culture always at odds within himself," Stedman objected to having his name associated with a ludicrous effort put forth, as was Field's wont, with the appearance of deadly earnest.

Field, of course, might be depended upon to be even with Stedman for this refusal. The announcement that Stedman was to lecture on "Poetry" before the Twentieth Century Club in Chicago gave the paragrapher his chance. He heralded Stedman's advent with such wit and humor as set the country in a roar and made Stedman feel that it might be advisable to postpone his visit. As Stedman sped on his journey, he was uneasy as to the reception that awaited him at the end. From the "complex American" the least the poet-critic expected was a calathumpian band. He got out of the train with fear. Only a few friends greeted him. Field was among them, "his face agrin like a schoolboy's."

In a copy of "Culture's Garland" which I carried to him from a friend in Boston, Field wrote:

"I am not ashamed of this little book, but, like the boy with the measles, I am sorry for it in spots."

The reception of his book piqued his pride somewhat, but it was not his nature to grieve long over the
thing. Soon came his incomparable lullabies and fascinating fairy-tales which delighted the world and
brought him fame.

The two books upon which Field's reputation and
popularity mainly rest are "A Little Book of Western
Verse" and "A Little Book of Profitable Tales." They
were first issued privately by subscription. Field was
in Europe when they appeared, 1889. A popular edition
followed. Before this came out, I pleased Field by
offering to put in book form any material of his he felt
worthy to be so placed. He had nothing on hand, except
some paraphrases of the Odes of Horace which he had
been printing in his daily column. He had not thought
to make a book of them. A great inducement to the
publication of books are subscribers. Field still being
absent, I forwarded my check to his literary adviser,
Slason Thompson, for the number one copy of a
limited edition. We all went into leisurely conference
with the result that two years later "Echoes from the
Sabine Farm" appeared. Except to a certain class of
readers, it is not at all the most interesting of Field's
productions. Their issue in a permanent form was
gratifying to Field's taste for the classics.

The "Echoes from the Sabine Farm" was privately
printed. A hundred copies only were made, thirty on
Japan, and seventy on Whatman, paper. Field proposed that he should take one copy and I a second, and
that we should then destroy all the others. The idea

Yours faithfully
Hub. T. Smith.

HUBBARD T. SMITH

He found Eugene Field's "A Little Peach," uncredited, in a country newspaper. He set it to a tune which everybody hummed.

was that we should be concerned in the issue of a de luxe edition of a work so rare, so scarce that succeeding generations of bibliomaniacs would weep and wail over their inability to secure a copy. That sort of thing delighted Field, and was extremely interesting to me. Somehow he sensed that certain forms of what he wrote would ultimately be sought by bibliophiles.

However, we agreed upon the plan. But when the etched vignettes and the graceful head- and tail-pieces by Edmund H. Garrett, whom I secured to illustrate the work, came along, with the beautiful specimen pages, both Field and I weakened. There were too many dear friends whom neither he nor I could find it in our hearts to deny.

Much fun has been poked at me because I have cared to collect "number one" copies of certain issues of books. When an author sets aside a particular volume of a limited edition and attests with his signature that he has given it the distinction of first place, it somehow, for me, takes on an additional interest. Of course he might have selected any other copy and given it first choice, but he did not. He chose that particular book. However, in this matter of books I have ever agreed with "Tony Lumpkin" that the inside of the letter is always the cream of the correspondence.

Until 1889, when these books of "Western Verse" and "Profitable Tales" appeared, I think Field never wanted to be anything so much as he wanted to be an actor. He did little or nothing at the three colleges he had attended, and from none of which he graduated, to

accomplish a command of the thing in which he finally
excelled, technic, facility of expression. In boyhood, at
college, as his brother Roswell said of him, "He was a
genial, sportive, song-singing, fun-making companion"
— "prolific of harmless pranks," and "his school life
was a big joke." But he never missed an opportunity
to declaim! In all amateur entertainments Field
excelled. With a deep bass voice he always "brought
down the house" with "The Old Sexton," who, to a
taking melody, was always, quite after the fashion of
the real old sexton of the song, "gather! — gather! —
gather-er-er-ing them in!" I am wondering if, in the
manner of our common friend, the comedian William
H. Crane, Field, after delighting his audience with the
serious rendering of the song, hilariously convulsed
them by topping it off with a darkey breakdown!

Ida Comstock Below,[1] Field's sister-in-law, tells us
that as a young man he was always in demand for entertainments and amateur theatricals. "His vivacity, his
sparkling wit, his keen sense of humor, and his wonderful ability to attract people to himself, made him the life
of every social gathering." "The Old Man" which he
wrote and sang was a rollicking production of words
and action and showed, Mrs. Below declares, "to
perfection his talents as a comedian." A take-off on
"Mrs. Jarley," of waxwork fame, was another of his
early creations and, with Field's talent for mimicry and
facial expression, must have been worth seeing. Not
more so, I think, than his imitations of Henry Irving

[1] *Eugene Field in his Home.* E. P. Dutton & Company.

which he had the courage to give before that great English actor. I should like to have been present to study Irving's expression as Field was holding forth Though he poked fun at Irving's "matchless legs" and the "Naw, naw!" of his negations, Field was a sincere admirer of the tragedian and said so with felicitous phrase in many tributes he paid him and his art.

Both Field and Sol Smith Russell were New Englanders. Though born in St. Louis, Field was educated in New England, where he lived with his grandmother and his cousin Mary Field French, and was brought up, as he would quizzically say, "in the nurture and admonition of the Lord." Russell was an actor with a charming personality and the possessor of a smile that has won its way long ere this past the guardian of the Pearly Gates. He excelled in reciting stories of New England life in dialect — the very thing which Field could do skillfully. The two were drawn together by common interests and mutual admiration. Field told Russell's stories — with embellishments. The stories were all the better for those embellishments, we may be sure. He wrote stories for Russell to recite, as "Our Two Opinions," etc., and Russell told them delightfully with no other broidery than a pathos, a quaintness for which he was famous. In Russell, Field recognized the master in such things and sat admiringly at his feet and learned as he sat.

In his humorous effort to keep his friend Russell before the public he wrote of him severally as the owner of rich coal-mines which had been accidentally unearthed at the Russell homestead, the chosen or prospective candidate for President of the National Prohibition Party, and the bountiful contributor to countrywide institutions of charity. This did not add much to Russell's comfort and peace of mind. He found himself the constant target of hordes of solicitors of charity with which his friend of the humorous paragraphs had intentionally showered him.

All through life Field kept up his friendships and his affection with people of the stage and, in full measure, they returned both. After the play was over, at table, in private, even along the street in conversation, they exerted themselves to interest and delight this wonderful man with the heart of a child who loved them and their profession and whose deep regret it was that he also was not one of those whose privilege it was to entertain and refresh mankind. Yet all the while, in another direction, he was working rapidly toward that very thing and in a permanency of form not possible to the actor.

> I'd ruther have your happy knack
> Than all the arts that critics praise,
> The knack o' takin' old folks back
> To childhood homes and childhood days,

he said in his tribute to Denman Thompson, after seeing him in "The Old Homestead."

It was the same with James Whitcomb Riley, who once told me that the height of his ambition as a boy was to be a minstrel, wear a "plug" hat, and march in the street parade! Like his friend Riley, Field never

quite got over being "stage-struck." In a copy of that beautiful limited edition of "Old-Fashioned Roses" Riley wrote for me the following:

> I'd ruther be an actor man
> That makes the sad world laugh,
> Than any other kind o' man
> That sports a' ortergraph.

Few people achieve anything without enthusiasm. Field had it in abundance, and loved it in others. He adored it in his actor friends, who seconded his propensity for pranks and jokes with as much celerity and interest as he himself had in their origin and execution. In our love for Field we of the stage were absolutely at his command. If he kept us seriously and humorously before the public, we, in turn, heralded his poems and stories, acclaimed them, and were delighted to help popularize them and him. It was a tacit pact of appreciation and affection. If he were ill, those of us who owned ranches or country places put them at his disposal, as witness Madame Modjeska. We were ready to send his children to college, to publish his books, and, in a word, to stand at his beck and call. If he had written plays, we should have done our utmost in their presentation with the hope of adding to his renown, as, in the performance of "Rip Van Winkle," Jefferson has added to the renown of Washington Irving. Like Robert Louis Stevenson, Field had no skill as a dramatist. Both tried. It was another art which neither took the pains, perhaps had no time, to acquire. Both had ample creative, inventive faculty. If his genius and industry had not made it unnecessary, his friends of the drama would unquestionably have provided for his family. The matter was considered on his demise.

Field was an inspiration to those who were ripe for interest in books, and not a little work on his part was done in a pioneer way for those who were not so interested and who had scarcely dreamed of becoming readers.

He was a discerning "prowler" among bookstalls, or in old bookshops at home and abroad, for the quaint and curious that might serve in his work. At such times he remembered his friends, and would frequently adorn the fly-leaves of his gifts with a verse or two of appreciative regard. From London, in 1889, he sent me a battered copy of F. Somner Merryweather's "Bibliomania in the Middle Ages" in which he had written as follows:

To FRANCIS WILSON

Herein again speak valiant men
        Of all nativities and ages;
I hear and smile with rapture while
        I turn these musty, magic pages.

And you, dear friend (to whom I send
        This charming work of Merryweather),
Perchance you'll find herein to bind
        Our hearts the closer still together.

For he who looks on good old books
        With such sincere regard as you do,
Is worthy of those sweets of love
        Which no vain worldliness can hoodoo.

At any rate, I beg to state
    That with this gift my love I send you;
And if I pray this Christmas Day
    'Twill be that blessings may attend you.

Bo't in the Brompton Road, Dec. 6, 1889.
    Henry Selwyn, dealer.

Then, of course, one would read and study like mad with the hope of living up to such a compliment. It was a charming way Field had of inciting the ambition of a friend.

As Field's reputation grew, he was much importuned for autographs, inscriptions, etc. People who knew of our friendship often persuaded me to ask him for this or that autographic favor. Only occasionally would he hesitate to comply, and even then with a comic assumption of dignity and importance that was enjoyable to witness. However frequent such a request, I am sure it must be too flattering ever to become an annoyance. Once at the Saints' and Sinners' Corner [1] of McClurg's Book Store, Chicago, I laid down before him two or three of his books with the bantering remark that the half a dozen demands for his autograph in the last year or two must be evidence to him of some growth, however slight, in popularity. He gave a funny little half laugh, half grunt, and, picking up a pad of scratch paper which lay at hand, penciled off, in a few moments, the following:

[1] So named by Field and frequented by him and a number of kindred spirits who loved books.

The Passing of Eugene [1]

When Eugene Field lay dying
    The death all good men die,
Came Francis Wilson flying
    As only he can fly.

"My friend, before you peter
    And seek the shining shore
Write me in common meter
    Some autographic lore!"

Then Eugene Field smiled sadly,
    And his face grew wan and dim,
But he wrote the verses gladly
    His friend required of him.

And having done this duty,
    From out its home of clay
That soul of spotless beauty
    To Canaan soared away.

April 5, 1893

One of the methods which Field employed to joke his actor friends, as we have seen, was to credit them with qualities they did not possess, with weaknesses they did not have, and, yea, with literary offspring that were never born to them. He greatly admired that fine Polish actress, Madame Modjeska, and lo, he must make her a poetess by ascribing to her the authorship of:

The Wanderer

Upon a mountain height, far from the sea,
    I found a shell.
And to my listening ear this lonely thing

---

[1] The late George M. Millard supplied the title.

EUGENE FIELD

He would spend hours with colored inks, a pointed pen, and a magnify-
ing glass inditing, decorating poems and letters to friends.

Ever a song of ocean seemed to sing —
    Ever a tale of ocean seemed to tell.

  . . . .

Strange was it not? Far from its native deep,
    One song it sang;
Sang of the awful mysteries of the tide,
Sang of the restless sea, profound and wide —
    Ever with echoes of the ocean rang.
And as the shell upon the mountain height
    Sang of the sea,
So do I ever, leagues and leagues away —
So do I ever, wandering where I may,
    Sing, O my home! sing, O my home! of thee!

Though not at all her composition, it expressed unquestionably the sentiments of Madame Modjeska (Countess Bozenta) who because of her patriotism had been expatriated.

Under the impression that she had actually written the poem, her numerous admirers throughout the country constantly deluged her with newspaper clippings of it with requests for her signature. Her denials were in vain. She was merely thought to be modest. Field was delighted. In a sweetly humorous way he had called attention to her banishment and the reason for it. Far from being displeased, Modjeska was flattered at the sympathetic position in which Field had placed her before the public. She went on denying the authorship and hugely enjoyed Field's enjoyment of his hoax. Field finally reclaimed his "Wanderer" by publishing it in his "A Little Book of Western Verse."

He not only wrote a review of the Life of Emma

Abbott, "Ten Years a Song Bird — Memoirs of a Busy Life," memoirs which never existed except in the fertile imagination of Field, but he mischievously credited Miss Abbott (who was Mrs. Wetherell) with knowing the happiness of motherhood. She never had. And "he wrote at least a bookful of startling and funny adventures" concerning the "infant."

He invented a baby for the William H. Cranes, who were childless, and named it Stuart Robson Crane, after Crane's associate. He wrote a poem of many stanzas to Mrs. Crane who for years was deservedly the most popular woman in the dramatic profession, though not of it.

Here is the eighth stanza:

Dear little lady Ella (let me call you that once more
    In memory of the happy days in Utica of yore),
I might keep one small share myself, but most of 'em should go
    To you — yes, riches, happiness, and health should surely
        rain
Upon the temporal estate of Mrs. "Billy" Crane.

As, according to Eastern tradition in the performance of one's duty, I had built a house, planted a tree, and was producing a family, Field had to look elsewhere for material concerning myself. Here is an allusion printed in his "Sharps and Flats" column. It has never stopped going the rounds:

We regard Mr. Francis Wilson's legs as the greatest curiosities on the American stage at the present time. We call them curiosities when perhaps we should term them prodigies.

The truth is, they are so versatile, so changeful, that we hardly know what epithet could be applied to them most properly. They are twins, yet totally unalike, reminding one of the well-mated man and wife, who are so different that we speak of them as well-matched. The left leg is apparently of serious turn, as may be observed on all occasions requiring a portrayal of those emotions which bespeak elevated thought and philosophic tendencies. The right leg is mercurial, obliquitous, passionate to a marked degree, whimsical, fantastic, and grotesque. The contrast between the two gives us comedy in itself which is very pleasing, for the constant struggle between the perennial levity of the right leg and the melancholy demeanor of the left leg is funnier by far than most of the horse-play which passes for comedy in these times.

> While one with sad emotion throbs
>   And wildly palpitates,
> The other makes its grievous sobs
>   And loudly cachinnates.
> While this one jigs along the floor
>   Intent on noisy pleasure,
> The other treads the carpet o'er
>   In many a stately measure.

The combination is a happy one. The left leg pleases the serious-minded, sentimental, and the lovers of the emotional style of dramatic art; the right leg solaces those who believe there is nothing more enjoyable than mirth. Here we find two legs capable of every variety of action. They can shake you out a jig or stride you a minuet; they can sob plaintively or titter hysterically; they can strut imperiously or wabble ludicrously; they can suggest a spondaic pentameter of the best old classic poets or a bit of modern doggerel from "Puck." Their name is Versatility, and in them we find the passions clearly defined and deftly combined.

Ever after during my professional tours, while people did not inquire after my "legs" as they did after the Emma Abbott or the Crane baby, or send "Congratulations" as they did to Modjeska on her writing "The

Wanderer" — I can see, of course, that it might be awkward to send, or even receive, congratulations on "a mercurial right leg" or the "melancholy demeanor" of a left ditto — but ever after, I repeat, I received few professional criticisms which did not have some allusion to the thing which Field's trenchant humor had fastened upon me.

There was praise enough for other qualities, some of which I hope was not unmerited and for much of which I have ever been grateful, but I did sometimes feel as if I would like once in a while — not always, but just once in a while — to escape that eternal repetition. It would have been a great relief! and it would have been a greater relief still if only some paragrapher had discovered the truth under Field's delicious humor, discovered that it was the skill of the owner of those Adonis-like underpinnings that made them put an antic curvature on as occasion demanded. It was so simple. As the twist of an expression may make literature or bosh, so may the turn of an ankle give us "Versatility," as Field called it — or a sprain.

Field's stories about his friends on the stage were often the reflections of the moods in which he found them. It must have been a dolorous moment of meeting that suggested the following to which Field appended the name of Richard Mansfield:

> Amber clouds on a cobalt sky,
> The hour for work is drawing nigh!
>
> An all-night journey and an aching head,
> A longing to strike and go to bed!

Not a friend to greet or a friend to meet,
  A lonely room on a noisy street!

A silent meal in a crowded room,
  A silent smoke in a cloud of gloom.

A scene rehearsal, a stammering crew,
  Letters received, and more work to do.

Business bothers, intrigues and war;
  The future a blank, the present a bore.

A cup of strong tea, a smoke, and I better
  Screw up my courage and seek the theater.

Dress for an hour in a cell that is stifling
  And then play a part with a heart — but
    I'm trifling

Nobody could enumerate the petty annoyances of the traveling player's existence or set them forth with more sarcastic humor than Richard Mansfield — I have heard him do it many a time — and Field probably jotted them down in the order in which they fell from his lips. The long and short "jumps" are not as frequent as formerly, but they are frequent enough even now to make facing an audience, after "the all-night journey with an aching head" and that "dress for an hour in a cell that is stifling," no joyful experience. I have seen it stated somewhere that among many requirements for the successful pursuit of the actor's art were the "delicacy of a flower and the hide of a rhinoceros." They are very essential. But on the stage one is forced reluctantly to admit that a certain kind of

success is sometimes observed without the joy of the
one or the comfort of the other.

Field had a queer theory that in all matters pertaining to the possession of books or curios the collector
ought never to hesitate to secure the coveted prize.
The trifling matter of an exchange of money as a
necessary part of such a transaction bothered him not
at all. The important thing was possession. Paying
might be done at leisure. He put this thought, after the
fashion of Dr. Watts, into verse and printed it with an
introductory paragraph in his "Sharps and Flats"
column:

Francis Wilson, the comedian, is the possessor of a chair
which Sir Walter Scott used in his library at Abbotsford. A
beautiful bit of furniture it is, and well worth, aside from all
sentimental consideration, the large price paid by the enterprising and discriminating curio. As we understand it, Bouton,
the New York dealer, had this chair on exhibition for several
months. Mr. Wilson happened along one day, having just
returned from a professional tour in the West. Mr. William
Winter, dramatic critic of "The Tribune," was looking at the
chair; he had been after it for some time, but had been waiting
for the price to abate somewhat.

"The Players Club should have that chair," said he to Bouton, "and if you'll give better terms I'll get a number of men to
chip in together and buy it."

To this appeal Bouton steadily remained deaf. After Mr.
Winter had left the place, Wilson said to Bouton, "Send the
chair up to my house; here is a check for the money."

There are rumors to the effect that when Mr. Winter heard
of this transaction, he rent his garments and gnashed his teeth,
and wildly implored somebody to hang a millstone about his
neck and cast him into outer darkness.

Horace Greeley used to say that the best way to resume was
to resume; so, in the science of collecting, it behooves the col-

Brist; Epit: in imitatione Skeltonis - circa 1530.

Under yᵉ stone (bet none deface it!)
Sanctissimus vir in pace jacet;
Bibliothecam habens, moriens donavit
To unum Tygrem quum amavit;
"Nemine Tyger," ipse dixit,
"If my epitaph's writ, be sure you fix it,
And say to yᵉ dampned and yᵉ fiends yᵗ rule 'em
Yᵗ diabolus osculet mei culum!"

Explicit

Eugenius Tyger fec-t

lector never to put off till to-morrow what he can pick up to-day. This theory has been most succinctly and beautifully set forth in one of the hymns recently compiled by the Archbishop of the North Side (page 217):

> How foolish of a man to wait
>   When once his chance is nigh:
> To-morrow it may be too late —
>   Some other man may buy.
> Nay, brother, comprehend the boon
>   That's offered in a trice,
> Or else some other all too soon
>   Will pay the needful price.
>
> Though undue haste may be a crime,
>   Procrastination's worse;
> Now — now is the accepted time
>   To eviscerate your purse!
> So buy what finds you find to-day —
>   That is the safest plan;
> And if you find you cannot pay,
>   Why, settle when you can.

It is quite true, as said, that "scattered throughout his [Field's] writings from 1887 onward were paragraphs, ballads, and jests, praising, berating, and 'joshing' the maniac crew who held that 'binding's the surest test,' and who bought books, as some would-be connoisseurs do wine, or once did, by label." If that were not so, we should miss many of the most delectable things Field has written, but it scarcely measures up to the fact to speak of his "*professions* of sympathy with the maniacs," etc. Except at first, there was no pretense about Field's interest and enthusiasm in these friends and their collections, however weird and bizarre. He

not only urged them on by word, but by deed. As far
as his limited means would permit, and they were unquestionably limited, Field surrounded himself with
the most extraordinary collection — conglomeration
would be a better word — of what he called "plunder,"
but what some unappreciative people would firmly
designate as "junk." He had sheet-music copies of
songs with stupid or over-sentimental titles; as:
"Don't Go Back on Your Mother, Tom," "Never
Kick Your Mother When She's Down," "The Moon
Looks Coldly and Sad on the Tomb of My Love," etc.
He had bells of various shapes and sizes with faces
some of which, when the bells were rung, would
mockingly protrude their tongues. On specially arranged shelves there were mechanical toys that performed attractive, human-like tricks. There were a
score or more of envelopes printed during the Civil War
as their labels or inscriptions showed. There were odd-
looking bottles, beautiful in color, fine or odd in shape,
and of historic interest. Here was the axe which
Gladstone used in his wood-chopping experiences at
Hawarden,[1] and there, Field's prize possession, the
shears which Charles A. Dana wielded in his editorial
capacity on "The New York Sun."

None of these things, particularly as exhibited and
descanted upon by Field, was, or could possibly be,
uninteresting, though the possession of some of them

[1] Another such axe went to the National Liberal Club of London in
1922, as a souvenir gift from the great Premier's son, Henry Neville
Gladstone.

might seem odd in a man like Field, who was a Horatian
student and who wrote charmingly in an old-world,
archaic style of expression. As for his books, to the un-
knowing they appeared as drolly chosen as his clothes,
his toys, and his innumerable trinkets. He had many
of the standard works found in "every gentleman's
library," and he also had books on medicine, dreams,
marriage, monogamy, polygamy, celibacy, ancient
customs and superstitions, fans, sewing, tobacco,
armor, crime, punishments, worships, rings, pottery,
watches, witch-craft, sorcery, opium, lace, etc. It has
been remarked with a good deal of verity that his
knowledge of literature of the gay, frail, rakish, mere-
tricious, gallant type was by no means inconsiderable.
His was an inquiring mind, curious, and all was fish
that came to his mental net.

The bibliomaniacal clan that gathered at the
"Saints' and Sinners' Corner," the clan which Field
had "so humorously maligned" over many years, had
ample compensation, if such a thing were needed, in
"The Love Affairs of a Bibliomaniac," the last of the
Field publications, the work upon which he was engaged at the time he laid aside the pen forever. The
work was not only a joy and comfort to the author, but
was also an attestation of his leadership in that clan, a
glad confession of his having been a willing victim to
the joy that physics pain in the pursuit, the doubt and
delight of ultimate possession that comes to those
initiated in the mysteries and raptures that dwell in the
Land of Bibliomania. He said nothing plainer in that

book than that he had remained to pray after having come to scoff.

Eugene Field was ever a boy, an enthusiast bent upon having what Roosevelt called "a bully good time" with life, and he had it. And having enjoyed it, he left life far richer for his possession of it. Imagine what that meant and means to his friends, to the world!

He was anything but a reformer, a world-straightener; he abominated the thought of being regarded as such. The nearest approach being his hatred for sham, pretense, which he lashed with joyous vigor and scorn.

He took as much pains to perpetrate a joke on a crony, "putting his friendship to a test," as he did in concocting and carrying out successfully an international hoax so skillfully arranged as to deceive even a Labouchere, of the London "Truth." His attitude toward Chicago was analogous to that of Dr. Johnson toward David Garrick. Johnson would roundly abuse the English "Roscius," but woe to any one else who attempted to do so!

Field was almost unmerciful — but always winningly humorous — in the way he would satirize the good citizens of the Windy City, citizens whose literary pretentions or realities he would purposely confuse with their sale of "green hams," or what not of a commercial character. No greater pleasure could come to Field than an opportunity to defend Chicago and the West. He was not above being anonymously satirical at their expense, or even at the expense of a friend, for the opportunity he had made to defend or eulogize them.

Chicagoans had a fine appreciation of Eugene Field
— except (of all men!) the bookseller and publisher
General Alexander C. McClurg. While Field was
busy inventing the "Saints' and Sinners' Corner" of
McClurg's store and thereby adding to the popularity
and prosperity of the place, McClurg was equally busy
regarding Field with doubt and disfavor. He had no
appreciation of Field's fun, which he felt was the
lightest of light persiflage, and he was quite convinced
for a long time that Field's jocular reference in "The
News" to the book-lovers who frequented the McClurg
store was detrimental to the interest of the business
there carried on. It was not until four or five years
after Field had issued the books that brought him
repute that McClurg would consent to become a
publisher of anything Field offered.

Lack of humor appeared to be at the bottom of
McClurg's attitude toward the author of "Little Boy
Blue." And this worried Field not at all. He thought
the General pompous and too self-important — and
was amused. McClurg did not escape Field's irrever-
ence — few things did, except women and the worthy
things in literature! Circulated among the book-loving,
book-collecting, bibliomaniacal bravos, who, for a
decade, gathered in that "corner," drawn thither, of
course, by the books, but mainly by the magnetic
presence of the quaint, fun-loving, wondrous Field,
was a sheet of paper upon which, remembering likely
the Johnsonian remark in connection with Hannah
More and "fundament," Field had written:

Bibliomaniac, beware
How you sit upon this chair,
For herein McClurg hath sat
With his consequential —

Field knew all the children in his neighborhood.
They went riding with him in the donkey cart he had
provided for his kiddies. One of my most amusing remembrances of the man is of his taking me down into
the cellar where the burro was stabled, "to hear it
talk." Field pitched his voice into a weird key and the
donkey brayed back like mad. If Field uttered a plain-
tive cry, the beast answered in like strain. If short,
quick, angry notes were given, they were returned in
kind. In the obscure light of the cellar, with Field standing with his hands to his mouth uttering those mournful
sounds which had such a startling, imitative effect upon
the animal, the situation was not without humor. We
all three enjoyed it! The donkey strayed from home.
Field offered books for its return. Neighborhood boys
earned the reward.

He bought a goat for his children. Mrs. Field complained of its odor. When the parents were absent one
day, the youngsters hauled "Billy" upstairs, gave him
a hot bath, and tried to perfume him from a bottle of
cologne. The first application stung badly and "Billy"
showed swift resentment by leaping out of the tub and
through the window, disappearing forever. If dinner
at home were not to Field's taste, or, especially, if he
scented apple-pie in the vicinity, he would search out
the table at which it was to be served and seat himself

FRANCIS WILSON AND EUGENE FIELD AS CHERUBS

Out strolling one day in Chicago, Field suggested being "taken."
The likenesses of him are excellent. Field's circulation seemed defective. He declared he had done most of his writing "freezing to
death."

unceremoniously. No man knew better how to "earn his dinner." It was ever a privilege to be present with him at a board.

Field was an industriously practical joker, but, strange to say, he was of that kind who could stand being joked. He once sent me the "Autobiography" of Joseph Jefferson together with a print of the comedian. I knew, of course, why he sent them and what he wanted done with them. Before his letter of explanation had time to reach me, I telegraphed my cordial thanks for the book and the picture which I declared added much to my collection. His characteristic reply follows:

Good God, my child, do you think I am a millionaire? That book is not for you; neither is the portrait. You get them autographed and embellished and pack them back to me as quick as you know how. The thought of this narrow escape makes me sweat blood like a behemoth!

He delighted in surprises. It was difficult to get him to name a time or hour for a visit. Then of a sudden when hope of seeing him had been given up, he would walk in unannounced. It happened so during one of his infrequent visits to New York. It was Sunday at New Rochelle, where I lived, and the house was full of guests. In he came followed by his daughter "Trotty" (Mary French Field), his brother, "Rose" (Roswell), and three other friends — ten minutes before dinnertime. With any one else this would have been embarrassing. With Field, no matter how numerously accompanied, it was a joy. However, the thought of the generous proportions of the turkey that day gave a real sigh of relief to the hostess. What a day of delight it was! Then, indeed, was Field a youngster! How finely he held his audience! How we laughed — and admired! In one of the bedrooms an old, quilted, blue-and-white spread caught his gaze. He seized it in the center, declaring it had no business in that house, stuffed as much as he could into his coat-pocket, and marched downstairs into the drawing-room with the ends dragging after him.

The world has long since bowed down to the charm of Field's "Little Boy Blue"and continues to be touched by its emotion, though, to me, "The Lyttel Boy" "that wolde not renne and play," and that "ben allwais in the way," is scarcely less beautiful.

There is one of Field's poems that all too unworthily has led a shameful sort of existence ever since he wrote it. He never included it in any of his publications, though he loved it beyond measure. It is as quaint and as tender as anything which came from his pen, and when he would recite it, as he often did to a chosen few, it never failed to touch the heart of those who were privileged to hear him. Yet through the squeamishness of publishers, fearful, no doubt, that the great outside world, which knows everything, would learn of a perfectly normal condition in childhood which has existed since Adam and Eve and will continue to exist till Doomsday, it has been frowned upon and never accorded a place among Field's published creations. It has often been privately printed, but always circulated as if it were a libidinous thing which could appeal only to the prurient-minded. Here for the first time between the covers of a book regularly published I had hoped to include the dreadful thing which is so beautiful, but my publishers have shown the white feather and I have reluctantly agreed to the omission of all but a part of the first verse:

> When Willie was a little boy,
> not more than five or six,
> Right constantly he would annoy
> his mother with his tricks;
> But not a picayune cared I
> for what he did or said,
> Unless, as happened constantly,
> that rascal — etc., etc.

Thus Field went on giving expression to himself, voicing the things no one else felt were worthy to be voiced and binding people's hearts to himself with hoops of steel. Went on saying and doing even the things other people had said and done, but giving them a twist of his own that made them as new, that were indeed as new, seen through the light of his personality. It is true that he was a fellow of infinite jest, but it is also true, thank Heaven, that he was a fellow of infinite tenderness, a new note, a lovely light in the world. It seems a thousand pities he could not have remained longer with us, this great big, gentle-hearted, generous fellow whose kindnesses and courtesies were many and frequent.

His friends at last have raised a statue to his memory, but the finest statue that could be fashioned in bronze or stone will always be feeble as a memorial by comparison with the one he himself has built in writing "A Little Book of Western Verse," "Horatian Odes," "The Love Affairs of a Bibliomaniac," and "A Little Book of Profitable Tales."

Field died suddenly one November night in 1895. A great wave of sympathetic regret swept over the country. A worthy man of letters, "intensely, whimsically American," had passed on. From Europe came this message from Henry Irving:

The death of Eugene Field is a loss not only to his many friends, but to the world at large. He was distinctly a man of genius, and he was dowered with a nature whose sweetness endeared him to all who knew him. To me he was a loved and honored friend, and the world seems vastly the poorer without him.

CHAPTER XI

JOSEPH JEFFERSON — "RIP" AND "THE RIVALS"

JEFFERSON said he thought Eugene Field an odd sort of man to go about the country as he did when at leisure picking up queer gimcracks such as old watches, rings, mechanical toys, editorial scissors, etc. When I told him that Field had much the same opinion of him and of his painting with a raw-egg mixture on a piece of tin and transferring the painting to velvet and other cloths by means of a washringer, and calling the squashed result a "monotype," Jefferson laughed heartily.

"That's it, that's it!" he said; "one half of the world always thinks the other half is crazy."

But what would Field have said if I had told him that a practice which Jefferson greatly enjoyed was resting in a recumbent position and having some one of his family tickle his stockinged feet with a feather.

Apart from his gifts as an actor, what I liked most in Jefferson was his gentleness, his modesty, and his love of children and home. Our "Rip" was assuredly a family man. He had homes everywhere — except in the city — at Hohokus, New Jersey, at Jefferson Island, in Louisiana, and at Buzzard's Bay. "Crow's Nest," the Massachusetts home, was "the big house," with the homes of his children nestling about it in a "comfy," affectionate way.

The Grover Clevelands were Jefferson's neighbors

at "Gray Gables," Buzzard's Bay. Cleveland and the comedian were fishing companions. In matters that were new and startling, Jefferson was very credulous. In a world full of wonders he could almost accept the happening of miracles. Once, while Jefferson was listening to some remarkable tale, Cleveland was fretting to be gone on one of their many fishing trips. The narrator, having overwhelmed the comedian, sought to interest "the President," but was headed off by the great Democrat with:

"Oh, keep on telling it to Jefferson. He'll believe anything!"

Jefferson was one of the real Peter Pans of the stage. He kept a lot of his boyishness till past seventy. His curiosity never abated as to inventions and pastimes. I can see him now, close to threescore and ten, whirling, under the direction of a "professor," around a hall where people were taught to ride a new-fangled, two-wheeled thing — called a bicycle. He looked very uncomfortable and out of place which, not being aware of it, worried him not at all. When he would roll a short distance without too much wobbling, he was thrilled with the joy of his accomplishment. As soon as he found he could go along without falling off, he lost interest and abandoned the wheel with the remark that he felt safer walking than "zigzagging over the face of the earth."

At his island home in Acadia, the land Longfellow made famous through "Evangeline," Jefferson had about as much success as with the bicycle in his effort

JOSEPH JEFFERSON AS RIP VAN WINKLE

Jefferson never saw a picture that pleased him of "Rip" gazing for the first time, after the mysterious sleep of twenty years, on the village of Falling Waters. He and his friend the late Charles A. Walker of Boston were constantly striving for one that was acceptable. The above was not developed until after Jefferson's death. It might have pleased him.

to keep up with one of the pastimes of the place, duck-shooting. On a time he had visiting him a mutual friend, Edward Kemble, the cartoonist. One day the host suggested to his guest that they take their guns and go out for a little sport. Kemble had no skill as a shot, and Jefferson had less, but he thought it a good opportunity to test the floating qualities of a newly arrived rubber boat of collapsible type. They started out bravely. Presently some ducks came in view. Kemble was urged to fire. He did so — and missed. Jefferson seized the gun, took deliberate aim — and also missed. Declaring that he had had a full day of duck-shooting, Jefferson ordered the boat headed for the shore. The vent cork in the boat came loose and was not easily replaced. When land was reached, the boat was half filled with water. Both amateur sportsmen were wet — and scared. There are alligators in Acadian waters.

Besides fishing, Jefferson was passionately devoted to painting. He easily persuaded himself that he required much time in winter to paint and fish. The fact is, Jefferson was a sun-hunter, and a successful one. He was thin, and quickly chilled. Once caught North by an advance spell of cold weather, he appeared at a "stag" dinner and seemed suddenly to have gained a great deal of flesh. This was not so, however. He was dressed for the season, "and looked the part." As his son Charles explained to us: "Father has on his arctic overshoes, the thickest clothes he owns, and two or three suits of underwear." Jefferson even permitted

Charles to roll up the leg of his (Jefferson's) trousers to expose the Esquimaux-like outfit.

When the temperature went down in the North, Jefferson was generally to be found in the South, at New Orleans, at Jefferson Island, and, toward the last, at Palm Beach where he had a cottage called "The Reefes," in which he died. His death must have been a great surprise to him. He had gone on so long, so vigorously, holding his own in his beloved profession; he stood so high in the esteem of the public, that he had begun to believe that the end might almost be indefinitely postponed.

There is a picture, the last one taken of him, sitting on a bench at Palm Beach, and all too evidently thinking it over, and trying to realize with Sarah Siddons: "This is the end of all!" It is the saddest picture I have ever seen of one who gave so much pleasure.

Unless one is a student of the drama or an old playgoer, it is hard to realize the popularity, the influence Jefferson had in his time and day. In 1870, he named "The Little Church Around the Corner." In 1889–90, he published his "Autobiography." In 1892, Yale University gave him the degree of M.A. Harvard University followed suit with the degree of M.A. in 1895. Previously, the members of his profession had presented him with a great loving-cup in silver bearing figures of himself in various characters. Though he deeply appreciated his college preferments, it did not prevent his writing to friends facetiously that he was glad that to his new titles had not been added those of his old friend Dr. Peter Pangloss, namely, LL.D., A.S.S.

Some years ago, everybody was reciting and even composing what were called "limericks." One could scarcely pay a visit and stay half an hour without having the conversation swung into these four, six, or eight line drolleries. Many were cleverly wrought and all were humorous. Not a few (always told in private) were distinctly naughty. Those like:

> There was a young lady from Siam
> Who said to her lover, young Priam:
> If you kiss me, of course, you'll have to use force,
> But God knows you're stronger than I am!

Or

> There was a young sculptor named Phidias
> Whose work most people thought hideous.
> He made Aphrodite without any "nightie,"
> Thus shocking the ultra-fastidious.

And

> There was a young woman named Banker
> Who slept when the ship came to anchor.
> She awoke in dismay when she heard the mate say:
> "Hoist up the top sheets and spanker!" —

all amused Jefferson, but the one that most caught his fancy was that beginning with

> There was an old monk of Siberia —

Sitting in the company's private car (All-Star Rivals Company, 1896), fidgeting lest Nat Goodwin would not return from a visit in time to play his part of "Sir Lucius O'Trigger," Jefferson treated me to an "appreciation" of this last-named "limerick." It was delightful to hear him expatiate on the skill of its construction and to note the many-sided view the man took of the thing that interested him. The peculiar quality of his voice, the little whistling sound on the sibilants, caused by a "complete set of upper and lower," the enthusiasm and infectious laugh, made it a fascinating performance. As near as I can recall his exposition, it ran thus:

"There was an old monk of Siberia —

You see, Francis, we are struck at once with the cleverness of the author in giving us the name of the hero and the locale in the very first line. This is the epitome of condensation. But that is not all he gives us in that first line — by no means! He also gives us age and despair. It must be a mighty lonesome thing to be a monk anywhere, but just imagine the sadness and dismay of being old and a monk in Siberia! If I could bring myself to be a monk, Siberia is the last place on earth I should hope to find myself.

Whose life grew weary and wearier —

Of course it did. Nothing else is to be hoped for in such a God-forsaken place! Even a comedian's life would grow weary and wearier in Siberia — what, then, could be expected of a monk's? Note, Francis, how all that loneliness hinted in the first line is expressed in two words in the second, *weary* and *wearier*. Clever, mighty clever!"

With an anticipatory chuckle which he seemed unable to restrain, Jefferson ushered in the third line of the quatrain —

> With a hell of a yell, he burst through his cell —

"There!" he cried, "note the dramatic effect, the climax, the third act, the broken suspense the audience has been hungering for, and which, by gad, they ought always to have. Isn't it wonderful? It couldn't be better!" And back went his head in a laugh so infectious it was impossible not to join in it. Then half audibly he repeated the line, nodding time with his head. "No use talking," he added, "he certainly made the most of that climax! I think it is wonderful. But here, Francis, here is the extraordinary finish, the lovely capstone to the whole edifice:

> And eloped with the Mother Superior! —

By Jove, that's electric!" And back went his head again and there was another full exposure of his dental arrangements together with a renewal of that contagious laughter.

"For the ordinary author it would have been enough that the monk, overcome by the terror of Siberian life, had broken through his cell and escaped. The reader, the audience, too, would have been satisfied, but this is no ordinary author, Francis — no! Having begun and gone on so artistically he meant that it should continue so to a triumphant ending —

> He eloped with the Mother Superior! —

An elopement, you know, is not an abduction! We

easily realize that the Mother Superior's life, also, has grown weary and wearier, as of course it would, and that she was glad to escape. Here, then, we have willingness and consent — all rounding out, as all good stories should round out, in marriage and the promise of everlasting happiness. I tell you, Francis, it's a *multum in parvo* of a story — and beautiful."

It has been said that, though Joseph Jefferson stood high in popular affection, and though he reflected honor upon his profession, he was not entitled to a place among really great actors.

That, however, is a matter of personal opinion, not only as to the possession of individual power, but as to whether or not anything other than tragic acting is to be regarded as great acting. Whether, in short, it is as eminent a thing to evoke laughter as to call forth tears.

Garrick, a past-master in both comedy and tragedy, declared that he played the latter with ease, but that comedy was "serious business." "It may be as difficult to act well in tragedy as in comedy," as has been said, "but it is always easier to produce a successful effect by tragedy than by comedy, and tragedy can often be made to disguise imperfect acting." [1]

As to the difficulty of creating an effect in comedy, I once had a corroboration from Henry Irving — he had not then had the distinction of knighthood conferred upon him. I had gone to see him as "Malvolio," in "Twelfth Night," at the Lyceum, in London. It was an exquisite production, of course, a delight to behold, but

[1] William Winter.

HORACE HOWARD FURNESS, JR., AND FRANCIS WILSON PLACING
THE MEMORIAL TABLET ON THE HOUSE IN WHICH JOSEPH
JEFFERSON WAS BORN

The house stands on the Southwest corner of Sixth and Spruce Streets,
Philadelphia.

Irving was not wholly happy as the grinning steward; in fact, he did not grin at all. The pit on first night had called "Better luck, next time, 'Arry!" Irving the manager had "miscast" Irving the actor. One important omission in his interpretation of the character was "that horrible laugh of ugly conceit" which Boaden tells us, in speaking of the actor Bensley, "rendered him Shakespeare's 'Malvolio' at all points." When the play had ended, I went back to Irving's dressing-room to pay my respects. We talked for a few moments as the great man unmade his face, and then, after a brief pause, and punctuating his remarks with a grease-rag which he held in his hand, he said, with much earnestness:

"No tragedian or serious actor ought ever to play 'Malvolio.' The character needs the services of a man thoroughly equipped with the command and devices of comedy."

He had discovered the difficulty of producing an effect in comedy. Who was I to dispute the wise words of a master! Opinions will differ, of course, as to Irving's judgment in this, and certain it is that many players with small gift for comedy have made satisfactory "Malvolios." In acting, however, there is a great gap between giving satisfaction and being wholly equal to a splendid opportunity. When "Twelfth Night" was last played at Daly's Theater, the comedian Henry E. Dixey was "Malvolio." Daly's judgment coincided with Irving's. It was the absurdity of such a man as "Malvolio" aspiring to the hand of the delicate and brilliant "Olivia" that Shakespeare had in mind, and not "Malvolio's" fitness for such an aspiration, though it is evident, of course, that too comic a personality would never have risen to the position of a "Malvolio" in "Olivia's" household. There is a nice balance of judgment required here which has been too infrequently observed when this play has been given.

Irving had no illusion about his acting. He knew what he did best, and what he could not do at all. Most actors know that, however loath they may be to admit it.

"Don't make a mistake about it!" said Jefferson to me once when I had smiled at what I thought was a touch of egotism on his part. "Every man who is clever knows it. Vanity does not consist in the knowledge that one is clever, but in parading that knowledge."

But was Jefferson entitled to a place among really great actors? If the test of great acting, as is sometimes set down, be the ability to play a number of characters well without too great an intrusion of the actor's personality, then, to my thinking, Joseph Jefferson was a great actor. His "Rip" was not at all like his "Acres," nor "Acres" like his "Caleb Plummer," or "Dr. Pangloss," or "Golightly." We knew, of course, that it was Jefferson who was playing the different parts and we welcomed the delightful man we had learned to love. It was that which took us to the theater. We should have felt cheated had he been able, as no actor ever was, to make that personality unrecognizable. Jefferson knew all the secrets of expression. He had the splendid gift of character presentation. With equal facility he evoked laughter or tears. Bountifully equipped for the extraordinary success he attained, I shall always be convinced that if he be denied the distinction of being regarded as a great actor, then it is likely no actor may be so characterized.

If genius, greatness in acting, is to be accorded only to actors who have distinctive creative force, the title cannot be withheld from Jefferson. He had extraordinary power to create stage illusion. The illusion of the first time was an art with him. Things he had said and done hundreds, thousands of times, he said and did with the freedom and delight of an impromptu. And much of the by-play and many of the speeches which his audiences so greatly appreciated were Jefferson's and became an integral part of the play.

Not much dependence is to be placed on genius in acting that rests upon versatility as its test. On that score Beerbohm Tree as an actor would rank with Shakespeare as a poet. Tree was not an ingratiating actor. He had fine technical skill, and was as versatile as Proteus. He lacked charm, magnetism, though he believed himself gifted in this direction.

Through his ancestors, Jefferson began to be an actor years before he was born. His great-great-grandfather, Thomas Jefferson, acted with Garrick at Drury Lane. His great-great-grandmother, "the most complete figure in beauty of countenance and symmetry of form" — as Davies wrote of her — died on the stage in the midst of a hearty laugh. His grandfather was for twenty-five years "the pride and adornment of the Chestnut Street Theater, Philadelphia, at a time when that city was the most important of the Colonial places of residence, having just ceased to be the Capital of the New World Republic." Ludlow says of this Jefferson: "There was a perfection of delineation that I have seldom if ever seen in any other comedian of his line of characters; not the least attempt at exaggeration to obtain applause, but a naturalness and truthfulness that secured it. The nearest approach to his style is that of his grandson, of the same name."

Elizabeth Jefferson (Chapman), daughter of the above and our "Rip's" aunt, was declared by Forrest to be the best tragic actress on the stage. He added that she is "the best 'Lady Macbeth' we have, and the only 'Pauline.'" She was "Julia" in "The Hunchback" when that play was first produced at the Park Theater, New York, by its famous author, Sheridan Knowles, with whom she acted.

Jefferson's father, Joseph Jefferson (they loved the name of Joseph!), acted, managed, and painted scenery all his life. He was manager and scene painter at the old Franklin Theater in Chatham Street, New York. There, in 1836, he painted the scenery for a play called "Mobb, the Outlaw, or, Jemmy Twitcher in France." It was a version of Lemaître's "Robert Macaire" from which "Erminie" was taken. The highest claim to distinction and remembrance of this Joseph Jefferson was that he was the father of our "Rip Van Winkle"

Jefferson, the greatest of all the Jeffersons and who became an American institution.

Jefferson had come to him what many men of fine powers have lacked — opportunity. This good fairy often does little but tap at our door, when she deigns to visit us at all. With favoring persistency she made herself known to him again and again, beginning with the day in the Pennsylvania haymow when she whispered that Washington Irving's "Rip Van Winkle" would be his Aladdin's Lamp, if he had but the wit to polish it, to trim its wick so that it might give forth its proper light. He heard the whisper and made an effort. He revised the play which his father, his half-brother Charles Burke, and the elder Hackett had performed. He gave it to the public, who would have none of it. Still, thanks to the continued whispering of the fairy, he did not lose faith in the chief character "Rip," though he had none in the play.

All the years of the American Civil War he spent in Australia and in South America, going thence to London, in 1865. Almost the first person he met in the English Capital was his old manager, Dion Boucicault.

"Do you intend to act in London?" asked Boucicault.

"I certainly do," Jefferson replied, "if I see an opening offering a fair chance of success."

"What material have you?"

"A great part in an indifferent play, 'Rip Van Winkle,'" said Jefferson.

Boucicault thought the subject "stale," but, agreeing on a price, he undertook to rewrite the play. "And so," says Clement Scott, discussing the play's evolution, "it was Dion Boucicault that placed the pinnacle on a solid foundation and crowned the work built up stone by stone."

In a book written for The Dunlap Society in 1915, and called "The Career of Dion Boucicault," the author, Townsend Walsh, speaks of Christopher J. Smith, the pantomimist, who enacted the part of "the dwarf with the keg" containing the Schnapps that sent Rip on his sleep of twenty years. He tells of the "business" arranged by him for the scene of the gnomes in the Catskills, "business" scrupulously followed by those who succeeded him in the rôle, as Jefferson always demanded. Well might Jefferson insist! What Smith brought to the play was a master stroke which lent conviction to the weird scenes enacted among the mountain peaks, and added greatly to the chances of the play's acceptance.

In his "Autobiography," Jefferson tells the story of Boucicault's connection with "Rip Van Winkle." Though much less known, here is a fuller and I think a more interesting account as given by Boucicault and quoted in the Townsend Walsh book mentioned above: "He [Jefferson] walked into my study in London," said Boucicault, "and with sincere pleasure I rose to greet my old colleague. This was in 1865, and in summertime. Who remembers the Winter Garden where he played 'Caleb Plummer' in 'Dot,' and 'Salem Scudder' in 'The Octoroon'? During these intervening years he had been in Australia; I had been in London.

"Jefferson was anxious to appear in London, but all his pieces had been played there. The managers would not give him an appearance unless he could offer them a new play. He had played a piece called 'Rip Van Winkle,' but when submitted to their perusal they rejected it. Still he was so desirous of playing 'Rip' that I took down Washington Irving's story and read it over. It was hopelessly undramatic. 'Joe,' I said, 'this old sot is not a pleasant figure. He lacks romance. I dare say you made a fine sketch of the old beast, but there is no interest in him. He may be picturesque, but he is not dramatic. I would prefer to start him in a play as a young scamp — thoughtless, gay, just such a curly-headed, good-humored fellow as all the village girls would love and the children and dogs would run after.'

"Jefferson threw up his hands in despair. It was totally opposed to his artistic preconception. But I insisted, and he reluctantly yielded. Well, I wrote the play as he plays it now. It was not much of a literary production, and it was with some apology that it was handed to him. He read it, and when we met I said: 'It's a poor thing, Joe.' 'Well,' he replied, 'it is good enough for me!' It was produced. Three or four weeks afterwards, he called on me, and his first words were: 'You were right about making "Rip" a young man. Now I could not conceive and play him in any other shape!'"

Walsh thought with Boucicault that no masterpiece had been created; that as a literary production it was nil, in fact, "the veriest pot-boiler"; that without Boucicault's clever turn of the wrist and the efforts of "the subtlest of actors," Joseph Jefferson, "Rip" could not have been made attractive; that the play would not have long endured.

From most of this I dissent. I believe the play will always endure and be successful if played by an actor of imagination and ability. Furthermore, in the interest of American drama and authorship, in the interest of public pleasure, it should always endure, for, if the literature of it be small, the conception of the story as put forth by Washington Irving, and developed and embellished by Jefferson and Boucicault, is of the highest value and importance, far too high to be permitted to diminish in the minds and imaginations of Americans. Like "Uncle Tom's Cabin" by Harriet Beecher Stowe, "The Old Homestead" by Denman Thompson, and "'Way Down East" by Lottie Blair Parker, to which, however, it is far superior, it holds and deserves to hold an active place in the affections of our public and in the annals of our drama. The play has three qualities which any author would be proud, if able, to utilize — mystery, humor, and emotion.

The play is not now performed because Jefferson's quaint and magnetic interpretation of "Rip" is too fresh in the public mind. No player would soon care to risk comparison with him in a part which was so eminently his own. Time will remedy this, and "Rip Van Winkle" will see many a revival. It is one of our few folklore stories. Americans are brought up upon it. They should always be able to see it as a play, for only in that way may its rich, full humor, and its quaint, weird fancy be wholly realized.

Having this idea in mind, Equity Players, of which I happen to be the president, thought to give "Rip," in 1924. As no one else seemed available for the sacrifice, I took the manuscript and went off to Bermuda with it for the winter. We had a cottage up Pitts Bay way, just opposite Bay House, so tenderly associated with the last days of Mark Twain. When my family were shut in for the night, I would often pace the road near by to talk out, act out, the scenes of "Rip." It is a lonely road, and the shadows are deep, but lit up every few moments by an instant's flash from the powerful Gibbs Hill Light. One night, the Dwarf, whom "Rip" helps up the mountain with the keg, and I were having it out together on this lonely road. I had just said:

"Go long, pick up my gun, and I'll follow mit der keg," when just before me appeared the dwarf! Of course it was not the dwarf at all, nothing but neighbor Allen's gate swinging in the wind, as I soon realized, but with my mind full of the Kaatskill and the keg of Schnapps to be toted up to Hendrick Hudson and his specter crew, the gate outlined itself easily as a moving figure. It gave me such a spooky feeling that I — was glad to go indoors.

I have known actors whom I thought as gifted as

Joseph Jefferson, but who, unlike him, never had the good fortune to obtain a vehicle by which their unquestioned powers might be successfully brought forward. William Warren was one. Charles R. Thorne was another, and so, too, was Robert Craig. These never ventured far out on the open ocean of the drama, because of the insecurity of the ships in which they sailed. Warren had great talent, but no ambition. Preferring comfort to travel, he became a delightful fixture in Boston, and throughout New England, where everybody knew and loved him. Craig's name was a household word in Philadelphia, while Thorne was an attractive power at the Union Square Theater, in New York. An exclamation from him, often uttered as a whisper, was more expressive than long speeches from most actors. Because of the possession of extraordinary magnetism, Thorne must have gone far in fame and public affection had not his untimely death deprived him of the opportunity.

They all had chances for success in plays as good as "The Cricket on the Hearth," "The Octoroon," or "The Heir at Law," in which Jefferson found favor, but never a "Rip Van Winkle" to bring them beyond local repute into nation-wide celebrity — never a play of their very own in which they were loved, in which their genius shone out as Booth's did in "Hamlet," as Salvini's did in "Othello," as Mayo's did in "Davy Crockett," or Jefferson's in "Rip." The best example of delayed but well-deserved success within my time is that of the late Frank Bacon. Always the possessor of a gracious personality, coupled with technical facility, it was not until time had whitened the luxuriant locks of Bacon that he evolved the play, "Lightnin'," which, with the Boucicaultian touch of Winchell Smith, brought him enviable popularity and success.

Mention of Jefferson involves mention of his gifted associate, Mrs. John Drew. She was an incomparable artist. Her "Mrs. Malaprop" was a delightful performance, one which the great comedian never tired of extolling. And no wonder, for his performance of "Bob Acres," rich and satisfying as it was, did not contribute more to the enjoyment of the play than her distinguished impersonation of Sheridan's Grande Dame of Mispronunciation.

In some respects Mrs. Drew's career paralleled that of Mrs. Stirling, the accepted and popular "Mrs. Malaprop" of London during the last half of the nineteenth century. At one time or another, nearly all the characters assumed by Mrs. Stirling in England were played by Mrs. Drew in America. A touch of additional interest to us is given the English actress when we remember that she was the "Desdemona" and the "Cordelia" to the "Othello" and "King Lear" of Edwin Forrest when the American tragedian appeared in London.

Both John Drew (father of the present John Drew) and his wife, our own "Mrs. Malaprop," appeared with Jefferson in "The Rivals" before the days of the Jeffersonian revision of that play. The elder Drew played "Sir Lucius O'Trigger," and his wife, the romantic-minded "Lydia Languish," the part played later by Julia Marlowe and recently by the dainty Violet Hemming.

When Jefferson came to rearrange and condense "The Rivals," he felt the need of so sterling an artist as Mrs. Drew to support him in the liberties he felt he was taking with a masterpiece. These changes did not affect the part of "Mrs. Malaprop." She and "Acres" do not meet during the play, except for a brief moment at the end, and then do not address each other. So sincere was Jefferson's admiration for Mrs. Drew's art that I do not recall an evening during the All-Star tour in 1896 that he was not in the "wings" enjoying her acting in what is called the "Letter-Scene." Her confusion on carelessly handing the detested "Beverley" a love-letter sent to her by "Sir Lucius" was delightful. Jefferson called it "the perfection of comedy."

John Drew tells us, in his "My Years on the Stage," of the dinner he gave to the cast of the All-Star Rivals Company at Chicago, where he was also playing. It was there he saw his mother act for the last time. As a member of that unusual association of players, at the head of which were Jefferson and Mrs. Drew, with such small-fry as Julia Marlowe, William H. Crane, Nat Goodwin, Robert Taber, Edward Holland, Joseph Holland (Jefferson's godson), Fanny Rice, and Francis Wilson filling up the ranks, I well remember that dinner. I especially recall "the stories of the old days" told by Jefferson and Mrs. Drew — they had been telling equally wonderful experiences all through the season — for, at that time, and for a number of years previously, I was taking notes of the sayings and doings of Jefferson which were later issued in book form by Charles Scribner's Sons.

There was also present a young lady by the name of Ethel Barrymore, a niece of Drew's. She was playing a small part in a piece called "Rosemary" by a young dramatist named Barrie, who was thought to be "promising." The play was Drew's vehicle for the season. After dinner, this young lady sang for us, and I remember how enchantingly embarrassed she was when I expressed delight at having, at last, heard a singing voice worse than my own.

In those days the youthful and undeveloped Ethel was quite uncertain as to what line of dramatic work she would turn her attention. From something she and her grandmother had said, I thought it might be along the broad way of light opera. She was already a capable musician, "soothing her young heart with catches and glees," and, notwithstanding my jest at our respective voices, sang with taste and intelligence. I was all the more impressed with this feeling of uncertainty on her part when I recalled what her uncle Lewis Baker said to me about this time. I had expressed some doubt as to Ethel having inherited the family talent. "My dear Francis, why be in doubt?" he replied; "in the family, Ethel's ability has long been a matter of hilarious jest." In this connection, and apropos of the fact that prediction is never a safe indulgence, I remember reading an interview by one of our well-known dramatic critics with Georgie Drew Barrymore. Her three children, Ethel, Lionel, and John, were mentioned. It was confidently declared that no one of these children would ever figure prominently on the stage. Not more than three of them did. I wish her mother had lived to see Ethel's exquisite performance of "Lady Teazle!"

There was another player about whose ability I had the gravest misgiving. He was a member of my company and was — still is — one of the most modestly intelligent young men who have permitted me to claim their friendship. He had given much time to the study of law. I presumed to point out to him that that time might be wasted, if he followed his ambition for the drama. I could see but little promise of his becoming a player of importance, just as the elder Sothern saw no talent in his son Edward. My young friend was in no way halted, and despite my discouragement has gone steadily on from one success to another, as will be recognized when I give his name — Grant Mitchell.

Jefferson did not make his revision of "The Rivals" until after "Rip Van Winkle" was in the full swing of success. Not able to guess the duration of that success, he wisely sought a play with which to follow it, or to use alternately. He had been in close association with "the adaptive Mr. Boucicault," and felt that he had profited thereby. He had well noted the Irish dramatist's ability and resourcefulness in manufacturing successes by bringing a character out into bold relief while at the same time keeping the other characters

subordinate. He now determined to try his own hand
at that sort of thing. He did a fine piece of work. His
revision of "The Rivals" was a great success and became a worthy companion piece to his "Rip."

What Jefferson did was to conserve so much of
Sheridan's text as would enhance the part of "Bob
Acres"; in short, to make a star rôle of it. After his
extraordinary success in the play of "Rip Van Winkle,"
he believed the public would welcome a similar treatment of "The Rivals." Except from the public, Jefferson underwent much serious and facetious criticism for
what was regarded as his temerity in tampering with a
classic. The grand council of Wallack's Theater were
outraged. They were the legitimate inheritors, the
guardians, of all things of age and dramatic repute hail-
ing from England, and it was thought barbarous that
an American comedian should presume to take such a
liberty.

John Gilbert, who loved every punctuation mark in
English comedy, yet who was not averse to a good
"gag," or an illuminating bit of "business," provided
it had the stamp of foreign approval, thought the
alterations "sacrilegious"; that Jefferson should be
haunted by the shade of Sheridan, giving no thought
of the haunting to which Sheridan himself should have
been subjected, along with such arch-appropriators as
Shakespeare, Molière, Dryden, et al.

William Warren, Jefferson's cousin, was credited
with saying something clever reflecting on Jefferson's
audacity, that it was "The Rivals," as Jefferson played

it, "with Sheridan twenty miles away." But that remark was first made, Jefferson declared, "by a member
of my company." That "member" was likely the
brilliant Maurice Barrymore, who one Christmas
amused everybody, including Jefferson, by presenting
him with a copy of "The Rivals" with every part
scissorsed out but that of "Bob Acres." This was like
the witty Barrymore, who was much given to such
pranks. It is said that once, about to sign his name
in a hotel register, he observed in the space above:
"Richard Harding Davis — and valet," and that
instantly Barrymore wrote beneath: "Maurice Barrymore — and valise." To give them vogue, conceits of
this nature must be attached to the names of prominent
men — indeed, they are too often so attached. While
we laugh at the jest, our respect for the men, or their
memory, is no whit lessened. Richard Harding Davis
was not only a skillful, popular writer, but a brave and
tender-hearted man.

One thing is clearly evident about Jefferson's revision of "The Rivals" — that because of the adroit
arrangement into three acts — the original is in five —
the action of the play is not only accelerated, but in-
tensified. Jefferson even ventured on an epilogue which
was not only characterful, but humorous, if not witty
or brilliant. Later, Oliver Herford greatly helped in
this respect. Jefferson and he followed where Sheridan
had not done himself justice. No matter how great was
Jefferson's desire to enhance the part of "Acres," he
was far too wise to cut out any of the fun of the play

and, therefore, too knowing to curtail the speeches of "Mrs. Malaprop." Indeed, he encouraged Mrs. Drew in all the additions she made, and they were many, to that most delightfully humorous among finer stage creations.

I have often wondered how much Jefferson thought the parts of "Julia" (which he omitted) and "Falkland," if permitted to remain intact, would have detracted from "Acres." I wish now I had had the courage to ask him. The tragedian Macready, who played only the best parts, once impersonated "Falkland," proof that it must have been highly considered. Perhaps the attitude of moderns toward such sentiments as "Falkland" holds is different from that of our elders; that we laugh at things which the older audiences regarded as heroic and romantic. I believe it likely that modern audiences would not patiently endure much that Jefferson omitted from the Sheridan masterpiece. In Sheridan's time "Julia" spoke the author's epilogue.

In The Players Club production of "The Rivals," in which I played "Acres," June, 1922, there were liberal restorations of the speeches of "Julia" and "Falkland." "Julia" did not appear, her lines being spoken, and consistently so, by "Lucy," delightfully played by Patricia Collinge. It was thought that these restorations clarified the plot and added to the enjoyment of the play. Indeed, the audiences took so eagerly and amusedly to "Falkland's" temperamentally exacting attitude toward love and life as to lend the conviction that the complete omission of "Julia" and the drastic curtailing of "Falkland's" speeches had been a mistake, and unfair to both play and author. In the four weeks' performance of "The Rivals" given in June, 1923, for the Equity Players, I took the *liberty* of making further restorations, not only of speeches, but of the part of "Julia," which was charmingly played by Eva Le Gallienne. This brought additional clearness to the comedy and gave meaning and richer interest to the temperamental "Falkland" in which McKay Morris distinguished himself. Such scholars and critics as William Lyon Phelps, Lawrence F. Abbott, and John Jay Chapman were warm in their praise of these performances of "The Rivals."

As for my own performance of "Bob Acres," a character which I assumed for the first time, it is a fact that, but for the decision of The Players, I should likely never have attempted the rôle. The original plan was to give "The School for Scandal" with John Drew and the three Barrymores in the cast — Ethel Barrymore as "Lady Teazle," John Barrymore as "Charles," Lionel Barrymore as "Joseph," and John Drew as "Sir Peter," which would have made an interesting event,[1] but professional engagements made that impossible and it was decided, rather than abandon the project, to substitute "The Rivals."

The success was instant and the attendance tremendous in face of unprecedentedly warm weather.

[1] A year later, *The School for Scandal* was given by The Players, June, 1923.

FRANCIS WILSON AS BOB ACRES IN SHERIDAN'S
"THE RIVALS"

In the Players Club production of this comedy in 1921 there was a liberal
restoration of omitted lines.

The moment Mary Shaw, as "Mrs. Malaprop," began her scene at the opening of the play down to the final word of the "tag," spoken by "Acres," the audiences were laughing and applauding. I had deep interest in the number of young people who attended. As in the last revival of "Erminie," in 1921, these young people came with older folks as if brought to see and hear something they ought to admire, a sort of visit of duty, but were soon overtaken by the felicity of the occasion and the contagion of laughter which was in the air.

The wisdom of the colleges in fostering a taste for dramatic literature was having its reward. Students flocked to see the realization of one of their classic studies and the professional touch to rôles they had acted *en amateur*. An encouraging sign of the times in which play-reading has become so general.

I was but one in a cast of even excellence which brought aptitude and, in a majority of instances, long experience to the play — a cast that generously gave its services of a month of mental and physical effort for an ideal, and in appreciation of the club which Edwin Booth founded. A portion of the receipts were set aside for the Actors' Fund of America. While in one instance a critic said we did not know what we were talking about, the press as a whole was favorable, even enthusiastic. The audience for whom the play was given told us what we wanted most to hear. They did not miss the point of the matter, which was to bring the public better acquainted with a beautiful old comedy masterpiece.

As manager, along with Louis Evan Shipman and Daniel Frohman, I thought the "Bob Acres" of Francis Wilson might have been improved upon and that, judging from the first performance, when, as is the case with most actors, Wilson was evidently scared blue with a sense of responsibility, it would have been profanation to mention his performance in the same breath with that of the man whose version of the play — with restorations — we were giving, Joseph Jefferson. But as performance succeeded performance, there was evident improvement, giving color to the feeling, at last, that if, like Jefferson, Wilson could have had twenty-five or thirty years at the part, he might have been able to make a perceptible dent in the realization of the character.

The surprising part of the matter was the favor he found with the audiences, which rippled, laughed, and applauded as judiciously as if an artist were before them. The explanation being, probably, that he was carried along with favor through the brilliance of the assemblage and the superb efforts of the other comedians, not to mention the wit of Richard Brinsley Sheridan.

There was certainly no acting in what Wilson did. He was really the marplot lout, really scared to find himself penning a challenge, and wholly overcome at the bare thought of fighting a duel. He cut the sorriest kind of a figure in his attempt to ape the fads and fashions of the play's period. This being so, Shipman, Frohman, and I could hardly find sufficient warrant to dismiss him. Besides, we were embarrassed by the fact that he had originated the whole plan of the performance, had yielded reluctantly to the request to play its chief rôle, and, like the other Players, had volunteered his services. What is to be done with such a man? More embarrassing still, such was Wilson's diplomacy, the Board of Directors of The Players felt impelled to vote him an expression of thanks and a silver souvenir for his well-meant if inept and profitable efforts. The "Sir Anthony" of Tyrone Power was a fine, virile performance, while the "David" of James T. Powers was most unusual. I thought it excruciatingly funny, and so did the audience.

Jefferson lingered so long on the stage he was afraid at times that he might wear out his welcome. There was little danger of such a thing. He determined, however, that it should never happen. He kept a sensitive finger on the public pulse, meaning to retire the moment he felt enthusiasm in his behalf was beating slowly. A favorite expression of his on the matter was that he meant, like a well-bred dog, to withdraw the moment he detected any intention to kick him out.

A social idiot said to him one day: "When are you going to stop acting, Mr. Jefferson?"

"I am only waiting for you, the public," he replied, "to say the word."

"Stop acting?" he said to Mary Shaw; "I am afraid to quit acting, for fear I shall die! So many men stop working because they have gained a competence, and then, having nothing to do to occupy their minds, they sink into oblivion, death. However, I shall never be at loss to occupy my mind. I have my painting to turn to, and in which I am ambitious to do something that will live after I am gone." He never felt for long that he had accomplished this.

"Come over to the studio. I did something really fine, this morning!" was a message he would send out. But when the studio was reached, the "something really fine" had vanished. It had been blotted out. Subsequent inspection made him feel that it was "not so good" as he thought.

He had a superb way of disconcerting tactless questioners.

"It isn't true, Mr. Jefferson, is it," said one such to him, "that your son is going to marry a chorus girl?"

"Why not?" "Rip" replied, with a charming smile; "his mother was a chorus girl."

He could be as playful as a child, and would often bowl one over with a winsomely juvenile remark. Once he had hooked a fish, Cleveland told me, Jefferson had a bad habit of "yanking his line."

"Don't do that, Joe!" called the ex-President to him; "why do you jerk the fish like that?"

"Because he jerked me!" retorted Jefferson, like a resentful schoolboy.

In the long, long service Jefferson gave to the stage, he played hundreds of parts. Yet, because he narrowed himself to a few, or the public narrowed him to one, from the time of his success with "Rip Van Winkle," it was said that he did nothing for his profession.

This is best answered by quoting an extract from the tribute paid him by Henry Watterson:

He [Jefferson] did in America quite as much as Sir Charles Wyndham or Sir Henry Irving did in England to elevate the personality, the social and intellectual standing of the actor and the stage, effecting in a lifetime a revolution in the attitude of the people and the clergy of both countries to the theater and all things in it.

CHAPTER XII

WALT WHITMAN AND "LEAVES OF GRASS"

INVITED one day to go and see Walt Whitman, I was not at all sure I cared to accept. As a boy I had often seen "the good gray poet," as he was called — and many people, especially those of the tender sex, frowned when he was so called — sail down Market Street, market-basket on arm to the ferry which he crossed *en route* to his home in Camden.

"There goes the filthiest old rascal in Philadelphia," some one said to me, as he pointed out Whitman with his long hair, Kossuth hat, flowing white cuffs, and breast "bared to the breeze" because of the wide-open, soft, broad collar thrown back from his throat and neck. He was tall, and, though he seemed to walk a trifle hesitantly, as if each step hurt and the walker determined notwithstanding to walk if it killed him, I liked the eagle-like cock of his head and glance of his eye. He looked clean enough with his spotless linen.

"Why is he the filthiest old rascal in Philadelphia?" I asked.

"Why?" This "Why?" with much hesitation, because, as I came to know later, my informant had no knowledge on the subject, except that of hearsay.

"Oh, you are too little to understand, but he is a woman-lover, and prints the most awful things about them in plain language, right in his books."

I soon forgot all about that explanation, but never forgot to keep a sharp lookout for the proud old man with the market-basket, the lame man who was determined to walk. The mysterious thing to me about him was the absurdity of coming to Philadelphia to market. Why not market in Camden? There were markets over there. I had seen them and, for all I knew to the contrary at the time, it was the home of all the country's produce. I had seen the ferryboat crowded with filled and empty country wagons coming and going to and from Jersey farms to supply the city's demands.

Stranger still, I saw no chicken or turkey legs protruding from that market-basket of Whitman's, nor yet any celery tops such as I had seen thousands of times peeping out from the covered, or from the more democratic uncovered, tops of genuine market-baskets. No, indeed! Other people might be deceived about the marketing of that "lusty-begotten and various boy of the Mannahatta," but there was one youngster who was not to be taken in. Whatever it was that "old rascal" was carrying in that basket I was sure it was not vegetables. Neither was it meat or poultry. It was evident that he was a deeper-dyed villain than was suspected and was making bi-weekly or weekly journeys through the city with something concealed at the bottom of that basket. What was it? How was I to find out? Once or twice I had tried to peep and discover, but he was too tall and imposing to permit me to get a fair look. I know now that he would have told me had I had the courage to ask him. Some one explained finally that the basket was filled with books — copies of a book ("Leaves of Grass") which the old man had written himself and was trying to sell, but that he was having a hard time disposing of them for many reasons, chief among which were the awful things said in the books, things, too, that Whitman called poetry when there was not even a rhyme in it! Whoever heard of such a thing as poetry without rhyme in it! And, furthermore, it was all about himself. In fact it began, "I celebrate myself," which did not seem too modest, and, lastly, so the story ran, it called a spade a spade in telling of Whitman's amours. Who wanted to bother with such stuff as that? I did, from curiosity, but I did not have the price.

It was not many years thereafter that I got hold of a copy and read it misunderstandingly from cover to cover. I was mystified at "breathing the fragrance of myself" — and — "liking it," and about "the smoke of my own breath"; and especially about the importance of "the song of me rising from bed and meeting the sun." I did like "An individual is as superb as a nation when he has the qualities that make a superb nation," and the picture of the grass which seemed to Whitman to be "the beautiful uncut hair of the grave," but I shied at the question of "Who need be afraid of the merge?" I had no need to fear it — I did not even know what it meant. For all me, it might be a typhoon, or some unknown animal. I saw inde-

WALT WHITMAN

The good gray poet." His poems, expurgated, were first accepted by
England.

pendence but no poetry in "I cock my hat as I please indoor and out," and I got little but laughter from "washes and razors for foofoos — for me freckles and a bristling beard," which seemed rustic and healthy enough if not unclean, as did "beetles rolling balls of dung," which only recently was so extraordinarily portrayed in the play "The World We Live In" by the Czecho-Slovakian dramatists Karel Kapek and his brother Joseph. "Foofoo," however, would not disassociate itself in my mind from a bird in the storyhour of the nursery.

The fact was, the philosophy of the book was beyond my grasp and the greater part was confusing and unintelligible, but, boy-like, I memorized the questionable expressions and thought it "smart" to quote and misapply them as evidence of the man's coarseness and, especially, of his enormous conceit. When I read the passage:

> I conned old times,
> I sat studying at the feet of the great masters;
> Now, if eligible, oh that the great masters
> might return and study me! —

it was difficult to understand that such an expression could be the emanation of any but an arrant egotist, perhaps that of "a once noble mind o'erthrown." It was the same with:

> Divine am I, inside and out; I make holy whatever
> I touch or am touched from.

I could not make up my mind whether it was the

usual self-consciousness of some noted persons, regarding themselves as "a boon for the age in which
they lived," or plain lunacy. That it was not himself
individually he was "celebrating," but man, mankind "developed through individualism, comradeship,
spirituality," that it was his intention, as he himself
says, to sing of

> The greatness of Love and Democracy,
> and the greatness of Religion,

did not come to me until long years after when I was
able to grasp the subject, long years after the visit to
him which I started out to relate.

There were several of us, an editor and his daughter and their friend, a granddaughter of Nathaniel
Hawthorne, Hildegarde, who, evidently imbibing the
family distaste for Whitman, determined on meeting
him that he should not kiss her, it having been freely
discussed *en route* that there was positively to be no
encouragement of what was declared to be Whitman's weakness. However, when we arrived, the
"good gray poet" looked so kind and patriarchal
that I could not help declaring to Whitman that the
ladies of our party, I felt sure, would be deeply disappointed with any greeting less than a chaste salute
of the lips, to which "the ladies of our party" submitted with more or less grace, with considerable
emphasis on the less, all of which, not unlikely, the
poet mistook for timidity and bashfulness.

I had primed myself with a lot of questions that I

wanted to ask about matters in connection with the
famous man, things that had been suggested by some
article I had read as to why Whitman did not do this,
that, or the other thing in a literary way, but had not
proceeded very far when I realized that I was taking
the wrong tack, and had better beat to windward. I
did so with as much skill as I could muster, which was
nothing to boast of, I now realize. Here was I asking
questions of a man that I came to know later abhorred
nothing more than being questioned. However, he
was rather gracious, smiled and said he believed he did
not care to enter into discussion of the matter — that
his physician forbade him to talk on the subject, which
was as good a way as any to halt a pest, who had
really no purpose in the matter beyond appearing in
his eyes and in those present to have some familiarity
with the subject. No doubt he had met many another
such unduly inquiring person and knew how to head
him off.

He seemed very white as he sat by that wonderfully
littered table in the midst of an equally wonderfully littered floor, yet able to put his hand instantly
upon anything he required. He was wan and spent
with illness, just how weak it was impossible for me
in the full flush of health and strength to comprehend.
As I looked at him, I could only think of "Rip Van
Winkle" — minus the rags — on his return to the
Village of Falling Waters after that mysterious sleep.
After the first false step on my part, the conversation
went on easily, as it was sure to do with a poet who

believed that "a leaf of grass is no less than the journey work of the stars."

How I wanted to ask him about the Lincoln poem — "Captain, O my Captain" — and how it was that England had accepted him and placed him among the great poets while his own America whose praises he sang so lustily had held aloof. I felt I knew why, but I wanted to ask him about it. It was well, indeed, that I did not venture. What might he not have replied! to me, a stranger, when he could say of his great admirer John Addington Symonds, who constantly sang his praise, but who had asked for information as to a certain poem, "Callicrates": "What right has he to ask questions? I suppose he'll have to be answered, damn him!" And again: "It always makes me a little testy to be catechized about the 'Leaves' — I prefer to have the book answer for itself."

I had not asked him about the "Leaves," and, of course, had now no intention of so doing. But what if I had! What if I, the slave of a frolicsome temperament, had put my hand on the knob of the Mickle Street door, for the purpose of easy egress, and asked why he found it necessary to horrify staid people, not yet accustomed to the return of Elizabethan freedom of speech, by his "shocking impropriety" in the message which was given to the world in "Leaves of Grass"? What if I had been bold enough to point out emphatically that his popularity in England, as Dr. Furness declared, came from the fact that his first published works there were expurgated, and that he must know that his disesteem here had come, of course, from the fact that his message was given to America in all its grossness. I wonder what would have happened! I can imagine him rising in all his gray grandeur and, trembling with rage — and Horace Traubel, who Boswellized him, told me that Whitman could rage! — and charging me with the possession of "altitudinous and Himalayan gall," as he had once charged a reporter who pretended to have interviewed him — order me from his presence in a voice bristling with elbowed oaths. It would have been dramatic and I should have enjoyed it — if not then, certainly in perspective — and Whitman, who lived a dramatic life and adored the theatric, would also have enjoyed it, later on!

Differing absolutely from many English and some American men of letters, Dr. Furness seems to have had little estimate of the character "of the so-called poems" of Whitman. In the charming collection of "Letters" edited by his grandson Horace Furness Jayne, the learned and witty editor of the Variorum Shakespeare has the following, written to his sister, Mrs. Caspar Wister:

No, the very best thing about Walt was his godlike face and mien, and this will die with the generation which was blest with the sight. I once went up to him when I saw him on Chestnut Street and said I must personally thank him for being so handsome, adding that I hoped he didn't mind. "No, Horace," he added, "I like it!" which was certainly delightfully honest. Ach Weh, lass ruhen die Todten (his brain is in the Wistar Institute for future microscopic examination).

But there was evidently much more to Whitman than his "godlike face and mien," much that insists upon living beyond his generation. It is all very well to condemn Whitman by intimating or asserting that he purposely used the obnoxious phrases in "Leaves of Grass" in order to draw attention to the book and its philosophy, that he deliberately chose the method of the quack to advertise his wares, but the real question is, Is that philosophy worth while, irrespective of the accompanying pornographic passages, which many people have come to regard as merely an amusing, if vulgar, idiosyncrasy? More and more it is felt that the answer to that query is in the affirmative.

Whitman must be given all credit for consistency in the attitude he assumed and grimly maintained to the end, declaring himself to be anything but a favorite of fortune — "unless it be a favorite victim." A two hours' talk with Emerson, who had written in high praise of "Leaves" — a two hours' walk and talk under the elms of the Boston Common, still found Whitman unwilling to yield. "To take out one of those passages," he told the sage of Concord, "would break the ensemble of my nature."

While Dr. Furness was damning Whitman's "ensemble," or, as he declared, wanting to, English men of letters were writing about "the intense emotional feeling for the universe," as portrayed in Whitman's writings, "his acute sense of the godliness of life in all its aspects, his human sympathy, his thrill of love and

comradeship which sent a current of vitalizing magnetism through the speculations of the world."

But so varied are the opinions of men, less than a
dozen years ago James Huneker, in "Ivory Apes and
Peacocks," said that though "there is rude red music
in the versicles of 'Leaves,'" and "they stimulate,
and, for some young hearts, they are a call to battle,"
the philosophy of Whitman is "fudge"; that "he is
destitute of humor—else he might have realized that
a Democracy based on the 'manly love of comrades'
is an absurdity."

Whitman was once endeavoring to explain a certain
poem and was not succeeding. He stopped and said:
"You see, at the time, the poem wrote itself — now
I am trying to write it." I am in that position exactly in the telling of a visit to a great man. At the
time, the visit just happened, and now I am trying to
tell of its happening, but thoughts and facts about
the picturesque personality of a dominant figure, a
strange and in some respects, crude, yet knowing,
man with an attractive philosophy of human love and
democracy intrude themselves, a poet who thought
it imperative to include in the description of that
philosophy "a brutal exposure of the mysteries of the
temple of love" such as no literature had ever previously known.

A miracle happened, through the simple medium of
a glass of water. I was thirsty and asked for it, and
was sent to the kitchen for it. When I returned,
Whitman's whole attitude had changed from grave to

gay. I suspect that some explanation made to Whitman during my absence had much to do with the miracle. He greeted my return with:

"Why, Wilson! I didn't understand. Actors are especially welcome here. I like their spirit, and they seem to be of mine."

The sun was out once more! — and thereafter all went as merry as a marriage bell. Much was said by everybody during the remainder of a pleasant visit, though I never mustered courage enough to touch upon the subject of "Leaves." The particular incident that has always stood out in that visit of mine to the apostle of the common and the commonplace has always been his allusion to Poe which suggests the "salty tang" of Whitman. I made a note of it in my copy of the 1855 "Leaves of Grass":

Edgar Allan Poe came up for discussion and Whitman must have detected that I had leanings toward him, perhaps Poe-maniacal symptoms — there are periods in life when nothing seems so important as the last thing we read — for, after listening for a while to the "talk," he said: "Come here, Wilson!"

It was such an abrupt break in the conversation that a wondering silence ensued. I went bravely forward and the ladies of the party were hopeful, I think, that I was about to be kissed, that I was to have a dose of the "freckles and bristling beard," but they were to be disappointed. He put one hand on my shoulder and with the other, which held his cane, he pointed to the window, and said: "Do you see the sun, the sky and the trees?"

I nodded.

"Out there, out there," he continued, "lies life, and not in the jim-jam writings of Edgar Allan Poe."

TO THE SUN-SET BREEZE.

Ah, whispering, something again, unseen,
Where late this heated day thou enteres' at my window, door,
Thou, laving, tempering all, cool-freshing, gently vitalizing
Me, old, alone, sick, weak-down, melted-worn with sweat;
Thou, nestling, folding close and firm yet soft, companion bet-
    ter than talk, book, art,
(Thou hast, O Nature! elements! utterance to my heart be-
    yond the rest — and this is of them,)
So sweet thy primitive taste to breathe within — thy soothing
    fingers on my face and hands,
Thou, messenger-magical strange bringer to body and spirit of
    me,
(Distances balk'd — occult medicines penetrating me from head
    to foot,)
I feel the sky, the prairies vast — I feel the mighty northern
    lakes,
I feel the ocean and the forest — somehow I feel the globe
    itself swift-swimming in space;
Thou blown from lips so loved, now gone — haply from end-
    less store, God-sent,
(For thou art spiritual, Godly, most of all known to my
    sense,)
Minister to speak to me, here and now, what word has never
    told, and cannot tell,
Art thou not universal concrete's distillation? Law's, all As-
    Astronomy's last refinement?
Hast thou no soul? Can I not know, identify thee?

Walt Whitman

1891
to Francis Wilson

When we parted I carried away with me his poem, "To the Sunset Breeze," at the bottom of which he inscribed his name and mine and the fact of the poem's presentation. I was delighted with my visit. On the way to Philadelphia, Stoddart told me as we crossed the ferry from Camden that, though many famous people journeyed to pay their respects to the great singer of Democracy, none really were more welcome than stage-folk, and how especially pleased he was of something Ellen Terry had said of him, and of a letter she had written thanking him "for the little, big book of poems"—as she described it—"As a Strong Bird," etc. This had led him on at the time to speak of people of the stage in a way that delighted me, of course, when I came upon it, much later on, however, in Horace Traubel's "Whitman in Camden."

These actor people [said Whitman] always make themselves at home with me and always make me easily at home with them. I feel rather close to them — very close — almost like one of their kind. When I was much younger — way back; in the Brooklyn days — and even behind Brooklyn — I was to be an orator — to go about the country to spout my pieces, proclaiming my faith. I trained for all that — spouted in the woods, down by the shore, in the noise of Broadway where nobody could hear me: spouted, eternally spouted, and spouted again. I thought I had something to say — I was afraid I would get no chance to say it through books: so I was to lecture and get myself delivered that way.... For a while I speechified in politics, but that, of course, would not satisfy me — that at the best was only come-day go-day palaver: what I really had to give out was something more serious, more off from politics and toward the general life. But the "Leaves" got out after all — in spite of the howl and slander of the opposition, got out under far better conditions than I expected: and once out went along — stormily, fiercely, rocked and shaken until within hail of its audience. I have wandered some distance from Terry: her letter made me reminiscent — this largely because the actors have always been more friendly to me than almost any other professional class, and she reminded me of it.

No doubt he found actors friendly to him because in their visits they brought cheer, pleasure, anecdote, even song to him, for which he could not but be far more appreciative than for the exceptional stupid one that wanted to question him as to things about which he had long since grown tired of being questioned, poor soul!

Immediately after my visit I sent to that ramshackle of a house in Mickle Street, from which, "old, alone, sick, weak-down, melted-worn with sweat," Whitman sounded his "barbaric yawp over the roofs of the world," a bottle of "Old Crow" whiskey, thinking that a stimulant to an elderly man might not be unwelcome. In a letter, I suggested that an occasional sip perhaps would prove a grateful accompaniment to "the sunset breeze." Then somebody told me that Whitman was as abstemious as myself in the use of liquors, and asked how I had come to make such a blunder. I could only reply that holding the same stupid opinion of poets as many people held of actors — that they might always be depended upon to neglect their duty to everything and everybody if only an opportunity offered to be convivial — I had given Whitman the final proof of a brilliant readiness to do the wrong thing. When I went to bed that night and rehearsed the personal doings of the day, I pulled the sheet over my head and shrieked at myself for a tactless fool!

A few days later some one left word at the theater that Whitman wanted to see me, but I paid no attention. Having had no acknowledgment of the "Old Crow" gift, I felt too wise to permit myself to be subjected to the extraordinary vocabulary of a man like Walt Whitman! When the Traubel book came out, I was astonished to read the following: "When we had helped him into the hallway, he said instantly, 'I came for a drink — oh! I'm thirsty for it. I could wait no longer — have had it in mind, could not get rid of it, for an hour past.' And a little later: ' I say, Tom [Harned], what's the matter with the tipple? Did you put the cork in again? What's the good of tipple with the cork in? I am in a good mood for gentle things — my philosophy sees a place and time for everybody.'" The fates seem to have arranged that I should blunder all along the line with the poet of whom it was wittily said that "he had too much Camden in his Cosmos."

It was a real sense of relief to feel that my well-meant gift of "Old Crow" had not been missent, and that I might have spared myself that bedtime abasement of pulling the sheet over my head. How much I regret not going to see him in response to that message which, after all, he meant to be a kindly one! Had I gone I should have tested by speech and anecdote the assertion that he was without humor, and, who can tell? He might have unbent sufficiently to speak of the things I wanted to know.

He is as vivid a figure to me to-day as when I last saw him, but I have a more vivid picture still of Walt Whitman, that of the proud old man with the market-basket, the lame man who was determined to walk, and who was peddling his "Leaves of Grass."

CHAPTER XIII
THE ACTORS' STRIKE

So far as his relations with managers were concerned, by 1912 the professional status of the American actor had become pitiable. Encroachment after encroachment had followed so swiftly that the actor had become little better than a "hired hand," something in the nature of a serf.

Despite his many protests in 1915 that nothing was further from his intentions than domination of the theatrical profession when he "cornered" the theaters and took complete possession of the "booking interests," the manager had now become not only supreme but autocratic. This was a reversal of the previous state of affairs when all, or nearly all, actors were managers which made for understanding, appreciation, and kinship. Control had passed into the hands of those who, having no opinion of the drama as an art, no sympathy or respect for its followers, were exploiting it as a commerce. They held, still hold, that all actors are temperamentally impossible and childlike. Since the advent of The Actors' Equity Association, however, this opinion is in process of swift amending.

This new régime in the theater has brought more formal business methods, perhaps more stability than its predecessors maintained, due to the fact that the newcomer is permanently located while the actor-manager was more or less a bird of passage. But in his contract relations with the actor, without whom nothing avails in the theater, this Syndicate manager brought to the conduct of his affairs a code of business ethics that was contemptible, the type of thing against which Roosevelt once waged war to the betterment of the country.

These managers proudly declare themselves to be "shopkeepers." The mere mention to them of the word "art," whether with a small or a large "A," in connection with the conduct of a theater is like waving the conventional red rag before the equally conventional mad bull. There is no way to put into print what one of the richest and most powerful of modern managers gave me as his opinion of acting as an art, adding that he sold performances to the public as a department store sold soap to its customers. Furthermore, he regarded his coarsely frank statement as a mark of honesty and freedom from affectation.

It seemed extraordinary to me that these Syndicate managers not only acknowledged that their contracts with actors were unfair, but gloated over it. They waved the matter off airily with such remarks as: "Yes, the contract may be one-sided, as you say, but you don't have to sign it. There it is, to be accepted or refused." More outrageous still was the admission and the defiance: "Yes, you are entitled to better treatment, but let's see you make us give it to you!" Refusal to accept these contracts meant setting one's self against a monopoly, a "closed shop," thoroughly organized to protect its interest, and it meant also being put on a list, perhaps, with those who were "not available for engagements." Such a thing as a "black-list" has always been strenuously denied, but, if it was never actually written out, there was certainly the strongest mental reservation and individual declaration concerning it.

Arrogantly enough managers sat back and exclaimed with "Boss" Tweed: "What are you going to do about it?" And for a long time actors did nothing about it, could do nothing about it, because they were weak and unorganized while the managers were banded and strong.

In whatever light the manager chooses to regard himself, "shopkeeper," "business man," or what not, there is no question but that he is in charge of a public institution which wields a powerful influence for good or evil. If he directs that influence so that it be detrimental to public morals and decency, he then becomes a public menace.

The theater is the people's sweetheart. It is a rational, beautiful amusement, a great emotional power with which long, long ago the world made up its mind never to part, resenting definitely any effort at separation.

That he, rightly or wrongly, has assumed the guardianship of this temple of the people, that he owes any civic duty to the public, the manager seems not to be aware. The thing he knows and appreciates most about the theater is that it is a profitable "business" and that he is in it "for all it is worth." That he is responsible in any way to the public for what he produces or for the effect upon the audiences he seems wholly unaware, shouting insult and defiance at those who dare, as he puts it, to tell him how he shall conduct *his* business. But it is not wholly his business. It is the business also of the actor, and, likewise, the business of the public.

The manager has chosen a public institution in which to invest his capital. Out of this investment he hopes to make money, does make money, but that does not lessen his responsibility to the public. There is no objection to the manager making money. He deserves to do so for the courage of his investments in a business which, to the uninitiated, and sometimes to the wisest, is dangerously speculative, but there is every objection to his making money by abasing the public mind, as is not infrequently done, in a sordid appeal to indecency.

But what of the actor in this respect? In what way, if at all, does he differ from the manager? Is he, as is sometimes asserted by the manager and the ignorant layman, tarred with the same stick for mere money-getting? or does he seek the stage because he has aptitude for it, and fights his way into the medium through which he can give expression to the only gifts he possesses, as personality, magnetism, power of presentation?

It may be that there are managers actuated by

finer artistic ambitions in connection with our stage, and there is much in William Gillette's terse declaration that "a manager must be either commercial or crazy," but I should like to say that in all my life I have never known an actor to whom, by comparison with his art, money was not a secondary consideration. His willingness to make a nomad of himself, his submission at times to humiliating conditions under which to labor, conditions of terms as well as surroundings, go a long way to prove this. And this he does for love of the thing he is doing, to compass the opportunity for self-expression. In that wide respect, at least, he differs in my opinion from the majority of manager.

I should think this interjection of doubtful value if some manager or person ignorant of the facts were not constantly declaring that the actor maintains the same attitude toward his profession as the manager.

Because of the unjust conditions spoken of, a great gulf had opened between the manager as employer and the actor as employee. It could not be otherwise. This gulf had been created, of course, not merely by the manager's opinion of the actor's art — that the actor has always borne with contemptuous indifference — but by the dishonest business relations forced with increasing severity upon the actor.

The old order of things was destroyed, the old harmony disrupted. The old relation between actor and manager had vanished never to return. The new relations, if more business-like, were far less sympathetic, and for that reason alone died and dies much of the actor's artistry. Actors were no longer engaged, they were "hired." Likewise they were never released, but "fired." Except for the few who vitally fitted into the business schemes of the new régime of managers, actors were boorishly made aware of the distinction. If anything but "strictly business" was expected of the managerial newcomers, that expectation, with rare exceptions, has been sadly unrealized.

For the increased demands made upon the time and application of actors there was no compensation, and injustices had become so flagrant as to be intolerable.

Originally, actors gave two weeks' rehearsal gratuitously, at the beginning of a season which lasted forty or more weeks. Now it had become no unusual practice to exact ten, even twelve weeks' rehearsal, without pay! Sometimes at the end of this period the manager has decided not to produce the play, and has arbitrarily dismissed the players without recompense. He had used the services of the actors to discover that the play was not worth producing and felt under no ethical or financial obligations. When I explained this to some business acquaintances who wanted to know about the "row" between the manager and actor, they could hardly credit the statement. Quite often, if the public did not make an immediate response, the "season" would be summarily closed after one or two performances and the actors paid only for these performances. Think of it! Four to eight weeks' rehearsals for one or two nights' pay! There was an instance or two of actors rehearsing as long as twenty weeks, for different managers, without pay, the plays in which they rehearsed having been abandoned. This seemed perfectly fair to the manager's warped sense of justice. The actor was helpless. Of what weight was his individual objection, if he dared to make it, against organized and arbitrary management?

Engaged to play leading or other rôles, actresses were obliged to lay out hundreds of dollars for costumes only to find that it was all a dead loss in a "season" that lasted but a few nights, or two or three weeks.

Until the "matinée performances" were inaugurated, actors played but six times a week. Then followed the Saturday matinée which soon became an unpaid part of the week's work. Boucicault began the midweek performances, which, being "extra," he always paid for. But Boucicault was human. With the incoming of the modern type of managers, all payment for the Wednesday matinée ceased. Matinée performances became more frequent. Managers immediately made their unilateral contract read that the number of performances would henceforth be governed by "the custom of the theater." Being their own theaters they then proceeded to make the custom what they would. The injustice was augmented until fourteen performances were given in a single week for which no extra salary was allowed. These were full dramatic performances lasting the entire afternoon or evening. Finally one manager declared that so long as he paid the usual salary (nothing being allowed for extra performances), actors had no right to object to any number of performances the manager might elect to give.

After a month or six weeks of free rehearsals, some managers declared the first two weeks' performances of the play to be "rehearsal weeks before the public," and only half salaries would be paid.

For Holy Week and the week before Christmas only half salaries were paid.

Contrary to all custom, some managers obliged actors to pay their fares to the point where the performances began. Engaged in New York, actors paid their way to Chicago or Denver, if the play began the season there. On the other hand, even though the actor was engaged in New York, if the season ended in Denver or Chicago, some managers obliged their companies to pay fares to New York.

An actor "engaged for the season," and giving six to eight weeks' rehearsals, gratis, would often be dismissed without pay before the first performance of the play.

At the option of the manager, at any time during the season the actor might be dismissed "without cause" on being given two weeks' notice. The actor had no reciprocal right.

Even in so small a thing as the collection of the company's baggage for the season's journey, and the release of that baggage at the end of the season, some managers compelled the actors to pay all, or a part, of the transfer charges.

Clearly something had to be done before managers proceeded to the extreme of requiring players to act as butlers at the managerial table or as chauffeurs on managerial automobiles. It was imperative, then, that the manager not only be reminded of his responsibility to the public, but also that he be compelled to deal honorably with the exponents of the art he was commercializing.

This was the situation when, in 1913, a few prominent actors, grieving at the increasing injustices done their fellows, met with the hope of threshing out a remedy. As the result of many conferences, there was formed an organization to which was given the name of The Actors' Equity Association. It was high time to take such a step for, up to that period, bookkeepers, scrubwomen, and actors were about the only body of people who had not combined for protective purposes. From the beginning the new association was in deadly earnest. It gave proof of that earnestness and also gave evidence of vision by declaring that the new association should be conducted on a purely economic and business basis. It carefully eschewed all "social" features which had been a strong factor in wrecking previous actor societies.

I was asked to be the president of the new organization, asked to lead the actors in the formation and up-building of a body of professional people strong enough to swing the pendulum of fair play back into the groove in which it had swung before the dollar hound had taken possession of the drama, asked to help make the

actors strong enough to oppose the unjust methods of
a powerful but seemingly conscienceless opposition. I
accepted and so for years brought upon myself volumes
of managerial vituperation.

The speculating managers received this new actor
organization with glee liberally mixed with contempt.
They seemed justified in being amused because of previous failure on the part of actors to check abuses.

The real struggle of Equity was with actors who had
to be educated as to the necessity of organizing.
Naturally they hesitated to ally themselves with an
association which might fail and so prejudice their
chances of engagement. All previous associations of
this character had failed, why not this one? Except in
individual instances, actors were now cowed beyond
belief. Some who were in demand held themselves
exasperatingly aloof from the newly formed Association,
through indifference or unwillingness to be concerned
in a struggle of any kind, now that their lives lay in
pleasant places.

Notwithstanding increasing abuses to which they
were being subjected, it took years of patient example,
daily, hourly argument, encouragement, and enthusiasm to bring actors into the Association and up to
the "sticking point." The Council sat as if for "company." Players were invited to meet them and state
their objections to becoming members, to answer arguments of the Council or prove such arguments false, to
acknowledge that the policies proposed, or in force,
were good, or to supply others that were better. This

won members, but not so rapidly as the feeling that spread through the acting profession that the unpaid Council, with the certainty of managerial disfavor, was unselfishly devoting time and mind, to the cause, that the Council was adopting the Syndicate's slogan of "business," and meant it.

Managers, however, continued quite unterrified, and absolutely indifferent to appeals from Equity for conference of any kind. By importunate correspondence, by occasional chance interviews with this or that manager, by publication of examples of the slave-driving methods of managers, in which both press and public were now manifesting interest and astonishment, the managers, after four years' evasion, deemed it prudent to meet as a body with Equity.

As a result of the meeting there came about a "standard contract" from which were omitted a few of the more flagrant injustices. It was far from being an equitable contract, and it was for a brief period, but it was a beginning. At the Hotel Astor in 1917, a Ratification Dinner was given and many complimentary declarations of faith were made by managers. One such, in the enthusiasm of a generous moment, was unintentionally amusing in trying to be emotional. This was his gemlike peroration: "I am proud of my part in this agreement, because I know it is just what 'C. F.' [his partner, the late Charles Frohman] would like me to do. And, now, when we meet on the other side, I can look him in the eye and, clasping his hand, say, 'C. F., I done it!'" Well, they are both on "the other side," and

I find it difficult to resist a strong feeling, that "C. F." is doing his utmost to avoid that handclasp.

This looked like an auspicious beginning of a more gracious epoch in the affairs of the drama. However, this promise of reform was short-lived, none of the managers caring long to keep faith. Our friend of the unconsciously humorous lapse was one of the first to break his word. Being specially organized for "business," Equity took cognizance of each breach of contract and, removing individual responsibility from the shoulders of its members, to their delight, haled the more flagrant offenders into court and beat them summarily. This led to a sitting-up all along the line and the taking of a good deal of notice.

Meanwhile, Equity was increasing in membership, in enthusiasm, and in determination. It evolved a set of new conditions by which it meant to stand, and took every means to bring about another meeting with the manager's association. Equity meant not only to insist upon the managers disciplining their faithless members, but, the first bond between the two associations being about to terminate, to present new conditions that would make for the wiping-out of further injustices, especially those relating to the number of performances included in a week's work. Eight performances, with four weeks' rehearsals, gratis, being the limit it meant to allow, a liberally fair allowance, indeed! But managers, running true to form, were evasive. Because of this or that, the time was never convenient for them to coöperate.

To me the problem had now shifted. While I felt that, in case of a crisis being reached, the actors would be likely to stand firm, I especially felt that, if the managers were to be made to accede to Equity's terms, they must be faced with something more than an organized body of players in whose ability to stand together they had no confidence. As a few of us in the Council saw it, our aggressive as well as our defensive move lay in alliance with The American Federation of Labor. Managers would have reason to fear such a coalition, for, in conjunction with it, after previous unsuccessful efforts without it, both the musicians and the theatrical mechanics associations had succeeded against managers. This made a precedent. But the bare thought of such an alliance was repugnant to many actors whose dignity was instantly outraged. However, many soon saw the light and being won over, became enthusiastic for the coalition. The contemplation of such a move on the part of Equity, if known, would give managers something to think of. Perhaps bring them to their senses, if anything could.

If managers were wise now, a "strike," with its attendant discomforts, expense, and dangers, might be averted. The wretched fear was that, accustomed to seeing actors yield to the power which employs, and blind to an inevitable reaction gathering strength under their very eyes, a reaction that had strong public sympathy, they would stubbornly force the issue. If the actor proved true to his principles, this could have but one result, namely, managerial defeat.

Strikes cost money and the Actors' Association was poor, with but a few thousand dollars in its treasury. Managers, on the other hand, had unlimited means at their command and were stubborn. A strike meant many unemployed actors for whom Equity, naturally, would have a sense of actual responsibility. How was Equity to meet this? Her funds would not permit much of a strain. How it was met will be told in due order.

At this juncture came the threatened dissolution in partnership of Klaw and Erlanger who controlled the "booking" interests, the dates of engagements of companies, of the powerful theatrical Syndicate. This led to the formation of The Producing Managers' Association by the younger and successful producing managers, who, doubtful as to what would result from that dissolution, thought it wise, through Equity, to propitiate actors. Through a member of this new organization, Equity was promised a cession of all its demands which were to be handed to it on a silver platter at a breakfast to be given at the Hotel Claridge. *Ad interim*, the old Bourbon-managerial-dyed-in-the-wool implacables came to the front in the new association and, in place of the promised love-feast at the Claridge, there was enacted a funeral wake of the most vigorous character in which every dead misunderstanding, recrimination, and grievance between actor and manager was rudely reanimated.

In all previous meetings with managers, Equity had practically to go cap in hand. This invitation, therefore, came as a great relief. It promised to be a big step to a satisfactory understanding. Little need to add that it was accepted. In the opening speech, I touched upon this point and congratulated all concerned on the change of sentiment that I was given to understand had been wrought and, closing, said that whatever fair proposal was to be made would, of a certainty, be met with whole-hearted acceptance by Equity.

Because of a willful or stupid misinterpretation, this opening address was the cue for a "brainstorm" on the part of the managers. I was accused of "gloating!"

Just what there was to gloat over I cannot yet imagine, but so the accusation ran. I was cheerful, for I thought understanding near, but I had no thought to exult. At all events, it was evident that I was not sufficiently humble. "Seeked on" by a brilliantly double-negatived guardian of the spoken drama, the most picturesquely behaired of all managers became so violent that he pounded his fist into his goblet which was smashed by the impact. It was his "great moment" and he must be credited with making the most of it. It also added to the "comedy relief." Though emotionally besought to seek surgical assistance for a scratch, he heroically refused. The Equity president was threatened with personal insult and responded by declaring that he would meet it with insult if he of the graceful plumage should make good his threat.

Instantly there was an uproar of serio-comic confusion which was greatly enjoyed by those whose sense of humor would not forsake them. The traditional contest of the monkey and the parrot was being re-staged, with fantastic embellishments. When quiet was restored and discussion resumed, so far as recitals of personal vauntings on the part of managers permitted, the droll spectacle was presented of the manager of America's most æsthetic theater repeating the astonishing argument, which had previously been voiced in the press by one of supposedly inferior mentality, that actors must of course share the responsibility of managerial enterprises; that if the manager's business declined, the actor should devote a part of his salary, never to be returned, to sustain managerial projects!

It mattered not that the actor would have no part in either the origin, arrangement, or direction of these enterprises; he must, perforce, become a peculiar kind of partner who shared the losses and participated in no profits! It was heads managers win, and tails the actors lose. Could anything be simpler! I replied that actors might be willing to come to the manager's assistance when there was a loss, but that it seemed only fair that he should share in case there were a profit. Judging from the astonished silence with which this proposition was received, I gathered the impression that if I had any regard whatever for managerial opinion I should instantly consult an alienist.

To precipitate an argument, to confuse the situation, and finally to dismiss the meeting with the declaration that it was impossible for managers to deal with impractical actors (and this is precisely what happened), the actors were sounded on the likelihood of joining the American Federation of Labor. It was admitted that Equity had given thought to such a step. Instantly the self-confessed "business men" were tremendously shocked that "artists" should dream of such an alliance. Here was a comic touch that called for unrestrained laughter, if one wanted to be impolite — that actors, upon whom managers had previously looked as mere property, commerce, pawns to be stuck on this square or that, as "hams," should now, in the opinion of these same "business men," suddenly blossom into "artists."

Considering that musicians and stage mechanics had won from these same managers by such an alliance, one was tempted to suspect a not too subtle motive on the part of the managers in applying this flattering epithet. It was too rich. It was so blatantly specious! The managers were told that they could stop such a move on the part of the actors by redressing the injustices, the abuses complained of. In that event Equity would then feel no necessity to join any other association, but that if it did seek an alliance with The American Federation of Labor, the unyielding managers themselves would be responsible.

A touch of delightful naïveté was given the occasion by America's best double-fisted manager, who roared him like any sucking dove, in indignation that his actress wife and daughter should be obliged to join any society against their wishes. To which it was said that there was no obligation whatever, but that they ought to be proud to enroll themselves in the only effective organization known in a quarter of a century for the protection of the peopl of their profession. He was especially eloquent and scornful as, with admonitory index finger, he demanded to know where and into what pitfalls Francis Wilson was leading these actors. "To victory," as I hoped, was the obvious answer, and so it was given. And, in conjunction with as fine and upstanding a body of men and women as I have ever known that victory came to pass.

But to none at this meeting was permitted as much indignation, whether real or assumed (I suspect the latter), as to the "Yankee Doodle Comedian" and manager George M. Cohan, who, because he had once had an unfortunate experience, as he stated, with a labor strike among theatrical mechanics, decided, impulsively, I thought, to lose forever the fairest opportunity any actor ever had to become a real hero to his fellow players. Generous and actually performing many individual acts of charity, it seems remarkable that, with his theatrical lineage, he could have set his face against the righting of long-standing abuses to the people of his profession. This attitude of his is still a matter of amazement.

The climax to this remarkable meeting came when the managers suddenly staged a melodramatic tableau having for its object, among other things, the teaching of actors how to act. Led by the talented and virile Henry Miller, who has reached management by skillful stage-directionship and individual power, but who, as I see it, has been warped in his judgment by the terror of

VIOLET HEMING

The beautiful "Lydia Languish" of the Players
Club performance of "The Rivals," 1921.

PATRICIA COLLINGE

The dainty and beautiful "Lucy" in The Players'
production (1921) of "The Rivals."

the "booking system" to which he and all others of his kind are subjected, the managers rose at his bidding and, actually lifting their pudgy hands to high heaven, declared they would never, no, never, employ an actor who belonged to a labor organization.

It was an extraordinary picture. Some of the managers could not make their hands behave — they *would* drop at right angles, while a few of the more curious "spoiled the picture" by looking around "to see how it was going."

I would not have missed that sight for bags of gold. It was better than the climax of any second act I have ever seen. I wish now I had yielded to my impulse to start a round of applause. I am confident it would have met with a much-needed burst of laughter and calmed the situation. The tableau did not much impress the audience of Equity actors; it lacked conviction.

If this "Three Musketeers" or "Rosedale" performance was intended to frighten Equity, it was a failure. As a "bum" show, as the man in the street would characterize it, it was a huge success. One thing it did. It furnished George M. Cohan with material for an hilarious sketch given at a gambol of The Lambs.

It would be pleasant to record that the managers at last realized that they were contending with people who were the heart and soul of the theater, people upon whom they depended for their daily bread, to say nothing of their luxurious automobiles; people to whom they owed a long future of kindness and courtesies for past injuries and injustices, that, in short, the managers saw the light, and finally consented that simple justice be done and thus avoid the humiliating checkmate to which ultimately they were obliged to submit. To do credit, a few of them were so inclined, but were overruled by the older, reactionary forces who could not admit the possibility of defeat by their "hired hands."

Having been invited to breakfast with the managers, not to discuss the situation, but, as Equity was led to believe, to receive confirmation of the abolishment of certain abuses, Equity was insulted and told to go home as a body of impossibles with which it was impractical to deal. A few days later, Equity had joined the American Federation of Labor. That was its answer to the hymn of hate which managers had sung to it at the Claridge breakfast.

The determined stand actors were making was having its effect. There were signs of much more complaisance on the part of managers who, through envoys, individual representatives, actually brought themselves to yield to all demands except that which limited the number of performances per week. On that they were adamant. For a brief moment, it was a question whether in order to avoid a "strike," it would not be advisable for Equity to submit without insistence on this point, but, considering how much this meant in freedom and independence, Equity refused to compromise. Days of parley followed, but in the end, managers relying on the unbroken precedent that actors had never been able to hold together in an emergency of this character, and fortifying themselves with the assurance that history would repeat itself, rejected the proposed demands.

The "strike," the only one of its kind, the most picturesque America has ever known, was on. Strange scenes, mostly good-humored, were enacted in the theater districts where costumed players, with speech and drolleries entertained the crowds turned away from the places of amusement which were closed because of "No Performance," "Actors on Strike."

A feature of the actors' strike was its parade. A friend who had arrived from Europe in time to see the players march down Broadway said: "I have seen many of the great processions of modern times, but when I saw that thin line of actor people walking down that broad street, as an earnest of their intentions, I thought it one of the most pathetic sights I had ever seen." This was a great shock to me; for those of us who were so deeply concerned felt it to be the biggest procession the world had ever known. I freely confess to a swelling of the heart and a lumpishness in the throat such as I had never known before. That, I am sure, was the state of all those who participated. It was the actors' declaration of independence parade. No colonial of 1776 marched with prouder step.

The contest seemed an unequal one even to some in the Equity fold, but I urged that failure was impossible if the actors stood loyal — I dinned that into the ears of the players until they must have grown weary with its iteration. I insisted, after so many years of patient effort, that it would be better to fail and try again than lose the chance to test the power of Equity through the fealty of its members.

Many efforts were made to shake and disrupt Equity, but nothing availed. Actors were firm and confident. The plans successfully used in a previous vaudeville "strike" were brought forward by the managers and pushed with much vigor. They consisted of vilification of the actor leaders, of tempting offers of extremely lucrative engagements and unusual opportunities to individual players. There was also a dash of "frightfulness" injected by the serving of quarter-million-dollar summonses and injunctions, and any procedure thought likely to discourage and carry terror into the heart of the actor body. But the greatest stress was laid on the instruction to use flattery. If all else failed, it was thought that actors, if told they were "great" or were the coming Garricks, or the future Rachels, would instantly surrender principles for which they had been fighting for years.

A touching incident in the "strike" was the response of Equity members to the call of the Council for funds. Men and women of the drama, who, as the world's goods go, had practically nothing, stepped forward bravely and paid their tributes in amounts they could ill afford to spare. It showed how much they were affected and how deeply determined they were to win their battle for fair play. No cause could be lost with such a valorous spirit.

In this war between managers and actors there was

no question of wages, great or small, but simply of the abatement — not abolition — but merely abatement of injustices which had grown with increasing severity, and a struggle for fairer conditions under which to labor. If I live for a thousand years I shall never understand how Equity's opponents dared to have their side of this contention made public.

Managers were markedly cunning in the way they bent certain prominent players to their will, persuading them to influence, or attempt to influence, their fellow actors against their best interests.

There was no more dramatic scene in the whole "strike" or in the days immediately preceding it than that of Edward H. Sothern coming to a crowded Equity meeting to explain that managers were willing to grant the demands of the players provided they would come into conference without their president, whom managers absolutely refused to recognize and with whom they would positively not deal. It was a courageous thing for Sothern to do, for the meeting was in no mood to receive such a message. He jeopardized his popularity with his kind, and all men love to stand well with their fellows.

Sothern's entrance with the Council at the meeting was the signal for great enthusiasm, his presence being interpreted as an open espousal of the actors' contention. Moreover, I, the president, whom the managers so discredited, was in the chair and had not only to "put the question," but restrain the assembly. I went further and advised the actors to think seriously of Sothern's proposal.

If the managers could be trusted, the struggle was at an end, and the injustices would be abolished. What more could be asked? The president declared his willingness to step aside to permit the actors to attain their object, that having been his only aim, his only ambition, in becoming their leader. The question was formulated to Sothern's liking and put to the meeting:

"Do you wish to treat with the managers independent of your president?"

The thundering "No" that came back was thrilling to me whatever it was to Sothern. If there had been a weakling in that assembly of actors and he had answered "Yes," I should have died of mortification.

No one questioned Sothern's sincerity. He thought he saw a way to end the fight and tried it. He had applauded Equity and its conduct in times past. The situation was tense and, like a few other actors — very few, thank Heaven — he had been misled and probably acted hastily.

William Hodge, of "The Man from Home" fame, told me an amusing incident indicative of the ire of the Lee Shubert manager during the strike period. Hodge was "trying out" a new play by Owen Davis in a town not far from New York and, as a financially interested party, Shubert had gone up to see the performance which had not made a strong impression, as sometimes happens with plays when first produced. For one reason or another, Hodge and Shubert had little opportunity that night to discuss the matter, but agreed to do so the following morning. Bright and early next day Shubert learned of the closing of a New York theater through the action of Equity in "calling out" its members, and he was bursting with anger when he encountered Hodge. On his part, Hodge was depressed with the reception given the play, but knew nothing of what had taken place in New York. At these cross-purposes the following conversation ensued:

Shubert. Seen the papers?
Hodge. Yes.
Shubert. Awful, ain't it!
Hodge. Pretty bad.
Shubert. By Gawd, somebody ought to kill that fellow!
Hodge. (Believing Shubert to be referring to the author of the play.) I think so, too.
Shubert. All his life, that Wilson —
Hodge. Wilson! What Wilson?
Shubert. Francis Wilson, of course.
Hodge. What's he got to do with it?
Shubert. Why, haven't you seen? That d—d Equity has been closing theaters!
Hodge. Oh, I thought you meant the dramatist!

As soon as the actors realized that they possessed unlimited earning power with which to support their cause and, above all, that public sympathy was with them and, therefore, against the managers, it became merely a question of days when actors might halt and listen to managers try out their voices on "The Swan Song."

By a series of extraordinary performances, given at the Lexington Avenue Opera House, all the great players of the day, with a few exceptions, volunteering their services, Equity speedily provided itself with the sinews of war.

As stated, every conceivable effort was made to break the loyalty of the actors. Twice within a short period, I had the unusual experience of being sued for an aggregate sum of half a million dollars. It gave one an altogether exaggerated feeling of importance. It is a joyful remembrance to me now that so great was my confidence that it never occurred to me to safeguard my property.

There were numerous threats on the part of managers, in the event of the "strike" succeeding, to abandon the theater forever — to seek more congenial pursuits. If memory is to be trusted, the operation of an elevator was contemplated by one of these guardians of public thought, and of another, retirement to a back room where, like King Ludwig of Bavaria, his players were to perform for him alone. What could possibly have been the object of these threats? It is not recalled that they brought out the slightest protest on the part of the public which assumed what must have been a painful, if not brutal, indifference. Under this dreadful menace, too, actors remained stoically calm.

With the hope of stampeding Equity members, an opposition association was formed. It represented the views of managers and was named "The Fidelity." It was nicknamed the "Fidos." As is known, its members were made up chiefly of relatives of managers, business associates and connections of managers, together with those who saw the advantage of open espousal of the managerial cause, and those who appear to be deaf, dumb, and blind to the well-being of their profession.

One of the bold reasons put forth by the producers for their unwillingness to grant the demands of the Actors' Association was that such demands were prohibitive and, therefore, impossible. If granted, the business part of the drama could not be conducted with profit. To the uninformed this seemed a reasonable statement. It nicely lent the impression that perhaps a body of easily excitable players, with vain and inordinate estimate of their own value, were trying to take advantage of a number of fair, clear-thinking business men by driving an impossible bargain. Perhaps that was the impression that was intended to be lent. It was argued that, though it might be well to humor players occasionally, they must be made to understand now that there is such a thing as reason, such a thing as limit to demands, that an individual was not to be lightly driven to the unprofitable pursuit of his business.

It was, therefore, something of a shock to those who supported this view when, not long after, these fair, clear-thinking business men offered, through their Fidelity Association, better terms and conditions than Equity was demanding for them.

It seemed incredible, yet there it was. A body of fair, clear-thinking business men stultifying themselves with such a fool proposition as:

"We cannot afford to do what you ask. It would ruin

us. Therefore, if you will accept, we will give you more than you ask."

When this tender of terms was made, people laughed for a week. Of course this offer had a "string" tied to it. For a quarter of a century producers have been busy tying strings to offers to actors. Acceptance necessitated desertion of Equity. This was Cohan's trump card which shriveled in the playing. He quit the managers' association to join the Fidelity. Through his leadership in the "Fidos" and the dangling of one hundred thousand dollars, the thought was, perhaps, to disrupt Equity. If such was the intention, and it certainly had that appearance, it had the same miserable success as Sothern's effort to send Equity leaderless to the producers. "All dressed up and nowhere to go," that one hundred thousand dollars wandered about aimlessly for a while and finally went to that noble charity The Actors' Fund of America. For Equity's part in swelling the treasury of The Actors' Fund, the directors of which, anomalously enough, are mostly managers, Equity has not yet received any grateful acknowledgment.

When the settlement of the strike came about, Equity of course insisted upon the better terms offered by the managers. They were granted, just as even still better conditions could have been granted and the actor still not have been upon a wholly equitable basis. It is worth recording that in this struggle it was "the excitable actor" who was calm and the stoic manager who was excitable.

Meanwhile, I had been speeding along under forced draft. With all actors I had been doing my "bit" in the disposal of Liberty Bonds and setting myself afire by trying to make ten thousand people hear with a voice geared to less than half that number. The inward part of me rebelled and, becoming frightened, I consulted an eminent specialist. I was informed that I was threatened with a serious condition of the heart. "With care, and by conforming to certain dietetic conditions, etc., etc., the end might be indefinitely postponed." Especially was I warned against all excitement! Coming out of a clear sky, and at a time when I needed all the force and energy I possessed, this bolt was like a sentence of death. I died every day for the next year, from apprehension. My family and close friends all died with me, from sympathy.

I was not only alarmed for myself, but, so great is the power of conceit, I was alarmed for Equity. I seemed so much a part of it, and it of me, that I wondered what would become of both if I ceased to guide.

A strike, like a monarchy, is best conducted autocratically. We deemed it best to place that power in the hands of our Executive Secretary, Frank Gillmore, who had every detail, of course, at his finger-tips. He conducted the affairs of the Association from this point to the end so splendidly as to shame all egotism out of me, and to make me wonder if it would not have been better if he had had control from the beginning.

However, I kept moderately busy in Equity's behalf in conducting the enthusiastic rallies at the Lexington

Avenue Opera House, in rushing off to Boston and to
Chicago to speechify to actors, in reminding them that
loyalty alone would bring victory which they held in
the palm of their hands, in informing the deputies of
various companies that Equity had decided to call upon
them to take action at once, and none failed to obey.

When I had time to think of it, I kept taking note of
myself to see if I were showing signs of collapse or com-
bustion. Neither happened, so I pegged away and
began to smile again. At first, this did not happen too
often, for, having been atrociously inoculated with
fear, every pinch of pain, previously unnoticed, became the signal for an anticipated crisis. I was not
afraid of anything so much as of being afraid, and I
wondered how I could rid myself of the feeling. After a
while a friend of mine by the name of Fate came to my
assistance. She burnt up my house in the middle of the
night, but was gracious enough to let me escape. She
tossed and gored me with an automobile and gave me
a number of minor shocks and excitements, any one
of which it was said ought to have proved fatal, and,
finally, by this means cured me completely of the
habit of fear into which I had fallen . Altogether I was
given a strenuous time, but the price was not too great
for the relief afforded.

The strike was a long, hard struggle both for the
managers and the actors, but the managers were
finally forced to capitulate. Equity made a new
record in such matters. Going into the contest with but
eleven thousand dollars, at the end of the struggle, after

paying many thousands of dollars to unemployed actors, Equity's bank account showed a credit of over a hundred thousand dollars.

The actors won their victory by their loyalty, by the force of public opinion, by the aid of their allies who stood by them unfalteringly, and by the justice of their cause. No small factor in that victory, too, were the earnest, determined men and women who stood high in the field of the drama and had nothing to gain in a personal way by the success of the cause and everything to lose by its failure, men and women who stood up bravely for an ideal, love of their profession and the protection of their less fortunate fellows.

There have been many explanations given as to the specific act or action which finally induced the managers to surrender after so determined a stand.

First, it was their conviction, at last, that the actors would never yield.

Second, it was the decision given against them by Levy Meyer, the legal representatives of Erlanger, Dillingham, and Ziegfield, after an interview held at the Ritz with Frank Gillmore and Francis Wilson.

Actors must never forget the reply of Ethel Barrymore when she was asked why she took their side of the contention:

"These are my people!"

Nor must it be forgotten that the lamented Frank Bacon, coming late in life to his success of "Lightnin'," put it aside to attest his love for his fellow players. Heavier than most actors are aware was the burden laid upon the shoulders of Paul Turner, Equity's Councilor. He was not only looked to for legal advice and guidance, but consultation on matters of policy, and for criticism and encouragement. He failed in none. A tower of strength was honest John Cope. Absolutely fearless, it was a joy to have his support on any question. No man I ever knew more hated sham, nor more vigorously did his best to smash it. The unruffled fidelity, the calm, sage advice of George Arliss were ever to be depended upon. In marked contrast of manner was Florence Reed, a fine spirit of enthusiastic determination. No more patient, loyal, and faithful service was rendered by any member of Equity's Council than that given by Grant Stewart, Josephine Hull, and Katharine Emmet. In generosity, loyalty, and in inspiration none exceeded the radiant Lillian Russell.

As for Frank Gillmore, it only remains to be said that Equity presidents and presidents emeritus may come and go, but if Equity is wise, Gillmore will go on forever. I wish I had space to mention everybody concerned in that fine old struggle for justice. We were of many kinds and characteristics, but we had but one heart the core of which was Equity.

Even as late as the hour of conference for the settlement of the strike, it was declared by Bainbridge Colby, the chief counsel for the managers, that the basic law of society being adherence to agreement, to plighted and written word, the actors had outraged it by refusing to keep their engagements and by "going out on strike," and staying out until their demands were met. Quite aside from the fact that from time immemorial managers had been industriously fracturing a large part of the Ten Commandments in their agreements with actors, it should be well noted, in regard to this specific charge of the former counsel, that there was no longer any agreement to violate. By serving notice upon the Actors' Association that they no longer intended to abide by their agreement, that henceforth, in all infractions of contract, they would act as judge and jury without the agreed-upon representative of the actor being present, the managers themselves had nullified their contract.

The actor, then, felt himself free to fight for this right of representation of which the manager had so summarily deprived him, as well as for the abolition of long-standing wrongs. Like his forbears of Revolutionary days, he refused longer to be taxed without representation.

It was well for the managers that the end came when it did. A few steps further on in the struggle, and there would have come an upheaval that would have revolutionized the theater in America, likely for its advantage. No one but the few cognizant of the matter knows how close that upheaval was.

Notwithstanding that the actors' strike had nothing to do with "minimum wage," nor wage of any kind, which is one of the first considerations of all labor organizations, producers willfully declare that the object of Equity's strike was no different from that of any labor strike. This is not the fact. It is, besides, misleading. Equity did "walk out," as any labor organization walks out, but not because it had been refused higher wages. Let me emphasize the statement that wages, money, had no part in the matter. Equity struck for the overthrow of injustices which had become intolerable. It was the principle, and not the money involved.

Another misleading statement is that Equity is a "closed shop" organization. In that it is affiliated with the American Federation of Labor, thanks to the stupidity of managers, Equity is a labor organization. It is, and must ever be, deeply grateful for the invaluable assistance and guidance given it by that body at a time when that assistance and guidance should have been made unnecessary by managers themselves. But Equity is not a labor organization as managers would have it understood. And its doors, its "shop," unlike the doors of the "syndicate" are never "closed" to any member of the theatrical profession.

Another "shop" over which managers are now, 1924, somewhat perturbed, is "Equity Shop," formulated by Equity for self-protection. It is not generally known that it costs Equity many thousands of dollars per year to bring home companies culpably abandoned by managers. These companies, as are all other companies, are composed of Equity and non-Equity actors. When the companies are deserted, Equity takes charge and pays *pro rata* when, as often happens, the apprehended managers are legally forced to "settle."

Payment to non-Equity actors bred discontent in the loyal actors, who resigned in great numbers, refusing to pay for what non-members got for nothing. What was the remedy?

There is no way now for any actor to escape protection and the enjoyment of many other advantages secured by Equity. To prevent disruption by secession, to hold all actors in line for the common good, even to protect managers from contract jumpers, was Equity's problem.

It will be solved, it is hoped, by Equity Shop which requires all actors who wish Equity protection to support their association by becoming Equity members. Managers may have all Equity companies, or all non-Equity companies. Equity actors claim the right to refuse to play with any but Equity members. Incorporation of "Equity Shop" has been asked for and granted in the new agreement with managers, June 1, 1924.[1]

Managers do not like it. Their main objection appears to be that it is an Equity suggestion. They believe that in some way it will give Equity too much power. This they fear. If, since Equity has had power she had in any way abused it, there might be reason to fear. Considering the fact that managers have, with remarkable unanimity, violated their agreements with

[1] To "save the face" of managers, Equity has compromised with them (July, 1924) on an 80–20 basis. This means that eighty per cent of the actors of all companies must be Equity members. This allows for the presence in companies of "conscientious objectors." As all actors profit by the advantages won by Equity, it is agreed that *all* actors, members or not, must pay the regular dues to Equity.

Equity while she has lived up religiously to every iota of hers, the fear does not appear to be well grounded.

Until recently, the aim of managers, their openly expressed wish, was for an association composed of themselves and actors to whom alone, it was feelingly said, should belong the right to guide the destiny of the theater. They would own the theaters, of course, and do the guiding. The actors would do the rest. However easy it would be to imagine a theater of that Pickwickian character, made up of employers and those to be employed, it assuredly would not be safe for the actor. It requires but little vision to judge the result. It might well be summed up in the quaint old interrogation addressed by one Herr Spider to Mademoiselle Fly.

I like to think that there are many indications of a theater belonging to the public and controlled by sympathetic people in conjunction with the actor. I hope this institution of the people, with its great emotional power of laughter and tears, will soon come gallantly into its own, for its own.

CHAPTER XIV

STORY OF AN AMBITION, A PLAY, AND
A DRAMATIST

It was Boswell who set the unapproachable standard in biographies. In a letter to his "worthy friend Temple," he asks: "What can be done to deaden the ambition which has ever raged in my veins as a fever?"

This ambition which weighed upon "Bozzy's" mind, until he caught the more congenial one of chasing celebrities, was "the delusion of Westminster Hall, of brilliant reputation and splendid future as a barrister," an ambition never to be realized.

There was a good deal of that same feeling in me in respect of the drama. I began to wonder if I should ever again set solid foot on the dramatic heath, disassociated from the music which I had rended with such facile indifference. But the time came, at last. Once more I bundled up my stage toggery and, with a grateful bow to it, "quothed," with the Raven: "Nevermore!" It took a much larger bundle than before. It comprised about a dozen elaborate play productions which had involved the outlay of a quarter of a million, and had necessitated an entire building for their housing. The situation, too, was entirely different. Some public favor and a modest fortune had come to me, but still the fever of ambition raged.

Visiting London, in the spring of 1904, I called upon

Charles Frohman, then, and until his death, the center
of most things dramatic in America. A few years earlier we had had an understanding that ultimately we
should form a partnership. Tugging at his hair, which
showed indications of telltale white at the temples, he
had advised haste. I now needed Frohman because I
needed a play, a real play, in which it was possible to
express a continued thought without having it broken
in upon by a soprano solo or a shuffle. I was not certain how I should be received — that he would not now
feel that it was too late, because of my long biding
in the world of song and comedy.

I had been anything but an afternoon man. This
tardiness of approach to the thing I loved had not only
enabled me to secure my own material interests for the
future, but similar interests of those dependent upon
me. Had I stood alone, I had leaped forward more
swiftly. But what now would be Frohman's attitude?
He received me cordially. Then followed one of those
rapid conclusions of business arrangements so characteristic of the man, arrangements involving years of
time and much money.

The greeting was barely over when he said:

"I know exactly why you are here. I'll take every
bit of responsibility off your shoulders, provide the
play and bear the expense of the production. You are
to have a certain amount per week secured and, after
the initial expense is deducted, we'll share the profits."

I did not want to be relieved of any responsibility,
but I did want a play, and plays were what he dealt in.

"Agreed," I said, "have you a play?"

"No, but I'll get one," he answered.

"The kind of a play that I think would—"

"Let me get the play and submit it to you," he broke in, "and if it doesn't appeal to you, don't do it."

"That's it!"

"Do you want a contract?" he asked.

"No, do you?"

"No," he replied.

"You are busy," I said, "for I saw a number of people in the outer office."

"Yes."

"Good-bye!"

"Good-bye!"

"Oh," I said, turning back with the thought of a restriction, "no Wednesday matinées."

"All right, no Wednesday matinées," he repeated, and then added, "Go with me to the theater, to-night?"

"With pleasure."

"Good; I'll pick you up at the hotel."

"Thanks."

That was all the contract we had between us during the ten or twelve years of our association. The only kind of an agreement he had with nearly, if not all, the people with whom he did business. He was ever as good, and oftentimes better, than his word, which explains the general mourning at his death, the special sorrow of the actor world and the world in general, who saw little or nothing of this pudgy little Hebrew manager with the big brain and tender heart, this appealing, gentle man of unusual capability and perennial youth.

How came such a man as this to be the head and front of the Theatrical Syndicate with its lack of consideration for anything but a grinding ambition for money-getting? As a matter of fact, he was not the head — far from it. It was because his name was more in the public eye than that of other managers that he was so regarded. He knew very little about the Syndicate and cared less. Charles Frohman really loved the theater. His only ambition was the production of plays, which was impossible without money. That money was furnished by Al Hayman, and, after Hayman's death, by his brother, Alf Hayman. The Haymans wanted the money and Frohman wanted the glory. He knew no use for money except in connection with plays and, as I believe, kept women out of his life that he might have more time for his real passion — the drama. He spent little money on anything else, wore no jewels — did not even carry a watch, at least, when I knew him — and had much difficulty in bothering to keep himself fittingly attired.

Frohman was the despair of the Haymans who died every time a play of Frohman's choice failed to attract the public.

"Give 'C. F.' and Maude Adams a chance," the younger Hayman said to me, once, "and they'd spend all the money in the world with their d——d fool ideas about art!" The Haymans moved Frohman around like a chessman, in every other respect except as to his dealings with authors. There he was supreme. But no matter what Frohman paid for a play, Alf Hayman was always sure it might have been got for less. Without plays a theater is merely a hall. Frohman could get plays. He was in touch with the world's best dramatists who loved him for his personal qualities — his rich humor, his enthusiasm, and his liberality. He was in familiar touch with geniuses whom the Haymans, with all their money, could not even meet.

The selection of a play for me was not too easy. Frohman doubted if I knew what I could do in the new field. But I knew exactly what I could not do, and when with enthusiasm he brought me Jacobs's comedy "Beauty and the Barge," in which Cyril Maude had made a fine impression, in London, and I declined it, "C. F." (Frohman's title among his familiars) was clearly disappointed. Nat Goodwin snapped it up, but it had a disastrously short run. The next choice was "The Honor of the Family," which I also rejected. When it had proved a success, Frohman was able to say: "I don't want to seem to crow, but I told you so, didn't I?" But how was I to grasp that, sitting at a rehearsal, he would suddenly switch the play from grave to gay, a change that was to make for success? In any event, supposing I could have convincingly impersonated the swaggering, ex-military relation, the play's chief character, blusteringly bent upon his rights, I feel sure it would not have been as artistic a creation as that which was given it by Otis Skinner for whom it seemed made.

Beginning to fear we should never find a play for our venture, I was delighted when "C. F." wrote that Clyde Fitch had undertaken for me an adaptation of the French classic "Le Voyage de M. Périchon," a play that so drolly sets forth the annoyance which may arise from being continually grateful to another for the saving of one's life. We finally gave it under the absurd title of "Cousin Billy."

After the first performance, Frohman, Fitch, and I sat up for hours pruning the comedy. Frohman called it, "Letting the audience write the play," by taking out the speeches and actions which had not met with responses of interest, laughter, or applause. I marveled not only at their skill in the task, but most of all at Fitch's seeming lack of author's pride in the sacrifice. On the morrow, however, he made clever substitutions.

Now follows the Story of the Play. Not the play of "Cousin Billy," an entirely different one, but done on the same evening. When Frohman had eliminated from "Cousin Billy" the things which he, as auditor, discerned were not wanted by the audience, the play was much shortened. A one-act play, then, would nicely fill out the evening's requirement. Just at this time, Austin Strong, the author of "The Three Wise Fools," "The Seventh Heaven," etc., with aspirations for the drama, was eating his heart out as a landscape engineer. "I have always fancied you in the part of a little priest," he said to me, one day at the club, "and sometime I am going to write a piece for you around such a character."

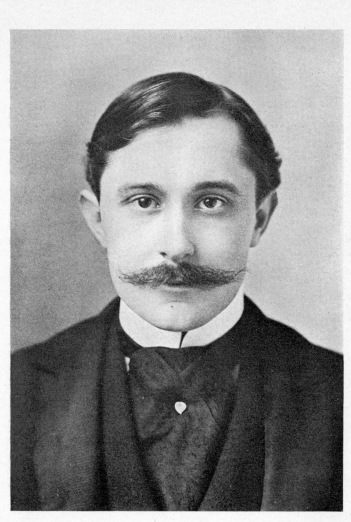

CLYDE FITCH

The skillful and prolific American dramatist. He had five plays running at the same time in New York.

"Why not write it now?" I asked. "Make it in one act and I'll give it at once."

"By Heck, I'll do it!" he replied.

In fourteen days, the play was written, accepted, produced, and heralded as a success. Strong carried his idea to his uncle, Lloyd Osbourne, and the two men, in that incredibly short space of time, wrote a veritable little masterpiece that has never failed to go straight to the hearts of all who saw it. For novelty, quaintness of humor and emotion, that tiny one-act play cast the French classic, even with Clyde Fitch's facile adaptation, into deep shade.

It was the simple story of a village priest. He has been summoned to court by his sovereign, Louis XV, and hoping tremblingly that it may be for services rendered as a missionary in the wilds of Canada, when that country was New France. Louis has heard that the priest had been to Canada and has commanded him to appear merely to decide a foolish bet made with a courtier as to the height of Niagara Falls. Pressed to answer, the priest, "Père Marlotte," is obliged to decide against the king. This is not to Louis's liking. The little father of the wilderness is somewhat brusquely dismissed. Pitied by the king's mistress, he lingers in the background. He is completely lost sight of in the arrival from New France of the Chevalier de Frontenac, one of Louis's overseas warriors with a retinue of trappers and Indian allies. The king makes them a royal speech of welcome to which Frontenac replies.

Attracted by the familiarity of the voice, the priest comes forward modestly. He is recognized and greeted affectionately by his former parishioners and friends of the far western wilds. The Indians and the trappers crowd about him, kneel to him and kiss the hem of his frock. Louis is told by Fontenbras that, though he has deigned to praise the services of his soldiers in New France, greater credit still belonged to men like Père Marlotte who conserved the country to France through heroic example, suffering, and even torture. Thoroughly ashamed of his attitude towards the pathetic little man of God, Louis makes atonement by creating him Archbishop of Toulouse. He and the Court kneel before the odd old priest, who is so overcome in the act of blessing them that he hides his face to conceal his tears of joy and gratitude.

The presentation of such a character was a serious undertaking for a comedian, like myself, identified over many years wholly with laughter. I had little doubt of my power to play the part, to feel and speak the words, but how would the audience feel about it? Would they accept it? Men who make a mark in the world, great or small, are all labeled, and people resent having these labels falsified. My little label had spelled laughter.

Jefferson told me that when Boucicault gave him his first serious lines as "Caleb Plummer," in "The Cricket on the Hearth" ("Dot," Boucicault called it), he spoke the opening scenes at rehearsal with so sad a tone as to leave no opportunity for contrast. The dramatist warned the comedian in time. I profited by that, and all went well until the final dress rehearsal. Edward Abeles, who was to play "Frère Grégoire," the little priest's attendant, remarked, just before we made our joint entrance, that we looked like a couple of priests about to do a song and dance. He improvised words and raising his skirt proceeded to do a shuffle. I joined him. Later, in the midst of the most touching scene, the thought of our caper in the wings recurred to me so strongly that I began to laugh. The more our stage manager, William Seymour, hoped I would control myself, the more I laughed. What if I should not be able to control myself before the audience?

It was agreed that they, unused to seeing me in a play of that nature, might be puzzled, at first, and that only the most convincing acting would tide me over the moments of their doubt. Unless, therefore, I should be complete master of myself, there would be little conviction either on their part or mine. I was worried, apprehensive, not the best frame of mind in which to face an ordeal. But when the play was launched, that night, it took hold of the feelings of the audience so promptly and tenaciously, and I found myself so stirred and carried forward by the story and its impressive reception, that I never once thought of the morning's touch of hysteria.

The success of this play gave me more pleasure than any in which I have been concerned. An actor's power is not fully developed until he is able to touch an audience to tears as well as excite them to laughter. It was grateful evidence that I was rounding out as a player. It is often said satirically that the man being a comedian wanted, of course, to play tragedy. Never since I discovered just what my mission in life was have I ever had any such ambition. But I was ambitious, as the artist is ambitious, to provide my pictures with something else besides laughter. That was light. I longed for a touch of emotion. That was shade.

With all Frohman's facility in procuring plays, he never succeeded in getting me one that compared in importance and merit with "Erminie." He tried, but they were not to be had. Masterpieces do not present themselves every day, nor yet every year. Our best plays came through my own efforts.

We began, 1904, as stated, with "Cousin Billy," from the French, by Clyde Fitch. Through a chance talk with Austin Strong, "The Little Father of the Wilderness" gem appeared, April, 1905. Then, 1906, came "The Mountain Climber," from the German (*Der Hochtourist*), by Graatz and Neal. It was the story of a deceptive husband accounting for his summer absences from home by tales, filched from guidebooks, of perilous mountain climbing. The adoring wife is completely deceived. Gathering a large circle of his friends for a birthday party, she presents him with a book which she has had printed of his great deeds as described by himself. She has also summoned to the party the two alpine guides whose praises her husband has sung, but whom, in actuality, he has never met. In the character of the wife, May Robson was inimitable.

AUSTIN STRONG AND FRANCIS WILSON

"The Little Father of the Wilderness" was Austin Strong's first stage creation. He was so eager to visualize it that this picture was taken before the
play was given.

It was an extremely amusing play and ran beyond a season.

Our next play, 1907–08, was "When Knights Were Bold," by Charles Marlow, a pen-name for the actress-dramatist Harriett Jay. It duplicated the success made with it in London by the English comedian, James Welch. It was the quaint conception of a very modern knight whose romantic fiancée accuses him, much to his distress, of being lacking in gallantry and heroism of the knights of old. Doctoring for a dreadful cold in the head, the knight falls asleep at the chimney place. The balance of the play is made up of the enactment of his dream. In it he performs the most valorous deeds. The merit of the conceit lay in keeping the knight modern while the other characters were carried back several centuries.

There was much success in all this, but the nature of it did not quite satisfy me. Frohman not being able to find the kind of play I wanted, I decided to write it myself. I had been play-plotting all my life, and was responsible for much that has succeeded in every piece I had done. For years I had studied "The Principles of Playwriting," by William T. Price, who was the first, so far as I know, to formulate those principles.

"The Bachelor's Baby," I thought was a good title for my play. Through unfortunate experiences with children, the bachelor of my invention had come to hate them. By the accidental death of a twin brother and his wife, this despiser of children becomes the guardian of a baby girl who mistakes him for her father.

How she winds his heart about her, how he nearly loses her, is quite willing to fight to keep her, and how she is the means of bringing him a wife, make up the comedy.

When I took the play to Frohman, he thought the idea of it not bad, but "a little thin." He doubted that it would succeed. While he was away in Europe, I made an elaborate production of the comedy at a mid-week matinée in Baltimore, April 28, 1909, the expense being about eighty-seven dollars. It caught popular fancy at once. It ran about three years and netted Frohman and myself a small fortune. Best of all, it had in it the kind of thing I wanted to do, with which I wanted to be identified.

One paper, the "Sun," said it was "as delightful an example of child and father acting as has been seen in this city in many seasons." "Humorous and sympathetic," "bright lines and laughable situations," said the "Baltimore American." When the play was properly staged for the following season, opening in New York, December 27, 1909, the "New York Tribune" called it "a comedy that was filled with a note of unselfishness, of human sympathy and love that struck home to the heart."

By this time, it seemed to me that I could not fail at anything to which I turned my hand. It often happens when good fortune takes a fellow up she fairly over-whelms him with continued favor. Emboldened by my success as a dramatist, I wrote "The Spiritualist" involving the discovery of a crime through occult means.

To Mr Francis Wilson

Montreal
April 18th 1907

FRANCIS WILSON IN "THE LITTLE FATHER OF THE WILDERNESS"

The story of a heroic little priest. He hopes his summons to court may mean belated appreciation, promotion. Instead, he finds he has been sent for by his king to decide a foolish wager as to the height of Niagara Falls.

The chief character, which I played, was that of an individual terrified at discovering that he possessed mediumistic powers. The history of this effort may be summed up as follows: A few days after the production of the play I mustered up sufficient courage to go to the club, The Players. As I entered, I was hailed by my playwright-friend, George Middleton, who cried:

"Come on in! Thank God, you are human. At last you have made a failure!"

CHAPTER XV

TOLD AT THE CHIMNEY CORNER

IT is said that a bottle dropped into any ocean will sooner or later find its way into the Sargasso Sea. So with a good story. Sooner or later it will come to the chimney corner of a club.

At the Chimney Corner of The Players many good stories have been told, many strange and interesting events related. There, wit, humor, and fancy are given rein. Some of the jests, gibes, and anecdotes are given herewith, together with a fancy or two which took their rise from the events of the moment. All have had association with the present narrator. We shall begin with the fancy and follow with the anecdotes and a few of the topics that engaged the attention of the Corner.

Shakespeare's birthday, annually, is Ladies' Day at the club. A committee stands at the head of the stairs to welcome the coming and to God-speed the parting guests. On this day, 1921, as Henry E. Dixey and I were officiating, we talked, at intervals, of what the shades of the Founder, Edwin Booth, and our second President, Joseph Jefferson, might be saying standing, as we imagined, on the landing above us and peering down upon the scene. Reaching us as indistinctly as it did, their conversation seemed to run as follows:

Booth

Look, Joe, look! Isn't it lovely to see those two gray-headed boys laughing and smiling welcome to our guests? How fine!

Jefferson

Y-e-s — but wouldn't it be better if there were some one with a little less gayety — and shall I say — more grandeur of mien to —

Booth

Heaven forbid! I shouldn't care to come and look on if such a dreadful thing as "grandeur of mien" were a part of our receptions. My wish has always been that our Players should be smiling and happy, just as we see them now, in companionship with the brave and gifted of the other arts.

Jefferson

Y-e-e-s, but what in the world has become of John Drew?

Booth

He's gone below stairs, to arrange his necktie. He'll be back presently — meanwhile, look at the beautiful people, and see how they delight in our festival!

Jefferson

It's a wonderful sight, Edwin! How it must warm your heart to see your dream realized.

Booth

It does, it does! Look, Joe, look! There's dear Ida Vernon — my sweetheart when a boy! Wasn't she beautiful — *isn't* she beautiful!

Jefferson

Yes, but I knew a —

Booth

And there is Ida Conquest. How faithful she has been. She has never missed a Ladies' Day since they were inaugurated.

And there's young John Barrymore. He's done splendidly since we've been away, Joe. I wish I could whisper to him never to let success turn his head, and never to think of building a theater of his own to be wrecked as my folly of a theater was.

Jefferson

It wasn't a folly, Edwin. It was a public education, a public benediction.

Booth

Perhaps, but I couldn't manage to make the public believe in it.

Jefferson

You mean you couldn't manage to manage the theater. You were the right man acting, but the wrong man managing. Look, Edwin! Who is that beautiful creature sweeping up the stairs?

Booth

You speak as if she were a servant.

Jefferson

Don't be so literal, Edwin! Who *is* she?

Booth

Margalo Gillmore, one of those beautiful daughters of "Equity," destined to refresh and entertain the world. They appear as lovely and attractive as in our day, Joe, don't they?

Jefferson

They do not! Now, there was —

Booth

Ida Vernon is going. How graciously Dixey and Wilson take leave of her! Could we have done it so well, Joe?

Jefferson

Without half trying.

CARICATURE OF JOHN DREW

"All dressed up and nowhere to go."

Booth

Did you hear that, Joe? Did you hear what Dixey said to her? That he hoped she would run in any "Ladies' Day." As if we had them fresh every hour, instead of holding them but once a year.

Jefferson

Well, that's like him, flippant! Look, look, Edwin! Wilson bowed and smiled at Mary G—— as if he'd known her intimately all his life, and now he's asking Dixey who she is.

Booth

What does Dixey say?

Jefferson

That he is not sure, but that he thinks she is the old-woman-afraid-of-her-first-husband! Now, that's disrespectful. I call that disrespectful!

Booth

But she didn't hear it, and he was only jesting with Wilson.

Jefferson

I don't care! It's disrespectful. He's a light fellow, Dixey. He used to give a "rotten" imitation of me as "Rip." Hope we don't see him for a long time.

Booth

So does he. It was only said to Wilson, who'll never repeat it.

Jefferson

Repeat it? He'll publish it! He kept notes on me for fifteen years.

Booth

Yes, and you reveled in it! What makes you so pessimistic since the Passover, Joe? Look, there's Kate Claxton. How gracefully she has grown old! She little dreams how soon we shall welcome her! Let's bow to her, Joe. (*They bow.*)

Jefferson

Ah, here comes John Drew, at last! Let's go!

And satisfied that the full measure of dignity would no longer be lacking, Jefferson tugging at Booth's arm, as Dixey and I imagined it, vanished with him from view.

The subject of playwriting came up at the Corner. I told of once having written a play which I thought would nicely suit the talents of a certain leading actor since become an international figure in the drama. I spoke to him about it. He expressed the wish to hear the play read. We made an appointment — my room at the hotel — after the play. He arrived on time. I gave him an easy-chair and a good cigar. He settled himself back comfortably. I had not turned many pages of my manuscript before realizing, by his regular breathing, that my leading man was asleep. I kept on mumbling, tiptoed to the wall and pushed out the electric light, locked the door and went downstairs.

How he ever escaped I never knew, but when we met he was covered with confusion and full of apologies. He has since given me one or two elaborate dinners, always enjoining me not to mention his name in connection with the incident, and I promised that I never would — so I have no hesitancy in saying that it was my friend James K. Hackett, but I have a good deal of hesitancy in admitting that his going to sleep was perhaps thoroughly justified.

There came to the Chimney Corner one afternoon a man of culture who told to an interested group an experience of his friend, Thomas A. Edison, whom circumstance once obliged to sleep penniless in one of our city parks.

Edison, coming from Michigan, had secured a position in Boston as a telegrapher. Pursuing his inclination for experiments, he tampered with the office wires, put them out of commission, and was discharged. He resolved to go to New York where he had a friend who was also a telegrapher, and who might assist him to employment.

When he had bought his ticket and arrived in the Metropolis, he was penniless. Contact with his friend therefore became a necessity. He found the office where his friend was employed and learned that, being on night-duty, the friend was not at the office, of course, during the day. The future Wizard of Menlo Park was obliged to walk the streets till evening, mealless. Promptly on hand to greet his friend at the usual hour of his return to duty, Edison was dismayed to learn that it was the friend's night off!

He slept that night in Battery Park, when not told by the policeman to "move on!" Next morning, passing a store where a man was "tasting tea," his hunger forced him to enter and ask for a cup, after explaining that he had been twenty-four hours without food. His request was granted. He finally met his friend, who lent him a dollar, all the money he could spare. Edison dashed for the nearest eating-house, Smith and McNell's, opposite Washington Market.

He declares that never has he given greater thought to any problem in electricity than he gave to that bill of fare in selection of his first meal in New York. The choice fell ultimately upon a cup of coffee and an apple dumpling. Years later, promising his friend Walter Mallory a great treat, he took him to the same restaurant. They had coffee and apple dumpling.

"Were they good?" I asked Mallory.

"Not very," he replied.

Before his deafness increased, Edison was a frequent visitor to the Casino, where I was playing. He occupied seats well down front. We soon came to exchange glances. In those days he was experimenting with the phonograph. I had occasion to write him. He sent me a cordial letter inviting me to "come around and fool with the pesky thing." I saved it to reproduce in this autobiography which I felt even then might be written, but it was burned with many other treasures in the destruction of my home at Lake Mahopac. He writes an attractive, individual hand making one wonder just how he came by it. It seems as if one could not possibly write like that and ever be in a hurry. Edison, Eugene Field, and James Whitcomb Riley were the three star penmen of all my friends and acquaintance. It has not been my good fortune to be thrown as often as I wished in contact with Edison, but through a friend, I have helped to supply him with the amusing stories he craves.

Mark Twain was an enthusiastic member of The Players and came often to us there. When anything

MARK TWAIN.   THE PHILOSOPHIC HUMORIST

He wielded the weapon of laughter against the sins and humbug of the universe. He thought "humor must be one of God's chief attributes," and that "temperament is master of the man." This picture was taken before the gray came into his hair and softened his features.

SARAH BERNHARDT

The renowned French actress. She failed at the Comédie Française in tragedy. She tried burlesque and again failed. She was recalled by the Comédie and succeeded. She paid $20,000 to be released from the Française. Irving admired her as a manageress. "Of her superb power as an actress he never had a glimmering notion."

"How wonderful she looked in those days!" says Ellen Terry. "She was as transparent as an azalea, only more so. Her body was not the prison of her soul, but its shadow."

asked who in America had been responsible for the introduction of matinées. It is a common thing among players to anathematize Dion Boucicault as their inventor. But "a gentleman present" spoke up and said that Boucicault was blameless. That "the blue laws" of Massachusetts were responsible.

These not only forbade smoking and swearing on the streets, but also forbade any theatrical performance after sundown on Saturday when, as it had been decreed, the New England Sabbath began. To circumvent this law as to the theater, and, at the same time, to compass a full week's work — six days — the Boston managers instituted an afternoon performance on Saturday. Imitation and multiplication did the rest.

Many of the marriages and also many of the funerals of actors take place from The Little Church Around the Corner. The Players' Founder, Edwin Booth, was buried therefrom. I thought there was now no doubt as to the origin of the church's quaint name, but as late as 1922 an incorrect account was published by a Player. This led to a discussion of the subject at the Chimney Corner. I had heard the story from Jefferson's lips, but, stepping upstairs to the Library, I refreshed my memory from his "Autobiography." The facts are these:

On George Holland's death, Jefferson was requested by Mrs. Holland to call on the pastor of her own church relative to the funeral. Learning that Holland had been an actor, the pastor declined to hold the services in the church. Such a declination would have shocked Jefferson at any time, but the actor was accompanied by Holland's oldest son which made the matter doubly painful. Jefferson asked to be directed to another church from which his dead friend might be buried, and was told:

"There's a little church around the corner where it might be done."

"Then, if this be so," Jefferson replied to the minister, "God bless the little church around the corner!"

The minister had unwittingly performed an important christening, and his baptismal name of "The Little Church Around the Corner" still clings to it.

Speaking at the Corner of the knighting of Forbes Robertson, recalled an incident in connection with "The Third Floor Back" when Robertson came first with it to America. I gathered up some friends and went eagerly to a performance. I kept next me an attractive young woman who had a knowledge of play construction. When the curtain fell on the first act, which was novel and interesting, I fairly glowed in anticipation of the discussion to come. Turning toward me with a fine light in her eyes she exclaimed:

"Oh, Mr. Wilson, Forbes Robertson is bow-legged, *too!*"

I have never quite been sure just what she meant to imply.

.The visit of Sir Arthur Conan Doyle to America, and his ardent belief and espousal of spiritualism, together with the strange experiences and declarations of men like Sir Oliver Lodge and other eminent scientists as to the possibility of communicating with the world beyond the grave, has frequently come to the attention of the Chimney Corner.

Jefferson's inclination to flirt with this subject in which he grew deeply interested, is somewhat known, while the weird incidents in connection with the passing of Booth's wife, Mary Devlin—as related by Booth in his letter to Adam Badeau—caused Booth doubts which greatly puzzled him, doubts which were only dispelled, as Edward Simmons [1] would have us believe, by Kellar, the necromancer, who, to Booth's amazement, out-mediumed the mediums in the cleverness of his magic.

But Booth had a masterful friend in Dr. Horace Howard Furness, the Shakespearean scholar, to whom Booth's enfranchisement from belief in spiritism was likely due. When the Commission was appointed by the University of Pennsylvania to investigate Modern Spiritualism in accordance with the request of the late Henry Seybert, who was an "enthusiastic believer in modern spiritualism," Dr. Furness became the Acting-Chairman of the Committee. With characteristic thoroughness he set about his task by bringing himself in touch with Slade and other famous mediums of the day. He was told by the medium, Caffray, that he

[1] *Seven to Seventy*. Harper & Brothers.

possessed "unrivaled mediumistic powers" which with
application and practice would develop. He applied
himself to spiritual communications received by writings on slates between which pieces of pencils were
placed. But Dr. Furness's words are best:

> With these precious slates I sat every night, at the same hour,
> in darkness. I allowed nothing to interfere with this duty; no
> call of family, of friends, of society, was heeded. At the end of
> three weeks I searched every molecule of the slate for the in-
> dication of a zigzag line, but the surface was unsullied, and its
> black monotony returned stare for stare.
>
> Still hopeful and trustful I continued, day by day and week
> by week. The six weeks expired. Not a zig, nor a zag.

Clyde Fitch was such an industrious playwright that
he was not often to be met at The Players' Chimney
Corner, or, for that matter, at any club corner. Perhaps the most interesting circumstance under which I
ever met him was that on an autumn day in 1891, at
The Players. He had just come home from London
where his comedy "Pamela's Prodigy," though given
with the celebrated English actress, Mrs. John Wood,
had failed to find public favor.

Brimming over with happiness at the success of a
play I had just produced, "The Merry Monarch," I believe, I was a shining contrast to poor Fitch, who was
sorely depressed at the setback to his hope and ambition. We were alone in the "Grill," and he told me of his
struggle with the play which, in trying to amend, he
had rewritten again and again feeling each time that "it
was only another nail in the poor thing's coffin."

Like the Irishwoman making confession and being
told to omit particulars, and demurring because she
"loved to talk about it," Fitch, hungering for sympathy, wanted to unbosom himself. He did. I was
willing enough, but I had an engagement to play golf,
and should have been on my way. I could have done
quite well at the time with very little of Fitch's story,
but as he rattled on with express train speed, I had not
the heart to speak my mind and, before either of us
was aware of it, he was reading me (acting to me) scene
after scene of the play from the manuscript which lay
on the table before him.

He was a handsome man, though of delicate type.
As he read, his color mounted, and his fine dark eyes
glowed with excited interest. As was his wont, as I
afterwards came to know, he ran one hand through
his hair which fell in graceful waves on either side of
his head. There was, however, nothing studied or
theatrical in this action of his. I soon forgot my golf
engagement in Fitch's earnestness and enthusiasm, and
then in the play itself. As I smiled and laughed in
honest approval, he was frankly pleased. Putting down
the script, and with a deal of soul in his voice he said:

"Oh, Francis, you *like* it! I *knew* you would!"

"But why didn't it go in London?" I asked.

A shrug of the shoulders was his only reply. I got no
golf that day, but I had cheered a young dramatist
who became, as I did not predict, the most famous playwright of his day.

One of Fitch's early successes was "Nathan Hale,"

played by Nat C. Goodwin. In connection with the play's first night, Fitch told me of an incident that cut him to the quick, though I never could understand why it should. When the curtain fell, a number of acquaintances and friends sought the "star's" dressing-room to extend their congratulations. Fitch trailed them. Just in front of him walked two bull-necked managers one of whom said in a voice that would have filled any theater: "Well, by God, imagine a man like that [that is, a scholar and a gentleman] writing such a crack-a-jack play!" Why should Fitch have cared!

In his success he earned a great deal of money which he spent lavishly upon everything of an artistic nature which he craved — pictures, furniture, marbles, cloths of gold, satins and silks, glass, quaint old ceilings, doorways, columns of stone and wood, well-heads, baluster rails, etc., which he used most attractively to adorn the various homes in town and country which he built for himself and family. A number of his books on the drama came to The Players.

He had the quaint habit of pinning up around the room where he worked detached thoughts which, in his reading, had struck his fancy, either for the thought itself, or for the felicity of its expression. One of the last so arranged, as dwelt upon by Dr. Percy Stickney Grant in his "Remarks" at Fitch's funeral (October 1, 1909), was from the German:

> Where there is faith, there is love;
> Where there is love, there is peace;
> Where there is peace, there is God;
> Where there is God, there is no need.

These sentiments were not necessarily those of Fitch, though they might well have been. He was a dramatist, and could at any time create a character into whose mouth such ideas would fit. Perhaps such characters were already revolving in his mind. The pinned-up slips were suggestions. Opening the pages of a book, or even a dictionary, with a random glance at a word has more than once given the idea of a plot or story. This, however, is not an infallible procedure. Fitch had these speech-suggestions ready for his formed or partly formed characters.

"What puzzles me most," said a sculptor member of the Chimney Corner, as he leaned back in his Windsor chair, "is how you actors manage to keep your voices in such good condition. Do they never worry you?"

"Constantly," I replied. "And whether one has a good, bad, or an indifferent voice, if he uses it continually it is bound to give him many uncomfortable quarters of an hour. Speaking for myself, while I was in the lighter form of opera, mine was not a voice that enjoyed great repute, neither was it so bad as to merit such comment as the Abbé Galliani passed upon the voice of the celebrated Sophie Arnould, describing it as one of the best asthmas he had ever heard."

"What was the most amusing comment you've had on your own voice — if you don't object to saying?" asked the sculptor.

"Once in Chicago, I had gone to a throat specialist to ward off a cold I felt to be coming on. In no haste, I surrendered my turn to a bustling sort of patient who seemed in a mad hurry. I inquired about him from the doctor and learned that he was a stock-broker whose voice from wretched usage on exchange needed regular treatment. The doctor laughed, and then went on to say that, on entering, the broker remarked:

"'Doc, I saw Francis Wilson out there in the waiting room.'

"'Yes. You recognized him?'

"'Oh, yes; but, Great Grief, Doc, you can't do anything for *his* voice, can you?'"

The Chimney Corner was thrown into a hum of conversation, on a morning, by some one suddenly asking who was the first great American actor.

"Who would you say was worthy to be so called?" a member asked.

"Well, I suppose there *were* some great American actors, old dear," facetiously replied one of our English members, "but do you know, for the life of me, I can't recall them. Yes, come to think, I believe your Edwin Forrest fills the bill. At all events, I know he came to England, got on famously, and spoiled it all by raising a deuce of a row."

"What is said of him by his contemporaries?" some one asked.

James E. Murdock, a brilliant actor and scholar, says:

Never have I been able to find a fitting illustration of the massive and powerful acting of Forrest until, on a visit to

Rome, some years ago, I stood before the mighty works of Michelangelo . . . his Last Judgment, his gigantic Moses. Call it exaggeration, if you will, but there it is, beautiful in symmetry, impressive in proportions, sublime in majesty. Such was Edwin Forrest when personating the chosen characters of Shakespeare.

"Well, nothing halfway about that appreciation," a Cornerite said, "but his father being Scotch and his mother German, was Forrest an American actor?"

"God save us!" shouted an elderly Player, "if he were here and heard that, what would Edwin Forrest, with his concentrated Americanism and almost barbaric intensity, say and do!"

"He'd rip and swear and tear, just as he did in life, I suppose," laughed the objector.

"Forrest's father was Scotch, but his mother was an American-born woman of much intelligence," it was answered; "and though he gave way to explosive anger at times, his biographer, the Reverend Doctor Alger, declares in his own proper soul, from center to circumference, undisturbed by collisions, he was grand and sweet."

"To Doctor Alger, perhaps," the objector retorted. "What is there 'grand and sweet' in a person that hisses a fellow actor, as Forrest did Macready, because that actor had interpolated a bit of 'business,' the waving of a handkerchief, in a play — 'Hamlet'?"

"It is not to be defended, but one act does not make up the sum of a man's character," was replied. "Forrest had been hissed when playing 'Macbeth,' in London. Rightly or wrongly, he blamed Macready, laying the act to professional jealousy. Burning with resentment, he went to see Macready play 'Hamlet.' The air of gayety, with waving handkerchief, assumed by Macready, was offensive to Forrest. He stood up in his box and hissed. This defenseless act and, above all, Macready's tactlessness with respect to it, led, later on, to the Astor Place riot, in New York, in which twenty-one persons were killed and thirty-six wounded. Intelligent Americans condemned Forrest. The populace made a hero of him."

"Is it true that he was ever a clown in a circus?" some one asked.

"No," was the reply. " 'In a pet,' because Sol Smith, the theatrical manager, would not engage him, he went to a circus proprietor and engaged to go for a year 'as rider and tumbler.' Smith sought out Forrest at the circus and found him with the other performers. He turned flip-flaps for Smith to prove his ability. Smith speedily reasoned him out of his folly, and Forrest, who was but seventeen, went at once to fulfill his engagement with Caldwell, in New Orleans. Nor is it true that he was a ranter and 'scene chewer.' All tragedians employ full power in depicting rage and passion. Forrest was more powerful than others."

"His utterance was sometimes tender, almost to womanly sweetness," says Lawrence Barrett, in his "Life of Edwin Forrest." ". . . He left behind him the glorious reputation of having been the first and greatest of American tragedians."

Some one at the Corner asked which, of all the characters I had played, I liked best. After some thought, I decided that it was one that no audience had ever seen. The part of a servant in my own house to three elderly couples which, at my request, The Society for the Improvement of the Condition of the Poor had sent me. It was Christmas. I had become a widower. I was alone. I was lonely. Francis Wilson had extended the invitation, the guests were told. He might be able to drop in in the course of the evening, but it was not at all certain that he could. Meanwhile, his long-time butler, James, would do the honors. I was the butler, with properly combed hair, tufts of side-whiskers, gloved, and in correct livery.

The guests were punctual to the moment, and at once took "James" into their confidence. He was one of them, albeit with a touch of dignity. It was a rare evening. Shall I ever forget the elderly Scot who had lost his position as watchman because of defective hearing? He sat at the head of the table and insisted upon telling anecdotes of Napoleon, and became inarticulate from laughter just before the point of the story was reached. How I loved him for it! It was much funnier so!

Shall I ever forget the little old Irish woman who ate dinner in a pair of coarse white cotton gloves, saying, apologetically:

"Sure, I've bur-r-nt me hands in the foire!"

The real reason was, as she told "the maid" (a gentle confederate), she "was that 'shamed of her hands so red from the washin'." There were many inquiries about the "Boss"; would he come, did he say funny things?

They had heard about him. One of them — the little lame lady — had seen him, long ago. Was he as funny off the stage as on? "James" had to tell them about him. Not an easy task for "James" — the inquiry came so unexpectedly — but he managed to tell some of the things the "Boss" said, and, God bless 'em! they laughed. They would have roared, of course, even if what "James" told them had been tame. How amused they were when "James," the fraud, told them that at times he "was obliged" (suiting the action to the words) "to jiggle ice in the pitcher" to conceal the fact that he was so far forgetting his position as to laugh!

There came a telephone from Mr. Wilson saying how much he regretted he could not be present. Then there was dancing, in which "James" and "the maid" took part, whereat the wise little lame lady declared that "James" danced as well as some professionals she had seen. At parting, "James" was thumped on the back and told he was a "good feller" and knew his place.

Next day, the agent of the Society telephoned that, on reaching the street on which they lived, Mr. Wilson's guests had the taxi-driver blow his horn every second or two so that the neighbors might know that the guests had come home on a Christmas night in an automobile.

Yes, I liked the character I played that night as well as any I ever performed.

A few days later, at the Chimney Corner, a companion said: "I was interested in your story of the butler. Did you never repeat the experience?"

"Yes, but not quite in the same manner."

"How then? Tell me about it."

"A year later, still a widower, I thought to have another such party, but decided this time to be one of the invited guests — one of the 'has beens,' accepting a Christmas courtesy. But how to manage it?"

"Exactly! Well, how *did* you manage it — for, of course, you did —?" he said.

"I learned from the Society mentioned that it had a Toy Shop where it employed elderly men at a nominal sum to make and paint toys. Dressed as a 'down-and-outer,' I applied for a position, and was set to work sawing chicks, lions, and camels, outlined in pencil, from soft wood. As I had no sense of mechanics, I oversawed the pencil lines, penetrated the chests and stomachs of the lions and camels, and had the greatest difficulty to keep from cutting the throats of the chicks. After I had snapped several saw blades, I was banished to the paint shop, the easiest and lowest form of service. I did better here. After a few efforts I was able to get an expression of humor or terror into the eyes of the animals. That brought commendation — and a smile — from the Superintendent. The pay was fifty cents a day, enough to keep any hard-lucker from starving, or crime. On Christmas Day I was called back and given fifty cents extra, same as the old hands, and I was delighted. That day a number of us were invited to dine and pass the evening at Francis Wilson's home in Gramercy Park. We accepted. To my surprise, I was the only one of our party who wore a flannel instead of a white shirt and collar. It made a difference in their attitude toward me.

"There were five of us: Our spokesman, whom I likened to William Dean Howells, because of the slight resemblance and because of his kindliness and his ease of expression; the tall de Puyster, who boasted of his relationship to people of Colonial times; the Frenchman; the Irishman, and the Nondescript, myself.

"On our way over in the street car, from our place of meeting on the far west side of town, I made inquiries about this Francis Wilson to whose house we were going.

"'Good Lord!' said Howells, 'did you never hear of Joseph Jefferson and Edwin Booth?'

"Yes, I had heard of them.

"'Well,' he continued, and I could have hugged him for the compliment, 'he is in *their* class, and is as rich as Crœsus. Now, it's all right with ourselves, but be careful what you do and say if he or any of his friends come in on us. Keep your tongue between your teeth.'

"I nodded my determination to be careful.

"It was another rare evening. The Irishman wanted to leave as soon as the turkey and cranberry sauce had been disposed of, declaring, 'These people don't want to be too much bothered with the likes of us!'

"He was soon silenced by the Frenchman:

"'Doan you know nossing? Have you never been

to Delmonico's?' he hissed. 'Now come desser', black cof*fee* and de cigare!'

"This man is a broken-down nobleman, I thought.

"'Delmonico's?' I repeated. 'Were you ever there?'

"'Mais, certainly—for long time,' he replied.

"'For a long time, eh? What did you do there?'

"'Me?' proudly — 'I was waitaire!'

"I dared not smile, and I wanted so much to laugh outright.

"Our pictures were now taken by flashlight. Then we adjourned to the big living-room and were entertained with a concert by some singers provided by our host, really friends of his. Then came the speeches. 'Howells' acquitted himself admirably, both in sentiment and choice of words. De Puyster did not say much, but his manner was imposing. The Frenchman now dashed to his feet and poured forth a burning discourse, without head or tail, about the mother, the child, home, the Star-Spangled Banner, France, and 'Thou shalt not pass.' Something had to be done, so we applauded.

"The Irishman refused to say a word, evidently disgusted with the oratorical turn matters had taken, and quite eager to be gone. Then the Nondescript, I, was asked to speak. The Irishman began to squirm, and could only be prevailed upon to remain on its being hinted by one of the ladies that it would be impolite to go.

"The Nondescript's speech was halting. It was so intended. The more it halted the more his companions fidgeted, except 'William Dean Howells,' who beamed encouragement. The Nondescript struggled to say something worth while, but became hopelessly confused. It was evident by the coughing and uneasiness of his companions that they felt he was disgracing them, and finally 'Howells' kindly suggested that perhaps it would be better if he sat down. This only served to rouse the Nondescript. From that moment words came more readily to him. He denied warmly that there was anything to be grateful for to Mr. Wilson, which was the truth, but the denial brought groans from some and an expression of 'Holy Moses!' from the Irishman. 'Mr. Wilson is indebted to *us!*' cried the Nondescript, 'for in giving him the chance to be kind, we have given him the chance to be happy' — which precisely expressed my sentiments.

"By this time, however, the Nondescript was too deep in everybody's bad graces to recover even a jot of lost prestige — and, now, no one was listening to him, except the 'entertainers.' When he and his comrades had got outside, the Irishman bolted precipitately, calling back a not too cordial 'Good-night!' The Nondescript walked awhile with the others in gloomy silence. When it came time to part, he said to 'William Dean Howells':

"'I made a darned fool of myself, didn't I!'

"'Howells' put his hand kindly on the Nondescript's shoulder, and said:

"'We all do that at times.'"

I had the pleasure of introducing a distinguished professor of Princeton University to the frequenters of the Chimney Corner. He told us the most interesting anecdote of the afternoon. It concerned his friend and fellow townswoman Frances Folsom Cleveland-Preston — Mrs. Grover Cleveland, as she will always be nationally known. She went as a bride to the White House, the loveliest and probably the most tactful and best-beloved "first lady of the land" America has known.

"Mrs. Cleveland," our professor told us, on taking a train one day, at Trenton, sat down beside a woman busy peering out the window. As the train rolled on, the woman ventured to ask:

"Did you get on the cars at Princeton?"

"I did," said Mrs. Cleveland.

"Do you live there?"

"Yes, I do," Mrs. Cleveland answered. At once the woman was alive with interest — and questions.

"I wonder if you happen to know Mrs. Cleveland?" And Mrs. Cleveland acknowledged some acquaintance with the lady mentioned.

"Oh, tell me about her," went on the curious passenger; "is she as handsome as she was, or has she gone off?"

"Well," replied Mrs. Cleveland, "some people think she has 'gone off,' but there are others who believe she is as handsome as she ever was, and I am among that number."

A friend at the Corner, rejoicing in my possession of

the Sir Walter Scott Library Chair, asked if I had any remembrance which gave me greater pleasure.

Yes; I am delighted with the thought of having probably been instrumental in supplying to The Players the lacking First Folio Shakespeare. Busy one day arranging the other three Folios in a safe where they are kept, I was earnestly lamenting the absence of the First, the 1623 treasure. A fellow member, John D. Batchelder, standing by, remarked that he owned a First Folio. I persuaded him that no greater honor could come to him and to the Folio than by its presentation to The Players. He magnanimously consented, and this consent has been signed and sealed.

Asked if I owned such a memento in connection with Shakespeare, I was reluctantly obliged to admit that I did not. I was vain enough to add, however, that I possessed a Shakespeare memoir which I highly prized, some pew doors, made into armchairs, from the Stratford-on-Avon church which the Bard of all time attended and where his ashes lie — pew doors any one of which, or many of which Shakespeare likely handled.

An enterprising owner of a Boston Gift Shop, on reading that because of the high-church tendencies of the new rector, the ancient pew doors of the church were to be replaced by praying stools, rushed to Stratford in the hope of purchasing the discarded doors, with their carved Prince of Wales plumes and Stratford coat of arms. She found them in a joiner's loft and bought them, and had them duly attested. On consultation with the joiner, armchairs were made of them, the pew doors supplying the backs. Passing through Boston to Worcester, where I was to play, I was one of the first to purchase a chair. Harvard and Leland Stanford Universities each has one. What good was a single chair? How much wiser were I, an actor, I reasoned on the train from Boston, to have bought a dozen such extraordinary souvenirs in which to seat my friends in and out of Shakespeare's profession! I scarcely slept a wink that night. I was sure the shop containing the precious chairs would be burned down before morning. I took the earliest possible train next day to Boston town — and gratified my desire.

"What is the quaintest remembrance in book form you have in connection with the stage?" asked my friend and fellow player, Professor George O'Dell.

"A book I received from Henry Irving. After his retirement from his Lyceum Theater in London, a number of his books, somehow, were sold at auction. I picked up his personal copy of Calcraft's 'Defense of the Stage,' containing his bookplate. I took it to him and asked if he would not present it to me.

"'How can I?' he asked; 'it is no longer mine.'

"'Very well,' I replied; 'I'll sell it to you for a penny.'

"'Too cheap,' he said; 'I'll give you ten cents for it.' The bargain being struck, the exchange was made and, duly inscribed, he presented the book."

We spoke of Frank Bacon and his long-delayed advance to prominence and of his untimely death which occurred so soon after he had reached the goal of his ambition. It was recalled that another player, the lamented Shelley Hull, had been in the same company with Bacon when that popular play, "The Fortune Hunter," was first given. John Barrymore was also a member of the cast.

Then one of the Cornerites related this little-known incident of Bacon and Hull in connection with the aforementioned play: The first performances of "The Fortune Hunter" were given *en route* to Chicago where a long engagement would be undertaken. As is customary after first performances "on the road," the company manager wired his report into headquarters. It stated that the piece had gone well, that the cast was satisfactory except as to two members, and asked if they should be given their release. Questioned by telegraph as to the names of the two unsatisfactory actors, the answer was: "Frank Bacon and Shelley Hull"!

This greatly amused "headquarters," who, wiser than their representative, understood that no actor, however skillful, is able to give in his first performances anything but a hint of the developed product. This was proved in the Chicago performances in which Bacon and Hull triumphed.

There is a pretty sequel to this. I had it from Mrs. Hull. Hull had come splendidly to the front, and when Frank Bacon produced his "Lightnin'," Hull's telephone bell rang at eight o'clock the following morning. Always a light sleeper and an early riser, Bacon had awakened this morning to find himself famous. Unable to restrain his joy, he sought to rouse his friend with whom he was eager at the earliest possible moment to share his happiness. Mrs. Hull received his message over the telephone which stood at the head of her bed. Mindful of the comfort of her husband, who was by no means such an early bird as Bacon, there ensued a subdued conversation over the wire.

"I've been up for hours," said Bacon, "and have read all the papers. When he wakes, give my love to Shelley and tell him I think that it has turned out very well for two no-account actors who were once threatened with dismissal for inability."

Gatherers at the Chimney Corner were rejoicing over Walter Hampden's fine success of his revival (1923–24) of Rostand's romantic play of "Cyrano de Bergerac."

"I once saw you in that play," said a member to me, "and a beautiful production you gave us! How did you come to include it in your repertoire?"

As the man in the play says, I replied, "It was like this": The furore which Coquelin created in Europe as "Cyrano," followed by the success made of the character in America by Mansfield, made me look upon it as fair game for travesty. With Victor Herbert to write the music and Harry B. Smith the lyrics and do the paraphrasing, it was given at Abbey's (now the Knickerbocker) Theater.

Something happened during the rehearsals to swing our version closer to Rostand's than was my intention. The appealing quality of the versification so overcame us, as it had overcome everybody, that we could not resist incorporating large parts of the original into our text, sweeping out much of the paraphrasing, and I ended by acting, or trying to, many scenes in actual earnestness, just as I had always done, for sake of contrast, some scenes in the operas I had played. But in "Cyrano de Bergerac" I leaned still more to the serious, causing some adherents to wonder and ask why the change when the other form had been so acceptable. There was no answer save the sudden determination to have a fling at a character so humanly tragi-comic, a being with the mind and heart of a poet — and the nose of a "Bardolph." I grew enthusiastic; nothing could sway me. There was one scene in which I believed I could not fail to make a deep impression — the Scene of the *Ballade* — in that I had had long practice and some honor with the sword, and that I was not devoid of stage experience and a moderate amount of intelligence.

I was confident that I could fight that duel and, at the same time, speak the supposedly improvised *ballade* in a way that must win favor from the audience and praise from the commentators, meaning the dramatic critics. I did it so well that, on the morning after the première, no review that I remember mentioned either the fencing or the *ballade*.

Not all the dramatic situations happen on the stage. There was one that took place at The Players which greatly impressed me. As it occurred many years ago and the chief actors are dead, perhaps no harm can come of its telling. As told one day at the Chimney Corner, it ran like this:

Joseph Jefferson was in the chair at a directors' meeting. The annual election was over and club officers were being chosen. Augustin Daly had been vice-president of The Players from the beginning, but had never attended a meeting; that is, not within the memory of the president. A more active official was sought. A. M. Palmer, the manager, was placed in nomination. In great surprise, Judge Daly, a valued and dignified Board member, asked why his brother's name had been passed over. Jefferson explained, eloquently, that it was necessary to have directors who would be present and direct. That, otherwise, no club could function properly. His argument, convincing to everybody else, left Judge Daly quite cold, not to say frigid. When Jefferson had finished, Daly rose stiffly and said:

"Since Augustin Daly's name is to be passed over, I cannot consent to sit at this Board. Please accept my resignation."

An impressive silence followed. As the Judge, whom we all loved and respected, rose, the entire Board rose, and stood mute until he had departed. I was a new-comer to the Council Room. I had been elected to fill the place made vacant by the death of the Founder.

To me the scene which I had just witnessed was an interesting example of austere parliamentary procedure.

Many years later, after the death of his distinguished brother, Judge Daly, on solicitation, came back to the Board, and served as The Players' vice-president, the same position which his brother, Augustin, had occupied. No allusion was ever made, so far as I know, to the incident just related.

This time the talk at the Corner was of "mistaken identity," and of the complications that sometimes arise from it both in life and in plays. We have all been mistaken for others, but once I had the experience of being taken for myself which led to a humorous compliment.

Journeying from that place, Chautauqua, which Roosevelt called "the most American thing in America," to New York, I had two hours to wait at Buffalo. Gazing into windows, I found one, a pawnbroker's, containing, among other attractive articles, a box of rings. Making a choice I by no means approved, I entered the shop and inquired the price. A bright-looking Hebrew young man came forward and, after a little time spent in parleying, he suddenly asked:

"Pardon me, but are you an actor?"

Indulging my sportive proclivity, and with a slightly injured air, I answered:

"No, sir, I'm a minister!"

This somewhat abashed the questioner, and the parleying was renewed. The young man was evidently not to be denied, for, gathering courage, after a little, he ventured again with:

"I beg your pardon, but has anybody ever told you that you look like Francis Wilson?"

"The *comedian?*"

"Yes, sir."

By this time the cleric in me was completely shocked and, laying down the ring I had been pricing as if I had no further intention of its consideration, and with measured tones, I said:

"I have been told that I resembled many people, but never that I looked like such a grotesque, such a joke-making buffoon as Francis Wilson!"

"Oh!" came sharp and clear from the young man, "he's not so 'rotten'!"

I had not the courage to spoil that picture, so I was obliged to stalk out of the shop, apparently furious, in order to keep from leaning over the counter and thumping my defender gratefully on the back.

With two productions back of it, "The Rivals" and "The School for Scandal," what more natural than that the Corner, at The Players, should come to discuss all-star casts.

"They are generally poor affairs," it was said, "because, being made up of 'stars,' of people who, accustomed to shoulder all responsibility, are unable or unwilling to adapt themselves to a perfect *ensemble*. Each individual will strive to outdo the other —"

"With the result," broke in another objector, "that

there's a flash of merit here, a dash there, and — well — only that and nothing more."

"Ending in a coöperative eclipse," snapped in one who is accustomed to deal in stings at the tail of a sentence.

"Ungenerously urged," said 'a gentleman present.' "I observe," he continued, "that the objections come from two quarters, those who are not 'stars' and, so, are excluded from participation in such a performance, and those, I believe, who seek an excuse, because of the price, to stay away."

Speaking of a gifted actress, Julia Marlowe once said that, given a bouquet of graces, it was not difficult to charm. Nothing is more applicable than this to all-star casts which are made up of a myriad instead of a limited number of accomplishments. With a strongly developed sense of responsibility, feeling the necessity of living up to a reputation already earned, how is it possible for all-star actors to be less skillful, less acceptable in any performance than those less gifted, less prominent? A barometer in the matter is the public, which adores all-star casts and goes in droves to witness them and, in the long run, the public will be found to be right.

"To be frank," said a member, sinking down in his chair as if not quite proud of the thought he was going to voice, "I don't attend all-star performances because I have had no interest in seeing an old play done by popular players."

"Preferring, no doubt, to see it done by unpopular, or mediocre, players," some one ventured.

From time immemorial competition in mental, moral, and physical excellence, prowess, has been the world's most pleasing spectacle, from the dramatic competitions of the Greeks to the races at Sheepshead, or the contests at Boyle's Thirty Acres.

"What, then, are all-star casts competing for?" was asked.

"Excellence," was the reply.

"Oh, it's a grab-bag affair in which curiosity and cupidity are excited, greediness to get as much as possible for one's money, as I see it."

"Exactly; both as you see it and in getting one's money's worth. However, grab-bag games are usually cheap games. There is nothing cheap about all-star performances. The quality is high and so are the prices. They are usually given for charity or to serve some noble purpose, or, as in the instance of The Players — mainly to do something worthy their Founder, something of which he might well be proud; and such performances, involving weeks of study and effort, are given *con amore*, with no thought of financial gain to any of the individual participants."

It stands to reason that all-star casts are superior. Their people bring, besides a knowledge of tradition, experience, and a delightfully satisfying air of authority which none but seasoned players could muster. In 1853, when Joseph Jefferson played "Moses" in "The School for Scandal" to the scholarly "Charles" of James E. Murdock, with both Placides, James W. Wallack and Edwin Adams, in the cast, he was unfavorable to such performances, but in 1896, when he gave the all-star revival of "The Rivals," with Mrs. John Drew, Julia Marlowe, Fanny Rice, Joseph Jefferson, William H. Crane, Robert Taber, Nat C. Goodwin, Edward Holland, Joseph Holland, and Francis Wilson, he changed front and applauded such combinations.

In trying to make a speech, somebody had been walking on stilts and had stumbled. This led to a talk in the Chimney Corner about embarrassments in speechmaking. Challenged to be truthful, I recalled the following:

At Christmas time it was the custom of a Philadelphia newspaper to give the newsboys of the city a free vaudeville entertainment. This would be followed by Christmas dinner and appropriate gifts of the season. At one of these entertainments — I think it was the first — I was asked to make the opening address, and I felt myself honored. I was born in Philadelphia — and am even willing to admit it! After living for fifty years in New York, it is easy to imagine how proud a man must be of having been born in Philadelphia. I felt that I could say something to these youngsters that would prove of service, something that would incite their ambitions and strengthen their resolutions.

The entertainment for the boys was to be given at the Academy of Music, just opposite the theater in which I was playing, and I must needs speak first in order to return in time to my own performance. As I watched

those youngsters piling into that huge auditorium and
noted them springing up and down on those cushioned
seats, I realized that many of them had never sat on
any but wooden chairs and that some of them evidently
were in a theater for the first time. My heart went out
to them, and I resolved to make as big an impression as
possible upon their little minds.

The lights went up, and I advanced to speak.
"Fellow Boys!" I began — and thought it rather a
happy phrase. To my surprise, I made no impression
upon them whatever. Bumble, bumble, bumble all over
the house went the holiday hum of those eager boys who
wanted to be played to, gifted to, dined to, anything
but speechified to — and I felt rather silly. Could it be
possible that I was not going to be given the opportunity
to make that speech I had so carefully prepared! My
pride was piqued. I must try again.

"Boys! Oh, boys! Listen!" I cried, and again I got
the same bumble, bumble, bumble of inattention. I
must be strategic, I reasoned. Going nearly to the back
of the stage, I turned and came down with a rush, and
yelled:

"Boys! Boys! Boys!"

There was an instant's lull — just long enough to let
an apple-faced youngster poke his head above the brass
rail of the orchestra and, with hands to his mouth, cry:

"Ah, cheese it, Francis!"

And I did. Those boys will never know what they
missed, and, what is more, they will never care.

On an afternoon at the Chimney Corner there was much laughter over many stories. Talk followed as to what it was that caused people to laugh — at anything. It was agreed that the element of the unexpected had most to do with it. Then came more stories, arising, of course, out of the experience of the narrators. Note was taken of the effect, and confirmation renewed that in surprise, in the unexpected, lay the chief cause of laughter. All of which serves for as good an excuse as any to introduce the following:

I had gone with a friend to the beautiful Sleepy Hollow Golf Club. As we approached the place I thought of "Ichabod Crane," "The Headless Horseman," and of the gentle Washington Irving lying at rest, not far away. My mind reverted to the story of the Catskill, to "Rip Van Winkle," and, of course, to Jefferson. As we drove up to the clubhouse and a liveried footman opened the door of the automobile, I could not resist leaning forward and asking:

"Is Mr. Van Winkle in?"

"No, sir," was the reply, in all seriousness, "but we are expecting him at any moment."

At the World's Fair in San Francisco, I persuaded a dear friend, William H. Crane the comedian, to accompany a number of us to Los Angeles and speak with us in behalf of The Actors' Equity Association. We found Los Angeles in the hands of the Elks who were giving one of their elaborate street parades. On reaching the hotel, the proprietor, a friend of Crane's, invited us to a second-story window to witness the procession, a courtesy we were glad to accept. Once there, strangers were met and introductions followed. On hearing Crane's name, one of the ladies present became enthusiastic and said:

"Oh, Mr. Crane! I am so glad to meet you! I have seen you in everything you have played, but I never dreamed I should have the pleasure of meeting you off the stage."

Crane beamed, and it would have been wise if the good woman had gone no further.

"Let me see, what *was* the last play I saw you in?" she continued.

Envious of Crane's immediate popularity, and, being mischievously inclined, I said:

"Could it have been 'Wang,'" which, as everybody knew, and I felt the lady would not (they never do!), was DeWolf Hopper's *pièce de résistance*. As I believed she would, she clutched the straw and went on excitedly:

"Oh, yes! 'Wang'! Delightful 'Wang'! And, oh, Mr. Crane, you *were* so *comic* when you slid down off that elephant!"

In the theater when the unexpected happens, it is always a moment of great hilarity. Dealing as the drama does with the big questions of life — as love, marriage, jealousy, fear, revenge, avarice, etc. — the moment the unexpected arrives, that moment the slender thread of illusion is snapped — that illusion which is the soul of the drama — and all seriousness vanishes while mirth prevails.

The unexpected does not exist alone for its effect in wit and humor. Life is full of it, especially dramatic life, as witness the following:

I knew a little girl of long theatrical lineage whose aspiration for the stage was the jest of her family. However, that little girl got her chance, ultimately, and outstripped the rest of her family, sustaining some of them in their dramatic and financial discouragements — and that little girl was my friend Ethel Barrymore.

I knew a little boy who was so highly energized, so full of mischief, that prison, or at least "no good end," was frequently predicted for him — a little fellow whose stage ambitions were the horror of his Quaker relatives. He won something of a name for himself and a substantial something for his family, and was clever enough to remain a long time in the dramatic profession without permitting the public to discover how little talent he had — and — and — a sudden burst of modesty forbids my mentioning his name.

Whether or not there is a fire in the Chimney at the Corner, we gather there, back up, part our coat-tails, and the talk begins. Originally this chapter was made up largely of anecdotes of other story-tellers who gathered at the Corner. Critical friends, however, pointed out that fine as these anecdotes were, they did not specially concern the individual, meaning myself, with whom this book is to be associated. This was thought to be a mistake, and I have been reluctantly prevailed upon to omit a number of fine things. I am sorry. The reader has missed much. Those other stories were wonderful.

CHAPTER XVI

"ERMINIE" OF TO-DAY

"WHOEVER it was that thought of reviving 'Erminie,'" says a writer of to-day, "did something worth while. It is hardly beside the mark to say that nothing will be seen this year, or any other year, that will excel in brilliance, in sparkling wit, in airy grace, this classic 'Erminie.'"

Considering all that might be brought forward of Sheridan, Shaw, or Barrie, it must be confessed that this seems an extreme statement. However, I shall not challenge it, for I have long been as prejudiced in the play's favor as old Sir Fisherman Walton was in respect to strawberries, than which, he declared, God never made a better berry, even while admitting that it was in His power to do so.

There seemed not only to be a pleasant but a sentimental interest attached to the revival of "Erminie" in 1920–21. The reviewers outdid themselves in the invention of terms of welcome. One Middle Western paragrapher, in sporting phrase, said that if "Erminie" was a hit thirty-five years ago, it was unquestionably a home run at the present time.

Long ago I had promised myself that if I ever gained a certain competence and reached a certain age, I would give myself some deserved leisure. Gladly I attained the competence and sadly I reached the age, then I treated myself to an unannounced retirement. I have been periodically retiring, ever since. However, I did none of the things in leisure that I had so long been promising myself to do. I did something much better. There came to me the rare opportunity to devote a few years to the affairs of the Actors' Equity Association in an ultimately successful effort to better wretchedly unjust contract relations between actors and managers.

Meanwhile, that playful matter of systematized murder, the German War, came on. The Kaiser was telling his well-tutored subjects that he was already supreme in America. The income tax and the high cost of living became disturbing entities and left many people doubtful and discouraged at what had been thought sufficient incomes. I was among the number. My wife having died in 1915, there had come to me, as the result of a second marriage, two additional children. One of these was a boy, thus gratifying a lifelong ambition. For me the advent of these beautiful but unexpected strangers changed the whole course of future events. If the same status of affairs was to be preserved as before their coming, and their future properly guarded, the income must be slightly increased. Then, again, seven years is a long time to be absent from the profession one adores.

I was burning with a desire, greater than I admitted, to see if I still possessed the power to make an audience laugh, to excite sympathy at will. Only those who have enjoyed such an experience can fully understand and appreciate its meaning, its delight. It is the kind of thing which Dickens, coming from the study to the lecture platform, wrote about so sympathetically. What went straight to his heart was the joy of bringing himself into personal touch with those for whom he had written. Now, so to speak, he could take great numbers of them into his arms — and revel in the visual and audible evidence of their affectionate appreciation. That is precisely how I felt. In my humbler way, I longed for a little more reveling, a little more incense snuffing! Several years is a long time for an actor in good health to miss a round of applause, a burst of laughter! Then, too, one remains so long dead.

A new generation of theater-goers had sprung up. I wanted to make its acquaintance. I wondered if it would accept me. I had still spirit enough to be willing to make the trial. Unquestionably vain, but none the less human. A strong factor in the matter was my desire to have my boy meet some one who had seen his father play which, because of the disparity of our years, would not otherwise be probable. Of course I was overweening enough to hope the report of me would not be unfavorable—the dead are never too much abused.

The world was suffering from the aftermath of the German War, but notwithstanding the high cost of tickets, people crowded the theaters as never before. Then came the oft-repeated request for the "Erminie" revival, and with it came DeWolf Hopper as minister plenipotentiary from Manager George C. Tyler. Hopper was eager to appear as "Ravennes," the Robert Macaire character of the play which, with Lemaître, Fechter, Irving *et al*, had had so many illustrious impersonators. Hopper's willingness to participate added zest to the whole matter, and I declared that he might report me as not being at all averse to the scheme.

"Erminie" now belonged to me, by right of purchase. Years after its drawing power was thought to be exhausted, I had had the courage to pay a goodly price for it. I never made a more profitable investment. Though the play has been revived many times, it was never more artistically staged, never more hailed by the press nor acclaimed by the public than in this 1920–21 reproduction. Those of us who were in touch with the audience when the play was first given remembered that it then took days for the press to catch up with the fervor of the public, but in this last revival it was a joy to find instant appreciation. With perfect judgment, Tyler entrusted the dress and scenic creations to that constructive young master Norman Bel-Geddes, of whom I knew but little. It was a rich pleasure to approve and applaud when the designs were presented. Taste and generosity were apparent throughout.

In writing of "Erminie" of to-day, how am I to do so without mentioning the names of living people? Mentioning only those who have passed on is what is called playing safe. If I were egotistical enough to imagine I were writing an episodical biography that was to rank with the Cibber, Sol Smith, and Jefferson books, I, too, might be willing to "play safe," but holding no such delusion I feel myself free to mention both the quick and the dead. Giving myself this liberty not only gives me freedom of speech as to others, but allows one to prattle of himself, "an enticing luxury — and cheap," as has been well said. How else is a man to say things he wants to say, fearing they may never be said, repeat things that have been said, fearing no one else will think them worthy repetition?

In any account of the "Erminie" of to-day, or even of yesterday, I should want it known what the late James Gibbons Huneker thought of it. The flattering nature of his remarks gives a clue to my anxiety in the matter. His reminiscent outpouring on the operetta was among the last reviews, if not the last, he wrote, and contains all the old fire of enthusiastic appreciation and constructive condemnation which characterized the man. When Huneker reflected on the inartistic in the performance of an actor or a musician, it was something into which one could sink one's teeth for the betterment of one's art. There was always the comforting feeling that the man knew what he was talking about, and was not seeking to be "funny" or flippant for the purpose of "holding down his job," nor yet merely writing against time in the closing "forms" for publication. Galli Curci expressed much when she said of Huneker: "We all waited on his verdict, fearful of his condemnation, grateful for his slightest praise."

However much one disagreed with Huneker, and disagreement at times was possible, one always appreciated his enthusiasm and directness. In the critique which follows, he has his fling at "Wilson's tone production" which he notes is of the "same crusty old vintage of the eighties." This is a slanderous description of a voice that was actually splendid, but misplaced — for the purposes of ballad rendition. This is of a piece with the injustice Eugene Field did the writer's legs. Huneker speaks of "The Beggar's Opera" which was not more famous, not more tuneful, though more indelicate than "Erminie."

OHE "ERMINIE!"

By James Gibbons Huneker

ANCIENT RECOLLECTIONS

Possibly the old-timer — who is as mythical as the "man in the street" — may say "Oh, hell!" and not "Ohe, 'Erminie'!" when he visits the present revival made by George C. Tyler, at the Park Theatre [Columbus Circle]. Old timers, so called, are an uncertain quantity at any revival. With their memories of "better days," they hitch up their grouch. The other night in the lobbies of the Park I met a dozen old boys, and all exclaimed: "Not a bit like it — not for a moment!" Now, as a mere matter of history, the new production is very much like the Casino production of May, 1886, in one important point. And that was, and still is, the essential quality of the pretty, insignificant opera; the legs, the squeak, and the inimitable personality of Francis Wilson. Erminies have come, have sung, have gone, leaving no abiding recollection, but Francis Wilson goes on forever (at least, we hope he will). Francis Wilson is "Erminie." Don't let any of those old inhabitants with the glittering eyes of the Ancient Mariner fool you. In 1886 it was Francis Wilson. In 1903 it was Francis Wilson. In 1921 it is Francis Wilson. It is Francis Wilson first, last, and all the time. (How he must hate to see his name peppering this paragraph!)

The same was the case of "Adonis." Aut Harry Dixey aut nihil. Although one of the original Erminieites, like George Tyler himself, I didn't participate in the hurrah of the first night, a night that hasn't been often duplicated in New York. ("Trilby" at the Garden was another such triumph, when they looked for Paul Potter all over town to drag him before the footlights.) But I soon got the "Erminie" habit, especially as I was a friend of that best of fellows, Rudolph Aronson and had access to the house. The music is the weak sister of the work, the book clever, although a dilution of a characteristic play, "Robert Macaire." Curiously enough, a secondary rôle became the stellar one, thanks to Mr. Wilson's racy interpretation. (What a Filch he would make in "The Beggar's Opera"!) A genuine low-comedy part played in the old-fashioned low-comedy manner. Mugging and gagging, making the audience a confidant of every "aside," winking and blinking and cutting up the very old Nick at every pause. Withal, of a comic force undeniable. A cockney rascal from the Seven Dials as full of the joy of life as Sam Weller and of original sin as the Artful Dodger. The unction of Mr. Wilson has increased. His Caddy — originally Jacques Strop — is a capitally conceived, admirably executed portrait of a laughter-breeding blackguard. It has served since as the model for hundreds of low-comedy characters in and out of operetta. Even the younger generation of fun-makers copy his formula, though they may not have seen him. Tradition which is tenacious in the theatre, has handed it down for their benefit.

With joy I noted that Francis Wilson's vocal tone production is the same crusty old vintage of the eighties. In his days of "The Merry Monarch," when Jeff De Angelis was playing elsewhere, he and Frank studied the same old Italian method of voice-placing. They usually practiced on the train from Tarrytown, imitating the whistle of the locomotive, not without a certain success. The result was tremendous. Not even Jeff could make such queer, throaty, gurgling tones as Wilson, who has a comical larynx. Legs, larynx, the "glance of the eye, Reginald," and that devilish leer fetch an audience every time. There is only one Francis Wilson — thank God! If there were two we would all die of apoplectic laughter. Like the character in the Goldsmith comedy, he could raise a horse-laugh in the pews of a tabernacle.

Now I'm going to give a jolt to the Old Guard that dyes but never pays for a cent. W. S. Daboll, the original Ravennes of the Casino production, was an excellent actor, but he never impressed me as did DeWolf Hopper last week. There is so much buncombe in the boasts of old actors that certain rôles can never be re-created that I had considerable satisfaction in watching Mr. Hopper pull off the trick so neatly. There are no peculiar difficulties in the part. Henry Irving, who excelled in the eccentric, made of it a canvas for all his creaking mannerisms. (Irving was the worst "great actor" in the history of the English stage; and as soon as he became a British institution, like Madge Kendal — the apotheosis of middle-class stodginess — it was blasphemy to criticise his freakish Hamlet, his ghastly Macbeth. So I shan't.)

Mr. Hopper, while illustrating the soundness of the Hopper dramatic and musical schooling, played Ravvy in the mock-heroic style. He still boasts the "grand manner" in comic opera and he still retains more than a moiety of his fine, natural basso. I first saw DeWolf as a music student at Alexander's Conservatory in the upper seventies on the east side. This was about the year 1887. He kept the class, including his master, in roars. He was as lively as an electrified rainbow. Like Eugene Cowles, Hopper had grand opera aspirations. Luckily for the larger public, he became the breeziest, most vital and individual singing comedian in the profession. I assure you that when Hopper and Wilson aren't "on" the present performance of "Erminie" is markedly slow.

And that's where the Casino show outpointed this one. We had Pauline Hall, dark-eyed, vivacious Pauline with the shapely underpinnings; we had sprightly Marie Jansen and charmng Marian Manola. These girls diverted our attention from the banalities of the book and music. The young ladies at The Park are hardly mediocre. One compassed the feat of singing flat throughout the evening. Consistency, thou art a mule. Another delivered the interpolated "Ohe Mamma" with the weighty earnestness of a bale of hay. But I do not wish to be impolite. Young women rush in nowadays, where "angels" once feared to tread. A dozen vocal and dramatic lessons and then — zip, bang! On the boards they go — but not on the pitch. However, Alice Nielsens and Eleanor Painters are not born every day.

Vocally the most artistic Erminie was Amanda Fabris, a young, stately beauty and a well trained singer. Jennie Weathersby, in her original rôle of the Princess, seems as if 1886 were only yesterday. Madge Lessing, who appeared in the 1903 revival, has mastered the same trick of stopping the clock. . . . Good-bye to "Erminie." I hope I shan't live to witness another revival. Its venerable bones are beginning to rattle. Youth alone is wise: when aged we grow foolish. But there is consolation in the assertion of Mr. Wilson that even if his hair is grayer his legs and his heart are young. Hooray for François Vilson! [1]

Huneker was a skilled musician. He gave up the organ because "the foot work was too strenuous," and sought some honest toil which could be "pursued in a sitting posture." Conversant with the output of the best musical minds, he found, as was natural, perhaps, the music of "Erminie" to be its "weak sister," but he was by no means deaf to its melodic, popular appeal. Perhaps it was this popularity that grated on him, but as I watched him sitting in his orchestra seat I noted well that, with the rest of the audience, his eye lit up and his head swayed as the familiar and tuneful numbers were given. He was a good auditor, and never lost his enjoyment of the theater. I am glad to have contributed to his pleasure, and to have evoked his appreciation. I always loved the man for his splendid Americanism, and especially for his determination to become a critic on discovering that criticism in this country was

[1] From the *New York World*, January 16, 1921.

mostly in the hands of foreigners. Vale, Huneker, you died too soon!

The real joy of the "Erminie" of to-day production, to me, lay not in the quaint and fascinating scenic setting given it by Norman Bel-Geddes, quaint and fascinating as it was, nor in the whole-hearted reception the public gave it, as delightful as that was, but rather in the insistence of press and public that in all respects the spirit and quality of the earlier productions were preserved, perhaps surpassed. Happily there were no indications that the two original members of the cast, Miss Weathersby and myself, lagged superfluous upon the stage, but rather that "time had mellowed their art."

Many came to witness the revival with grave misgiving, the misgiving of those whom time had not touched too lightly, or, escaping, feared it was not too well with us. With still more misgiving, though not devoid of hope, they brought with them children of the present generation, young people, many of them educated in the alluring syncopation of "Jazz." One of these older revisitants was the author of "The Virginian," who sent me singing for joy with the following letter:

THE COPLEY PLAZA
BOSTON

Thursday, November 25, 1920

MY DEAR FRANCIS WILSON,

To the thanks I am giving to-day, I add thanks for seeing you in "Erminie," last night. My son is a sophomore. I said to him and two other college boys, "You will go with me to hear Wilson in 'Erminie.' You may not enjoy it. You're of the musical comedy and 'Jazz' epoch. But at least you will have the chance to see what I used to enjoy and what made me laugh when I was your age." Well — they liked it every bit as much as I did. They fell over each other with joy. You are a wonderful man, and it was a great pleasure to shake your hand again.

Yours sincerely

OWEN WISTER

In the original production of "Erminie" there was no artistic scheme for the costumes, and not overmuch for the scenery. The chief actors, according to custom, furnished their own dresses, with suggestions from author Harry Paulton. The costumes for the chorus, as was said, were from revamped dresses of other and older plays. The scenes were painted by a capable artist, Henry E. Hoyt. The "Pink Ball-Room Scene" made a deep impression, much to Hoyt's joyful amusement. There was hope, but no confidence whatever that the play would be successful. It was an acknowledged stop-gap. It would be doing well to repeat the somewhat tepid success it had had in England. In those days we had no one in America who was really skilled in the decorative side of the stage, no men like Norman Bel-Geddes, Robert Edmond Jones, Rollo Peters, or Woodman Thompson to whom one could appeal in framing a stage picture, and frame it in a way that would be a sympathetic adjunct, a development of the dramatist's intention.

If it was true, as Huneker declared, that criticism in America was mostly in the hands of foreigners, it was truer of stage embellishment. For years many of us had to go to Europe for such things. Percy Anderson, the English water-color artist, furnished me the sketches from which were produced the costumes for all the period plays in which I produced. We had largely got over our contempt for people who devoted their lives to the art of acting, and felt there really might be something worth while in it, as the Greeks thought, 500 B.C.; but making an art of stage decoration, horrors! It seemed effeminate. We do these things better now in America. We do them as well here as is done anywhere.

Newspaper scribes do not like curtain calls and speeches. They prolong the performance and shorten the all-too brief time in which to write the review of the play. On the other hand, the public adores them. They bring the auditors in intimate touch with the players whose personality and skill may have charmed them. These speeches are something in addition to the play and, when well given, afford a peculiar pleasure.

Macready, according to Bernard Sobel, was the first actor to indulge in a speech before the curtain: "The crowd sat silent and expectant," he says. "Then an actor, still dressed in his play costume, stepped forth and walked down to the audience, and bowed, as if he were personally thanking every one for the applause. Just such a scene must have taken place at Covent Garden when Macready responded to the first curtain call. . . . Since then the curtain call and speech have become stock features of theatrical performances, and have so developed that they have formed a separate history of their own."

In the "Erminie" revival Hopper and I knew that a speech would be expected, but we were so busy rehearsing that we put off consulting about it. At last, time pressing, we sat down for the consideration of what some people were rude enough to say was the best thing in the performance. This is how it was planned:

"What are you going to say? What have you in mind?" I asked Hopper.

"Nothing in particular, except to jest about your name — Francis — if you don't mind," he replied.

"Not at all," I said, "if in return, I may poke a little fun at yours."

It was not too difficult to walk out to the audience and say a few conventional somethings along the line agreed upon, but what would be the exit? That puzzled us for a moment. Finally, we agreed that having said nothing as brilliantly as we could, we would declare our intention of withdrawing to think up something worth saying. That was as much, or as little thread as we had to weave what gradually grew into a ten-minute curtain talk which gave a great deal of pleasure, judging from the shouts of laughter it provoked. Two things in the speech made for its success — the slight element of truth in the personalities indulged in, and the appearance of shocked surprise and astonishment each of us gave at the audacity of the reflections. No matter how often the speech was given, the illusion had to be lent that it was being spoken for the first time, or the effect would be lost. Let me say, to the credit of the principals, that not once during the

entire season did that speech come tardy off. Hopper
and I not only enjoyed it, but we especially enjoyed the
public's enjoyment of it.

Not we, but the audience, really made that speech.
We experimented nightly with it until they told us that
it was about what they wanted, and then we let it alone
— even while changing it, paradoxical as that may
seem. It was thenceforth always the same speech —
but ever different.

We came on the stage as if merely to bow, grew
puzzled at the heartiness of the applause, edged forward, as if impelled to speak. Now, in pantomime, it
became a question as to who should begin. With
deference, Hopper said shyly:

"I think you should speak first." Nodding my
thanks to him, I advanced and began with:

"Ladies and Gentlemen: Among the very agreeable—" I stopped, as if feeling that I had been too swift
to accept the courtesy of speaking first, and, turning to
Hopper, I indicated that perhaps he should make the
opening remarks. Somewhat provoked that I should
have thought it at all necessary to halt, being under
way, he insisted that I should go on.

"But why?" I asked.

"There is a reason why you should speak first," he
replied.

"What reason?" I inquired, much puzzled.

"For one thing," said Hopper, "your name is first
on the printing. Heaven knows why it should be, but
it is!" — which he delivered as if not at all sorry for the

chance to say it. Here the audience entered delightfully into the situation, keen and curious to know
where such a lead might end. Feeling that the remark
was one that should have been left unmade, I replied
soothingly:

"Somebody's name had to be first. Probably mine
got there by mistake," whereupon Hopper sniffed a
trifle contemptuously.

"Then there is another reason," he went on, as one
bound to speak his mind.

"Another reason?"

"Yes, and a potent one." This is a phrase much to
Hopper's taste at all times. "What 'potent' reason?"
I sent back.

"I hesitate to mention it before all these people," he
retorted.

Venturing to take up the Hopper manner and
method, I replied by saying:

"Cease to hesitate, give vent."

"Well, then — you are the older!"

This came to me as a great shock, and with rising
indignation the more the audience seemed to enjoy my
discomfiture. Being a palpable hit, it had, of course, to
be countered. I prolonged my indignation until I could
think of a fitting reply. It came. Not as I wished it, at
first, but ultimately as:

"What do you mean by 'older'? Older! I couldn't
keep the gray out of my hair, but I kept it out of my
heart and legs — which was the best I could do." Said
with feeling by a little gray-headed fellow who had

been picked upon by a black-headed giant, this was warmly greeted. It was a phrase that went the rounds of the press. When the audience had got through laughing and applauding, Hopper set them going again by sneering:

"Mush!"

Not to be denied full indulgence in my indignation, I went on with:

"Older! I don't know about being older, Mr. Whopper! I remember that my father used to take me to see you play when I wore pantalettes."

"And now, having reached second childhood," retorted Hopper, "you are still wearing the pantalettes."

The allusion was evident in the white lace ruffle of "Cadeau's" knee-breeches, one leg of which would insist upon falling to the ankle. Though the quarrel was patched up in a few words, Hopper seemed unable to maintain peaceful relations, for, taking the audience into his confidence, he began to chuckle, and with much disdain, finally said:

"Francis! Did you ever hear of such a silly name for a *man?*" and off he went into a gale of laughter, carrying the audience with him, "It's a *girl's* name!" he insisted. "Why," he continued, "he gets letters from corset manufacturers all over the country!"—which was not far from the fact. This last sally of Hopper's amused the women part of the audience intensely. But the climax of his lance-breaking came when he keeled over the audience with:

"Why, lots of people think he's my wife!"

Now, whether because the audience thought it daring for the much-married Hopper to allude to a little matter like a wife, or were amused at the expression of amazement with which I received the astonishing declaration, or both, which is most likely, certain it is the result was a tremendous roar of laughter. Nor was it lessened when, struggling to repress my outraged feelings, I was able to exclaim:

"Oh, God forbid!"

Defending Francis as a name, I now made a few inquiries as to the DeWolf part of Hopper's name, about which I had always been curious.

"Tell me," I asked, "is that your maiden name?"

After recovering from his amusement at my ignorance, he explained learnedly his relation to the wolf that had suckled Romulus and Remus and from whom, or which, his name had been acquired. At this juncture it was thought advisable to remind each other that, inasmuch as the call before the curtain was likely to be made at each performance — Hopper injecting the information that it had never yet failed to be demanded — instead of indulging in personalities, it would be but courteous to thank the audience, which should have been done at the beginning, in a few well-chosen words. In endeavoring to carry out that suggestion, another outbreak was threatened by Hopper declaring that I was stereotyped in expression and should say something scintillating and refreshing, which he patronizingly intimated I was able to do. I replied that it was the fear of being conventional that made me feel that he,

Hopper, should speak first, and I was not surprised to find him in full accord. We finally decided that the exact thing we needed was:

Hopper

A brief —

Wilson

Impromptu —

Hopper

Extemporaneous appreciation, a fleeting something born of the moment.

And, then, thoroughly pleased at having discovered what was required, we told of our intention to set about the composition of a masterly impromptu speech to be given the next time we were honored with a call before the curtain.

Like the words of some orators who electrify their auditors and yet whose speeches read tamely enough the next morning, this little bit of stage raillery seems a mere nothing, as I review it. Yet it was a tiny drama in itself. A trifle of fooling that more than paid for itself in the pleasure it gave, in the laughter it evoked.

It would be difficult to meet a more companionable man than the multi-married DeWolf Hopper — a great big good-natured susceptible boy! — one whose philosophy has never permitted him to take anything too seriously, especially trouble. After his enthusiasm for baseball, I think perhaps his most marked characteristic is sympathy. If he feels sorry, he wants to throw his arms about you and say so. If I were distressed about anything, or in pain, as I was in Milwaukee, where I had the misfortune to be bowled over by an automobile, he would hover over me like a Gargantuan mother, waving his huge arms as if ready at any moment to snatch me up from further danger. He so Couéd me out of the belief that I was hurt and unable to play that I actually went through a week's performances when I should have been in bed.

I never knew an actor more loyal to an audience than Hopper. Again and again he dared to face the people with his big voice reduced by cold or congestion to a tiny whisper, yet, somehow, he carried on to the end which found him quite buoyant while the rest of us were worn out with the fear we had had that he might break down. He has one great love that exceeds any affection that he has ever known, a passion for poly-syllables. Any sentence which does not contain at least one of these is not for Hopper. Many-sectioned words roll from the man as the conventional water rolls off the back of the conventional duck. It is a picturesque expression full of vivid contrasts at which one marvels, but it is not strained and seems to go with the big body and vibrant voice.

Hopper is fond of the pleasures of the table. He would sometimes reach the theater regretting that he had not had an additional hour or two for a more leisurely digestion.

"If ever you see anybody of prominence in the audience," he said to me once, "let me know, won't you. It bucks me up."

Thereafter, we had as auditors an increasing number

of distinguished people. This worked very well until I happened to mention as being present some one who had been dead for weeks, but whose passing on had escaped my, but not Hopper's, attention. I lost caste with him at once as a teller of truths.

On a night in Philadelphia, as the melodies were being repeated in the finale, I said to him in half voice: "Another performance over."

"Yes," he replied; "do you observe how swiftly we approach the termination of our existence? Say, Frawncis, hereafter, let's play the piece slower!"

I had gone to the theater in Cleveland in search of that joy of the traveling actor — the mail. It is the actor's severest disappointment to arrive in a new place of endeavor to find no letter to greet him! As I approached the box office to make my inquiry, two women swished by me in evident anger. One said:

"Three dollars and thirty cents for a seat!"

"Yes," replied her equally angry companion, "and they are both old men!"

When I repeated this to Hopper that night, he put his head on top of his make-up box and groaned.

At Minneapolis I went with a friend, Dr. Richard Burton, to a matinée performance of the local stock company. We sat well down toward the stage. Two strangers came in and occupied seats immediately in front of us. As they were taking off their overcoats, one said to the other:

"Have you seen the Hopper show yet?"

"No, not yet; but they tell me it is great."

"It sure is," responded the first speaker. "He has a little fellow with him named Wilson who is very clever."

Hopper was telling the incident to some friends.

Said one: "Oh, *don't* tell that to Mr. Wilson!"

"Why, you poor Fish" (the gentleman's name), "Wilson told it to me!" Hopper replied.

Richard Mansfield was one of Hopper's admirations. On witnessing a performance of "Dr. Jekyll and Mr. Hyde," and having been thrilled by the sudden transformation by the actor from the gracious "Jekyll" to the hideous "Hyde," Hopper rushed back to Mansfield's dressing-room to offer his congratulations.

"Mar-vel-ous, Dick! Mar-vel-ous! Simply cyclonic!" cried the enthusiastic Hopper. "How *did* you do it?" Sitting under the green-shaded light of his room, Mansfield instantly repeated the transformation. Taken wholly by surprise, Hopper caught his breath, steadied himself, and paid Mansfield a fine compliment in the following original manner:

"You d——d rascal!" he exclaimed. "If you ever frighten me again like that, I'll never speak to you as long as I live!"

The revival of "Erminie" afforded the people of my profession an opportunity to pay me a great honor, the public presentation of a silver loving-cup bearing flattering inscriptions. I strove, feebly enough, to say how I felt about it, but such things are never told. They can only be felt. The gift came about through small contributions from a number of players. My professional comrades believed that I had rendered them service in devoting a number of years to better the conditions under which they had been laboring. Few of them have realized what a labor of love mine was, and fortunate it was for me that they should have postponed the adjustment of their long-standing grievances until I could be of assistance.

I have ever adored a contest. This was very much to my liking. The odds were overwhelmingly against success. There were picturesque and dramatic features — managerial steeds pawing the earth, sniffing the battle from near and afar; humorous and enthusiastic actors overflowing with newborn determination, wide-eyed and confident after their Rip Van Winkle sleep of twenty years or more; surges of disappointment followed by waves of discouragement, and then the thrill of conquest, success! It seems to me that not the actors but I should have presented the loving-cup filled with gratitude for my opportunity to serve. From an out-of-town paper there follows a description of the presentation:

The first night of the revival in New York was turned into one of those occasions that keeps the street corners and the curbstones of the theater district abuzz next day. Within five minutes of the opera's conclusion, and just as Caddy and Ravvy were about to be turned over to the police, some one stopped the performance to report that the "house was full of the prisoners' confederates." Whereupon Mrs. Whiffen, in the costume of the old Southern lady in "Just Suppose," walked into view, followed by Laurette Taylor, as "Peg"; Fred Stone, straight from "Tip Top," Frank Bacon as the "Bill Jones" or "Lightnin'," and John Drew.

Mr. Drew, being in what his reviewers used to speak of as "immaculate evening dress," explained that he was just a young fellow who had stepped in off the street "to see what the stage of a theater was like."

This committee was followed by John Emerson, the new president of the Actors' Equity, his right arm raised to quiet the tumult, his left arm encircling a silver loving cup, which looked to be about twice as big as the one Sir Thomas Lipton has been trying to lift for so many years.

Followed speeches in which Mr. Hopper told Mr. Wilson how much everybody loved him, especially the actors whom he had so successfully led through the strike of 1918, and Mr. Wilson with tears in his voice, replied that this was the greatest and proudest and most affecting moment of his life — which, undoubtedly it was. After which some one started the finale, and the performance was concluded.

Earlier in the chapter, I gave as one of the reasons for return to the stage the desire to have my son meet some one in later years who had seen his father play. But strange to say, the little tike took matters into his own hands, made my stage acquaintance for himself, and even took part in the stage performance, though inadvertently. At a matinée in Boston, Hopper and I were called before the curtain as usual for a speech. As we stood pantomiming each other to begin, the house meanwhile in perfect silence, that very small boy of two and a half, who had been watching the play from a box, where he sat engulfed in the velvet folds of a huge armchair, created much laughter and applause by piping up in a clear childish treble:

"Jump down here, Daddy!"

Having now had an opportunity to revisit the chief cities of the country, to regreet old friends and acquaintances and to revive affectionate memories, I had little joy in the prospect of the professional grind of a cross-

THE LOVING CUP

country tour to California. But there seemed no way out of it. One came, however, in the shape of an unheated dressing-room in St. Louis where, November 21, 1921, we began what was to be, likely, my final appearance in "Erminie."

With the weather at a low point, I caught cold, developed temperature, and was bowled off to a hospital, having given St. Louis but three performances of a promised eight. Never having been ill before in my life, that I remember, this was a depressing experience. Told that I had earned the right to be careful of my health, I became apprehensive.

The papers were pessimistic. I was a more interesting item of news close to death than if merely ill. They declared that a major operation was pending, that the outcome was doubtful. This was no encouragement whatever to a man sixty-seven years young. In two or three days I had reasserted myself and was the joy of the medical staff. I was ready to resume playing. Such, however, was not to be. I was significantly advised that it was imperative that I undergo a series of health tests. This I did with honor, if not distinction, and, with a skillful minor operation by Dr. Bransford Lewis, upon whom later I revenged myself at golf, I was whole once more, but too late to rejoin my companions, who, drifting on without me, finally halted altogether.

Like a prisoner who had earned liberty for good conduct, I was permitted during my month's stay at Saint John's hospital, to stroll outside for air and exercise. One day, passing the half-opened door of a patient yellow with jaundice, or blood poisoning, I halted to extend a word of cheer. He was grateful and became communicative. Could I do any errand for him?

"For gawdsake, pard, bring me back a cigarette!"

"What kind?" I asked.

"Aw, it don't make no difference to me. Just a cigarette!" he replied.

I got a package, but in fear of going contrary to orders, I ventured on his having one on learning that the doctor "hadn't give no orders about the weed." As I started to leave the room he said, as he puffed in languid enjoyment: "Say, you're all right"; but there was a lack of heartiness in his tone due, doubtless, to my unwillingness to let him have the entire package. As he survived the night, I contributed another cigarette, which served as an excuse for a new call. He was pleased, or seemed so. I waved to him daily from my window on seeing him propped up in his cot. With the prospect of an operation — even though a minor one — I forgot all about my new-found friend for a day or two. Before daylight on the morning of my first appearance on any operating table, my door was quietly pushed open. By aid of the dim night-lamp I recognized my cigarette-loving friend.

"Say, pard, they tell me they are goin' to do things to you this morning."

I admitted it.

"Well," he continued, "you never can tell what'll

happen, so before you went, I thought I'd drop in to see if you had any more of them cigarettes left."

"You'll find the package in the top drawer of the bureau there," I directed from my bed.

"Can I have what's left?" he asked.

"Yes."

"Every one of them!" he said.

"Every one," I repeated.

"Say, you're a prince!" he replied heartily.

He found the package, and, selecting a cigarette, put the others into the pocket of his dressing-gown. We chatted a few moments. He took his leave of me with this phrase of encouragement:

"Say, pard, don't be scared. Them fellows upstairs know how to bite. But I guess you're all right, anyway. So-long!"

The next day but one, he was not in his cot by the window, for I had my bed wheeled up for his greeting. On inquiry, I learned that friends had come for him, that he had gone, and was well on his way to recovery. The nurse told me laughingly that he had left his love "for that guy in number 315."

After my fright and my month in a hospital, it was a real joy to reach home again, which happened "jest afore Christmas." Next day I had occasion to speak quickly to my small boy who had had a collision with his tiny sister. Taking me by the hand he led me silently along the hallway to the door, and said:

"Go straight back to the hospital!"

CHAPTER XVII

A WORD TO BEGINNERS

INCREASINGLY, a number of young people, noting the fame and fortune gained by those no better endowed than themselves, as they believe — and often correctly — are taking up the stage as a profession. In childhood they have played at tiny dramas in the nursery, belonged to amateur theatric associations in adolescence, have felt the universality of the dramatic instinct, and, with the innate ability they are confident they possess — all great actors must have begun with the same confidence — they cannot understand that that instinct should not be obeyed.

Doing their own thinking these ambitious youngsters find it impossible to reconcile parental and grandparental prejudices with open knowledge. They realize that a profession so much to their liking is not to be ignored as a vocation because its followers work with head instead of hand. They even find this a recommendation. From their association with it for charity, for fun, or for love, they have come to know something of its difficulties and much of its beauty and attraction. With the innocence and necessity of all amusements now generally recognized, they note well that the positive instead of the negative influence of the public is fully enlisted in behalf of the theater. They are not at all unmindful of the large space in the press and the deep interest actors and acting occupy in the public mind, and with appraising eye and longing heart, they especially note the knighthoods, decorations, honors, fame and fortune conferred on many actors. It is not at all surprising, then, that a number of young men and women of all classes should prefer to make the effort to share these benefits rather than dawdle through life, accept a place in the counting-house, finger-point at the typewriter, or apprentice themselves to necktie-cutting or to other occupations for which they have neither appetite nor taste.

For women the stage is especially alluring. Besides acclaim, there is always the seductive chance of marriage with royalty, or with some king of finance, or with some prince of letters, or, perchance, a Charles Lamb for the refusal of a Fanny Kelly. No soul-mate is less attractive because of family or wealth or mentality. And it has happened that when wealth has flown, the actress-wife has become the family's chief support. Sometimes, too, the wife so surpasses the husband in public affection that he is known by her name, as — Mr. Sarah Siddons. Too great a fame in an actress may thus dull the chances of a "great" marriage.

This is to be said of the drama and acting: there is likely no profession in the world which offers so many startling and unexpected opportunities for advancement both to the talented and the mediocre player. Progress toward success may be summed up in two words — ability and opportunity. Readiness to take advantage of opportunity often explains the sudden leap into public favor made by actors. This readiness involves study and understudy, willingness and alertness, the very price, of course, the ambitious only are willing to pay.

In the drama, as said, the prizes go to the "gifted and beautiful." However, the theater has its plodders, many of them, as have medicine, law, and the ministry. If with the talented readiness is the great necessity, so plodding mediocrity requires industry. An intelligent, reliable man or woman with presentable appearance, and some aptitude, even though lacking distinctive individuality, may gain an excellent livelihood and a position of respect. Macready's father was such a plodder. After ten years' service at Drury Lane he retired to provincial management. It was then said of him:

> Though than M'Cready there are many better,
> Who, pray, like him, so perfect to a letter?

Though being "perfect to a letter" always brings a "steady job," it gathers no great wealth — and no knighthoods.

Few things are more important than the choice of an occupation. A false start so delays one's chance of success in other directions. Before deciding, then, one ought to place one's cards face upward on the table. This done, there will be far less chance of misapprehension as to the play. If ever there were a time when one should be honest with one's self it is at this moment. In adopting the stage as a profession, account of stock ought to be taken, so to speak, and a searching and pitiless examination of one's qualities and accomplishments should be made, because what one is, what one can do, has a more intimate association with one than is the case in other professions. Defeat is ever tragic. Defeat as an actor is particularly so, because one's pride, personal, intellectual, and spiritual, is so completely demolished.

The painter's canvas, the sculptor's marble, and the musician's compositions may be criticized apart from the artist. But not so the actor. He is his own medium. It is his intimate, personal self in conjunction with his efforts that must come in for comment by those "present and voting." It is this which makes commendation so sweet and dispraise so bitter.

Few young men and women seeking the stage as a profession stop to consider fully the requirements for such an undertaking. The most many of them realize is that they have youth, looks, and tremendous ambition, three wonderful qualities.

It is the nature of youth not to appreciate the struggle, rebuffs, and infinite toil lying between it and the realization of its ambitions. And, too, youth has a disconcerting way of knowing all about the exceptional few who, by reason of possessing extraordinary qualities, have stepped over the heads of their confrères and, at a single bound, have reached the top.

The recruit should know at once that no man on the stage becomes a public favorite, and remains one, without qualities that entitle him to that position. Back of all artists who have won the attention and admiration of the world there is an indefinable something, a gift, that has come to him at birth. This endowment has been given various names; such as: personal magnetism, fascination, enchantment, attraction, etc.

Somewhere, wondering what caused one of his characters to succeed where another of a more plodding nature had failed, Barrie calls this quality "that damned charm," which is about as good a definition as we shall ever have of it. Call it what we may, but if, in one's equipment as an actor, one has the power to charm, one goes far. If he is also studious, he goes farther still. If the elements have not been so mixed in him at birth that this property be included, then the gods have but made faces at him. If it come about that such a person should choose acting as his profession, he will never reach the top.

What Lewes saw on one of his visits to the theaters of Paris is quite possible to see in almost any theatrical season in New York; that is, an almost or quite unknown actor standing out in a performance because of the possession of an attractive personality.

"On his very first appearance," says Lewes, of Montal, whom he saw in "Vingt Ans Après," "as he stood silent in the background, there was no mistaking that an impressive actor was before us. He had the rare power of being silently eloquent; of standing quite still and yet riveting attention on himself. . . . So effective were his make-up, looks, and manners, that on quitting the theater, and for many days afterwards, my imagination was haunted by the vision."

Having the power, "the rare power of being silently eloquent, of standing quite still yet riveting attention," is not to be acquired in the theater, whatever one's industry. It is an individual possession, a gift, and one either has it, or has it not. The measure, then, of one's success as an actor depends upon the possession or non-possession of this quality.

"No man can make progress," says Henry Irving, in his preface to "Talma, or the Actor's Art," "until he has mastered a certain mechanism which is within the scope of patient intelligence. Beyond that is the sphere in which magnetic personality exercises a power of sympathy which is irresistible and indefinable." And in the introduction to William Gillette's "The Illusion of the First Time in Acting," George Arliss says of this personality in connection with the actor: "It is part of him as he speaks and lives and has his being. He didn't put it there in order to be noticed; he didn't even know he had it until we told him so."

It is important, then, for the beginner to discover whether or not he has this quality. Without it, he starts woefully handicapped in his effort to achieve distinction as an actor. But how is he to make such a discovery? It is not an easy matter. A strong indication would be that if in private life people seem to gravitate toward him for no apparent reason, or in relating an occurrence or telling an anecdote he enlists the eager attention of his listeners. Another absolutely certain way of determining if one has this precious gift is one's power, on a golf course, to make a sensitive "duffer" forget his misery long enough to listen to "a good story." However, in making such a test as this, one should be prepared to risk personal injury.

Seriously, earnestness, energy, modesty, delicacy, enthusiasm, great good health, and tact are comprised in personality, but there is something else besides, an indefinable quality, like a sourceless light making all radiant. Even those wise enough to imitate these qualities go farther than those who ignore them. This wonderful gift has been an integral part of every great character the world has known, from Cæsar to Napoleon and from Napoleon to Roosevelt, and, despite all that may be said to the contrary, it is a gift and never an acquisition.

The second qualification of the actor should be power of perception and emotion; sensibility it is called. Like the sensitized plate in photography, the actor should be capable at will of receiving and giving off impressions of human characteristics and subtle peculiarities. Many examples could be given. Two or three will suffice. Leaving a dock on a boating expedition, Garrick swore at some laborers on shore in order to note the effect. He got the effect, but was nearly swamped for his pains. The outraged workmen not only showed great anger, as Garrick hoped, but nearly sunk his boat by the huge stones they threw at it. "Charley" Backus, the minstrel, told me of a similar instance. Standing on the platform of a train as it was leaving the station, he "swore horribly" at a burly individual who had come to see his family off. To Backus's delight, the man became frantic, swore back, and raced vainly after the departing train while Backus goaded him with taunts, observing keenly the man's actions and speech. Presently the train stopped, and then slowly backed into the station. Backus locked himself in the washroom and stayed there until the train was again well on its way. In searching after impressions of rage, anger, etc., the too ambitious may pay dearly for their whistle.

In further illustration of the above, I have always greatly enjoyed the anecdote as told by Knight of Garrick and his friend Préville, the French comedian, Garrick's "compagnon en ivresse," returning from a trip on horseback to the Bois de Boulogne. About to enter the village of Passy, Garrick suggested that they imitate drunkenness. They did so. Not a word was spoken, but the village was emptied, to see two intoxicated cavaliers. Young folk derided them, women cried out for fear they would fall from their horses, and old men shrugged their shoulders in pity, or burst into laughter, according to their temperaments.

"How have I acquitted myself, O master?" said Préville, as they issued from the village.

"Well, very well," said Garrick, "but you were not drunk in your legs."

It was Garrick's acuteness of perception that enabled him to detect the flaw in Préville's effort, a flaw, we may be sure, that was not present in his own.

Not long since was seen a similar instance in neglect of details. When the incomparable Duse gave her touching portrayal of The Mother in "Cosa Sia," at the Century Theater (November, 1923), The Blind One and The Cripple were well done by Gallio and Robert, respectively. When still in view of the audience, and while calling their grateful adieus to The Mother as they were leaving the stage, each, apparently, became so engrossed in the farewells, or in the finish of the scene, as no longer to be blind of eye or crippled of leg.

If to personality and sensibility one can add aptitude and enthusiasm, radiant enthusiasm, and then crown all with industry, golden industry, one will find himself perfectly equipped for the art of acting. But the beginner should not be too discouraged if, in his self-analysis a quality here and there should be found missing. An authority says that Charles Mathews could not laugh heartily, and that the renowned William Farren had no gayety, no geniality, and, most extraordinary for a comedian, had no unction. By the same critic, Macready was thought to be a poor "Hamlet" whose passion degenerated into irritability, though he could not be excelled for tenderness, in other rôles.

Most stage aspirants are convinced that if given but a chance to appear before an audience they would instantly touch it with fire, and be wafted back waves of lucific appreciation. Such a thing is possible, but attended with considerable risk. Audiences on such occasions have been known to do more heaving than waving.

To those who wish to adopt the stage from mere fancy, or from motives of vanity, Punch's advice to those who are about to marry seems pertinent: "Don't." Ethel Barrymore adopted it "to earn a living," as seemed natural to one in her position, she tells us. That is always a reason. A better one would have been the fulfillment of an irresistible impulse. Others, again, "take up" with the stage as they would "take up" with marriage, because of accident, propinquity, and even affection. Strangely enough, so fascinating is the calling, that once having ventured, few players ever regard themselves unsuited to it. All are determined to do or die. The unexpected arrives so constantly that even the least successful seldom abandon hope. Stage history is rife with accounts of failure after failure followed ultimately by success.

The uncomfortable thing about learning to act is that all one's efforts are made in public. Of course one blunders at first, and the publicity of the thing makes it doubly humiliating. If one makes an apprentice mistake in compounding a prescription, nothing but death may result. A gentle reproof in private may follow. But on the stage, if one fails to take up his cue, or sends an audience into gales of laughter when it should be in tears, or is unable to speak because his tongue cleaves to the roof of his mouth, one gets laughed at publicly, which is a much more serious matter. There is no balm in Gilead for that. A few such catastrophes give the beginner the feeling of which Napoleon spoke when he said that one soon grows old on the field of battle.

Under such grueling performances, one cannot easily recover one's equanimity.

Such occurrences as the following are not likely to happen nowadays, because of the non-existence of the traveling star, formerly a part of each season's routine in many stock companies, but they were not infrequent in "the palmy days."

One of these stars was C. W. Couldock, the English tragedian and character actor who had come first to America in support of Charlotte Cushman. Couldock was a talented actor possessing a fiery temper under no control whatever. Clara Morris tells us[1] that while he was filling one of his annual engagements at Cleveland, an actor, John Ogden, playing the small part of "Salanio" in "The Merchant of Venice," "in some way had given offense to Couldock." The next day, after rehearsal, Ogden was asked to look in at his (Couldock's) dressing-room that evening before the play began. Poor John was uneasy all the afternoon; still he drew some comfort from the calmness of Mr. Couldock's manner. Evening came and John was before the bar. The star was particularly gentle. He removed his coat leisurely and said:

"You played 'Salanio,' last?"

"Yes, sir."

"And your name is — er?"

"Ogden, sir," replied John.

"Ah, yes, Ogden. Well, how long have you been at it, Ogden?"

[1] *Life on the Stage.*

"About three years," answered the now confident and composed prisoner at the bar.

"Three years, huh! Well, will you let me give you a little bit of advice, Ogden?"

"Why, yes, sir, I shall be glad to listen to any advice from you," earnestly protested the infatuated one.

"Well," snapped the star rather sharply, "I want you to follow it as well as listen to it. Now, you take some money — you *have* some money saved, I suppose? —"

"Oh, yes, sir!" answered John.

"Well, then" — he turned his queer eye on him, he took a long, full breath — "well, then, you just get some of that money, and go to a hardware store" — his rage was rising visibly — "and you buy a good sharp hatchet, and then I want you to take it home and chop your d——d fool head off!"

Contrary to the opinion of many people, I do not believe that the best way to proceed in order to become an actor is to secure an engagement, "however small," in some stock company and rough out one's technique, as miners rough out the precious metal. That is one way, the old conventional way to do it, and good actors have been developed as a result, but I believe it to be a crude, hazardous way. The development has come, I feel, despite the method, as strong children survive neglect.

The ideal way to go on the stage is to begin by selecting grandparents who have served long and honorable apprenticeships in acting, grandparents possessing the power to transmit aptitude, if nothing else. Failing grandparents, the second choice is parents of that character having great pride in their profession and confident that, by the law of average, if nothing else, their immediate descendants are destined to take high rank in the acting world.

What if the beginner is unable to select his grandparents, or parents, and is to be forbidden the stage as a child, under proper guardianship? How is he to compass his object, and satisfy an ambition which refuses to be denied? Shall he attach himself to one of the stock companies now established in many of the smaller cities of the country, cities which the better traveling companies find it too unremunerative to visit? Given my choice, I should do no such thing. To be sure, it is a cheaper method and, oftentimes, the only one open to the beginner, but, as pointed out, it subjects the student to no end of humiliation. Just as where there is no sympathy there is no real criticism, so where there is no sensitiveness there is no real acting, and I would have no sensitive person so shamed and humbled. There are few or no actors who have begun in this stock-company way who have not lifelong remembrances of such humiliations.

There are now dramatic schools intelligently conducted which have many advantages over the older system of training the beginner. These schools systematically and progressively teach the rudiments of acting, a knowledge of which was demanded of the

major members of a stock company, and bludgeoned
into beginners. To my thinking, then, one is much
better off with a two years' study of the history of one's
art, together with such practice as one gains acting
en amateur, frequently before competent, professional
judges, than those who, ignorant of such rudiments and
devoid of such practice, begin at once with professional
acting.

There is, too, much to be hoped for in this respect in
the fact that our universities, after progressive and
helpful experience in teaching play-writing, as at
Harvard, are now taking up the matter of play-acting,
as at Columbia. Of course no university can teach
play-writing or play-acting. Neither is an exact science.
Both are arts. But a school or a university, properly
equipped, may put the student in the way of skillfully
doing either — provided he has aptitude or genius for
the undertaking.

In schools of acting one pays to learn and blunder
privately. By the other method, going into a stock
company, one is paid to learn and blunder publicly. In
the first instance, one does what he is naturally expected
to do, in the way of awkwardness. In the second, he is
doing what nobody wants him to do, especially the
audience, and he is damned if he does it. The difference
lies in holding up one's head, or in hanging it down.

It is a difficult thing to get an engagement in any
company unless one has had stage experience, which is
not to be had unless one acts on the stage. The Gordian
knot is cut by attending a school of acting whose

graduates are infinitely more acceptable to managers than those who have had no instruction, or no experience. Some of our most promising young men and women at the present time on the stage have come from schools of acting. Care should be taken in selecting the school. Elocutionists who combine the teaching of their "art" with that of acting are to be mistrusted, because most elocutionists are without experience in acting. Retired actors who combine the teaching of both arts are also to be looked at askance, because likely to engraft personal peculiarities upon pupils. Besides, either study is too big to permit the intrusion of the other for purposes of combined instruction.

The tyro should know something about his voice, at least how to produce it. It need not have the cultivation that a prima donna's voice requires, but if one wishes to retain that voice for any length of time as a professional instrument, one will need to be taught how not to impair it. A dozen lessons from a master, not a fakir, will be sufficient. Masters of this kind are scarce and do not travel with theatrical companies, nor do they necessarily ally themselves with stock companies or schools of acting. It is understood, of course, that one must have a voice to cultivate.

A sympathetic voice in an actor is an absolute necessity, a primal requisite. Voice is his chief means of communicating with his audience. The less that voice appeals, the less the impression. This is equally true in private life. It is through voice, facial expression, and gesture that the great gift of personality

works its charm. It cannot be said too emphatically
that the actor who, possessing a magnetic personality,
a sympathetic voice, emotional change of expression,
and graceful gesture, and refuses to crown them with
industry, is but a gifted mental loafer. These qualities,
including industry, are rarely found in a single individual, but when so found, we meet a Forrest, a Booth,
a Charlotte Cushman.

Perhaps the most beautiful, most powerful voice our
stage has known was that of Edwin Forrest. Edwin
Booth's voice was not less beautiful, though less powerful. People in all spheres of life — auditors, musicians,
and critics — sang the praise of Forrest's voice. I have
heard James E. Murdock and Frank Mayo, famous
actors with beautiful voices of their own, rave about it.
Twice as a boy, I heard it myself at the Walnut Street
Theater, in Philadelphia, in "Metamora" and "Jack
Cade," and the memory of it still lives with me.
Forrest was such a conscientious student that he would
not admit that his wonderful voice was a natural gift.

"The world thinks," he told Alfred Ayres, "that my
voice is God-given. Not at all. It is the product of
culture, practice. When I went on the stage, I got Dr.
Rush's book and studied it. When I didn't understand
anything I went to Dr. Rush and got him to explain it.
Then I practiced. That's how I came by my voice."
He did not place much of the credit where it belonged,
which is nothing new to the Almighty.

Among the voices on the stage of my time, I liked
Ada Rehan's. It had a soft, velvety quality, and seemed

easily under control to express many shades of subtle thought and emotion. And what a comédienne she was! After seeing her as Katherine, in "Taming of the Shrew," Irving declared her a great actress. And that she was, indeed, both in comedy and serious drama. How delightfully she could sparkle in the former, and how convincing she could be in the latter! A beautiful woman, too, and charmingly modest. In the height of her career, a bust of her was placed on exhibition. She was eager to see it after the sculptor had given it the final touch. It was interesting to watch how carefully she avoided it until there was no one by, and the furtive glances she shot in its direction until the coast was clear for her inspection. Over many years what a favorite, what a joy she was to the loyal frequenters of Daly's Theater, the legitimate competitor and successor to Wallack's. It was at Wallack's that the scholarly Richard Grant White insisted that one heard the best English spoken in America. Among the many lovely actresses whose talents were developed under Augustin Daly, from Agnes Ethel, Fanny Davenport, Clara Morris on down, none was more gifted, more worthy than Ada Rehan.

Any mention or discussion of fine voices on the stage would be incomplete which does not include the voice of Tomasso Salvini. It was a noble organ, rich, mellow, flexible, powerful, and of great range. In his tribute to Edwin Booth, at the Booth Commemoration Services, Madison Square Garden Concert Hall, November 13, 1893, the anniversary of Booth's sixtieth

ADA REHAN
For many years the keystone to the Daly Theater edifice

birthday, I thought I never heard anything so rich, so polished as the tones of the Italian tragedian's voice. However, I was less touched with the pathos of that tribute than with the beauty and glitter of its delivery.

Edwin Adams was another actor of my time with "a golden voice" of penetrating pathos. It was deep, rich, and possessed great carrying quality. Adams had won success as "Enoch Arden." It shortened his life. He was murdered by the social attentions of friends, convivial attentions which this able actor and man of many fine parts was unable to resist.

For want of voice I have seen the noblest dramatic intentions defeated. At a benefit performance, given at the Academy of Music for that gifted player "Tony" Hart, of Harrigan and Hart fame, an act of "Julius Cæsar" was presented. Stuart Robson was the "Brutus," William H. Crane the "Cassius," Nat C. Goodwin the "Marc Anthony," with Frank Mayo, Steele MacKaye, and a number of us making up the "mob" or playing the minor rôles. It was agreed that all should be done in the utmost seriousness. Goodwin came out the most victorious, Robson the most disgruntled. There was no doubt about his earnestness, and less about his determination, but both, alas! were defeated by his peculiar vocal squeak. The more he strove to induce the people to accept him gravely by riding over their laughter, the more they guffawed. Worn down with trying, and completely disgusted, he turned and swore at them — under cover of their laughter. Not being able to hear him, and supposing it was an additional part of his earnestness, they laughed the louder.

If one wishes to read how important the voice is to the actor in the estimate of one who himself was an actor, a dramatist, manager of Drury Lane Theater for many years, who became Poet Laureate of England, and finally wrote what many regard as the best of two or three theatrical super-excellent biographies, one should read what Colley Cibber has to say in his "Apology" of the voice of Thomas Betterton, "at a period of rant in the actor and fustian in the dramatist." "If there is no pathos in the tones," says Lewes, "the actor's soul may be a sob, yet we shall remain unmoved" — which is also much to consider. Richard Mansfield had a beautiful voice, with a tear, a shout, or a crackle of laughter in it, as he chose, while the voice of Julia Marlowe has had but few equals.

There is no question that voice is a prime factor in acting, but something more is required. One must have a knowledge of that which is the main reason for voice — speech. But, more important still, if one is going to be an actor one must be able to speak words and make gestures to accompany those words as if they were being spoken and being made for the first time. And what an art that is! Lending this illusion of the first time is one of the strong creative qualifications of the actor's art.

Anybody, not an idiot, may memorize lines and repeat them. Repeating them as if they rose to the lips from the mind and heart for the first time is quite another thing again. A body of actors would like no richer enjoyment than to witness the attempt, of those fond of denying creative quality to acting, to accomplish this illusion. But that would scarcely be a fair test. "Every man to his trade," as Edwin Booth penciled against the paragraph in which Lewes challenged Macready to edit and illustrate, from the wealth of his experience, an edition of Shakespeare.

Nor is this illusion the only creative force the actor brings to bear upon the play. While it is true the author creates the characters, there are myriads of illustrative actions emanating from the mind and soul of the gifted actor in the representation of a character which he alone could create and bring into play. For instance? A meaningful look of the eye, an eloquent pause, an equally eloquent gesture, and a wealth of inventive additions, multiplying with each performance, making for the success not only of the character but of the play — and of which the author never dreamed. Then there are illuminative repetitions of another character's speech in order to heighten an effect, and then come additions of exclamations not supplied by the author, but which cry aloud for inclusion, the reforming of speeches gaining force for the change, and, more often than given credit for or imagined, the addition of the electric word or speech which the author would have been only too happy to have given had it occurred to him.

Sometimes the author will have his manuscript returned to him at the end of a season with additions by the actor, and incorporated by the prompter, which were better omitted, but more often there is much there from the actor which in subsequent productions is never left out. Something of all this may be gathered from a letter Garrick wrote from Paris, in 1765. Speaking of his friend Préville, the comedian of the Théâtre Français whom we have previously mentioned. He says: "His genius never appears to such advantage as when the author leaves him to shift for himself; it is then Préville supplies the poet's deficiencies, and will throw a truth and brilliancy into his character which the author never imagined."

As Brander Matthews has pointed out: "The younger Dumas, in the preface to the 'Père Prodigue,' declared dramatic effect to be sometimes so intangible that the spectator cannot find in the printed text the point which delighted him in the performance of a play and which was due perhaps to 'a word, a look, a gesture, a silence, a purely atmospheric condition.' It is too often forgotten, or not known at all, that the actor alone supplies these intangible effects, these atmospheric, electric conditions."

Nor are authors backward in acknowledging their indebtedness to actors in this respect, as, even abating the enthusiasm of success and praise of the moment, Dumas's expressions of gratitude to Mademoiselle Clairon and Victor Hugo's compliments to Lemaître attest. Speaking of Bret Harte's comedy of "Sue," which Annie Russell played in London, it was said by a sympathetic critic (J. T. Grein): "I admire Bret Harte, the novelist, but in this case the actress is the thing. There are moments in this simple little story of Sue's awakening to love when we are pitched and tossed from laughter to sobs which are nothing short of exquisite." And Bronson Howard said that he did not realize how good a play he had written, in "The Banker's Daughter," until Charles R. Thorne had acted in it. There is no wish here to take away from the credit of the author without whom the actor would be reduced almost to impotency, but merely the desire to resent the charge of there being no creative power in the actor's art, by pointing out the great gulf lying between the conception of a character and its presentation, a gulf bridged by the actor.

Through the exercise of intelligence, through proper timing and pause, the actor permits the auditor to catch the full significance of what is being said and done, and lends the impression that the speaker is really thinking out his replies, and not racing them off by rote. By this the effect of naturalness and spontaneity is imparted. Jefferson got the greatest compliment and encouragement in this respect from a boy at a hotel table. Silent for a moment after he had been told that Jefferson was the man he had seen in "Rip Van Winkle," the boy, bubbling with delightful recollections, cried out: "Don't you remember that time when your gun fell apart?"

The gun had fallen apart thousands of times for Jefferson, but he was proud to know that he had made it fall apart for the boy as if for the first time.

Going bravely into a sentence, halting occasionally as if not too sure how you will round it out, a thoughtful "er, er," now and then, but still holding the confidence of the audience in your ability to bring it off, is a sample of what is meant by giving naturalness to speech on the stage. There are illimitable variations to the practice. There is no teacher for such things. None could be more instructive and profitable than one's self, if one could, or would, take note of one's self in the next conversation, or in observing critically some skilled orator or actor. For purposes of practice and reproduction, the observation should extend to one's own tones, alteration of voice, one's appearance and action in times of stress and sorrow, pleasure and joy. Talma, the great French tragedian, was dismayed to find he was doing just this, despite himself, and, of all places, at his mother's funeral. The artist overcame the man. Try as he would, he could not refrain from noting how he was affected by the sorrow of which he was the center. Willy-nilly, Talma was studying from nature — drinking in knowledge at the source. With his power to give off an impression once received, he could now depict this phase of grief, to the life.

However, we are told, and truly, that it makes no difference what the actor feels, "it is what he can express [that] gives him his distinctive value." I recall a sad confirmation of this fact. The Chestnut Street Theater, Philadelphia, in the 1870's was conducted by a number of public-spirited citizens. They wanted to see clean, classic plays at moderate prices. I had a season or two there in many old tragedies, comedies, and dramas, as mentioned. As the enterprise lagged, only one person, William D. Gemmill, held on to the management, to his financial undoing. He was an ambitious amateur, wrapped up heart and soul in the stage. He was, as well, a man of taste, refinement, and intelligence. As an actor, though he drank in all that the most sensitive soul could absorb of the drama, he could express — nothing. His acting as the tragic "Hamlet" was almost comic, and he was publicly advised as a manager to discharge himself as an actor. Thus cracked a noble heart!

This power to express a feeling, whether grave or gay, is described in vaudeville parlance as "getting it over." When the beginner has made several ineffectual efforts to "get it over," it is time to quit. He seldom or never does. And it is sometimes well that he does not, for as said, dramatic history is crowded with instances of victory after seemingly hopeless defeat. It is as if all disappointed players remembered that even the great Siddons was once dismissed for incompetency, and so they "carry on" hoping for ultimate success.

That was a pertinent inquiry of a certain manager who startled a company at rehearsal by advancing to the footlights in the auditorium (managers seldom venture on the stage at rehearsals!) and asking if the play were written in language.

"Why — er — yes," was the wondering reply.

"Then, I'd like to hear it," he said emphatically.

And that is the desire of the present-day audience

with respect to the play; they would like to hear it. Not as that particular manager wanted to hear it, rattled off like a fusillade, with no chance of light or shade in expression, but given with intelligence and taste.

If the public does not hear, or hears confusedly what the actor is saying, then author, public, actor, and manager suffer alike. The actor owes it, then, to all concerned to speak so that he may be heard and understood. That acting which in the interest of supposed naturalness turns its back upon the audience and speaks unintelligibly is not only unintelligible, but unintelligent.

To make one's self heard on the stage is not a matter of bellowing, nor yet of speaking like a continuous discharge of firearms. It is merely a question of correct reading; that is, with proper emphasis. Not personality, good looks, clothes, nor audacity will answer as a substitute. The speeches must be accurately stressed, then they will carry understanding and conviction. Here study and intelligence count. The supposed deafness of many theater-goers is to be explained by the false emphasis of actors. People do not understand what is being said and imagine they are becoming deaf.

Samuel Rogers says that Jack Bannister told him that one night he was behind the scenes when Garrick was playing "Lear," and that the tones in which Garrick uttered the words, "O fool, I shall go mad!" absolutely thrilled him. Imagine how impossible it would have been for "Davy" to produce that effect upon Bannister, or upon any one else, if, with the present-day stage practice of emphasizing pronouns, he had read: "O fool, *I* shall go mad!" Or, as a variant: "O fool, I *shall* go mad!"

The sin of false emphasis is not confined to the actors of our time. In her "Story of My Life," Ellen Terry tells humorously of Henry Irving eagerly seizing the opportunity of hearing Frances Anne Kemble read. He was delighted at the prospect of learning something of the famous "Kemble tradition" from an immediate descendant.

"Ham-a-lette," began the reader, and Irving was disheartened. Then swiftly followed one false reading after another, and Irving sat disillusioned, amazed. In the Closet Scene of the third act when Mrs. Kemble boomed out, "Let not thy mother lose *her* prayers, Ham-a-lette," there being no question of any one else's prayers, Irving was further startled. And when his ear was assaulted with "I shall in all respects obey *you*, Ham-a-lette," Irving stole away, refusing to accept what he had heard as a faithful reproduction of the "Kemble tradition."

It is saddening to sit in the theater and see the handsome, well-groomed, graceful young men and women actors — graceful, handsome old men and women actors, too, playing shuttlecock and battledore with misstressed words, and, so, hermetically sealing themselves into perpetual mediocrity. Nor have actors any monopoly of this failing. It is to be met with in many orators, public speakers, and clergymen. It also explains the failure of numerous actors, plays, and preachers. Here then is food for thought and determination on the part of the beginner. What the recruit goes to the theater for is craftsmanship. Failing this, he might just as well get out, or, if he stays in, make up his mind to get nowhere. It is easily possible for him, without technique, to ruin the fairest idea a dramatist ever presented. There are assassins of thought as well as of persons. Then he must tie up this craftsmanship with the thought he is presenting, and put something into it all that was not there before, something that not only gives the audience a thrill, but also the dramatist. The actor who does not bring something to the part he is playing, something other than that which has been set down in the lines, as color, spirit, intelligence, soul, is not an actor at all, but a laboring man on the wrong job.

The modern method of selecting actors to fit the characters they are to play, "engaging types," it is called, is well enough, if less attention were paid to selecting physical types of resemblance and more to types of intelligence and creative force.

In the next chapter I shall have something to say about the way managers defeat the very object for which they produce plays. That object, of course, being success. You will hear much about being "natural" on the stage, and of "facing the audience," and still more about "hogging the center of the stage."

Do not worry over such things. You cannot be successful and be unnatural. If you are not successful nothing much matters. If you face the audience like a wooden soldier and talk like a parrot you will be ridiculous and swiftly lose all chance of facing anything but failure. Face the audience whenever you feel you should. Be clever about it! Success will depend upon your being able to make the public feel that that is the very thing you should do, the thing they wish you to do. You ought never to forget that it is easier for an audience to understand you if it *sees* as well as hears what you say — this is as true off as on the stage — that it understands better for seeing your lips move and your eyes speak than by peering into your back hair.

About monopolizing the center of the stage. It is worth considering. Do not, as you won't, overlook its importance. All things, the architecture, the lights, the chief action, the audience and especially the chief actors, converge toward this center. If you have something vital to do or say in the play, do not imagine you will be permitted to do or say it obscurely in a corner. You will come center. The stage director will attend to that. You should know though that if you insist upon thrusting yourself forward in season and out, not only the stage director, the leading man and the leading woman will resent you, but the audience.

Arliss says that acting is "a bag of tricks." So it is. I should add, however, that they are tricks of taste, judgment, and discretion — born of experience.

The beginner should be careful not to be classed with those actors who feel they have done their whole duty if they come "perfect," as the stage phrase runs, to the last rehearsal of a play, and even manage to go glibly through their lines on first performances. That is the least expected of an actor. Given an agreeable personality and a pleasing voice, what one does with his lines after having memorized them largely determines whether one is going to be an eagle or a buzzard.

When a novice explained why he had given a reading to which Forrest objected, the tragedian looked up in pleased surprise and said:

"By God, the man thinks!"

It harms no man to have a reputation for thinking, and the stage is precisely the place where one may do a good deal of fine thinking profitably. If it is not done, it is amazing how swiftly detection follows. There is much, too, in being alert about the thing one is doing. Failing alertness, one would better be doing something other than acting. I remember an actor in a pique with a manager, quitting the stage in the middle of the play, "The Merchant of Venice." His defection caused no embarrassment. A little fellow of no importance in the company stepped forward and spoke the lines, saved the situation, though the speeches, those of "Gratiano," were the last he would be supposed to know anything about. The manager's and the company's feeling and expression of appreciation were as nothing compared with my joy at being the "Johnny on the spot." I do not offer this because I happen to have been the hero of the tiny drama so much as a hint to those of the right kidney to be prepared for the unexpected with

The first great American tragedian

which the stage bristles. These sudden opportunities make actors of those who never thought to act, and "stars" of those who planned to do so.

The student is not to be discouraged when told that "acting is an art very much more dependent upon special aptitudes than on general intellectual vigor." The admission that acting is at all an art is comparatively recent. Like virtues and vices, "general intellectual vigor" is distributed among actors in about the same proportion as among people of other arts and professions. The remark on "general intellectual vigor" was made in connection with William Farren, the great "Sir Peter Teazle" of his day. It was said that Farren was rather stupid off stage. What of it? That was his privilege, perhaps his duty. Must he be always "showing off" and striking twelve? Do we not know poets, painters, sculptors, and writers who, off stage, are marvels of seeming vacuity? Perhaps like clocks they take time to be wound up. Corneille was known to have "a fertile pen and a sterile mouth," as he declared of himself. Without a pen in his hand, Goldsmith, though he talked much, said little, and generally said it poorly. Walpole dubbed him "an inspired idiot." Garrick's playful epitaph on "Goldy" is well known:

Here lies Nolly Goldsmith, for shortness called Noll,
Who wrote like an angel and talked like poor Poll.[1]

[1] Goldsmith showed that he could also write like a wit, and was not to be outdone in the matter of humorous epitaphs, as his, to Garrick, proves. After lauding Garrick to the skies, "As an actor, confessed

It were easy to multiply instances. Because a man excels in one direction is no true reason to expect him to excel in another, however admirable such versatility might prove.

After the novice has graduated from his school of acting, there will come a time, many times, in early professional life when he will be puzzled as to the stage direction he will receive in acting: puzzled because he will not know what to do about it. Some of this direction will be excellent, some of it, impossible. Here the actor must employ tact — and determination. Tact in listening and determination to play the part in his own way. Many successes have come out of the actor going absolutely contrary to direction which it was impossible he could follow. Lemaître actually turning a tragedy into a comedy is the most notable instance.

The situation in question arises because of failure to see that nobody can get into the heart of a character like the person who represents it. It is not mere compliment which makes the dramatist say, as he often does when speaking of a successful impersonation: "I never dreamed there was so much in it!" And it is not strange that he did not. Bearing the burden of the composition of the play as a whole, it is rare that he is able to develop a part as fully and as minutely, with a

without rival to shine," and "As a wit, if not first, in the very first line," he drops him to earth with:

"On the stage he was natural, simple, affecting,
'Twas only when off the stage he was acting."

⁵ 'Twas only that when he was off he was acting

thousand shades and inflections, as the actor possessing aptitude and delicate sensibility plus personality. Some dramatists, as has been said, are broad enough to admit this, nay, to proclaim it. Lamb knew it. Lewes and William Winter knew it. They wrote with sympathy. A few of our present-day critics know it. Men like Brander Matthews have always known it. It was Sheridan, the dramatist, who wrote of Garrick, the actor:

> The grace of action, the adapted mien —
> Faithful as nature to the varied scene;
> Th' expressive glance — whose subtle comment draws
> Entranced attention and mute applause;
> Gesture that marks, with force and feeling fraught,
> A sense in silence and a will in thought;
> Harmonious speech, whose pure and liquid tone
> Gives verse a music scarce confessed its own.

Listen, then, to all directions. Be careful to sift and accept anything that may serve. But once before the throne — that is, face to face with the audience — cast all thought of direction, all thought of everything but your representation to the wind, and play only as your mind and heart and soul dictate. If you are the kind of actor whose mind and heart and soul are not given to dictating, do not play anything so much as politics.

No really capable director presumes to tell an intelligent actor how to play a part. Such an actor is engaged not only with the thought of his bringing out the best in the rôle, but as well for what it is hoped he will contribute to the rôle. William Sampson rehearsed two weeks with Belasco before being spoken to about the character he was to play. The direction he got was significant. Said Belasco: "I needn't tell *you* what to do!" Imagine Belasco telling Mrs. Fiske how to act!

The difficulty with the smaller director — we have so many small directors! — lies in coming in contact with actors about whose intelligence he is ignorant. Often, in this situation, much ridiculous assumption will be met, on both sides. I was once a chance witness of a rehearsal delayed for an hour in a dispute over the right word to emphasize, both contenders being wrong.

The capable director, after consultation with the manager and agreeing that the author is "incompetent, irrelevant and — impossible," as a director, and limiting his power to do harm, will go about his task of preparing the play for production in a manner to bring out its maximum effect. He will attend to the entrances and exeunts of the characters and the "business" of the scenes in which these characters move and speak. He will offer many wise suggestions, drop hints as to the play's intent, and show appreciation at the development and progress of the play's unfolding. He will superintend the arrangement of the scenery, the lighting of the stage, and perform such a multitude of intricate, technical, helpful things, matters usually beyond the ken of most managers, authors, and actors, as will leave him at the end in a state of admiring bewilderment as to what the play would have done without him. The stage director, not stage manager, is of incalculable æsthetic and financial value in the theater.

In the production of a play the best results are achieved when the director and the actor work in harmony. When either foolishly attempts to usurp the province of the other, the author and his play suffer. The actor seldom offends in this respect, and the wise director never. He knows that the skill of an impersonation and the destiny of the play lie in the hands of the actor, depending upon his power of representation.

Here follow ten little stage commandments which may be of service to the beginner, to whom this chapter has been dedicated. If any more seasoned player should find in them aught to his liking, he is privileged to help himself. They are not offered because thought to be pearls of wisdom, but as useful suggestions arising from an extended experience. They are taken from an address delivered by the writer at the Empire Theater, in New York City, in 1907, to the graduates of the American Academy of Dramatic Arts.

1. Act on the stage, not off.
2. Be modest in bearing and speech.
3. Speak English, not slang.
4. Be earnest in acting.
5. Know a great deal about your own art, and as much as you can about everything else.
6. Do not accept success as too personal. Hamlets and Juliets have come and gone, but the plays go on forever.
7. Do not ascribe failure to bad luck. "Luck," as Lowell wrote, "is the prerogative of valiant souls."
8. So be valiant.
9. Be prudent with your earnings. The earning period with the average actor is often brief.
10. Be true to your art, and, above all, to yourselves.

CHAPTER XVIII
ADVENTURES IN LOVE

IT is said that, in any full and candid document of one's self, one should not fail to treat of the sex relation, the love passion in one's life. The proportion in which it is mentioned, so it is declared, bears to one's self-delineation precisely that which it has borne to one's mind and life.

Again, that it is "a great loss to educators that autobiographers have failed to record the symptoms in themselves accompanying the development of the sexual instinct." [1]

Far be it from me to disappoint an educator. And since it is put in that light, almost any kind of an autobiographer would go far to avoid disappointment in this respect. If he were of the proper texture, I believe he might even go to the extreme of inventing the development of a sexual instinct, not having been endowed with one of his own.

Of course, one does not wish to be behind the age in such matters, and if one is writing a self-study, or if one thinks he is, which to him is much the same thing, one wishes it to contain all the ingredients which go to make up the most approved kind of autobiographic pudding. The real self-delineating person will want the up-to-date thing or nothing. I am determined, then, in the

[1] Anna Robeson Burr: *The Autobiography*.

interest of education and educators — purely in their interest — to set forth some of the amatory experiences that have come into my life. It is not too agreeable to impale one's self, like a grub on the pin-point of scrutiny for purposes of research autobiographic or otherwise, but there are sacrifices to duty in the interest of science, as the transfusion of blood, race warning or encouragement, etc., from which under certain conditions one should never shrink. Perhaps the record I shall make of the symptoms in these love experiences may not prove uninteresting even if they are of no scientific value. But we shall see. I shall also take the liberty of calling attention to one or two love stories of other people of my profession, romances which for one reason or other have seemed to me intensely interesting.

What, then, is the truth as to the sex relation, the "breast to breast" confidences, as Whitman would put it, of my life? According to conceived notions in some quarters, being an actor, constantly associated with beautiful and attractive women, I must have had many conquests, or opportunities for conquests. All the more so, if I possessed the least attractive quality of my own, which love of truth compels me not to deny. On one thing I am determined, I shall be frank and honest in the revelations.

Heine tells us that he so loved women that when he was deprived of their society at Göttingen, he got him a cat. Right here, then, in this respect, I rise to the highest sexual and educational importance if cats are to be of weight in the development of sex instinct. I went the Franco-German philosopher and humorist many times better. I got me a mother, the "Emily" of this story, who surrounded herself with many cats. I have always taken the utmost pleasure in their society, but I have found, as Heine found, that they were pretty poor substitutes for women.

"Emily" was my first, my constant love until death did us part — nothing but filial affection and not at all what the psychoanalysts mean by that affection which arises between the sexes, of course; but none the less interesting on that account and yet not unrelated either through the bearing it had on the judgment of other women with whom the present autobiographer came in contact. The reader must not be discouraged at this early allusion to "Emily" in the account of these love affairs. It is in no wise meant as a damper on the experiences which are to be brought forward, experiences which the author in the absence of a cool disposition feels — like as not, may even interdict the publication of this august tome. But having had it pointed out to us where the path of educational duty lies, we, editorially, are not to be restrained.

My first recollection of sex attraction, then, was of "Lizzie," the mortgaged sweetheart of the confectioner's son, Sam Baker. She was pretty and flirtatious — and susceptible. She had great skill in wafting kisses stealthily at immense distances while apparently engaged in duties to her perambulated sister. She was a girl of extraordinary vision, judging from her ability to perceive unerringly the return of those osculatory messages from the hand of a small boy in shirt-sleeves *en route* to back lots for the daily game of ball.

There must go with every spark of the true feeling in this sex attraction, I believe, a certain quantity of real chivalry. I had it, for I recall that when challenged by the confectioner's son for poaching upon his preserves, even though it was not so nominated, I accepted joyfully. It seemed a radiant thing to fight in such a cause. I remember that I vanquished my rival, after the fashion of Cyrano de Bergerac, singing the while. My opponent rudely declared I was "showing off." Far from the truth. I sang to keep up my courage.

So far as my recollection serves, "Lizzie" was not tremendously overcome at the account of the struggle in which I had met several unpleasant thumps in her behalf. There was an absence of enthusiastic appreciation to which I felt myself clearly entitled. But the next day she was at the old love rally in kiss-wafting and I analyzed her nature, therefore, as fervent but hardly sufficiently worshipful. There was nothing approaching the freedom of the Abélard and Héloïse stage in our association. I was nine, and she was twelve. And that is the story. It is to be hoped that this is going to give the analysis a tremendous urge forward. It is my loss that I cannot see how, but the educators will attend to that. Dear "Lizzie," I wonder whose grandmother you are now!

My next conquest was an actress. We are coming

on! A woman who caused the shedding of numberless sympathetic tears. More, perhaps, than any other actress of her time, except perhaps Clara Morris. But, oh, the happiness she gave to the myriad who love to shed sympathetic tears!

She won my heart, my admiration, not by tears, but by the portrayal of a character called "the dumb boy" in a drama named "The French Spy." She was the spy who adroitly liberated her countrymen from an Algerian fortress. When discovered, the spy unloosed a lot of back hair, and the gallant Colonel de Courcey, from behind his prison bars, cried: "Cowards! Would you shoot a woman!" It was such a thrill.

Ours was a Dante-Beatrice worship, from afar. I never spoke to her but once. She did not reply — in words. She could have done so. But it would have meant the disillusionment of an audience, the ruination of a story, and my love was an artist. It was Christmas night, at the old Walnut Street Theater, Philadelphia. I sat far down front, quite far — on the musical conductor's stool, the musicians having been driven out by the great crowd in attendance. The object of my adoration advanced upon the stage almost to the edge of the footlights. She knelt to attach a message to the arrow she was to shoot over the walls of the fortress into the camp of the besieging French. I could have reached out my hand and touched her. She could have gathered me in her arms. My nature urged me on. I spoke — just loud enough for her to hear.

"Hello, Lucille!" I murmured.

There, the name is out! Lucille Western, the most famous emotional actress of her day. Thousands of times as "Lady Isobel" and "Madame Vine" in "East Lynne," she preached a matchless, powerful sermon on the harm and injustice that may come from thoughtless, hasty jealousy. But let us not be impolite. The lady is standing before us on the stage and I have just addressed her. She tried not to betray the fact that she had heard. There were several involuntary quiverings of the eyelids, and then, with her gaze still fastened on the arrow, her lips trembled, she smiled. I have carried that smile all through my life. We never met.

It was old Herbert Spencer who lamented the absence of emotion from his experience, a sad admission coming from one who felt that emotion was as large a factor of life as thought. So far, I have the great scientist at a disadvantage in that I am but two deep in my amours and have already had a world of idealized feeling.

When I was eighteen or nineteen, I met my first widow. She was a thing of beauty and probably became a joy forever. Attractive, motherly, admonitory and tender, she was worth while. During a professional visit to Chicago shortly after its great fire, I had a room on Michigan Avenue. The widow was a relative of the landlady's.

Somehow I came in for a great deal of solicitude on the part of that widow. She expressed herself as alarmed that "a studious young man" like myself should be under the necessity of going about the world a prey to all its wickedness — that he should be devoting his young life and energy, of all things, to the stage. She sought to dissuade me from this. I was unused to so much thoughtful attention on my travels, especially from handsome widows, and it interested me.

She opened my eyes to much of which she thought I had not dreamed, explained about types of worldly men and women, and besides showing the proper astonishment, I gave her to understand that I was appreciative and grateful. Occasionally the widow puzzled me. At times she seemed aglow with the moral lessons she meant to inculcate and then again she would overshoot the mark a trifle by the display of an affection that I felt exceeded the bounds of preceptorship.

I spoke of her to my mature friend Dutassy. He was another well-wisher who longed to start me somewhere along the paths of commerce, anywhere so that it led away from the stage. Dutassy not only gave me advice, but also lessons in Italian, and seemed pleased with my power to memorize pages of what he called "la più bella lingua del mondo." His eyes went very wide and his mouth seemed to water at my account of the widow. He led me on to tell him repeatedly all that I knew of her. He shook his head sadly when I described how cordially she would greet me on my return to the house. But what astonished me most on his part was the great shout of derision he gave when I told him how the widow would have me recount the happenings of the day upon which she would comment, adding bits of sage advice, and that in her enthusiasm she would sometimes follow me to my room to make sure she had sufficiently emphasized her directions and that I had been properly impressed.

Toward the close of my engagement in Chicago the widow talked more and more of love, what it meant to the world in general and to young men like myself in particular. I was impressed, and wondered if there were no way to be properly instructed in such things. Finally, after what seemed a noble impulse to be chivalrous and perhaps sacrificial in a good cause, the widow declared that before I left town she meant, just for the incalculable service it would be to me all through life, to give me a lesson in love.

Overcome with gratitude I rushed off to Dutassy and told him all about it, expressing at the same time my pleasure at having met some one who took such a motherly interest in me, to which he ungraciously retorted, "Motherly fiddlesticks!" He declared his determination to call on that widow and find out things for himself, but to this I would not listen. He emphatically enjoined me not to keep that appointment for the lesson in love. I would not promise. Dutassy's attitude and exclamations had greatly whetted my curiosity concerning it. I argued that the widow had been notably kind to me, that she was evidently a woman of experience, that it would not only be discourteous to her but unjust to myself not to take advantage of the widow's generosity.

Dutassy thought it wise to disregard my protest. He called, and was delighted to find the widow as lovely and as worthy as I had depicted her. He congratulated me on my good fortune to encounter so charming a person. From this point on the widow's interest in me waned. Presently tactful friends began to speak of the frequency with which the widow and the erstwhile lonely Dutassy were seen dining together at various restaurants. It was evident that I had been the indirect means of his meeting an entertaining companion.

I have often thought that perhaps nobody needed a lesson in love so much as my friend Dutassy.

For a long time after the Lucille Western episode, there was no romance that carried with it any symptoms worth recording. I was a grown man with strong bachelor determinations before I was dispossessed of the idea that any woman, no matter how gifted or charming, could change my belief that marriage was anything but a convenience for carrying on the life principle. One is so cocksure at twenty-seven!

Then came a beautiful awakening. It was the days of the "Pinafore" craze, and many young women came into professional stage life from church choirs, then active in the formation of amateur companies in giving the charming Gilbert and Sullivan opera. As a temporary substitute there came, to a company "Our Goblins, or Fun on the Rhine," in which I was a chief comedian, a young lady fresh from such a Gilbert and Sullivan opera. She was a radiant creature that quite took one's breath away merely to behold. I was instantly smitten with admiration and thrown completely off my balance. All the more so in realizing that no attentions seemed so welcome as mine. With a mellow contralto voice, matchless complexion, wondrous eyes and teeth, and a gift of silence that hinted at philosophic depths, I longed for nothing so much as possession. It was a beautiful experience in which I would hang upon her every look, and she upon mine, as if increase of appetite grew by what it fed on. Each day seemed made solely for opportunity to meet and meet again. Every place I looked I saw her. Every place she looked I was to be found.

There seemed to be no bar to the consummation of my happiness except the young lady's consent which, with the instinct of all young people mutually attracted, we knew was but a formality. After some months, I proposed and — was accepted. We were married. I was radiantly happy. I redoubled my efforts for professional success that I might surround her and our prospective family with every creature comfort. I had a deep-seated conviction that enduring happiness lay in the home with children. I could not imagine a home without them. But the lady also had views of home life. Sadly enough, they did not include the idea of children. I was puzzled, discouraged. It made a difference. After some years two children came, unbidden. I was overjoyed. Absence from home now became a hardship. I thought nothing of rushing across the continent and back again in order to spend a few hours with my family. Gradually, however, fundamental differences in character made us more and more unhappy. One day, much later than she herself discovered, we awoke to the fact that we were singularly ill-suited. It was something neither of us could control, one of those mistakes of selection of which the history of the world is full.

With wider experience and, probably, keener comprehension, I might have avoided many misunderstandings had I possessed more patience. It is so easy to be wise after the fact. Unquestionably I was often to blame. In all things except the preservation of the family, there came to be little sympathy and no understanding. I thought I should never again be happy. I did not realize how much temperament is master of the man, how much he is its absolute slave.

Until death came to one of us, we lived on in alternate storm and calm. This going on unhappily was perhaps a mistake, an injustice to all concerned, though many will take issue with the statement. I have ever regretted that fate should have cheated her out of the serenity she would have enjoyed with another man. We talked about it; she also regretted it. In my opinion, it is better that four people should be given a chance to be happy than that two should be continually miserable.

One of the tenderest love stories of which I have known among the people of my profession was that of Julia Dean and Joseph Jefferson. All the tenderer with

JULIA DEAN

Joseph Jefferson's "first sweetheart." A beautiful woman and an accomplished actress. Daughter-in-law of Daniel Webster's opponent in the celebrated Webster-Hayne debates.

a touch of sadness, because it did not end as all love stories ought to end — in marriage.

Side-tracked in the Pullman of the All Star Rivals Company on a day in 1896, Jefferson told me all about it. As we sat alone, at dusk, he grew mellowly reminiscent and spoke of a lovely girl to whom he had been much attached, of her beauty, her charm, and of her rapid rise from the lowest to the highest rank in her profession, and that over all the years the memory of her was fragrant and dear. She was the daughter, he said, of a celebrated Western actress, Mrs. Drake, and that her name was Julia Dean, and of whom he thought I had perhaps never heard.

"How came you not to marry her?" I asked.

"Well, we drifted away from each other into different companies," he replied. "She went swiftly forward while I had to bide my time in the ranks. With youth, beauty, and skill she was soon able, as 'Julia' in 'The Hunchback,' to fill that huge Old Bowery Theater even as long as for two weeks, a remarkable achievement in the very early days of our theater when there were no such things as long 'runs' as we now know them. She was also the loveliest 'Juliet' I have ever seen!"

"Whom did she marry?" I asked.

"A son of Senator Hayne: the Hayne that Daniel Webster defeated in the celebrated debate," he replied.

To my question as to what made him remember her so keenly, after such a length of years, he paused a moment as if in reverie, and then said tenderly:

"Why — she was my first sweetheart."

Several months later, on finding a copy of "Cymbeline" with her name in gilt on the cover, I sent it to him, together with a newspaper clipping which told of the neglected condition of her grave at Port Jervis, New York. In thanking me he expressed his intention of having the grave renovated. I have always understood he did so. He returned the book with the following written on some of the blank, interleaved pages:

MY DEAR FRANCIS WILSON:

Yes, this little book must have belonged to dear Julia Dean and, as you say, does awaken memories of olden time. This sweet girl and I fought our early professional battles side by side. We were in the ballet — front row — together, happy peasants and gypsies, alternately Protestants and Catholics, Whigs and Tories, ready to change our religious or political opinions for six dollars a week. We led the choruses, too. Where we led them, God only knows, for the leader (Musical Conductor) never did.

May we meet in another world where there are no matinées and but few managers.

J. JEFFERSON

BOSTON, *Oct.* 7, 1902

What I have greatly loved about Maude Adams, next to her acting, was the determined way she kept herself to herself, the time she gave to herself to get acquainted with Maude Adams after strenuous hours given over to professional life. This was not wholly original with her. Booth did it. So, too, did Julia Marlowe, at one time. It is so unusual with people much in the public eye as to appear to be a mark of personal peculiarity.

This action aroused curiosity as to Maude Adams's

private life with which, in common with other thoughtful and modest people, she felt the world should have
no concern. There was no pose in this, simply the
natural reserve of one who values privacy as a compensation, as a necessary reaction to public effort.

We have all known actors, politicians, lawyers,
doctors, and ministers who in season and out have
sought publicity with the persistency and enthusiasm
of well-trained bird-dogs on the scent, and who have
felt with Oscar Wilde that aside from themselves, as
subjects of discussion, nothing, absolutely nothing, was
so interesting. But we may be sure that Wilde never
really thought that. He was far too clever a man. He
said it, as brilliant men are wont to say things, because
it was an audaciously witty thing to say.

Another of the wonderments of the curious public,
and the wonder extended as well to the people of her
own profession, was that Maude Adams never married.
It was none of our business, any more than it was the
public's, but she is so charming a woman and so original an actress that many of us — and perhaps the public also feels that way about it — are tenderly desirous
that such charm and originality should be reproduced
and perpetuated. Of course this shunning of wedlock
could not be because of lack of opportunity. From the
"spindle-legged little girl, unusually tall for her age,
with a funny little pigtail, and one of the quaintest
little faces you ever saw," of David Belasco's remembrance, up through her successes in "The Masked
Ball," "Rosemary," "The Bauble Shop," "The Little

Minister" (in which she first starred), "L'Aiglon," and "Peter Pan," to one of the most extraordinarily successful actresses of modern times, is a far cry. It is the kind of career likely to bring matrimonial opportunities even to less gifted, less masterful persons than Maude Adams. Perhaps I shall not be able to gratify curiosity to the extent of an explanation on the subject. I have never enjoyed the confidence of Maude Adams, but the lady will bear me out in the declaration that I did what I could to change conditions, in short, that I proposed to her.

It was like this: I had just witnessed a performance of "The Little Minister" and both play and player had gone entirely to my head and heart. I was mooning around the block tingling with joyful remembrance of it all, thinking how clever it was of Barrie to have written such a play, and how fortunate he was to find such an ideal representative as Maude Adams for his impish little devil of a woman, "Lady Babbie," with an expression on her face of quizzical good humor like nothing so much as Hogarth's "Shrimp Girl," thinking that if — when lo, and behold, I came upon "Lady Babbie" herself sitting in her carriage at the stage door.

It were easy to pour out a string of compliments of my enjoyment of her acting and of the play, easy and trite, and she would have been pleased, perhaps, as from one player to another, but I had been moved to such heights of enjoyment of the play and her playing that I was impelled to offer the highest compliment man has it in his power to offer woman, and I proceeded to do so. After the greeting, I said to her:

"I saw the play this afternoon, and as evidence of my deep appreciation I come to ask your hand in marriage. Being already a benedict as you know, you may perhaps regard me as 'shop-worn,' and therefore unacceptable as matrimonial material; that rests with you; but let me urge as to myself that I am house-broken, eminently docile, and have other qualities which might appeal if one were not over-punctilious."

Not at all overwhelmed, "Lady Babbie" smiled. I felt encouraged, though not necessarily hopeful. The proposal had not startled her, which decidedly comforted me, considering the abruptness and fervor with which it was made. When I left her, I cannot truly say that I was convinced that she would accept the proposal. She never made any reply — but — but — Maude Adams has never married!

All mankind loves a lover and hails a romance. Furthermore, most mankind may be depended upon not only to advertise said romance, but to make generous contributions to it. About the romance of the poet D'Annunzio and the actress Duse the light of poesy and drama has blazed with constantly increasing strength — and upon the slightest encouragement, nay, even upon the slightest hint of encouragement. It grew in interest because the world hungered for it, reveled in it. It made no difference that it was a poet and an actress. Priest and nun would have served as well, so the romance was there and the romancers interesting and attractive.

Around the love story of Duse and D'Annunzio there has been woven much that never really happened and still more that will never be known. When they met, Duse was a giantess and, in point of reputation and importance, D'Annunzio a comparative Lilliputian, a minor Italian poet and novelist. Duse was at the very peak of her power as an actress. She recognized the young poet's talent and encouraged it, stimulated him. At the time if there was any condescension in the association of the two, it was distinctly felt that it came from her and not from him. He was greatly flattered that an artist of Duse's caliber, one before whom the world was bowing, should regard him as worthy of encouragement, that she should trouble herself to inspire him to poetic creations worthy her interpretations. Could she have imagined that he was the type of man who would make commerce of their association to be published in a book for money, there never would have been this particular Italian romance and, likely, "the hero of Fiume" would have remained a minor Italian poet and novelist.

D'Annunzio rose splendidly to the extraordinary opportunity afforded him, which naturally increased the admiration of the great actress for the spirited poet and successful dramatist. His plays gave her, his gifted compatriot, the chance to show her unusual powers in new and varied phases, "to put reality into realism," as some one has finely said of her. Between them there was established inevitably a bond of professional, intellectual, and poetic sympathy. To the delight of the world, the talent, the genius of each supplemented and complemented the talent and genius of the other. For a while they were interdependent, and upon terms of great intimacy, no doubt.

We catch a glimpse of them at this time from Emma Calvé's conversation with Daniel Frohman:

"While in Venice," said the great songstress, "we were much with D'Annunzio. To please him Duse and I would array ourselves in various costumes, that he might be more inspired in reading his poems and stories as we floated languorously on the waters of the Queen City of the Adriatic to the rhythmic oars of our gondoliers." Duse disclosed to Calvé that, though she had great admiration for D'Annunzio, there was nothing of the nature of idolatry in her regard for him — which might have come as the result of a lover's quarrel or the revelation of one of the unlovely traits of which the temperamental D'Annunzio was not free.

Then came the time Gabrielle D'Annunzio attested his gratitude and appreciation of what Duse had done for him — what she had meant to him. He published the book called "Il Fuoco" ("The Flame"), in which, without reserve, he disclosed to the world the nature of this intimacy, and boasted of his power over the actress. Overwhelmed, amazed, and rendered desperately ill at such an inconceivable action, for twenty years Duse never again appeared upon the stage — nor would she have ever appeared again, had not necessity forced her out of retirement. The European war had broken her fortune and placed her in debt. Though old at sixty, frail, white-haired, and with face showing the emotion through which she had passed, scorning the artifices of mitigating make-up, she came back to the stage the same great actress she was when she left it, her art perhaps a little mellower for the sorrow through which she had passed.

The successful struggle to repair her fortune prematurely cost her her life. She was no longer able to withstand the hardships of acting and travel try as she would to soften them by infrequency. Through the Italian Ambassador, Italy at once took charge of the remains of its gifted daughter. About her as she lay in state in the Church of Saint Vincent Ferrer, in New York, there was heaped a great profusion of beautiful flowers, emblems of affectionate respect and remembrance. Upon her coffin there was permitted but a single wreath, from the King of Italy, a token of sorrow from his people. Her burial in her own country, to which she was borne on an Italian battleship, was a remarkable expression of sorrow and honor.

When D'Annunzio passes, it may be that the world will remember him for much that he has contributed to it, but it will remember him for nothing so much as that he proved himself an ignoble figure in one of its darling romances.

I have given some account of a little boy, unconscious of the presence of an audience, halting me in the midst of a performance with the request to "Jump down here!" in order to play with *him*.

A little girl, not yet four, ran to me recently and begged me excitedly to "come see something won'ful, how caterpillows turn themselves into butterflies." "We put the caterpillows into a big bottle," she went on, "they made themselves into funny balls, and now they are coming out pretty, pretty butterflies." Then pausing and, looking up at me, she said: "Caterpillow? Cat and pillow! What a funny name to give a thing. Daddy, how did they get that name? Look it up in your book."

How these two children came to be mine involves a love story which may or may not prove interesting according as I have the wit to tell it. It may possess symptoms worth recording.

How so many handsome and gifted girls leave home and come to New York to have their voices misplaced by fake teachers might well be a matter of investigation and protection by the proper authorities. Semi-occasionally, however, some of them come in contact with a capable instructor and all goes well until home funds give out, or dependence upon home-town patrons grows irksome. Then something must be done to avoid defeat. The particular young lady who found herself in this latter position — that is, determined to carry on without further dependence — applied to me for a small-part position in my company. I was glad to engage her. I was always on the lookout for just her kind. Such were always given the preference. She was young, slim as a lily, beautiful and accomplished. A convent graduate, refinement and gentility characterized her manner and speech. Later on, I discovered that she had unusual mental quality. She proved a valuable addition. She rose gradually to a position second only to the highest.

When I had made the change to the field of comedy without music, I feared that I had seen the last of the young lady, for I admired her and had become interested in her; but fate willed it otherwise. I was astonished one day to receive a letter from her asking if I would not favorably consider her application for a position. She, too, had come to regard the musical field as narrower in opportunity than that of the drama and had determined upon a change. I replied that the desire to act did not necessarily carry with it the ability to do so, that though akin, acting in the drama was quite a different thing from acting in light opera. I then proceeded to give her a lot of fatherly advice. I gladly admitted her beauty and charm, but, if she would pardon me for saying so, I thought perhaps her talent did not lay along the line of the drama. I knew of no one who would grace a home better than she, and with this thought in mind, I even took it upon myself to suggest that she should marry.

She took me at my word. She was years, however, following my counsel to the letter. Meanwhile, she accepted a minor part in my company and, proving how easy it is for advisers not to know too much about anything, she rose by right of ability to be the highest

FRANCIS WILSON AT HOME

salaried member in it as its leading actress. What especially interested me in this young lady, whose name was Edna Bruns, was the comprehensive nature of her ambition. I flattered myself that I had a peculiar quality of the same article in that, differing from some ambitions I had met, it compelled me joyously to slave in its behalf. So with her. She wanted to sing, and she did so. She wanted to act, and she acted. She was eager to pass triumphantly through summer college courses, and she did it.

Interested in playwriting, she absorbed much that was to be learned in the teachings of William Thompson Price, who was probably the first to formulate the principles of that art. Besides writing several plays, she finished by becoming an analyst of real power. My interest could not help growing in such an unusual person, and I was glad to be of any assistance. With wealthy, good-looking suitors buzzing about, the marvel was that such a handsome and accomplished young woman stayed single. She reveled in her independence, though I knew that her ultimate aspiration was for a home with children, a matter that was to be attended to when she met the man of her choice and had sufficiently proved to herself the possession of practical, worth-while qualities making for happiness in such a home.

I took great pleasure in discussing with her the type of man she had in mind for a helpmeet and, dullard that I was, the true state of my feelings toward her did not dawn upon me until I found myself picking flaws in all prospective candidates except those who possessed qualities similar to my own, or what I believed my own to be. That discovery when it came was a twister. It alternately alarmed and elated me, as such things will. I had fully determined never again to marry, there being so much attending risk. Often I quieted myself with the thought that I need give myself no uneasiness, for, being somewhat the young woman's senior, there would be little likelihood of her giving me the preference over youth and brawn. Notwithstanding, I grew uneasy. Although like Johnny Walker, I might truly be said to be going strong, I had also been going long, and this might readily be the deciding factor against me. The more I considered the subject, the more intensely interesting, not to say puzzling, it became. There was about it the triumph of hope over experience, as the great lexicographer expresses it. And yet at times I would, like squibs in a Fourth-of-July celebration, flash off in the opposite direction, convinced that I was foolish to think of such a step, suspicious that the young lady knew all along and, à la Shaw, never meant to give me a chance to escape, but always coming back to the fear that I should surely lose the opportunity to compass an ideal existence.

No very close observation was needed to prove that I was betraying all the beautiful symptoms of the world-old story — that it was evident I was deeply in love. After what seemed an interminable time, I proposed — and was rejected, not because the young

woman did not love me but because she thought I
needed more time to consider such a momentous step.
I took time. Thought my deepest about the matter for
three additional days. No desire to escape presenting
itself, I again proposed and was accepted. We were
married. Then an extraordinary thing happened. My
two daughters, by my first marriage, were not blessed
with children. This gave me great concern, for I had
longed for the privilege of grandfatherdom — had, in
fact, felt myself cheated in this respect. How to remedy this! Out of the harmony and complete state of
understanding that had come to me in my new-found
happiness, my wife and I evolved a plan of gratifying
my ambition. And behold it came to pass through the
arrival of the tiny persons whose remarks began this
little history. For though I am their father in fact, I
am their grandfather in — experience!

When the author of that heart-taking fantasy,
"Peter Pan," came to America, he one day expressed
a desire to see The Players Club. Now, unless with
cronies, Barrie is noted for taciturnity. In his visit to
the shrine of Edwin Booth, in Gramercy Park, he did
not belie his reputation for brevity of speech. After
two hours or more of inspection of the many rare possessions of The Players, two "Ah's?" and an actual
sentence were the extent of Sir James's utterance.

The "Ah's?" mattered little. What was of much
more significance was that taken to the rooms where
the great tragedian had passed the last days of his life,

Barrie halted instinctively before the portrait of Mary
Devlin, Booth's first wife. Long and admiringly the
dramatist gazed upon it and said thoughtfully with
appreciative nods of the head:

"A verra byutiful face, a verra byutiful face!"

As he spoke, he was looking at the counterfeit presentment of a woman who had been a part of the saddest love story in the dramatic history of my time.

"The lovely Mary Devlin" was a ward of Joseph
Jefferson's. During the three years she lived in the
family of the comedian, "she rose," said Jefferson, "to
be one of the leading actresses of the stage." On the
other hand, a new star had risen, not in the east, but
in the west. That star was a young and extraordinarily handsome young actor named Edwin Booth.
He wended his way eastward, contrary to the motion
of many stars, conquering as he came, to be speedily
conquered in turn by a charming young woman before
whose portrait, fifty years later, Barrie, the skillful
Scottish weaver of eerie dreams, stood in rapture.

After Mary Devlin had rehearsed but a single week
as "Juliet" to Edwin Booth's "Romeo," they became
affianced lovers. They married. They were perfectly
mated. They were ideally happy. In less than three
years she was dead, leaving behind her a broken-
hearted, lover-husband and a baby girl, Edwina.

The story is best told in a letter to Adam Badeau,
Booth's closest friend, who declared it the saddest
message he had ever received:

By the time this reaches you, you will have heard of the

MARY DEVLIN BOOTH

Edwin Booth's wife "Mollie." At her death, though far away, he
declared he heard her voice calling him.

terrible blow I have received, a blow which renders life aimless, hopeless, darker than it was before I caught the glimpse of heaven in true devotion of her, the sweetest being who made man's home a something to be loved. My heart is crushed, dried up and desolate. I have no ambition now, no one to please, no one to cheer me — I left her in the bloom of health and hope, joyful and loving, throwing kisses to me as I parted from her. Two little tiny weeks slipped by and I was summoned to her bedside. I came *too late:* the baby wife lay dead, after one week's illness.[1]

I think she is somewhere near me now; I see her, feel her, hear her every minute of the day. I call her, look for her every time the door opens. In every car that passes our little cottage door, where we anticipated so much joy, I expect to see the loved form of her who was my *world.* . . . My acting was studied to please her, and after I had left the theater, and we were alone, her advice was all I asked, all I valued. . . . I lie awake at night and look for her in the darkness. I hold my breath and listen, and can sometimes fancy I can feel her speak away in somewhere, in my soul, perhaps, for I know if it were possible for spirits to come back, she'll come to me some night. . . .

I have received kind words of consolation and advice. I do not need advice or sympathy, although it is good in them to give it and I appreciate it; but I do need some sign of her, some little breath of wind, nothing more, whispering comfortable words of her. Didn't you tell me once that you saw me standing near you when I was in reality far away?

I'll tell you what happened two nights before Mary left me. I was awake. I felt a strange puff of air strike my right cheek twice. It startled me so that I was thoroughly aroused. I

---

[1] It has been stated that Booth might have reached the bedside of his wife before her death had he opened telegrams lying on his table at the theater. Booth denied this bitterly to his daughter Edwina. If his denial were not sufficient, it must be remembered that it was the invariable rule in his time to withhold all telegrams for actors until after performances. The practice is still in force in some theaters. This is done on the principle that good news will keep and bad news if disclosed often injures or disrupts a performance without being of any advantage to the recipient.

turned in bed, when I felt the same on the left cheek. Two puffs of wind, ghost kisses. I lay wondering what it could mean, when I distinctly heard these words, "Come to me, darling, I am almost frozen," as plainly as I hear this pen scratching over the paper.... What does all this mean? I, who have ever laughed at such things, now feel mystified and half believe such things may be....

Every day now seems endless, the night seems lengthened into a century ... God help me! Madness would be a relief to me, and I have often thought I stood very near the brink of it. ... I should not complain even in my grief of woe, for surely God is just, is good, is wiser than we, and nothing has ever so impressed me with the truth of this as Mollie's death.... Is there anything of Mollie's that would please you to have? Her guitar is hanging on the wall, mute and tuneless now.... Set not your heart on anything in this world. If good comes to you, take it, but be ready always to relinquish it without a groan.

CHAPTER XIX

THOUGHTS OF THE THEATER

I HAVE about reached the end of all I care to say. It is not all I could say, but let us not proceed to the vulgarity of a checkmate.

It is not certain that anybody will care to make my autobiographic acquaintance, but, waiving false modesty, I am hoping, for the publisher's sake, and of course for my own, that I shall find myself mistaken.

Some one[1] says, "Any aspect of the human creature has its poignant interest." Here, then, thought I, is a wire under which any old kind of a self-delineating animal may trot with impunity. On this hint I acted, and set down an account of some of the stirring events of the theater of my time and in which I had a part.

Biography, autobiography, are no strangers to me. I have never cared so much for any other form of literature. I came early under the influence of that skillful and pervasive creation known as "Boswell's Life of Samuel Johnson," and I have never recovered from its charm.

Soon thereafter, also, I made the acquaintance of that humorous old philosopher and utilitarian autobiographer, Benjamin Franklin, whose sage advice ranged from statesmanship to lightning rods, from wealth to widows. It was but a step from him into the

[1] Anna Robeson Burr: *The Autobiography.*

world of self-analysts in whose company it is always a delight to dwell. They are a finely human, entertaining, and informative people, from the indiscreet and apologetic Père Abélard to Alfieri and Béranger, who penned their own lives for purposes of self-study; to Lamartine, who wrote his because friends requested it. Then there is the charming Locker-Lamson, who wrote "for the uses of his children," and Goldoni, Cibber, and Mrs. Oliphant, who sought to explain themselves, because "no one else was likely to do it, or to do it so well." Enter the masculine Catherine II of Russia, who treated her love affairs "like a gentleman" and who, we may depend upon it, was anything but "a perfect lady," whatever her mental strength.

Here come Gibbon, Georges Sand, Wordsworth, and Gosse, who became autobiographical with the hope of better self-acquaintance, and old George Quaker Fox, whose wife, as he declared, God had specifically selected for him. And Carlyle, Darwin, Hunt, and Shaftesbury, who laid bare personal peculiarities "for amusement," as did the "a-babe-in-the-house-is-a-well-spring-of-pleasure man," Martin Farquhar Tupper. Then there was Sarah Bernhardt, who was silent about her love affairs, in contradistinction to Mademoiselle Georges, who was blatantly open about hers; and then Ellen Terry who makes the refreshing admission that she "was in love with love"! Clear on down to the *apologia pro sua vita* of John L. Sullivan. As a further urge to the adoption of the autobiographic form, I had already written an intimate personal remembrance of Eugene

Field, and, later on, had Boswellized Joseph Jefferson.

As Roosevelt said of the Presidency when he turned it over to Taft, "I have had a bully good time" with life, an altogether charming time, and within the limits imposed upon all by Mother Nature, I have done my utmost to make some return.

As I floated through life — I seem never to have walked — I dare say I have been the *enfant terrible* of many a situation, been, wittingly or unwittingly, even the cause of unhappiness — who has not! — but no such recollection brings me joyless days or sleepless nights. If, on the other hand, I have done anything deserving to be placed on the credit side of the ledger — and who has not! — it is enough credit for any man. At all events, he is not likely to get more.

But this I know, and say thankfully, that no human being ever got more joy than I out of such faculty as he possessed for humor and comedy. Success in the theater seems to give an especial satisfaction in the realization of one's ambition. I cannot speak for others, of course, but to me this satisfaction was as nothing compared to the discovery that, in the pursuit of one's profession, one was making daily contributions to the pleasure and well-being of others. It seemed a shame to take money for it! I never spoke to any manager about it, but I have a suspicion that he would have seen the point and would have been eager to co-operate.

In the theater there is one thing in which managers show extraordinary unanimity — retrenchment. When it is necessary — and it is practiced as rigorously, often-times, in success as in failure — it begins first with the reduction of actors' salaries. Next, in the reduction of actors' salaries, and, finally, in more reduction of actors' salaries.

One of the favorite pastimes of those whose future lies mostly behind them, so to speak, is speculating on what they would do if they had life to live over again. Were youth and the choice of a profession again given me, what should I do? For one thing, I should not incline to a clerical life. In the light of recent events the temptations there seem wholly irresistible. Jesting aside, I should choose, and choose again, the stage, which has brought me so much gladness, and where, as I hope, I have not been found wanting in contributing to the general store of public enjoyment.

In this choice I should be as gay and unrestrained as the boy with the insatiable love of custard pie, and cared not a whoop how much it mussed his ears. I think we should not grieve much over mussing any-thing in life — except our character. That, at least, should be kept clean.

I have always rejoiced in the stage as the most perfect form of wisdom-coated relaxation the world has yet devised. I doubt if there will ever be a better or stronger. Prejudiced? Of course. But what is to be expected of an enthusiast who does not know too much of anything but the theater? Then, too, one should not be ashamed to have the courage, not only of his convictions, but also of his prejudices.

Like every other actor I have known who has had a measure of success, and especially those who have had no such measure, my first thoughts of the theater were born of love for it. The ambition, secret at first, to shine in it, to be worthy to shine in it, came early and came strong. Present-day psychologists implore us to search out the bent of our children's minds and give it all encouragement — full swing. I swung. Not, however, from any special direction or encouragement, but from sheer inclination — and necessity. What the truly ambitious person thinks of in connection with the medium in which he longs to work is not money, but the opportunity to express himself. It was so with me. I did not think of money in relation to acting. I just thought of acting. With your true actor money is always a secondary consideration. On no other theory is it possible to explain the hardships, even the humiliations, the devoted actor will undergo for the privilege of practicing his art. Managers know about this. How well they know about it! How they will pinch the novice to pay the " star," who has come to know and to exact his value. It seems to be an inherited trait. Colley Cibber was satirically merry over the "menagers" of his day in this respect. They "menaged" so skillfully that the "shares" of the actors showed no profit.

Once confident that his services are in demand, it is a poor creature who is not able to match wits with even a deft bidder seeking something one has to offer. Indeed, it is not the recognized actor that is worsted in these transactions, but those who are not able to make a pretense to position.

At first one cares only for opportunity. That once obtained and taken advantage of, ho, for the delectable journey into the fairyland of the theater! What a joy-starred place it has been in my day! How could it be else? There held forth the towering Forrest, the superb Murdock, the versatile Davenport, the emotional Lucille "East Lynne" Western and her beautiful sister, Helen "Satan in Paris" Western, Jean Davenport Lander, Charlotte "Meg Merrilies" Cushman, Lester "Rosedale" Wallack, Charles "Monte Cristo" Fechter, Joseph "Nick of the Woods" Proctor, Mrs. D. P. "Lady Audley's Secret" Bowers, and those two delightful comedians Frank "Mazzeppa" Drew and John "Colonel Sellers" Raymond, John E. "Solon Shingle" Owens, who charmed two hemispheres and was responsible for the popularity of that sprightly melody "Dixie" over which Southerners and pseudo-Southerners squeal enthusiastically when it is played by the restaurant bands.

Then, too, there were Mr. and Mrs. Barney "Emerald Ring" Williams, Frank "Mose" Chanfrau, Maggie "Fanchon" Mitchell, George L. "Humpty Dumpty" Fox, Edwin "Enoch Arden" Adams, Oliver Doud "Across the Continent" Byron, and those other stars which continued to shine when the foregoing had paled: Edwin "Hamlet" Booth, Lawrence "Cassius" Barrett, Joseph "Rip Van Winkle" Jefferson, John "Virginius" McCullough, Edward A. "Dundreary" Sothern, Miss

"Little Nell" Lotta, Dion "Shaughraun" Boucicault, Countess Helena "Rosalind" Modjeska, Olga "Sapho" Nethersole, Clara "Miss Multon" Morris, Mr. and Mrs. "Almighty Dollar" Florence, Annie "M'liss" Pixley, Minnie "My Sweetheart" Palmer, James A. "Hearts of Oak" Herne, Louis "My Partner" Aldrich, Harry "Diplomacy" Montague, Maurice "Captain Swift" Barrymore, Stuart Robson "Two Dromios" William H. Crane, Denman "Old Homestead" Thompson, Eleanor "Salomy Jane" Robson, William "Secret Service" Gillette, Henry E. "Adonis" Dixey, Minnie Maddern "Becky Sharp" Fiske, Maxine "Her Own Way" Elliott, Arnold "Candida" Daly, William "Svengali" Lackaye, Robert "Monbars" Mantell, Cyril "Prince Chap" Scott, and that brilliant personality and fascinating actor, Joseph K. "Fritz" Emmet, and the lovely Lillian "La Grande Duchesse" Russell, etc., etc.

Not for a moment must I forget those two players so beloved of New Yorkers, Harrigan "Mulligan Guards" Hart, Harrigan the creator and character actor, and Hart the magnetic and versatile, and those other players like the minstrels Birch, Wambold, Bernard and Backus, "Ad" Ryman and "Bob" Hart, who, as "stump speakers," so humorously satirized the foibles of the time, nor "the Water-Melon Man," J. W. McAndrews, whose narrow little "specialty," done to the life, amused the audiences continually, nor Delehanty and Hengler, who brought the song and dance to such a pitch of ease and artistry as to be veritable "crazes" of their day, and Dan Bryant, who, when he was not at the head of his minstrel company in his own theater on Twenty-Third Street and Sixth Avenue, was to be found at Wallack's delighting great audiences in a round of Irish characters of the Handy Andy type. Like Tony Pastor, he occupied a niche of his own in the affections of the people of the metropolis, as did John Brougham, who would not in the least have thought this an odd collocation of names. Nor must I omit the incomparable Weber and Fields, for so many years the joy of New York.

They were all, all gifted people who charmed the audiences of their day. A few still do. Many of them were closing brilliant careers when, as a boy, I came upon the scene. I sat as audience to all of them, knew many of them, played on the same stage with some of them, and, now, except to the advanced in years, or the student of the drama, many of them are unknown, have never even been heard of, by the present-day theater-goer, so swiftly effaced are the stage heroes of yesterday. Yet, as I remember well, how tellingly alive they were, as it seems, but a few nights ago. What charm they had for their numerous and enthusiastic followers. Well might one exclaim with "Rip": "Are we so soon forgot when we are gone!"

However, not much regret should be indulged in over the evanescence of the actor's fame. He is the most blest of artists in that he receives his reward of merit here and now, while merit in other fields waits a century oftentimes for its just recognition.

"How fortunate you are, my dear fellow," said George Meredith to David Bispham the baritone, "to find yourself appreciated while you are in the prime of manhood and can still enjoy it. Here am I, hanging on to my chair, and only in my declining years am I known to exist by the world at large."

As I lie in bed o' mornings, loath to rise to begin the daily "Dirty Dozen" which are to give assurance that the old coördinations are still unimpaired, I often think what a wonderful period in our life of the drama was that which I was fortunate enough to witness and of which to be a part. How did it compare with the present? Have we anything to-day to match it? Oh, so much.

There would be a deal more youthfulness in the world if only graying people kept the gray out of their minds and hearts. There never was a period in the drama when there was not lamenting that that drama was going to "the demnition bow-wows." And there never was a time, likely, that it was true.

Autres temps, autres mœurs, other days, other ways, applies here as elsewhere. There is much in the stage of to-day that is just as good as it ever was and something, surely, that is better. It is different, that is all, different in treatment, in presentation, and adapted to the requirements of the time. The gods and goddesses of youth, of personality, charm, and magnetism still occupy thrones, and are still receiving homage from their grateful subjects — they are merely other gods and goddesses, and other subjects.

We have the spectacle now of the best minds in literature devoting themselves to the stage. Not apologizing for it, as some men of mind thought necessary in the past, but proud of the association — Hauptman, Maeterlinck, D'Annunzio, Pirondello, Shaw, Pinero, Barrie, Galsworthy, de Curel, Molnar, Benevente, Kapek, etc., etc. Here in America, we have men like Eugene O'Neill who are beginning to receive worldwide recognition. In addition there are writers vividly picturing different phases of American life; as, Augustus Thomas, Booth Tarkington, Frank Craven, George H. Broadhurst, Langdon Mitchell, Winchell Smith, Edwin Milton Royle, J. Hartley Manners, George Ade, Rachel Crothers, Eugene Walter, Channing Pollock, Owen Davis, Porter Emerson Browne, Marc Connelly, George S. Kaufman, Gilbert Emery, Austin Strong, George Kelly, Harvey O'Higgins, Harry Leon Wilson, Montagu Glass, Lee Wilson Dodd, Brian Hooker, Arthur Goodrich, Lulu Vollmer, Zoe Akins, Susan Glaspel, Zona Gale, etc. Nor must the poetic Percy MacKaye be overlooked, nor the classic Charles Rann Kennedy, and we always have with us the versatile and effective George M. Cohan.

Men of literary feeling and cultural background are more and more turning to the stage. And what I regard as most significant with us is the great number of college men who are devoting themselves to playwriting, men who have already made names for themselves; as, Edward Sheldon, William C. De Mille, Albert E. Thomas, George E. Middleton, Phillip Barry, Arthur Richman, etc.

Following the example of Brander Matthews, late of Columbia, and Professor George P. Baker, of Harvard, whose "47 Workshop" is familiar to all stage students, we now have courses in playwriting in nearly every college in America.

To one who cares a great deal for acting and not too much for scenic decoration there sometimes appears an overabundance of the latter to the confusion and disturbance of the former. The eliminating of the motive power of a classic, as the "Ghost" from "Hamlet," happily rectified, however, after many moons, goes on now as in the days of Garrick who provided "a happy ending" to his version of "Romeo and Juliet."

And it might be told in Gath, and even published in the streets of Askelon, that there are as good actors in America as elsewhere. Given the same conditions — that is to say, years of association and intelligent direction — nothing those fine artists of the Moscow Art Theater do but could be matched by American players. The coming to us of the Russian actors has been of inestimable service. It has pointed the way and well emphasized the homely adage that the proof of the pudding is in the eating. As a result, when we accepted their invitation, we sat down to an inviting repast. There was no startling individual effort. No one shone with more brilliancy than many actors of our own whom we could name, but there was nearly always a unanimity and harmony of performance, ripely excellent and richly satisfying. What is of the utmost importance is that these performances were imbued with a spirit, an enthusiasm on the part of actors and directors proud of a splendid achievement.

They spoke in a foreign tongue. Yet with the aid of such expression as could be gleaned from much-be-whiskered faces, from illuminating gesture and admirable hints from programmes, and especially from the swing of conviction with which the actors carried themselves, they were intelligible to many.

It was frequently asked by auditors and even by critics why we had no such artists here in America, the truth being, as said, we have many such. The further truth being, too, that we shall never have such perfect *ensemble* work as the Russian players showed until a number of our actors band together, as have the Russians, and, as they, are willing to fight, bleed, and die several times, until the educational value of their work is so conclusively demonstrated that it will not be permitted to languish.

It was declared that our managers defeat the object they have in producing plays — that object, of course, being success — and an explanation was promised. The Russian players give the cue. They devote weeks merely to the reading of a play. They gather about a table for the purpose. The most our managers give is a single such reading, and often not that. "They" (the actors) "will get it as they go on," it is declared in respect of the meaning of the play. As a consequence, actors frequently give several performances before they know what it is all about. With the manuscript, the manager and the director have an intimate acquaintance, mayhap have been pondering for months, not being dramatists, to botch the play by the insertion of a few devices of their own, and seldom fail to wax impatient that actors can be so stupid about something they have been given little or no opportunity to know anything.

Greatly to increase the chances of success, then, of a play, it would unquestionably be wise that rehearsals for the first week should begin with the reading of the play, script in hand, by the actors with explanations and comment of the detailed parts by the director. No feeling of irksomeness or impatience, or suggested "waste of time," should be permitted to curtail these readings. In the end, by this means, a better, swifter knowledge of the work in hand would be secured.

On first performances an actor may give, it often happens, a satisfactory, even a brilliant presentation, but, as should be quite apparent, it is impossible at such times and under such conditions that any actor should be at "more than fifty per cent of his best." What with a sense of responsibility weighing one down, together with the ordeal of "the first time," it is not infrequently a struggle to hold on to the mere lines of the part, let alone act. As old stagers know, there are always a word here, a word there, sometimes whole phrases, which behave like fiends, absolutely refusing to be held captive. They stand off, as it were, in mockery, just out of reach, beckoning to all the other words to follow suit. And it has happened that they do, the mind becoming a blank.

With public repetitions of a play, audiences are treated to a surer, more artistic effort, making for greater pleasure and enjoyment, but, at the best, it is a little unreasonable to expect at initial performances the confident attack, the mellowed *ensemble* and effect given by an organization like the Moscow Art Players who have been long associated and appeared before us in characters familiar to them for years.

Whether or not, as in the past, the theater of the future will keep pace with the other arts and professions depends upon the theater itself and upon the public which is its reason for existence. If the theater for a continued period should offer what is unworthy, it might easily become a public nuisance instead of being a public blessing and speedily suffer an eclipse, as in the time of Charles I when it became but a reflection of rotten public morals. If the public will but encourage the best the theater has to offer and stay away from the worst, the question of the theater of the future will be swiftly and happily decided.

There is no longer reason to doubt that a theater, being a public institution, is also a public trust. There is a conviction, however, in certain quarters that it is a private business in which it is an impertinence for others to meddle. But the theater, because of its influence for good or evil, passes the barrier of private enterprise and, therefore, includes responsibility to the public, a responsibility which is not to be shirked. It becomes the duty, therefore, not necessarily of the authorities, nor of a censor, but of the public to halt

the theater when it becomes a menace. How? I repeat, by staying away from it. Nothing would prove so
salutary in this case as heroic doses of absence.

But if the theater is a public institution and possesses such wonderful influence, why does not the
State in the interest of the people control it, accept its
profits and pay its losses? Some European and even
some South American states do, practically, and regard
it as a profitable investment, but it is thought our
democratic government ill adapted to such a thing.
And it is conceivable that the theater under political
control might develop into something worse even than
the worst of state or national legislatures.

It might.

If, then, we are going to confine the theater, with its
great power — and it is a great power — to commercial exploitation, it is surely an impertinence to
interfere with its direction so long as the exploiters
stay within the law and are equitable and just in the
conduct of their business.

Placing upon actors, as has been suggested, the responsibility of refusing to appear in plays of questionable taste offers no solution as to the nature of plays
to be produced. What they, or any body of people
might think unclean, might be thought otherwise by
another individual or a class of individuals of different education, temperament, or experience. A word
or a phrase that is questionable in one aspect of the
drama may be of the highest ethical importance in
another.

The power of censorship, then, is too arbitrary to be placed upon any form of literature or the drama. But what is to be done with that class of the public which glories, or seems to glory, in a degraded drama? How is it to be controlled?

There are certain dramas given yearly which are simply bald panderings to a public which likes salty fare, plays which have no wit, no moral, nothing but suggestiveness of situation, and about which no two minds, even those who love their theater with a tang, would disagree. Such plays are given a cordial preference by a certain type of producer and have no excuse for being except a nasty appeal to nasty minds, and but one purpose, commercial gain. Without the necessity of appointing and supporting a censor, there are, or should be, legal ways to halt such a thing. The cancellation of a license or two would work a startling change, and bring great satisfaction to the reputable producer who is constantly being brought into disrepute by less conscientious managers.

At the same time, great care is to be exercised. Worthy plays of unusual force and containing high morals have been condemned because of the presence of a plain, rude speech, and the moral blindly overlooked. Nor are all those who attend such performances to be set down as prurient-minded. Curiosity is a powerful thing. Once satisfied it oftener than not proves its owner a force for cleanliness and the loudest in condemnation. We cannot well decry what we do not see or hear, and especially what we do not comprehend. Plain speech, such as is involuntarily spoken in anger or anguish by red-blooded people never hurt anybody worth hurting, no matter what the squeamish may say. If it has proved a lot of indelicacy and tactlessness, it, for all that, is quite natural, of daily, hourly occurrence, and is in no way criminal. Nor is a story which tells of life, if it be not downright disgusting, to be condemned if there is wit in the telling and inspiration in the moral.

It is true that a manager's initial outlay and financial responsibility are often tremendous. His is a highly speculative enterprise, depending upon the capricious taste of the public, and upon his ability to guess that taste, that whim, perhaps. If he should succeed three times out of five, he is a wonder. He is always guessing, anticipating and — sometimes — directing that taste, but seldom intentionally.

Conditions change so swiftly in the theater, where the unexpected plays such an important part, that within an hour, oftentimes, a manager is obliged to shift his plans with lightning rapidity in order to save his fortune from what but a little time previously appeared a brilliant prospect. Any public calamity, an earthquake, fire, pestilence, prevailing fever, death of a public official or public character, or the illness, caprice, or weakness of a chief player may ruin him overnight. Not being a philanthropist, it is small wonder, then, that he is "commercial." Failing care in this respect, no purse would be long enough to serve. This is what the comedian William Gillette meant when he said that a manager must be either "commercial or crazy." Let him be as commercial as he pleases, but not at the expense of public morals.

An urgent consideration of the theater of the future is the question of Stage Directors. I capitalize them because they are the great need of the stage of to-day. In many respects this directorship is the most important position in the theater. It requires great knowledge, extreme tact, extraordinary versatility, real vision, fine health, and energy. Without having been an actor, I doubt if any man could possibly fill such a position adequately. The French, Germans, Russians, and Italians are probably far beyond us in this respect. We have some dramatists who are, as Clyde Fitch was, skillful stage directors of their own plays, about which, naturally, they have an intimate knowledge of details, with the ability to suggest and secure the effects they seek.

There are few present-day managers capable of making artistic suggestions as to *mise-en-scène* or play, and most of them are wise enough to refrain. Others, again, from sheer desire to assume knowledge and because their investment gives them power to meddle, make merry history for ineptitude. Belasco is the great exception. In certain respects he is masterful. I have never been associated with him in a stage production, but actor friends who have are loud in praise of his patience, insight, consideration, and creative energy. His enthusiasm and love of his art are proverbial. The last of the Wallack, Daly tradition, he is one of the least purely commercial of producers. Like the American business man, it is not the dollar so much as success that he worships. Personal popularity is as the breath of his nostrils. He has had wide experience in all branches of the stage and drama. He confines his stage activities mostly to the discovery and development of promising and good-looking young actresses. Though he is seldom or never concerned in the production of a classic, he is the stage's great realist with no superior in producing strikingly beautiful effects. He has no conception of the modern woman as a heroine. His stage protagonist is the woman of a hundred years ago when she was the sport, the pleasure, and the chattel of man.

Within the last decade or two what is called "the new stagecraft" has come strongly forward. In it Gordon Craig stands for England, Max Reinhardt for Germany, Adolphe Appia for Italy, and Robert Edmond Jones, Joseph Urban, and Norman Bel-Geddes for America. All have made superb productions, though sometimes, Geddes excepted, overlaying, smothering the thing which they perhaps meant to aid and illustrate, to wit: the play.

When the house lights go down and the stage lights go up with the rising of the curtain, and the dramatist and the actor come forward with the story and its telling, it is futile, not to say presumptuous, of the scenic artist to essay the leading rôle.

Craig is the master spirit, the Trotsky of this new movement, which some fear has for its object the substitution of scenery for drama. He declares that we shall never have good drama until flesh-and-blood actors are replaced by puppets. It seems a strange statement from one who was for years an actor in Henry Irving's famous Lyceum Company and one whose mother, Ellen Terry, won distinction for her very unpuppet-like qualities in portraying emotion. There is no serious menace in the Craig averment which it is hoped will not come to the ears of his mother.

Happiness is the chief object of life. To contribute thereto is the object of the theater. Cheerfulness, kindness, courtesy, merriment, instruction, health, success, and love make up the perfect state of happiness. With its myriad tragedies, dramas, and comedies exemplifying each, the theater is a powerful factor, a ministrant force in the well-being of the world.

The atrabilious period of mankind has passed. The age has grown sensible and optimistic. We have given over the unfruitful idea that life is a melancholy preparation for something to come of which we know little or nothing. We are in accord with Kingsley in believing that the earth is "not the God-forsaken anteroom of Hell." More than ever is it realized that we must smile, laugh, and enjoy now lest we may never again have the opportunity. And it is felt that this may be done within reason without endangering our chances of salvation.

It is a real privilege to be able to contribute to the joy of the world, to steep annoyances, pain, and sor-

BRANDER MATTHEWS

Littérateur, dramatist. Professor of Dramatic Literature at Columbia College. A skilled and sympathetic writer on all matters pertaining to the stage.

DR. HENRY W. BELLOWS

A prominent Unitarian divine. In his "Relation of Public Amusements to Public Morality," he defends the stage, declaring that "amusement is not merely defensible, the want of it is a calamity."

row in forgetfulness, even temporarily. Maybe I have aided a little in this way. At all events I have been told so. People have written about it. I hope they meant it. Those who have been notable in pleasing the world have sometimes been called "public benefactors." It is a fine, high-sounding expression. I love it. I have a feeling, shared by others, that "public necessities" would be a better, perhaps a truer characterization.

Says Dr. Bellows: "The will that rests for a while is more vigorous than the will that is always strained." The laws of physical and moral health demand change of thought, relaxation, amusement, laughter. Failing this change, sooner or later, Nature avenges herself for the violation. The theater supplies this change; hence its importance, its necessity. The theater is the antithesis of routine, strain. It is the great contrast, relief and antidote to the toil and anxieties of life.

Nothing is farther from my wish than to create the impression that the theater has only to do with humor. Quite the contrary. Humor is only a part of its quality. Yes, the theater is for pastime, entertainment, splendidly so; but it is also for education, development, and evolution.

The theater has to do with that dynamic force called emotion, than which nature has nothing stronger. That which is impressed upon our minds and hearts through emotion, whether of laughter or tears, is deeply, indelibly impressed. Not, therefore, to make use of such a force in driving home the lessons, the truths of morality, religion, and history, the lessons of manners, customs, even of geography, seems a thousand pities. To abandon such a power to speculating commercialism, instead of organizing, directing, and protecting it for public well-being, is like using water merely to sprinkle flowers and neglecting it for the mighty purposes of steam.

I love the theater for many reasons, some of which I have been giving, but most of all I love it for the happiness I know it has brought and brings not only to me, but to the world.

In closing these remembrances, I feel with Renan, that unless life is reserving much sorrow for my final years, or hours, I shall have nothing but thanks to offer the Giver of all good for the charming passage that has been permitted me across reality.

T
H
E

E
N
D

INDEX

INDEX

Abbott, Emma, 181, 182.

Abbott, Lawrence F., praises performances of "The Rivals," 222.

Abélard, Père, 424.

Abeles, Edward, as "Frère Grégoire," in "The Little Father of the Wilderness," 287.

Acting, the profession of, aspirants to, 362, 363; allurements of, 363; offers startling opportunities for advancement, 363; readiness great necessity in, 363, 364; examination of aptitude before adoption of, 364, 365; a natural gift lies back of permanent success in, 365–67; how to determine possession of personality needed for, 367, 368; power of perception and emotion the second qualification for, 368; other requisites for, 370; reasons for adopting, 371; way of beginning, 373–76; sympathetic voice needed for, 376–80; creative force of, 380–83; depends on special aptitudes rather than on general intellectual vigor, 391.

Actor, the, three accomplishments of, 55; a trick of, 55–57; his voice, 309, 376–80; creative force of, 380–83; observation of self necessary to, 384; must express feeling, 385; must be heard and understood, 386–88; "engaging types" of, 388; must be natural, 388, 389; the importance of the center of the stage to, 389; who thinks his whole duty is to come "perfect," 389, 390; should be alert, 390; and stage direction, 392, 393; surpasses the dramatist in getting into the heart of characters, 392, 393.

Actor-managers, and Theatrical Syndicate, 148–59; "stock" companies maintained by, 154; more or less birds of passage, 244.

Actors, tributes to, 5–8; status of, in 1912, 243, 247; money secondary to art with, 247; subjected to injustices, 248–51; strike, 263–73; parade of, 263; broke no contract in striking, 275; reasons for their strike, 275, 276. *See* Theatrical Syndicate.

Actors' Equity Association, The, actor's status improved since advent of, 100, 101, 162, 166, 243; organized, 251; difficulty in bringing actors into, 252, 253; meeting of, with managers, 253; makes standard contract with managers, 253; tries to obtain second meeting, 254; alliance with American Federation of Labor considered, 255, 259; second meeting of, with managers, 256–62; joins American Federation of Labor, 262; parade of, 263; not to be disrupted, 264, 270; members answer call for funds, 264; secures funds through extraordinary performances, 267, 268; reasons for strike of, 275, 276; to what extent it is a labor organization, 276; is not a "closed shop," 276; "Equity Shop," 276, 277; Wilson devotes efforts to interests of, 337.

Actors' Fund of America, 223, 270.

Adams, Edwin, 329, 428; his voice, 379.

Adams, Maude, kept herself to herself, 408; never married, 409; proposed to, by Wilson, 410, 411.

Aldrich, Louis, 429.

Aldrich, T. B., 123, 137.

Alfieri, 424.

Alger, Reverend Doctor, biographer of Edwin Forrest, 311.

All-star casts, 327–30.
All-Star Rivals Company, 216, 330.
Amateurs, 109–11.
American Federation of Labor, Actors' Equity Association joins, 255, 259, 262.
Anderson, David, and Booth, 121, 137.
Anderson, Percy, water-color artist, 346, 347.
Annunzio, Gabrielle d', and Duse, 411–14.
Antier, Benjamin, and "Robert Macaire," 87, 88.
"Apajune, the Water Sprite," 70.
Appia, Adolphe, and "the new stagecraft," 441.
Arlington, "Billy," minstrel, 43, 130.
Arliss, George, in the actors' strike, 274; on personality in the actor, 367; says acting is a "bag of tricks," 389.
Arnold, Matthew, 301.
Arnould, Sophie, Abbé Galliani's comment on, 309.
Aronson, Rudolph, in partnership with McCaull, 63; separates from McCaull, 72; Wilson under, 72, 73; how he lost and secured a fortune through "Erminie," 77, 78; out of sympathy with "Erminie," 79–81; his father, 91; his proposal to Wilson, 92–94; his conduct puzzling, 99; had little qualification for management, 100; incensed at Wilson, 101, 102; his attempted revenge, 102–04.
Ayres, Alfred, 377.

"Bachelor's Baby, The," 289, 290.
Backus, Charles, minstrel, 43, 50; tests his sensibility, 368, 369; mentioned, 429.
Bacon, Frank, in "Lightnin'," 214, 215; in the actors' strike, 273; and Shelley Hall, incident of, 322, 323.
Badeau, Adam, 137; letter of Booth to, on wife's death, 420–22.
Baker, George P., 433.
Baker, Lewis, 217.
Baker, Sam, 398, 399.

Baldwin Theater Company, the, 47.
Bannister, Jack, thrilled by Garrick, 386.
Barber, Nellie, of Chestnut Street Theater Company, 51.
Barker, Richard, stage director, 107.
Barnum, P. T., 154.
Barrett, Lawrence, and Booth, 122, 129, 137; on Edwin Forrest as actor, 312; mentioned, 428.
Barrie, Sir James, his "Appreciation of Charles Frohman" quoted, 34; his "Rosemary," 217; and Mary Devlin, 420; mentioned, 35, 366.
Barrie, Mira, marries Francis Wilson, 61.
Barrymore, Ethel, early misgivings about her talent, 217, 218, 334; as "Lady Teazle," 222; why she took the actors' side in the strike, 273; her reason for adopting the stage, 371.
Barrymore, Georgie Drew, 218.
Barrymore, John, 218; in "The School for Scandal," 222; in Chimney Corner fancy, 294; in "The Fortune Hunter," 322.
Barrymore, Lionel, 218; in "The School for Scandal," 222.
Barrymore, Maurice, witticisms of, 220; mentioned, 429.
Barton, pooh-poohs "Erminie," 77.
Bartram, Ernest, of Chestnut Street Theater Company, 51.
Batchelder, John D., presents First Folio to The Players Club, 320.
Bave, Harry, of Chestnut Street Theater Company, 51, 52.
"Beggars' Opera, The," 76, 341.
Belasco, David, and the Theatrical Syndicate, 151, 152; and William Sampson, 393; his description of Maude Adams as a girl, 409; masterful, 440; one of least commercial producers, 441; discovers and develops actresses, 441.
Bel-Geddes, Norman, gives setting to new "Erminie," 339, 345; and "the new stagecraft," 346, 441.

Bellamy, Edward, writes lyrics of "Erminie," 89.

Bellows, Reverend Henry W., his tribute to the drama, 8; quoted, 443.

Below, Ida Comstock, sister-in-law of Eugene Field, 174.

Benedict, E. C., 133, 137.

Béranger, P. J., 424.

Bernard, minstrel, 429.

Bernhardt, Sarah, plays under tent, 158; at The Players, 301, 302; silent on her love affairs, 424.

Betterton, Thomas, his voice, 380.

Birch, "Billy," minstrel, 43, 50, 429.

Birch, Wambold, and Backus Minstrels, 50.

Bispham, David, 431.

Bispham, William, 123, 137; story of Booth told by, 144.

"Bob Acres," Wilson as, 221–25.

Booth, Edwin, in "Richard III," 48; as minstrel, 60; as "Robert Macaire," 118; envelope marked "Police Headquarters" sent to, 119; and David Anderson, 121; and Lawrence Barrett, 122; at Cos Cob, 122, 123; tells anecdote of Jefferson, 123; tells anecdote of his father, 124; in farcical parts, 124, 125; posts his own bills, 125, 126; alert to a humorous situation, 126, 127; his reserve, 127, 128; scintillates in talk, 129; his ideas on leadership, 129, 130; seemed to tower in certain parts, 132; at dedication of Actors' Fund Monument, 132, 133; makes acquaintance of Wilson, 133, 134; his swordsmanship, 135; on his father, 136; had few intimates, 137; founds The Players, 137, 143; portraits of, 137, 138; gives autograph to Wilson, 139–42; his view of Hamlet's insanity, 142; his admiration and affection for Dr. Furness, 142, 143; adored his profession, 143; confused by people greeting him, 144; rescues Robert Lincoln, 144–46; misfor-

tunes of, 146, 147; death, 147; in Chimney Corner fancy, 293–95; buried from the Little Church Around the Corner, 303; and spiritualism, 305; his voice, 377; Salvini's tribute to, 378; words of, 381; kept himself to himself, 408; marries Mary Devlin, 420; letter to Adam Badeau on his wife's death, 420–22; mentioned, 428.

Booth, Edwina, daughter of Edwin Booth, 122, 125, 142, 420.

Booth, John Wilkes, 135.

Booth, Junius Brutus, 46; pupil of Monsterey, 131; his swordsmanship, 135.

Booth, the elder, 124, 136, 146.

Boswell, James, quoted, 279; charm of his "Life of Samuel Johnson," 423.

Boucicault, Dion, saying of, 89; on "The Oolah," 105; rewrites "Rip Van Winkle," 209–12; began midweek performances, 249; warns Jefferson, 286, 287; as to his responsibility for matinées, 303; mentioned, 429.

Bowers, Mrs. D. P., 428.

Braham, David, 169.

Braham, John, 169.

Briggs, Claire, cartoonist, 112.

Brougham, John, 430.

Brower, Frank, minstrel, 43.

Bruns, Edna, Wilson's wife, 415–19.

Bryant, Dan, minstrel, 43, 430.

Buckley, "Ned," of Baldwin Theater Company, 47.

Burgess, Cool, minstrel, 43.

Burke, Charles, 209.

Burr, Anna Robeson, quoted, 423.

Burton, Dr. Richard, 355.

Byron, Lord, quotation from, 5.

Byron, Oliver Doud, 428.

Caffray, medium, 305.

Calcraft, his "Defense of the Stage" presented to Wilson, 321.

Calvé, Emma, 413.

Campbell, Bartley, assurance of, 54.

Campbell, Thomas, quotation from, 5.

Canby, Albert H., gives Wilson encouragement to become a "star," 100.

Carleton, William T., in "Don Sancho," 65; with the song "Woman, Fair Woman," 70, 71; in "Nanon," 73.

Carlyle, Thomas, 424.

Carncross, John L., minstrel, 43.

Carryl, Charles, 123.

Carter, "Billy," minstrel, 43.

Casino, the, New York, 89.

Castle, William, 73.

Catalani, self-appreciation of, 54.

Catenhusen, Ernst, director, 65.

Catherine II of Russia, 424.

Censorship of the drama, 438.

Chanfrau, Frank, 428.

Chapman, John Jay, praises performances of "The Rivals," 222.

Chatterton, John (Signor Perugini), 65.

Chestnut Street Theater, company, 51; how conducted, 384.

Chimney Corner. See Players Club.

Cibber, Colley, 424; on the voice of Thomas Betterton, 380; satirically merry over "menagers," 427.

Clairon, Mlle., 382.

Clapp, C. C., 125 n.

Clarke, John S., as minstrel, 60.

Claxton, Kate, in Chimney Corner fancy, 295.

Clemens, S. L. ("Mark Twain"), 82; at The Players, 298, 299; anecdotes of, 299–301.

Cleveland, Grover, neighbor of Joseph Jefferson, 198, 226.

Cleveland, Mrs. Grover, 319.

Cohan, George M., attitude in struggle between actors and managers, 260, 261, 270.

Colby, Bainbridge, counsel for managers in actors' strike, 274.

Collier, Jeremy, 7.

Collinge, Patricia, as "Lucy" in "The Rivals," 221.

Columbia University, play-acting in, 375.

Comedy and tragedy, relative merits and difficulties of, 204–06.

Comic opera, 62.

Conkling, George, Lion-tamer, 41.

Conkling, John, "strong man," 42.

Conkling, Peter, clown, 42.

Conquest, Ida, in Chimney Corner fancy, 293, 294.

Conried, Heinrich, stage director and impressario, 73.

Cope, John, in the actors' strike, 274.

Coquelin, Constant, 116, 323.

Corneille, had a "sterile mouth," 391.

Cotton, Ben, minstrel, 43, 49, 130.

Cottrelly, Mathilde, singing comédienne, 67.

Couldock, C. W., gives advice to actor, 372.

"Cousin Billy," 284, 288.

Crabtree, Charlotte, 58.

Craig, Gordon, and "the new stage-craft," 441, 442.

Craig, Robert, 214.

Crane, William H., of Baldwin Theater Company, 47; as minstrel, 59; manner of, 174; joked by Eugene Field, 182; in All-Star Rivals Company, 216, 330; anecdote of, 332, 333; in "Julius Cæsar," 379; mentioned, 429.

Crane, Mrs., poem of Field to, 182.

Curci, Galli, her opinion of James Gibbons Huneker, 340.

Curtain speeches, 347; of Hopper and Wilson, 348–53.

Curtis, Uncle John, 28.

Cushman, Charlotte, paraphrase of Tennyson addressed to, 6; supported by Couldock, 372; mentioned, 428.

Cutler, George, cannon-ball king, 41.

"Cyrano de Bergerac," 323, 324.

Daboll, William S., in "Erminie," 84; characterization of, 84; death, 85.

Daly, Arnold, 429.

INDEX

Daly, Augustin, vice-president of The Players Club, 325, 326; actresses developed under, 378.
Daly, Judge, 325, 326.
Dana, Charles A., 188.
Darwin, Charles, 424.
Davenport, Edward L., Wilson given letter of introduction to, 39, 40; mentioned, 428.
Davenport, Fanny, opposed to Theatrical Syndicate, 151, 152; developed under Augustin Daly, 378.
Davis, Richard Harding, 220.
"Davy Crockett," 214.
Dean, Julia, 406–08.
Delehanty, 429.
De Mott, James, bareback rider, 41.
DeNovellis, Antonio, conductor, 108.
"Denver Tribune Primer, The," 170.
Devlin, Mary, wife of Edwin Booth, 305, 420; death, 420; letter of Booth on her death, 420–22.
Dickens, Charles, 338.
Director, stage, the, 392–95, 440.
Dixey, E. F., minstrel, 43.
Dixey, Henry E., in "Adonis," 77; in "Evangeline," 106; recites poem of Field, 170; as "Malvolio," 205; fancy of, at the Chimney Corner, 292–96; mentioned, 429.
"Dixie," 428.
Doctor Polyanthe, 87, 88.
"Don Sancho," 64.
Dougherty, Hughey, minstrel, 43, 49.
Doyle, Sir Arthur Conan, 305.
Drake, Mrs., 407.
Drama, tributes to, 5–8; of to-day, 431; writers of, 432; control of, 438.
Dramatic schools, 374–76.
Drew, Frank, 428.
Drew, John, father, in "The Rivals," 215; in Chimney Corner fancy, 293–95.
Drew, John, son, gives dinner to cast of All-Star Rivals Company, 216; in "The School for Scandal," 222.
Drew, Mrs. John, 59; her "Mrs. Mala-

prop," 215; in the "Letter-Scene" of "The Rivals," 216; at head of All-Star Rivals Company, 216, 330.
Drew, Sidney, 169.
Dudley, Annabelle, of Chestnut Street Theater Company, 51.
Dumas, Alexandre, expressions of gratitude to Mlle. Clairon, 382.
Duse, actress, 369; and D'Annunzio, 411–14.
Dutassy, 402–04.

Edison, Thomas A., anecdote of, 296–98; penmanship of, 298.
Edouin, Willie, 77.
Elliott, Maxine, 429.
Elliston, Robert William, Charles Lamb's address to, 7.
Emerson, "Billy," minstrel, 43, 48–50.
Emerson, Ralph Waldo, and Walt Whitman, 236.
"Emily," mother of Francis Wilson, 10; an all-round good fellow, 10; not a "superior" woman, 11; her dancing, 11, 19; doubts "eternal damnation," 12; manner with her son, the grown man, 12; her modesty, 13; sensitiveness of, 13; her husband, 13–15; her love of children, 15; her love of animals, 15, 16; her prejudice against the negro, 16, 17; anecdotes of, 17–20; death of first daughter, 20; at theater at opening performances, 21; her influence on Francis, 22, 23; ruins Francis's new suit of clothes, 23–25; her love for ice-cream, 25; her singing, 25; her celestial occupation, 26; her first thought, to keep the family together, 36; Wilson's constant love, 398.
Emmet, Joseph K., 429.
Emmet, Katherine, in the actors' strike, 274.
Ensemble music, 66.
Equity Players, think to give "Rip Van Winkle," 213; "The Rivals" produced for, 222.
"Equity Shop," 276, 277.

Erlanger. *See* Klaw and Erlanger.

"Erminie," Lillian Russell in, 73; composer of, 74; Wilson hissed in, 75; most successful operetta of modern times, 76; a clean play, 77; lost and won a fortune for Aronson, 77; how Goodwin loses a fortune by, 77–79; how it goes to Aronson, 77, 78; vogue of, 79, 80; Aronson out of sympathy with, 79–81; Wilson's part in, 80; puns in, 82; cast of, 83–87; the music of, 83, 84; interpolated number, "Downy Jail Birds of a Feather," 85; history of origin of, 87–89; Wilson averts calamity in course of performance of, 90, 91; revival of, 336, 338, 339; received with acclamation, 339; Huneker's remarks on, 340–45; old spirit preserved in revival of, 345; letter of Owen Wister on, 345, 346.

Erroll, George, of Chestnut Street Theater Company, 51.

Ethel, Agnes, 378.

"Evangeline," 106.

"Falka," 68.

Farren, William, rather stupid off the stage, 370, 391.

Fechter, Charles, 428.

Ferguson, Elsie, begins in company of Wilson, 109.

Ferguson, W. J., of Chestnut Street Theater Company, 51.

"Fidelity, The," 268, 270.

"Fidos," the, 268, 270.

Field, Eugene, agrees that Wilson should make promises, 5; his verses to Marie Jansen, 113, 115, 116; verses of, on Wilson, 168; his "Little Boy Blue," 168; his poem "A Little Peach in an Orchard Grew," 169; recites "The Little Peach," 169; his story of the Peach in "The Denver Tribune Primer," 170; his "Culture's Garland," 170–72; and Stedman, 171; books on which his popularity rests, 172; his "Echoes from the Sabine Farm," 172, 173; wished to become an actor, 173; at college, 174; in demand for entertainments, 174; and Sol Smith Russell, 175, 176; his friendship with actors, 176, 177; had enthusiasm in abundance, 177; had no skill as a dramatist, 177; an inspiration to those interested in books, 178; verses of, addressed to Wilson, 178; incites ambition, 179; importuned for autograph, 179; "The Passing of Eugene," 180; his manner of joking actor friends, 180–84; and Madame Modjeska, 180; jests on Wilson's legs, 182, 183, 341; verses on Richard Mansfield, 184, 185; as a collector, 186–89, 197; his library, 189; his "The Love Affairs of a Bibliomaniac," 189; characteristics of, 190; satirical of Chicagoans, 190; and McClurg, 191, 192; imitates donkey, 192; fond of apple pie, 192; a practical joker, 193; delighted in surprises, 193; an unpublished poem of, 194, 195; tribute to, 195; death, 196; penmanship of, 298; remembrance of, written by Wilson, 424, 425.

Field, Roswell, brother of Eugene Field, 174, 193.

Fields, Weber and, 430.

Firmin, 88.

Fiske, Mrs., opposed to Theatrical Syndicate, 151, 156, 157; mentioned, 429.

Fitch, Clyde, makes changes in "Cousin Billy," 284; reads "Pamela's Prodigy" to Wilson, 306, 307; his "Nathan Hale," 307, 308; artistic collection of, 308; speech-suggestions of, 308, 309; skillful stage director, 440.

Florence, Mr. and Mrs., 429.

Folsom, Agnes, in "Erminie," 85.

Forrest, Edwin, three accomplishments of an actor, according to, 55; on Elizabeth Jefferson, 208; with Mrs. Stirling, 215; greatest Ameri-

can tragedian, 310–12; hissed Macready, 311, 312; his voice, 377; surprised at the man who thinks, 390; mentioned, 428.
"Fortune Hunter, The," 322.
Fox, George L., 428.
Fox, George Quaker, 424.
Franklin, Benjamin, 423.
Freeman, Max, in encounter with Wilson, 101, 102.
French, Mary Field, daughter of Eugene Field, 175, 193.
Frohman, Charles, from Sir James Barrie's "Appreciation" of, 34; member of Theatrical Syndicate, 148; makes agreement with Wilson, 280, 281; his passion, the drama, 282; in touch with best dramatists, 283; makes changes in "Cousin Billy," 284; his opinion of "The Bachelor's Baby," 290.
Frohman, Daniel, 224, 413.
Furness, Caroline, 143.
Furness, Dr. Horace Howard, and Booth, 142, 143; on Walt Whitman, 234; had little estimate of the character of Whitman's poems, 235; and spiritualism, 305, 306.
Furness, Dr. Horace Howard, Jr., 142.

Galliani, Abbé, his comment on Sophie Arnould's voice, 309.
Gallio, of "Cosa Sia," 370.
Garrett, Edmund H., his vignettes to "Echoes from the Sabine Farm," 173.
Garrick, David, Johnson on his death, 5; abused by Johnson, 190; on comedy- and tragedy-acting, 204; tests his sensibility, 368, 369; on Préville, 382; his tones thrilling, 386; his epitaph on Goldsmith, 391; epitaph of Goldsmith on, 391 n.; Sheridan's lines on, 393.
Gaston, George, 64.
Gemmill, William D., manager of Chestnut Street Theater, 51, 385.
Georges, Mlle., 424.

German War, the, 337, 338.
Gibbon, Edward, 424.
Gilbert, John, disapproved of Jefferson's alterations in "The Rivals," 219.
Gilbert, William, singing of, 66.
Gillette, William, on the manager, 247; his "The Illusion of the First Time in Acting," 367; on commercialism in managers, 439, 440; mentioned, 429.
Gillmore, Frank, Executive Secretary of Actors' Equity Association, 271, 273, 274.
Gillmore, Margalo, in Chimney Corner fancy, 294.
Gladstone, Henry Neville, 188 n.
Gladstone, W. E., axe of, 188.
Glaser, Lulu, 108, 109.
Glover, Lillie, of Chestnut Street Theater Company, 51.
Golden, Richard, in "Evangeline," 106.
Goldoni, Carlo, 68–70, 424.
Goldsmith, Oliver, his conversation not brilliant, 391; epitaph of Garrick on, 391; his epitaph on Garrick, 391 n.
Goodwin, J. Cheever, author of songs in "The Merry Monarch," 106.
Goodwin, Nat C., as minstrel, 60; how he lost a fortune from "Erminie," 77, 78; opposed to Theatrical Syndicate, 151, 152; his idea of a chain of theaters, 152; goes over to the Syndicate, 152, 156; in All-Star Rivals Company, 216, 330; unsuccessful with "Beauty and the Barge," 283; in "Nathan Hale," 307, 308; in "Julius Cæsar," 379.
Gosse, Edmund, 424.
Gotthold, Charles, anecdote of, 127.
Gouggenheim, Adelaide and Joey, 125 n.
Grant, Percy Stickney, his remarks at Fitch's funeral, 308.
Greensfelder, Joseph, 65.
Grein, J. T., critic, 382.

Grossman, Mrs. *See* Booth, Edwina.
Gunther, Archibald, 54.
"Gypsy Baron, The," 73, 74.

Hackett, James K., anecdote of, 296.
Hading, Jane, and Wilson, 116, 117.
Hall, Pauline, in "Erminie," 83.
Hamlet, Booth's view of his insanity, 142.
Hamlin, Harry, son of John Hamlin, 169.
Hamlin, John, theater manager, 169.
Hampden, Walter, in "Cyrano de Bergerac," 323.
Hardie, James, of Chestnut Street Theater Company, 51.
Harrigan, 429.
Hart, "Bob," 429.
Hart, "Tony," benefit preformance for, 379; magnetic and versatile, 429.
Harte, Bret, his "Sue," 382, 383.
Harvard University, play-writing in, 375.
Haverly, J. H., 61.
Hawthorne, Julian, his Introduction to Field's "Culture's Garland," 170.
Hawthorne, Nathaniel, his granddaughter, Hildegarde, 232.
Hayman, Al, member of Theatrical Syndicate, 148; and Charles Frohman, 282, 283.
Hayman, Alf, and Charles Frohman, 282, 283.
Heine, Heinrich, 397.
Heming, Violet, as "Lydia Languish," 216.
Hengler, 429.
Henley, William Ernest, his "Macaire," 88.
Herbert, Victor, 323.
Herford, Oliver, 220.
Herne, James A., 429; of Baldwin Theater Company, 47.
Hodge, William, and Lee Shubert, 266, 267.
Holland, Edmund, in All-Star Rivals Company, 216, 330.

Holland, George, Jr., of Chestnut Street Theater Company, 51.
Holland, George, Sr., death, 303.
Holland, Joseph J., of Chestnut Street Theater Company, 51; in All-Star Rivals Company, 216, 330.
Holland, Mrs., 303.
Hopper, DeWolf, appears in "Erminie," 338, 339; his curtain speech to "Erminie," 348–53; characteristics of, 353–56.
Horn, "Eph," minstrel, 43.
Howard, Bronson, his tribute to Charles R. Thorne, 383.
Howard Athenæum, 44.
Hoyt, Henry E., 346.
Hugo, Victor, 382.
Hull, Josephine, in the actors' strike, 274.
Hull, Shelley, and Frank Bacon, incident of, 322, 323.
Huneker, James Gibbons, on Walt Whitman, 237; his remarks on "Erminie" revived, 340–45.
Hunt, Leigh, 424.
Hutton, Laurence, 123; paraphrase of Tennyson, 6.
Hyacinthe, Père, 3, 4.

Irving, Henry, imitated by Eugene Field, 174, 175; on death of Field, 196; as "Malvolio," 204–06; presents Wilson with Calcraft's "Defense of the Stage," 321; on personality in the actress, 367; declared Ada Rehan a great actress, 378; disappointed in Fanny Kemble, 387.
Irving, Washington, 177.

Jacobowski, composer of "Erminie," 74, 83, 89.
James, Louis, of Baldwin Theater Company, 47.
"James," Wilson's butler, 313, 314.
Jansen, Marie, in "Erminie," 85; engaged for "The Oolah," 101; in "The Merry Monarch," 113; characterization of, 113; takes place of

Sadie Martinot in "Nadjy," 113, 114; Eugene Field's verses to, 115, 116; in duet, "The Little Peach," 169.

Jay, Harriett, authoress of "When Knights Were Bold," 289.

Jayne, Horace Furness, grandson of Dr. Furness, 235.

Jayne, Mrs. Horace. *See* Furness, Caroline.

Jefferson, Charles, son of Joseph Jefferson, 199, 200.

Jefferson, Elizabeth, aunt of Joseph Jefferson, 208.

Jefferson, Joseph, father of Joseph Jefferson ("Rip"), 209.

Jefferson, Joseph, tribute to, 7; as minstrel, 59; anecdote of, 123; opposed to Theatrical Syndicate, 151; Field's copy of his "Autobiography," 193; practices of, 197; a family man, 197; his credulousness, 198; riding the bicycle, 198; as duck-shooter, 199; devoted to painting, 199; a sun-hunter, 199, 200; his last picture, 200; his popularity and influence, 200; degrees of, 200; amused by limericks, 201–04; as regards his greatness as an actor, 204, 206, 207; had gift of character presentation, 207; his ancestors, 207–09; unsuccessful at first with "Rip Van Winkle," 209; gets Boucicault to rewrite "Rip Van Winkle," 209–12; in early version of "The Rivals," 215; revises "The Rivals," 216, 218–22; his enjoyment of Mrs. Drew's acting, 216; at head of All-Star Rivals Company, 216; sayings and doings of, issued in book form, 217; kept finger on public pulse, 225; his painting, 226; his fishing, 226; tribute of Henry Watterson to, 227; as "Caleb Plummer," 286; in Chimney Corner fancy, 293–95; and The Little Church Around the Corner, 303, 304; and spiritualism, 305; his views of all-star casts, 329, 330; spontaneity of, 383; and

Julia Dean, 406–08; Mary Devlin the ward of, 420; Boswellized by Wilson, 425; mentioned, 428.

Jefferson, Thomas, great-great-grand-father of Thomas Jefferson ("Rip"), 207.

John and Jess, 107.

Johnson, Robert Underwood, poet, 74.

Johnson, Samuel, quotations from, 5, 67; and Garrick, 190.

Jones, Robert Edmond, and "the new stagecraft," 346, 441.

Kapek, Karel and Joseph, dramatists, 231.

Kean, Edmund, words of Byron to, 5.

Kellar, necromancer, 305.

Kelly, George, "Leaper," 42.

Kemble, Edward, cartoonist, goes duck-shooting with Joseph Jefferson, 199.

Kemble, Frances Anne, her manner of reading, 387.

Kemble, John Phillip, Campbell's "Ode of Farewell" to, 5.

Kemble, John R., minstrel, 43, 130.

"Kemble tradition," the, 387.

Kennedy, M. A., of Baldwin Theater Company, 47.

Klaw and Erlanger, members of Theatrical Syndicate, 148; threatened dissolution of, 256.

Knight, tells story of Garrick and Préville, 369.

Knowles, Sheridan, 208.

Lackaye, Wilton, 429.

Lamartine, A. L. M., 424.

Lamb, Charles, quoted on Robert William Elliston, 7; quoted on Joseph Shepherd Munden, 7; hisses his own comedy, 75; wrote with sympathy, 393.

Lander, J. D., 428.

Laughing, the psychology of, 332.

Lay, Oliver, painter of Booth as "Hamlet," 137.

"Leaves of Grass," 230–32, 234–38.

Lee, Henry, of Chestnut Street Theater Company, 51.
Lemaître, Frédéric, his part of "Robert Macaire," 87, 88; his first appearance, 106; Hugo's compliments to, 382; goes contrary to stage direction, 392.
Levy, Jules, soloist, 70.
Lewes, on Montal in "Vingt Ans Après," 366; on the actor's voice, 380; challenge to Macready, 381; wrote with sympathy, 393.
Lewis, Dr. Bransford, 359.
"Lightnin'," 215, 322, 323.
Limericks, 201–04.
Lincoln, Robert, rescued by Edwin Booth, 144–46.
Little Church Around the Corner, The, 303, 304.
"Little Father of the Wilderness, The," 284–88.
"Little Peach, The," song, 169.
Locker-Lamson, 424.
Lodge, Sir Oliver, 305.
Lotta, Miss, 58, 429.
Love experiences, 396, 397.
Ludlow, on Jefferson, 208.

MacDonald, Christie, begins in company of Wilson, 109.
Mackay, John A., 170.
MacKaye, Steele, 379.
Mackin, James, partner of Wilson, 41–46; in fight with Wilson, 45, 46; last interview with Wilson, 59; death, 59.
Mackin & Wilson, 43–46.
Macready, William Charles, Tennyson on, 6; in "Falkland" in "The Rivals," 221; hissed by Edwin Forrest, 311, 312; introduced curtain speech, 347; his father, 364; challenged, 381.
Maguire, James, clown, 41.
Mallory, Walter, 298.
"Malvolio," the part, 204–06.
Managers, meet Actors' Equity Association, 253; make standard contract with actors, 253; evade second meeting, 254; come to second meeting with actors, 256–62; yield to certain demands, 262; at actors' strike, 264–73; why they yielded, 273; do not like "Equity Shop," 277, 278; their code of business ethics contemptible, 244; have no idea of art, 244; arrogance of, 244–47; vanishing of old relations, between actors and, 247; actors subjected to injustices by, 248–51; the aim of, 278; initial outlay of, 439; may be commercial, but not at expense of public morals, 439, 440. See Producing Managers' Association, Theatrical Syndicate.
Managers' Lockout. See Theatrical Syndicate.
Manning, "Billy," minstrel, 43.
Manola, Marion, in "Erminie," 85.
Mansfield, Alice, of Chestnut Street Theater Company, 51.
Mansfield, Richard, opposed to Theatrical Syndicate, 151, 152; verses of Field on, 184, 185; in "Cyrano de Bergerac," 323; and DeWolf Hopper, 356; his voice, 380.
Mantell, Robert, 429.
Mark Twain. See Clemens.
Marlow, Charles. See Jay, Harriett.
Marlowe, Julia, as "Lydia Languish," 216; in All-Star Rivals Company, 216, 330; remark of, 328; her voice, 380; kept herself to herself, 408.
Martinot, Sadie, in "Nanon," 73; withdraws from cast of "Nadjy," 114.
Mathews, Charles, 370.
Matinée performances, 249, 303.
Matthews, Brander, on good comedies without apparent moral, 66; writes letter to Mark Twain, 300; on dramatic effect produced by actor, 382; recognizes the actor's contribution to the character, 393; mentioned, 433.
Maude, Cyril, 283.
Mayo, Frank, 46, 214; on Edwin For-

rest's voice, 377; in "Julius Cæsar," 379.

McAndrews, J. W., 429; minstrel, 43.

McCaull, Colonel John A., becomes associated with Wilson, 63; anecdote of, 67; incensed at Wilson, 71; separates from Aronson, 72; characterization of, 72; death, 73.

McClurg, Alexander C., unappreciative of Eugene Field, 191.

McCullough, John, 428.

Melnotte, Violette, 77.

Melville, Emily, 72.

Meredith, George, 431.

"Merry Monarch, The," first performance of, 105; how Wilson came by, 106; introduction of John and Jess in, 107.

"Merry War, The," 68, 70.

Merryweather, F. Somner, copy of his "Bibliomania in the Middle Ages," 178.

Meyer, Levy, decision given by, in actors' strike, 273.

Middleton, George, 291.

Millard, George M., 180 n.

Miller, Henry, manager, 260.

Minstrelsy, vogue of, 43-45; discussion of, 59, 60.

Mitchell, Grant, 218.

Mitchell, Maggie, 428.

Mitchell's Pleasure Party, 60.

Modjeska, Madame, 177, 180, 429.

Monsterey, Colonel Thomas H., expert swordsman, 45-47; his redeeming weakness, 46; Junius Brutus pupil of, 131.

Montague, Harry, 429.

Montal, in "Vingt Ans Après," 366.

Moran, Frank, minstrel, 43.

Morris, Clara, 372, 378, 429.

Morse, Woolson, composer of music for songs in "The Merry Monarch," 106.

Moscow Art Theater, 433-36.

"Mountain Climber, The," 288.

Munden, Joseph Shepherd, Charles Lamb's address to, 7.

Murdock, James E., on Edwin Forrest's acting, 310, 311; in "The School for Scandal," 329; on Edwin Forrest's voice, 377; mentioned, 428.

"Nadjy," 113, 114, 169.

"Nanon," 73.

"Nathan Hale," 307, 308.

Nethersole, Olga, 429.

"New stagecraft, the," 441.

Nixon and Zimmerman, members of Theatrical Syndicate, 148, 161.

Nixon-Nirdlinger, Samuel F., makes bargain with Wilson, 161-64.

O'Dell, Professor George, 321.

Ogden, John, received advice from Couldock, 372, 373.

Oliphant, Mrs., 424.

O'Neill, James, 432; of Baldwin Theater Company, 47; opposed to Theatrical Syndicate, 151.

"Oolah, The," the story of, 98, 99; cast for, 101; first production of, 103; lacks skillful construction, 104; changed, 104; has successful season, 105; Jane Hading at performance of, 116, 117.

Osbourne, Lloyd, 285.

"Our Goblins," 60-62.

Owens, John E., 428.

Palmer, A. M., opposed to the Theatrical Syndicate, 152, 156; vice-president of The Players Club, 325.

Palmer, Minnie, 429.

"Pamela's Prodigy," 306, 307.

Pastor, Tony, 44, 430.

Paulton, Harry, author of "Erminie," 74, 80-82, 89, 346.

Performances, first, 435.

Personality, requisite for the actor, 367; how to determine possession of, 367, 368; qualities comprised in, 368; works through voice, facial expression, and gesture, 376, 377.

Perugini, Signor (John Chatterton), 65.

Peters, Rollo, 346.

Phelps, William Lyon, praises performances of "The Rivals," 222.

Phillips, Mrs. E. J., of Chestnut Street Theater Company, 51.

"Pinafore," 62.

Pixley, Annie, 57, 58, 429.

Play-acting, in universities, 375.

Play-reading, wisdom of, 223.

Players Club, The, founded, 137; Shakespeare's birthday at, 143; "The Rivals" produced by, 221–23; the Chimney Corner of, 292; anecdotes and fancy of, 292–335; the vice-presidency of, 325, 326.

Plays, of questionable taste, 437–39.

Playwriting, anecdote on, 296; in universities, 375, 433.

Poe, Edgar Allan, allusion of Whitman to, 238.

Post, Lillie, 65.

Power, Tyrone, as "Sir Anthony" in "The Rivals," 225.

Powers, James T., as "David" in "The Rivals," 225.

Préville, French comedian, 369; Garrick on, 382.

Price, William T., his "The Principles of Playwriting," 289.

"Prince Methusalem," 66, 68.

"Princess of Trebizonde," 68.

Proctor, Joseph, 428.

Producing Managers' Association, The, formation of, 256; attempts to propitiate actors, 256.

Quakers, the, 27, 28.

"Queen's Lace Handkerchief, The," 63, 67, 70.

Raymond, John, 428.

Reed, Florence, in the actor's strike, 274.

Rehan, Ada, 377, 378.

Rehearsals, exhaust nervous energy, 111; suggestions for, 435.

Reinhardt, Max, and "the new stagecraft," 441.

Rice, Fanny, in All-Star Rivals Company, 216, 330.

Riley, James Whitcomb, his ambition as a boy, 176; verses of, quoted, 177; penmanship of, 298.

Rip Van Winkle, asked for, at club, 332.

"Rip Van Winkle," Jefferson unsuccessful in, at first, 209; Boucicault rewrites, 209–12; qualities of, 212; a folklore story, 213.

"Rivals, The," before revision, 215; rearranged and condensed, 216, 218–21; the All-Star Rivals Company, 216–22; Players Club production of, 221–23; parts restored in, 221, 222; produced for the Equity Players, 222.

Robert, of "Cosa Sia," 370.

"Robert Macaire," "Erminie" a revamping of, 77; great actors in the drama of, 79; history of the part, 87–89; Booth in, 118; as afterpiece, 118 n.; programme for, 120.

Robertson, Forbes, 304.

Robson, Eleanor, 429.

Robson, May, in "The Mountain Climber," 288.

Robson, Stuart, his estimate of Booth, 127–29; his voice, 379; mentioned, 429.

Rogers, H. H., 299.

Rogers, Samuel, 6, 386.

Roosevelt, Theodore, 326, 425.

Rosenfield, Sydney, "The Dotlet on the I," 66.

Russell, Annie, 382.

Russell, Lillian, in "Erminie," 73; in the actors' strike, 274; mentioned, 429.

Russell, Sol Smith, regard of Eugene Field for, 168; recites "The Little Peach," 170; intercourse of, with Eugene Field, 175, 176.

Russian Players, 433–36.

Ryman, "Ad," 429.

Saint-Amand, and "Robert Macaire," 87, 88.

Saints' and Sinners' Corner, of Mc-Clurg's Book Store, 179, 189, 191.

Salvini, Tomasso, his voice, 378, 379.

Sampson, William, 393.

Sand, Georges, 424.

Sanford, Samuel S., his entertainments, 38, 39; gives Wilson note to Edward L. Davenport, 39.

Sanger, Frank W., secures rights in "Erminie," 77.

Sargent, Booth's portrait by, 137, 138.

Scenic decoration, over-abundance of, at times, 433, 441.

"School for Scandal, The," 222.

Schoolcraft, Luke, 49.

Schools of acting, 374-76.

Scott, Clement, on "Rip Van Winkle," 210.

Scott, Cyril, 429.

Sensibility, requisite for the actor, 368.

Sex relation, the, 396, 397.

Seybert, Henry, believer in spiritualism, 305.

Seymour, "Nelse," 43.

Seymour, William, manager, 287.

Shaftesbury, Earl of, 424.

Shakespeare, First Folio of, secured by Wilson for The Players Club, 320; mementoes of, owned by Wilson, 320, 321.

Shaw, Mary, as "Mrs. Malaprop," 223.

Sheridan, R. B., lines on Garrick, 393.

Sheridan, William E., of Chestnut Street Theater Company, 51.

Shipman, Louis Evan, 224.

Shubert, Lee, and William Hodge, 266, 267.

Shuberts, the, 153, 167.

Siddons, Mrs., 200; retires to private life, 6; dismissed for incompetency, 385.

Simmons, Edward, 138, 305.

Simmons, Lew, minstrel, 43.

Skinner, Otis, in "The Honor of the Family," 283.

Slade, medium, 305.

Slocum, E. N., minstrel, 43.

Smith, Christopher J., the dwarf in "Rip Van Winkle," 210.

Smith, Harry B., 323.

Smith, Hubbard T., composer of melody for song in "Nadjy," 169.

Smith, Sol, theatrical manager, 312.

Smith, Winchell, 215.

Sobel, Bernard, 347.

Society for the Improvement of the Condition of the Poor, 313.

Sothern, Edward A., 428.

Sothern, Edward H., brings managers' proposal, 265, 266.

Speech-making, 330, 331.

Spencer, Herbert, 401.

Spiritualism, 305, 306.

"Spiritualist, The," 290, 291.

Stage. See Acting.

Stage decoration, art of, 347.

Stage director, the, 392-95, 440.

Stanley, Charles, of Chestnut Street Theater Company, 51.

"Stars," Theatrical Syndicate applied to, 149; visited "stock" theaters, 154, 155; assistant managers of, 155. See All-star casts.

Stedman, Edmund Clarence, refuses to write Introduction to Field's "Culture's Garland," 171; sequel to his refusal, 171.

Stetson, John, manager of Howard Athenæum, 44; makes proposition to Wilson, 134.

Stevenson, Robert Louis, his "Macaire," 88; his idea of dramatic writing, 89; had no skill as a dramatist, 177.

Stewart, Grant, in the actors' strike, 274.

Stirling, Mrs., 215.

"Stock" companies, valuable training gained in, 53; maintained by actor-managers, 154; not good for beginners, 373-75.

Stoneall, Mrs., of Chestnut Street Theater Company, 51.

Stratford-on-Avon, mementoes of, owned by Wilson, 320, 321.

Strike, the Actors', 263–73; reasons for, 275, 276.

Strong, Austin, writes "The Little Father of the Wilderness" for Wilson, 284, 285, 288.

Sullivan, Barry, in "Richard III," 47, 48.

Sullivan, John L., 424.

Sweatnam, William, minstrel, 43.

Swift, Jonathan, anecdote of, 3, 4.

Symonds, John Addington, admirer of Walt Whitman, 234.

Taber, Robert, in All-Star Rivals Company, 216, 330.

Talma, tragedian, the artist overcame the man in, 384.

Tennyson, Alfred, paraphrased by Laurence Hutton, 6.

Terry, Ellen, and Whitman, 239; tells story of Irving and Fanny Kemble, 387; was "in love with love," 424; unpuppet-like, 442.

Thatcher, George, minstrel, 43.

Theater, Wilson's delight in, 34, 35; of the future, 436; a public trust, 436; and the State, 437.

Theatrical Syndicate, formed, 148; members of, 148; applied to "stars" only, 149; and out-of-town managers, 149, 150; sinister possibilities of, 150; prominent actors arrayed against, 151, 156; weak opposition to, 152; secures firm footing, 153; unnecessary, 153; receipts the first demand of, 154; how it grew up, 154–56; opposition of Wilson to, 156–62; Wilson makes bargain with, 162–66; injustices of, 166, 167; opposed by the Shuberts, 167; its code of business ethics contemptible, 244; have no idea of art, 244; arrogance of, 244–47.

Thomas, Augustus, tells anecdote of Bartley Campbell, 54.

Thompson, Denman, 176, 429.

Thompson, Slason, friend of Eugene Field, 168; Field's biographer, 170; literary adviser of Field, 172.

Thompson, Woodman, 346.

Thorne, Charles R., possessed extraordinary magnetism, 214; Bronson Howard's tribute to, 383.

Topical songs, 66.

Tragedy and comedy, relative merits and difficulties of, 204–06.

Traubel, Horace, on Walt Whitman, 235, 239, 241.

Tree, Beerbohm, 207.

Tupper, Martin Farquhar, 424.

Turner, Paul, Actors' Equity Association Councilor, 274.

Tyler, George C., 338.

Unexpected, the, 333, 334.

Universities, play-writing and play-acting at, 375, 433.

Urban, Joseph, and "the new stage-craft," 441.

Urquhart, Isabelle, in "Erminie," 85; makes innovation in dress, 86.

"Variety" theaters, 43, 44.

Vaudeville, formerly variety theater, 43, 44.

Vernon, Ida, in Chimney Corner fancy, 293–95.

Voice, sympathetic, requisite for the stage, 376–80.

Voices, noted, 377–79.

Wallack, James W., 329.

Wallack, Lester, 428.

Wallack's, 378.

Walpole, Horace, on Goldsmith, 391.

Walsh, Townsend, on "Rip Van Winkle," 210, 212.

Walters, Charles, 44.

Walton, Sir Fisherman, 336.

Wambold, 429.

"Wang," 333.

Warde, Frederick, tells anecdote of Booth, 126, 127.

Warren, William, a fixture in Boston,

93, 214; on Jefferson's version of "The Rivals," 219.

Watterson, Henry, tribute to Jefferson, 227.

Weathersby, Jennie, in "Erminie," 86; in "Erminie" revived, 345.

Weber and Fields, 430.

Welch, James, in "When Knights Were Bold," 289.

Western, Helen, 428.

Western, Lucille, 399–401, 428.

Wetherell, Mrs. *See* Abbott, Emma.

"When Knights Were Bold," 289.

White, Charles, minstrel, 43.

White, Richard Grant, on English spoken at Wallack's, 378.

Whitman, Walt, frowned upon, by many, 228; on the road from Camden to Philadelphia, 228–30; tries to sell his book, 230; misunderstood, 230–32; his philosophy, 232, 236; visited by Wilson, 232–38; his popularity in England, 234, 236; character of his poems little esteemed by Dr. Furness, 235; and Emerson, 236; allusion of, to Poe, 238; presents poem to Wilson, 239; interested in stage-folk, 238, 239; presented with bottle of whiskey by Wilson, 240–42.

Wilde, Oscar, 409.

Williams, Mr. and Mrs. Barney, 428.

Wilson, Francis, prejudice against his becoming an actor, 1, 2; legal studies of, 2, 3; his promise to Père Hyacinthe, 3, 4; inspired by tributes to the drama, 5–9; and his mother, their understanding of each other, 10, 11; as grown man, with his mother, 12; traits of mother in, 13, 19; traits of father in, 15, 19; eased by presence of mother at first performances, 21, 22; wanders from home, 21, 22; influence of his mother on, 22, 23; auctions off old furniture, 23; his new suit of clothes, 23–25; birth, 27; among the Quakers, 27, 28; disposition as a boy, 29; determines to become highwayman, 29–32; inclines to the stage, 32–34; his delight in the theater, 34, 35; gets engagement in "concert hall," 37; with Samuel S. Sanford, 38, 39; note of introduction to Edward L. Davenport, 39, 40; with circus troupes, 41–43; in company with Mackin, 43, 44; "utility man" at Chestnut Street Theater, 45, 51; fights Mackin, 45, 46; victorious in sword contest, 46; sees Baldwin Theater Company, 47; encouraged by William H. Crane and his wife, 47; with William (Billy) Emerson, 48; advanced to "Second Low Comedy" in Chestnut Street Theater, 51; applauded as "Lamp," 52; gains valuable experience in various parts, 52, 53; and the actor's three accomplishments, 55; a stage device of, 55–57; accepts engagement with Annie Pixley, 57; returns to Chestnut Street Theater, 59; joins Mitchell's Pleasure Party, 60; success in "Our Goblins," 61; marriage, 61; fails in "Our Goblins" in San Francisco, 61; life closely associated with musical plays, 62; specially interested in drama, 63; joins John A. McCaull, 63; with McCaull, 63–72; in "Don Sancho," 64; on topical songs, 66; in various parts, 68; visits Europe, 68; and Carlo Goldoni, 68–70; imitates Jules Levy, 70; plays trick on William T. Carleton, 71; under Aronson at Casino, 72, 73; plays joke on composer of "Erminie," 74; hissed in "Erminie," 75; his part of "Cadeaux" in "Erminie," 80; fights away from "Erminie," 81, 82; averts calamity in theater, 90, 91; makes favorable engagement with Casino management, 92–94; his luck as occupier of Stateroom Thirteen, 95–97; decides to become a "star," 100; engages company for "The Oolah," 101; in encounter with Max Freeman, 101, 102; Aronson tries to punish, 102–04; on first night of "The Merry Monarch," 105; how he came by "The Merry Monarch," 106; engages Lulu Glaser, 108; gives chance to amateurs, 110; attacked by an Irishman, 112, 113; and Jane Hading, 116, 117; tries joke on Edwin Booth, 118–21; beginning of his acquaintance with Booth, 130–36; collects autographs, 138, 139; his entrance in "The Merry Monarch," 139; secures Booth's autograph, 139–42; fights the Theatrical Syndicate, 151, 156–62; taught hatred of England, 158, 159; makes bargain with Syndicate, 162–66; Eugene Field's verses on, 168; sings "A Little Peach in an Orchard Grew" by Field, 169; forwards publication of Field's "Echoes from the Sabine Farm," 172; his liking for "number one" copies, 173; verses of Field addressed to, 178; joked on his legs, 182–84, 304, 341; believes in "Rip Van Winkle," 212; practices "Rip" at night, 213; in All-Star Rivals Company, 216, 330; early misgivings about Ethel Barrymore, 217; as "Bob Acres," 221–25; restores parts of "The Rivals" cut by Jefferson, 222; early ideas about Walt Whitman, 228–30; reads "Leaves of Grass," 230–32; visits Walt Whitman, 232–38; presented with poem by Whitman, 239; sends bottle of whiskey to Whitman, 240–42; accepts presidency of Actors' Equity Association, 251, 252; at second meeting with managers, 257–62; accused of gloating, 257; in actors' strike, 263–73; illness and misfortunes of, 271, 272; his ambition, to return to drama, 279; makes agreement with Charles Frohman, 280, 281; in "Cousin Billy," 284; in "The Little Father of the Wilderness," 284–88; in "The Mountain Climber," 288; in "When Knights Were Bold," 289; as play-writer, 289–91; in "The Bachelor's Baby," 289, 290; in "The Spiritualist," 290, 291; fancy of, at the Chimney Corner, 292–96; writes letter to Mark Twain, 300; with Sarah Bernhardt in the elevator, 302; his voice, 309, 310; as servant in his own house, 312–14; an invited guest at his own house, 315–18; secures First Folio Shakespeare for The Players Club, 320; armchairs made of pew doors owned by, 320, 321; presented by Henry Irving with Calcraft's "Defense of the Stage," 321; in "Cyrano de Bergerac," 323, 324; taken for himself, 326, 327; attempts to address newsboys, 330, 331; asks for Mr. Rip Van Winkle, 332; devotes efforts to interests of Actors' Equity Association, 337; death of wife, 337; second marriage of, 337; reasons for returning to the stage, 337–39, 358; appears in "Erminie" revived, 339; Huneker's remarks on his appearance in "Erminie" revived, 341–44; letter of Owen Wister to, on "Erminie, revived, 345, 346; his curtain speech to "Erminie," 348–53; presented with silver loving-cup, 356–58; adores a contest, 357; his son inadvertently takes part in performance, 358; illness of, 359; at the hospital, 359–61; ten suggestions for beginners, 395; his constant love for his mother, 398; and Lizzie, his first sex-love, 398, 399; and Lucille Western, 399–401; and the solicitous widow, 401–04; marries, 404, 405; his wife, 405, 406; proposed to Maude Adams, 410, 411; his second wife, 415–19; an admirer of biography and autobiography, 423, 424; his remembrance of Field and his Boswellized Joseph Jefferson, 424, 425; took satisfaction in his profession, 425, 426; his view of the stage as most perfect relaxation, 426; acted from love of acting, 427.

Winter, William, on relative difficulties of comedy- and tragedy-acting, 204; wrote with sympathy, 393.

Wister, Mrs. Caspar, letter of Dr. Furness to, 235.

Wister, Owen, letter to Wilson on "Erminie" revived, 345, 346.

Wood, Mrs. John, 306.

Wordsworth, William, 424.

Wright, "Billy," secures engagement for Wilson, 36, 37; his adeptness with knives, 37; gives Wilson note to Samuel S. Sanford, 38.

Zimmerman. See Nixon and Zimmerman.